Breaking through Schizophrenia

New Imago: Series in Theoretical, Clinical, and Applied Psychoanalysis

Series Editor

Jon Mills, Adler Graduate Professional School, Toronto

New Imago: Series in Theoretical, Clinical, and Applied Psychoanalysis is a scholarly and professional publishing imprint devoted to all aspects of psychoanalytic inquiry and research in theoretical, clinical, philosophical, and applied psychoanalysis. It is inclusive in focus, hence fostering a spirit of plurality, respect, and tolerance across the psychoanalytic domain. The series aspires to promote open and thoughtful dialogue across disciplinary and interdisciplinary fields in mental health, the humanities, and the social and behavioral sciences. It furthermore wishes to advance psychoanalytic thought and extend its applications to serve greater society, diverse cultures, and the public at large. The editorial board is comprised of the most noted and celebrated analysts, scholars, and academics in the English speaking world and is representative of every major school in the history of psychoanalytic thought.

Titles in the Series

Relating to God: Clinical Psychoanalysis, Spirituality, and Theism, by Dan Merkur
The Uses of Psychoanalysis in Working with Children's Emotional Lives, edited by Michael O'Loughlin
Psychodynamic Perspectives on Working with Children, Families, and Schools, edited by Michael O'Loughlin
Working with Trauma: Lessons from Bion and Lacan, by Marilyn Charles
Hypocrisy Unmasked: Dissociation, Shame, and the Ethics of Inauthenticity, by Ronald C. Naso
Searching for the Perfect Woman: The Story of a Complete Psychoanalysis, by Vamık D. Volkan with J. Christopher Fowler
In Freud's Tracks: Conversations from the Journal of European Analysis, edited by Sergio Benvenuto and Anthony Molino
Desire, Self, Mind, and the Psychotherapies: Unifying Psychological Science and Psychoanalysis, by R. Coleman Curtis
Transgenerational Trauma and the Aboriginal Preschool Child: Healing through Intervention, edited by Norma Tracey
Breaking through Schizophrenia: Lacan and Hegel for Talk Therapy, by Wilfried Ver Eecke

Breaking through Schizophrenia

Lacan and Hegel for Talk Therapy

Wilfried Ver Eecke

ROWMAN & LITTLEFIELD
Lanham • Boulder • New York • London

Published by Rowman & Littlefield
An imprint of The Rowman & Littlefield Publishing Group, Inc.
4501 Forbes Boulevard, Suite 200, Lanham, Maryland 20706
www.rowman.com

6 Tinworth Street, London SE11 5AL

British Library Cataloguing in Publication Information Available

Library of Congress Cataloging-in-Publication Data

Names: Ver Eecke, Wilfried, author.
Title: Breaking through schizophrenia : Lacan and Hegel for talk therapy / Wilfried Ver Eecke.
Description: Lanham : Rowman & Littlefield, [2019] | Series: New imago | Includes bibliographical references and index.
Identifiers: LCCN 2018055057 (print) | LCCN 2018056524 (ebook) | ISBN 9781538118023 (electronic) | ISBN 9781538118009 (cloth : alk. paper) | ISBN 9781538118016 (pbk. : alk. paper)
Subjects: | MESH: Lacan, Jacques, 1901–1981. | Hegel, Georg Wilhelm Friedrich, 1770–1831. | Schizophrenia—therapy | Psychoanalytic Therapy | Narrative Therapy | Psychoanalytic Theory
Classification: LCC RC514 (ebook) | LCC RC514 (print) | NLM WM 203 | DDC 616.89/8—dc23
LC record available at https://lccn.loc.gov/2018055057

∞ ™ The paper used in this publication meets the minimum requirements of American National Standard for Information Sciences Permanence of Paper for Printed Library Materials, ANSI/NISO Z39.48-1992.

Printed in the United States of America

For my grandchildren,
Maya, Josie, Michael, Eddie, Charlie, Ellie, Emily, Rogan,
Preston, Teagan, Virginia, and Natalie,
who continue to amaze me by their smiles and their questions.

Contents

Foreword

Wilfried Ver Eecke is a gifted Lacanian psychoanalyst and first-rate describer of psychoanalytic theories. To be sure of his understanding of Lacan's theories, he went to Paris and studied with Lacan for a year. He understands Lacan better and explains Lacan more clearly than anyone else in the United States, and probably elsewhere. While he uses Lacan effectively, he does not restrict his thinking to Lacan's ideas but uses all of psychoanalysis when it is relevant.

In this book, he describes effective treatments for schizophrenia. He describes what he believes accounts for the effectiveness of these treatments, in a way that will be useful to psychoanalysts and other therapists. He also offers real hope to patients suffering from serious mental disorders, who usually have been told they are hopeless. This book will help them know that it is not true.

—Bertram P. Karon, PhD, ABPP

Preface

Breaking through Schizophrenia: Lacan and Hegel for Talk Therapy is intended for anyone who comes in contact with people afflicted with schizophrenia or other psychotic disorders, whether those people are family members or medical professionals. By reading the last section of the book, in which I discuss successful talk therapies with those afflicted with schizophrenia, they will be able to borrow methods to communicate and thus stay in touch with their mentally ill family member. Also, in reading chapter 9 family members will learn to understand better their afflicted parent, child, brother, or sister. Professionals will be able to improve their understanding of their patients. Furthermore, medical professionals will be challenged to learn that severe mental illness is not a hopeless situation. It can, in certain circumstances, be cured. The "Open Dialogue" method in Sweden (Seikkula et al. 2003, 2006) and the Gifric method in Montreal (Apollon 1990; Apollon et al. 1990) report that more than 80% of patients diagnosed with schizophrenia can be cured to such a degree that they can return to their work or studies. Karon is willing to say to the patients who suffered from schizophrenia and who he treated that they will, in normal circumstances, not experience another psychotic episode (Karon 2018, 231). This hopeful view of severe mental illness will require that mental health professionals change their philosophy of mental illness. Mental illness will have to be seen and understood as a developmental challenge, not a biological condemnation.

This radically new view of severe mental illness will require from the medical profession that they view medication of mentally ill patients in a totally different way. Medication must be seen as secondary to talk therapy. It must be minimalized. I am happy to report that I am in contact with psychiatrists who are willing to diminish the medication of patients I see.

They are willing to do so because they have talk therapy as many as four times a week.

I saw a patient who reported that coming to see me four times a week had the result that in his daily life, both at work and at home, he was able to take a step back when he was disappointed and felt angry. He could ask himself why he was angry and then address the reason for his feeling angry instead of remaining the slave of his angry feelings and exploding in anger. The psychiatrist, in this case, was willing to drastically diminish the medication, which had been overprescribed by another psychiatrist. I myself saw a patient who was let go from a top American university because of a schizophrenic breakdown. I agreed to see the patient and used the ego-structuring method invented by Palle Villemoes, MD, on the basis of Lacan's ideas about schizophrenia—and discussed in chapter 14 (Villemoes 2002). Within eight months, the patient was able to return to college and finish his degree.

Serious mental illness is more widespread than is normally understood. Its consequences are dire. Furthermore, there is disagreement about its causes. The official position of the American Psychiatric Association, as presented in *DSM-IV-TR* and *DSM-V*, is that serious mental illnesses, like schizophrenia, are genetic and thus biological.[1] Professionals in another tradition, including Harry Stack Sullivan (1974) and Theodore Lidz (1973), but also Lacan and his followers, see "disturbed family communications and interactions" as the likely "origin of the disorder" (Freedman et al. 1975b, 856).

This book makes use of Lacan's ideas to defend the thesis that mental illnesses, including schizophrenia, can be understood as a failure in the psychosocial and linguistic development of the person when growing up. I am happy to report that some authors, adhering to a genetic and biological interpretation of schizophrenia, like the authors of the PORT reports,[2] are progressively giving psychosocial tools a more prominent place in their treatment recommendations. Still, they consider psychosocial tools secondary to medication and advise using such tools to increase adherence to psychotic medication (Dixon et al. 2009, 14).

I agree that medication has a role in the treatment of seriously mentally ill people; however, like Karon and Vergote, I consider medication a secondary tool compared to psychotherapy. Medication should be used when the patient cannot sleep or when the patient is in crisis. It can also be useful for a patient to have medication in his or her pocket because it provides reassurance to the patient that help is available in a potential sudden crisis, but medication for seriously mentally ill people is less effective in the long run than appropriate psychosocial treatment. As one psychiatrist said to me, "We, psychiatrists, can make schizophrenic persons good, but they do not improve. Your method promises improvement." That same psychiatrist summarized the biological approach to schizophrenia as follows: "Being more oriented to medication, [our therapy is limited to] wrap-around services and sometimes crisis [management]."[3]

We have empirical proof that a psychosocial approach to serious mental illness is effective. In the part of Finland, where "Open Dialogue" is used as an approach to dealing with schizophrenic patients, the following results are reported: "82% did not have any residual psychotic symptoms, 86% had returned to their studies or a full-time job, and 14% were on disability allowance. [Only] 17% had relapsed during the first two years and 19% during the next three years" (abstract in article by Seikkula et al. 2006). The method of "Open Dialogue" is described as follows: "The focus is primarily on promoting dialogue. . . . In dialogue, patients and families increase their sense of agency in their own lives by discussing the patient's difficulties and problems" (Seikkula et al. 2006, 216).

This book makes use of the theories of Lacan and child development to argue that serious mental illness can be attributed to the absence of a proper psychosocial and linguistic development in the childhood of the patients. This lack of proper development makes such people vulnerable to the challenges of human life, particularly in late adolescence and early adulthood.

PREVALENCE OF MENTAL ILLNESS AND ITS DIRE CONSEQUENCES

Mental illness is prevalent, both in its many forms and its most serious conditions. The National Institute of Health (NIH) reports that 18.5% of the adult population suffered from some form of mental health issue in 2013. Interestingly, the occurrence of mental illness is not spread evenly throughout the two sexes. Males have a prevalence rate of only 14.4%. Females have a prevalence rate of 22.3%. The prevalence rate also is not spread evenly based on age. The group of 26 to 49 years of age has the highest prevalence rate, at 21.5%.[4] NIH reports that in the same year, 2013, 4.2% of the population had serious mental health problems.[5]

Mental illness also has dire consequences for one's longevity. The median reduction in life expectancy for the mentally ill is 10.1 years (range from 1.4 to 32 years).[6] A Swedish study investigated a national cohort of more than 6 million adults between 2003 and 2009, to detect mortality and illness based on the results of every outpatient or inpatient visit nationwide. Among the 8,277 people diagnosed with schizophrenia, men died 15 years earlier than the rest of the population, and women died 13 years earlier. This early mortality was not due to completed suicide but rather cardiovascular disease, cancer, and pulmonary disease.[7]

Finally, mental illness is becoming, more often, experienced during teenage years. The number of young people aged 15 to 16 with depression almost doubled between the 1980s and the 2000s. The proportion of young people aged 15 to 16 with a conduct disorder more than doubled between 1974 and 1999.[8]

CAUSES OF MENTAL ILLNESS

There is no agreement about the causes of mental illness. Some authors stress genetic and thus biological causality. As recently as *DSM-IV*, it has been claimed that having a first-degree family relative with schizophrenia increases the risk of developing the condition by about 10 times (APA 2000, 309).[9] This claim is contradicted in *DSM-V*, where it is stated, "Most individuals who have been diagnosed with schizophrenia have no family history of psychosis" (APA 2013, 103). Still, *DSM-V* maintains, "There is a strong contribution for genetic factors in determining risk for schizophrenia" (APA 2013, 103).

Other authors stress environmental factors. Harry Stack Sullivan writes,

> As a result of some years' study of male patients suffering from schizophrenic mental disorders, I am inclined to the opinion that the occurrence of these illnesses is to be explained on the basis of experiential factors rather than by reference to an hereditary, or to a primarily organic, disorder. (Sullivan 1974, 246)

Bertram Karon uses the example of Nazi Germany to refute the thesis of the genetic origin of severe mental illness. He writes,

> For several years all schizophrenics in Nazi Germany were sterilized. Then, the annihilation gas chambers were designed by psychiatrists, originally not for Jews, but for mental patients. Hundreds of thousands of schizophrenics were annihilated. But a generation later, the rate of schizophrenia was not affected. (Karon 2003, 102)

Donald Winnicott says it as follows: "Psychoanalysis tends to show that the basis of mental health is not hereditary . . . ; the basis for mental health is being actively laid down in the course of every infancy when the mother is good enough at her job,[10] and in the span of every childhood that is being lived in a functioning family" (Winnicott 1990, 179).[11]

This book argues that Winnicott's "functioning family" includes the mother showing respect for the word of the father, which Lacan technically calls respect for the "Name-of-the-Father." I therefore consider as environmental factors the psychosocial conditions created by early family life, which optimally create certain relationships between mother and child, father and child, and mother and father. This network of relationships is the Oedipus complex and optimally guides the child to incorporate metaphors into its language, as the early Lacan teaches us.

In thinking about the causes of mental illness, one is faced with profound philosophical questions. Some people argue that the body dominates the mind and that thoughts are merely brain waves. In their view, delusions and hallucinations are indications of a malfunctioning brain. They support the use of medication to treat the malfunctioning brain. Other people argue that the mind dominates the body. They gain support from the curious phenomenon that cancer patients who are optimistic about the outcome of their treatment have a greater chance of survival.[12] Given that cancer is a bodily condition and optimism is a condition of the mind, these studies present evidence that, at least in some cases, the mind dominates the body. Since Husserl, Continental philosophy has argued that we are embodied minds. The mind makes use of the body and is thus to some degree dependent upon the body. Still, the mind is an active agent and uses the body as a means to express its thoughts and concerns. This idea of the mind–body connection is illustrated clearly in the case of a patient of Lacan. The patient was a French Muslim whose father had been falsely accused of stealing and could face the punishment of having his hand cut off. In this case, the mind of the child dominated his body to such an extent that he expressed, unconsciously, his deep empathy with his father's potential punishment by creating a paralysis of his own hand (Lacan 1988b, 129).

This book concentrates on the environmental factors of mental illness and argues that these factors reveal a possible important role for the mind in their treatment. In the most advanced treatments of cancer, the importance of the mind is already recognized. Hospitals create a pleasant environment for the children with cancer in their care. Hospitals do so despite the fact that it is not fully understood, precisely, how such environmental factors as a friendly environment contribute to the fight against cancer. Similarly, to provide the optimal environmental factors in the treatment of seriously mentally ill people, we wish to defend the use of psychosocial and linguistic approaches. The justification of the role of the mind in the treatment of mentally ill people can be increased if we can demonstrate the great importance of environmental factors in the development of schizophrenic symptoms. Giving a psychological and social rather than a biological interpretation of mental illness has the advantage of decreasing stigma (Read 2007). It also has the advantage of giving hope to the mentally ill. On the contrary, the idea that mental illness is attributable to biology tends to make patients feel condemned for life because they possess a defective brain. In addition, psychological treatment can avoid the side effects of long-term medication, which in the case of antipsychotic medication, can lead to tardive dyskinesia (Chakos et al. 1996; Karon and VandenBos 1981) and irreversible sexual difficulties.[13]

To decide whether schizophrenia is a biological disease or a psychosocial and linguistic maladaptation, it is worthwhile to look at empirical research. We find that in the Finnish research by Pekka Tienari.

The Finnish study by Tienari, which lasted 20 years, rejects the thesis, still presented in *DSM-V*, that biology or genetics is the determining factor in schizophrenia. Tienari looked up the women who had been hospitalized for schizophrenia or paranoid psychosis. Tienari then looked for any of these women who had children given up for adoption to nonfamily members in Finland (Tienari et al. 1992, 159–60). Tienari ended up with 179 children of 164 schizophrenic mothers (Tienari et al. 1992, 160). During the rest of the study, the number of adoptee children from schizophrenic mothers that could be followed diminished to 155. Tienari then categorized the adopting families, dividing them between those judged to be healthy, to be neurotic, and to have personality disorders, and those who were judged to have functional psychoses.

Tienari reports that zero children of psychotic mothers developed a "functional psychosis" if the adoptive family was classified as "healthy" (1992, 163). This research indicates that a nurturing family environment can overcome a genetic predisposition. In other words, genetics by itself cannot cause the outbreak of psychosis. On the other hand, if a child of a schizophrenic mother was adopted by a disturbed family, he or she was more likely to be seriously disturbed than the biological children of that disturbed family (61.7% of adoptee children grew up to become seriously disturbed as compared to 34% of biological children from such families) (Tienari et al. 1992, 162–63). Tienari's study clearly demonstrates that the environment in which one grows up mediates the process by which a genetic predisposition to schizophrenia becomes a reality.

If, for children of psychotic mothers, schizophrenia or other psychotic disorders are illnesses that only develop when those children are raised in disturbed families, then schizophrenia must be considered a psychological illness. Hence, we cannot hope that medication will heal people afflicted with schizophrenia. Medication will only be able to suppress the schizophrenic symptoms. We can argue that, in crises, suppression of symptoms is desirable. Bertram Karon, a psychotherapist who practiced psychotherapy with schizophrenic people, advised his patients that they should keep medication on them. Having medication, when the patient is fearing a sudden crisis, is very helpful (Karon and VandenBos 1981, 209–10). He continued by saying that the psychological reassurance is probably more effective to combat the crisis than the chemical compounds of the medication (Karon and VandenBos 1981, 210). Irwin Kirsch defends the same idea, in particular for people diagnosed with severe depression, by stating that the healing effect of medications is almost completely the result of the placebo effect (Kirsch 2010). Antoine Vergote, a psychoanalyst, provides an additional argument for the use of medication. He writes that a patient who cannot sleep does not have the energy or concentration to do talk therapy. Vergote continues by stating that he works together with a psychiatrist who prescribes medication for his patients who are severely ill (Vergote 2003, 246).[14]

Medication is, therefore, useful in the treatment of mentally ill people (Karon and VandenBos 1981, 208–10); however, the use of medication, as described by Karon, Kirsch, and Vergote, is auxiliary. It is considered a helpful tool for coping, although the real work to improve the patient is achieved through talk therapy. We can ask the question as to how we can understand how talk therapy is such a helpful tool to deal with mentally ill people. To begin with, we have statistical evidence that talk therapy, as used in Finland's "Open Dialogue," is efficient, even very efficient (Seikkula et al. 2006, 2003).

One way to explain why talk therapy is a helpful tool for mentally ill people is to understand that human development from child to mature person is a complicated process, which I like to compare to climbing a ladder. Going from one step of the ladder to the next requires a task that a person may fail to do well. Such failures lead to maladaptation, creating mental stress, which can become a contributing cause for possible mental illness.

Human development has an additional challenge discovered by psychoanalysis. Psychoanalysis emphasizes that as a baby, a human being must develop certain strategies that are only helpful at that stage in life. If continued into adulthood, these strategies would be maladaptive. These strategies cope with the fact that human infants are very dependent upon a supportive maternal figure. Still, a human baby has a developing consciousness, which makes total dependence upon another frightening or even unacceptable. Realistically, however, the child cannot escape this unacceptable situation. When one is faced with an unacceptable situation and can do nothing, one can fall back upon a typical human strategy: One can start fantasizing. Most children make use of two fantasies to deal with the psychologically unacceptable fact of total dependency. First, the child imagines that the mother (or the mother figure) is omnipotent; total dependence would not feel safe with a mother who is anything less than omnipotent and perfect. Second, the child imagines that he or she is everything the mother could want. This second fantasy assures the child that the omnipotent mother will take care of the child as the child fulfills all of the mother's wants and desires. Children who can create these two fantasies flourish.

However, these two fantasies are not always useful, since the feeling that one is the center of the world is not the best psychic attitude to succeed as an adult; therefore, to acquire a successful, mature psychic structure, human beings must undergo a radical change, which is unavoidably painful. This happens because of the introduction of a third person in the emotional life of a child. Psychoanalysis refers to this moment as the Oedipal phase. Normally, the person who is introduced as the third figure is the father.[15] But this introduction does not always facilitate the change when, for example, some references by mothers to the father are, at best, ambivalent. Another reason why the change might not happen is that single mothers may have a need for affection, which they satisfy by making the child a substitute for the missing partner. Finally, a father may be too narcissistic and grandiose to present a model with whom the child can identify (Lacan 2006, 482–83).[16] Any of these shaky beginnings for the child can lead to maladaptive strategies, which make the child, as an adult, more vulnerable to mental illness.

STRATEGIES FOR TREATING SERIOUSLY MENTALLY ILL PEOPLE

This book presents strategies for understanding and treating people that suffer from schizophrenia and psychosis. My proposed strategies depend upon the thesis that schizophrenia and psychosis result from failed psychological adaptation to the challenge of growing up. The psychosocial–linguistic theory of the cause of schizophrenia is preferable to the biological theory because it accommodates treatments that can cure the condition. The authors of the PORT report, who subscribe to the biological theory of schizophrenia, admit that for such patients, the prescribed medication will be needed for life (Lehman et al. 1998, 5: Recommendation 11).[17] Bertram Karon, who defends the thesis that failures in the psychosocial and linguistic development of the person are the cause of schizophrenia—a thesis I also defend—wrote, "The vast majority of hospitalized schizophrenic patients will be able to function as outpatients with two months of the five-time-per-week treatment" (Karon and VandenBos 1981, 168). Karon was also able to say to a patient he had treated that, in normal circumstances, the patient would not have a recurrence of a schizophrenic episode.[18]

ORGANIZATION OF THE BOOK

In the introduction, I present a picture of the many symptoms afflicting Daniel Paul Schreber, the famous case I use as the main clinical case for developing a theory of schizophrenia and psychosis. In the introduction, I also present the two theories of Lacan, which will be the basis for my psychological understanding of schizophrenia: i.e., the mirror stage and the idea of foreclosure of the "Name-of-the-Father."

Part I defends the idea that human growth is a complex phenomenon and that failure to master all the steps in the growth process can lead to a kind of psychic structure in a person that makes the person vulnerable to mental illness. Thus, I locate a principle cause of mental illness in the psychosocial–linguistic challenges that a person might not have mastered when growing up.

Chapter 1 argues that a child needs a radical psychological restructuring between 3 and 6 years of age, which invites the child to choose its own identity instead of allowing its identity to be determined by the desire of the mother.

Chapter 2 makes use of studies by Louis Sass, who interprets the alogia of schizophrenics not as a deficiency, but as a paralyzing hyperactivity connected with a deficient relation to their own body.

Chapter 3 elaborates on the ideas of the previous chapter by using Lacan's linguistic theory of psychosis, and I explain the meaning of Lacan's concept of "Paternal Metaphor?"[19]

Chapter 4 asks the question as to what happens to people who have not benefitted from a paternal function. I make use of ideas by A. Vergote and J. A. Miller's concept of "ordinary psychosis" to clarify that question.

Chapter 5 presents the later Lacan's claim that the "Paternal Metaphor" is only one possible way of avoiding schizophrenia. Based on his study of James Joyce, Lacan argues that the function of the father is to allow the child to have a name. If the paternal function does not work properly, the child has the challenge of creating a name for him or herself—a challenge Joyce pursued.

Chapter 6 uses the writings of De Waelhens to show that Lacan's approach to psychosis allows philosophy to overcome the mind-body dualism, which was first introduced by Descartes. Lacan shows that human beings must occupy and take ownership of their bodies by means of a triangular relationship with their parents. Many things can go wrong in taking up this challenge.

Part II points to the similarity between the theory of well-known philosopher Georg Wilhelm Friedrich Hegel and Jacques Lacan. Chapter 7 shows that Lacan is in need of a respectable framework for theorizing about his own psychoanalytic experience. I show that Lacan finds in Hegel's passage of the "Master/Slave" the desired framework for his theory of the mirror stage and in the passage of the "Law of the Heart" the desired framework for his theory of paranoia and aggression. Chapter 8 outlines the great similarity between Hegel and Lacan's theories on paranoia. I then continue by showing how Lacan points toward a developmental explanation of paranoia. Indeed, Lacan points out that children who later become paranoid were able to identify with and idealize their siblings but unable to fight them. Thus, they did not accept the challenge of becoming a separate self, separate from the idealized sibling.

Part III develops further the thesis that psychosis and schizophrenia are illnesses characterized by a defective relationship to language. Psychotic and schizophrenic people have great difficulty grasping the meaning of metaphors.[20] Thus, when told that they are handicapped, they might feel that they do not have hands. They translate a metaphor into a literal reality.[21] Chapter 9 uses Robert Sokolowski's idea that linguistic intentionality, for example, naming, superimposed on perception, not only represses the richness of sense data, but also provides a guide for action. Hence, naming objects for the very mentally ill can help them orient themselves in a world where they are overwhelmed by sense-impressions. Chapter 10 draws attention to the fact that the voices heard by Schreber have similar characteristics to the "social referencing" that is typical for young children. Hence, the hearing of voices is an indication of lack of psychic development and thus not a proof that the patient has a defective brain.

Part IV uses Lacan's theory of the "Paternal Metaphor" to clarify the famous case of Judge Schreber, which is much discussed in American psychoanalytic literature. Chapter 11 compares Morton Schatzman and Jacques Lacan's interpretation of the case of Schreber's mental illness. Whereas Schatzman emphasizes the role of the father's sadism, Lacan stresses the fact that Schreber's mother did not seem to show respect for the word of Schreber's father. He cites the mother's destruction, at the death of her husband, of his unpublished manuscripts, as evidence. According to Lacan, Schreber's mother's lack of respect for the word of the father obliterated the possibility for Schreber to create a "Paternal Metaphor." Chapter 12 addresses the problem of the breakdown of a schizophrenic or psychotic person. Lacan locates the cause of psychosis and schizophrenia in the absence of a "Paternal Metaphor." Lacan explains the breakdown of such a person by the presence of a protective maternal figure, who exercises paternal characteristics. Schiller seems to have played such a dual role in the emotional life of Hölderlin.

Lastly, part V analyzes, from a Lacanian point of view, three successful therapy approaches to cure the condition of schizophrenia. All three therapists stress that talk therapy for people afflicted with schizophrenia or other psychotic disorders must be of a very different kind than talk therapy for neurotic people.[22]

Chapter 13 uses the Lacanian concepts of the imaginary and the symbolic to analyze Bertram Karon's treatment of people afflicted with schizophrenia. Karon, a non-Lacanian therapist, first confirms the patient's imaginary needs by making statements like, "Who says it's wrong to want to kill a bitch like that (patient's stepmother)? The old bitch deserves to die, for what she did to you" or "Any time anyone hurts you, you hate them, you want to kill them. And that is healthy" (Karon and VandenBos 1981, 198). This allows the patient to reveal the suffering he experienced at the hands of his stepmother. Karon then introduces a prohibition by telling the patient, "The only reason for not killing her is that you'll get caught. If you're willing to die in order to kill her, she must be more important than you are. That sounds stupid to me" (Karon and VandenBos 1981, 198). That prohibition is based on a linguistic or symbolic connection presented by Karon and imaginarily understood and accepted by the patient.

Chapter 14 analyzes Palle Villemoes's method for treating schizophrenic people. Villemoes is impressed by the fact that schizophrenic people cannot properly use pronouns. Thus, when asked if his parents liked him, a schizophrenic person answered, "No, I did not like them." Hence, Villemoes concludes that the therapist cannot treat schizophrenic patients as dialogue partners. One way of doing so is to make the physical arrangement in the therapy room different from most other therapy methods. Instead of putting himself in front of the patient, Villemoes recommends that the therapist sits next to them. Villemoes also interprets the autistic symptoms demonstrated by schizophrenic people as a fear of human dialogue. People afflicted by schizophrenia fear communication because of their tendency to psychologically fuse with other people. This prevents them from maintaining a stable self-conception during the dialogue, which then culminates in self-alienation.[23] Hence, Villemoes is not asking questions from the schizophrenic person. Instead, Villemoes believes that a therapist must work indirectly with schizophrenic patients.

Villemoes's method consists of strengthening the relation of a schizophrenic patient with language. In a first phase, Villemoes describes objects in the consulting room, thereby inviting the patient to change her passive attitude of allowing herself to be bombarded by a multitude of sense impressions into a more active and aggressive attitude of cutting the continuous domain of sense impressions into pieces that are named and thus made into objects. When Villemoes then describes objects in the patient's own room, he elevates the patient to the guarantor of truth. This process normally leads to the patient starting to idolize the therapist.

The idolization by the patient is the sign, used by Villemoes, to start the second phase of the treatment, where Villemoes encourages the patient to describe objects in her memory, starting with the earliest ones and continuing up to the present. Villemoes observes that patients slowly introduce, in their description of past memories, references to their interactions with other people. This allows the patients to construct a story of who they have become. When that story is complete, Villemoes starts the third phase of the therapy, where he asks the patient to choose a date between the present and two months later. That date will be the last therapy session. The purpose of the third phase is for the therapist to give back to the patient the transferential power invested by the patient in the therapist so that the patient can finish the treatment without a feeling of loss. The patient is then ready to take her life back into her own hands.

Chapter 15 describes Gary Prouty's method of treating schizophrenic patients. Prouty emphasizes the patient's deficient relationship to the body. He uses five methods to improve the creation of a psychic body. One method is called bodily reflection. According to this technique, the therapist sits in front of the patient and either imitates the posture and bodily gestures of the patient (e.g., arm movements), or the therapist describes the bodily expressions of the patient (saying, "I see tears in your eyes"). In imitating the bodily gestures of his patient, Prouty is strengthening the imaginary relation of the patient to his or her body. In naming the bodily expressions of the patient, Prouty is strengthening the patient's relationship to language.

The chapters can be read on their own, but, of course, prior chapters might elucidate ideas in later chapters.

NOTES

1. APA 2013, 103: "There is a strong contribution for genetic factors in determining risk for schizophrenia"; however, no specific laboratory tests exist to prove the presence of the disease (Allen et al. 2008). For a more refined view, see Mark Solms and Oliver Turnbull 2004.
2. Lehman et al. 1998, 2004; Dixon et al. 2009.
3. Private communication.
4. http://www.nimh.nih.gov/health/statistics/prevalence/any-mental-illness-ami-among-adults.shtml.
5. For a paper that criticizes all papers about statistical data, including those about schizophrenia, see https://doi.org/10.1371/journal.pmed.0020124.
6. http://www.nimh.nih.gov/about/director/2015/mortality-and-mental-disorders.shtml.
7. http://www.nimh.nih.gov/about/director/2013/schizophrenia-as-a-health-disparity.shtml. See also Crump et al. 2013.
8. http://www.youngminds.org.uk/training_services/policy/mental_health_statistics.
9. Still the same *DSM-IV-TR* states, "No laboratory findings have been identified that are diagnostic of Schizophrenia," in APA 2000, 305.
10. Within the context of the theory presented in this book, the mother is "good enough" if the child experiences her in such a way that the child can develop and maintain the two fantasies: my mother is perfect and omnipotent, and I am everything my mother could want. André Green demonstrates how a depression in the mother can deprive the child of the necessary maternal presence to flourish (she is not experienced as omnipotent) (Green 1986, chapter 7, "The Dead Mother").
11. Robbins 2011, 210, concludes his cross-cultural book as follows: "Psychosis develops within a particular pathological family constellation that has distorted the infant's initial implicit learning by failure to meet basic psychological needs and by malignant admixtures of hostility, rejection, and distortion of meaning."
12. Carver et al. 2005; Allison et al. 2003.
13. "Sexual dysfunction often accompanies severe psychiatric illness and can be due to both the mental disorder itself and the use of psychotropic treatments. Many sexual symptoms resolve as the mental state improves, but treatment-related sexual adverse events tend to persist over time," in Montejo, Montejo, and Baldwin 2018, 3.
14. For a testimony about the interaction of medication and psychic self-determination see Nuland 2003.
15. In lesbian families, the partner, as a significant third, takes on the role that a father plays in a heterosexual couple. Alternatively, a single mother can introduce a third figure by looking at what her child is good at and pointing this out to the child, and then asking what the child imagines doing with that talent. The ability of the mother to make the talent of the child crucial for his or her future is one way for a single mother to introduce the idea of a third.
16. The first number refers to the normal page in the book (Lacan 2006). The second number refers to the corresponding page number in the French edition (Lacan 1966).

17. In their 2004 article, the authors argue against intermittent antipsychotic medication maintenance strategies (Lehman et al. 2004, 198: Recommendation 7).

18. This is consistent with the idea reported by Jonathan Shedler: "Psychodynamic therapy sets in motion psychological processes that lead to ongoing change, even after therapy has ended" (Shedler 2010, 101).

19. There are many books about Lacan. There is a one-volume work (Marcelle Marini 1986) and a two-volume work (Michael Clark 1988), with brief summaries of the work of Lacan and a full bibliography of Lacan's works and the secondary literature up to the date of the publication of the volumes. There are also several good books elaborating on Lacan's theory. The books by Jonathan S. Lee (1990), Mikkel Borch-Jacobson (1991), and Malcolm Bowie (1991) were some of the first English books on Lacan. The book by Stijn Vanheule (2014) stresses brilliantly the four phases of Lacan's thought. The book by Dany Nobus (2000) emphasizes the role of desire in Lacan's approach. The book by Colette Soler (2014) focuses on the later Lacan's idea of the "Real." In this book, I concentrate on the early Lacan, mainly covering the first two phases of his thought.

20. Langdon and Coltheart 2004. See also Mitchley et al. 1998 and Herold et al. 2002, both cited in Mo et al. 2008.

21. Whereas normal people are able to use metaphors as rhetorical devices, for a schizophrenic, metaphors "are not a rhetorical device." See Sini et al. 1985, 51.

22. This is also the main argument in an article by Bent Rosenbaum et al. 2013. The authors refer to appropriate therapy for people afflicted by psychosis as SSP (supportive psychodynamic psychotherapy). In Section V of this book I demonstrate that Bertram Karon, Palle Villemoes, and Gary Prouty, three therapists who developed a successful method for treating schizophrenic patients, indeed do not challenge the delusions and hallucinations of their patients. All three claim that their main task is finding a way to connect with their schizophrenic patients.

23. Note that Villemoes's view of the autism of schizophrenics is consonant with the view defended by Louis A. Sass, discussed in chapter 2.

Acknowledgments

I wish to thank two of my own professors at the University of Leuven. Professor Alphonse De Waelhens used his course on epistemology to introduce his students to the ideas of Jacques Lacan and argued that Lacan's theory of the unconscious is, for philosophers, a logical extension of Edmund Husserl's insight that all perception takes place against a background. That background includes, so argued De Waelhens, the unconscious. Professor Antoine Vergote accepted to be the director of my PhD thesis on Freud's article on negation. This forced me to reflect explicitly on the relationship between philosophy and psychoanalysis. Both professors used their contact with Lacan to introduce me to him so that I was able, in 1965–1966, to participate in his case presentations where only 10 to 15 people were present.

I also benefited from my psychoanalytic training in the Contemporary Freudian Society and my participation in the Lacan Forum of Washington, DC, which I cofounded with two former Georgetown students, Dr. Devra Simiu and Dr. Macario Giraldo. The monthly meetings of the Lacan Forum of Washington, DC, helped me test my theories of mental illness with real cases. I hereby thank all the participants in our Lacan Forum of Washington, DC.

Another series of monthly meetings on the ideas of Lacan with a group of scholars and clinicians under the leadership of William Richardson, SJ, kept me in touch with the latest developments in the field of philosophy of psychoanalysis.[1]

I have stayed in touch with two other students of De Waelhens and Vergote, who also work in the area of philosophy and psychoanalysis: Dr. Philippe Van Haute (professor at the University of Nijmegen) and Dr. Paul Moyaert (professor at the University of Leuven).[2] Their publications on philosophy of psychoanalysis continue to help me to see the wide application of

Lacan's ideas. I also have started contact with Stijn Vanheule, whose writings helped me deepen my understanding of the later Lacan, which are not the center of attention of this book.

For writing the different talks and papers that became chapters in this book, Bissie Bonner, Mark Nowacki, Brian Smith, Sigrid Fry, Thane Naberhaus, and Lynn Ilene Poss, most of whom were students of mine, provided helpful suggestions. I wish to also thank Jennifer Grady, with whom I jointly wrote the paper that became chapter 2, and Richard Cobb-Stevens, for allowing me to include his comments on a paper of mine, which together became chapter 9. Missy McMillan-Ver Eecke and two of my graduate students, Katherine Ward and Deirdre Nelms, helped improve substantially the English style of my manuscript. Thomas Matthew, a student at Rhodes College, volunteered suggestions for improvement of both content and style for my book. Finally, I wish to thank the anonymous reviewers of my manuscript. I accepted many of their suggestions.

I am very grateful to Dr. Bertram Karon for his kind foreword to this book. His ideas have been a great inspiration for me.

I could not have written this book without the continuous support of my wife, Josiane Berten-Ver Eecke. She also read the entire manuscript and suggested many improvements.

* * *

For this book, I made use of previously given talks and published articles. I made changes, mostly minor, to those talks or publications. I thank the previous publishers for their kind permission to use these talks or publications for this book.

Chapter 1, "Toward a Philosophy of Psychosis," was published in 1969, in French, as "Vers une Philosophie de la Psychose," in *Man and World*, 1, no. 4, 44–49. The original paper was translated into English by Arnold Davidson.

Chapter 2, "The Subjective Experience of the Person with Schizophrenia," was published jointly with Jennifer Grady in 1999, in *Personalist Forum*, 15, no. 2, 320–33.

Chapter 3, "Philosophical Questions about the Theory of Psychosis in the Early Lacan," was published in 2009, in *Psychoanalytic Notebooks: A Review of the London Society of the New Lacanian School*, 19, 233–39.

Chapter 4, part of "'Paternal Metaphor' and Ordinary Psychosis," was published in 1988, as "Phenomenology and 'Paternal Metaphor' in Lacan," in *Phenomenology and Psychoanalysis: The Sixth Annual Symposium of the Simon Silverman Phenomenology Center* [Pittsburgh], Simon Silverman Phenomenology Center Duquesne University, 91–119.

Chapter 5, "Theoretical and Therapeutic Implications of the Later Lacan's Complex Theory of Psychosis," was given as a talk in Istanbul in 2009. The talk was translated into Turkish and published as "Lacan'in Kompleks Psikoz Kuramina Dair Kuramsal ve Terapötik Çikarimlar" in *MonoKL*, 2009, 3, no. 6–7, 416–30.

Chapter 6, "A Post-Lacanian View on Schizophrenia," was originally given as a talk for the 13th ISPS symposium in 2000, in Stavanger, Norway. It was published in 2006, in Jan Olav Johannessen, Brian V. Martindale, and Johan Cullberg (eds.), *Evolving Psychosis: Different Stages, Different Treatments* (pp. 49–63). London: Routledge.

Chapter 7, "Hegel as Lacan's Source for Necessity in Psychoanalytic Theory," was published in 1983, in Joseph H. Smith and William Kerrigan (eds.), *Psychiatry and Humanities* (pp. 113–38). New Haven, CT: Yale University Press.

Chapter 9, "Phenomenology, Linguistic Intentionality, Affectivity, and Villemoes's New Therapy for Schizophrenics" was originally given as a talk in 2002, at the American Philosophical Association. Richard Cobb-Stevens commented on the paper. The paper and the comments were published in 2004, as "Phenomenology, Linguistic Intentionality, Affectivity, and Villemoes's New Therapy for Schizophrenics," in Anna-Teresa Tymieniecka (ed.), *Analecta Husserliana: The Yearbook of Phenomenological Research*, Vol. 84, (pp. 275–90). Dordrecht: Kluwer Academic.

Chapter 10, "Self-Referencing in the Language of the Severely Mentally Ill," was given as a talk at a conference in Calcutta on January 6–8, 2015, and has not been previously published.

Chapter 11, "Reflections on the Concept of 'Paternal Metaphor' at the Occasion of Lacan and Schatzman's Analyses of Schreber," was published in 1993, as "Lacan and Schatzman: Reflections on the Concept of 'Paternal Metaphor,'" in D. Boileau and J. Dick (eds.), *Tradition and Renewal: Philosophical Essays Commemorating the Centennial of Louvain's Institute of Philosophy* (pp. 1–19). Leuven: Leuven University Press.

Chapter 12, "The Concept of 'A-Father' or the Psychological Origin of Mental Breakdown in Schreber and Hölderlin," was published in 1995, as "Schreber and Hölderlin: The Concept of 'A-Father' or the Psychological Origin of Mental Breakdown," in *Journal of the American Academy of Psychoanalysis*, 23, no. 3, 449–60.

Chapter 13, "A Lacanian Interpretation of Karon's Psychoanalytic Treatment of People Afflicted with Schizophrenia," was first given as a talk, in Dutch, for the Third Symposium of the Centrum of Psychoanalysis and Philosophical Anthropology, organized by the universities of Nijmegen and Leuven in February 2000, and published in English in 2001, as “Lacan’s Theory, Karon’s Psychoanalytic Treatment of Schizophrenics,” in *Psychoanalysis and Contemporary Thought*, 24, no. 1, 79–105.

Chapter 14, “On Villemoes’s Lacanian-Inspired Treatment Method of People Afflicted with Schizophrenia,” was given as a talk at a conference in Cheng-Du in 2002. The talk appeared in 2002, as “On Villemoes’s Lacanian-Inspired Treatment Method of Schizophrenics,” in *Collection of International Symposium of Psychoanalysis 2002 ChengDu*, 287–99. ChengDu: University of Sichuan.

I also thank Harvard University Press for the quotations from Daniel Schreber’s *Memoirs of My Nervous Illness* (1988). Cambridge, MA: Harvard University Press.

NOTES

1. Muller and Richardson 1982.
2. I learned also from the publications of such philosophers as Jon Mills 2010, 2012; Jonathan Lear 2017; Rik Boothby 1991; Robert Samuels 1993; and George Graham 2013.

Introduction

This book relies heavily on the famous case of Daniel Paul Schreber and his own description of his experience with severe mental illness. For theoretically understanding severe mental illness, I will mainly rely on the theory developed by Jacques Lacan is the first half of his career. In this introduction I give a picture of Daniel Paul Schreber and a summary of the theories of the early Lacan.

THE CASE OF DANIEL PAUL SCHREBER (1842–1911)

Daniel Paul Schreber was one of five children from Daniel Gottlob Moritz Schreber and Pauline Haase. Daniel had three sisters and one brother, who committed suicide at the age of 38. The literature about Daniel Schreber has provided a lot of evidence about the role of the father. We know less about the influence of the mother except that we know that Daniel Schreber reacted to the death of his mother in 1907 with his third and final psychotic episode.

Daniel Paul Schreber had three mental illness breakdowns. Schreber describes his second mental illness (1983–1902) in his book *Memoirs of My Nervous Illness*. In that book he refers to his first mental illness (1884–1885). The first two breakdowns were connected with Daniel Schreber overworking himself. His third mental illness started with the death of his mother and lasted until he died (1907–1911).

The father of Daniel Schreber was a physician who became famous for his promotion of orthopedic gymnastics. He also became famous for his encouragement of city people to have small gardens, called the Schreber gardens. His push for orthopedic gymnastics was part of the elder Schreber's program for improving the German race. As part of this program, the elder Schreber developed tools to promote correct orthopedic development of people, including his own children. One of his tools was an armor that made sure the shoulders of the children remained straight even when they were sleeping. Another tool was a leatherhead cover, tied to a chair on which the children were sitting, so that their backs remained straight. His concern for the bodily well-being of his children also included swimming every morning, even if the ice had to be broken first during winter months.

The elder Schreber further promoted his care for the human body by publishing several books. One of them became a best seller. Mrs. Schreber helped edit the writings of her husband; however, when her husband died, she burned his unpublished notes, indicating less-than-full-hearted respect for his work. The idea of the mother's lack of respect for the "Name-of-the-Father" became a crucial idea in Lacan's theory of severe mental illness.

Daniel Schreber married Sabine Behr, who was considered below the dignity of the Schreber family tradition, which for three hundred years had produced outstanding lawyers and scholars. Daniel Schreber developed a successful judicial career. Later, he tried politics but was defeated in the Reichstag elections of 1984, which seems to have been the occasion or even the cause of his first mental illness, diagnosed as hypochondria. After six months of treatment in Professor Paul Flechsig's psychiatric clinic in Leipzig, he appeared fully recovered. Mrs. Schreber was so grateful for the contribution of Dr. Flechsig to the recovery of her husband that she put a picture of Dr. Flechsig in a prominent place of the house (Schreber 1988). Daniel Schreber himself wrote that the eight years after the recovery of his first mental breakdown were happy years, except that he was regularly disappointed in not having children, presumably because of multiple miscarriages by his wife (Schreber 1903, 36).[1]

In his career, Daniel Schreber achieved an important success when he was appointed "Senatspräsident" at the Dresden Superior State Court in 1893, which, at that time, was the second-highest court in Germany (Weber 1988, 3). Daniel Schreber was decades younger than the other judges. He wanted to prove that his appointment was deserved, so he worked hard. Actually, he overworked himself and became mentally ill for a second time in 1893 (Schreber 1903, 34, 37). This time his illness was more serious and was, by many, diagnosed as schizophrenia or psychosis (Baumeyer 1956). His illness would also last longer, and his recovery would actually take nine years instead of the one year it took for recovering from his first mental illness breakdown. Again, he consulted Dr. Flechsig, who had developed a program to make his patients recover in six months. Those who did not recover in that time span were moved from Dr. Pierson's asylum to Sonnenstein Castle, presumably a more permanent asylum (Schreber 1903, 117). Daniel Schreber seemed to have known about this program. The fear of not recovering in six months might have contributed to the aggravation of Daniel Schreber's despair and thus to the depth of his mental breakdown (Lothane 1992, 237).

During the latter part of his illness (1900–1902), Daniel Schreber wrote his *Memoirs* (Schreber 1903), in which he describes his symptoms.

Problems with Sexual Identity

Daniel Schreber considered as the first sign of his second mental breakdown the fact that, while half-sleeping, the thought came to him that "it really must be rather pleasant to be a woman succumbing to intercourse" (Schreber 1903, 36). He reports that, "This idea was so foreign to my whole nature that I may say that I would have rejected it with indignation if fully awake" (Schreber 1903, 36). He continues, "I cannot exclude the possibility that some external influences were at work to implant this idea in me" (Schreber 1903, 37).

In this passage, we find an idea that would become a crucial feature of Daniel Schreber's delusional system. The idea that women have special pleasures developed into the delusion that he himself was becoming a woman. At first, he resisted that idea, but then he provided different reasons to accept and even embrace it. He started by providing an egoistic justification to accept the idea that he was becoming a woman because that was the way in which he could have "high-grade voluptuousness" (Schreber 1903, 178). Schreber then, at some point, asked rhetorically, "Who, faced with the choice of either becoming a demented human being in male habitus or a spirited woman would not prefer the latter" (Schreber 1903, 178). Toward the end of his *Memoirs*, he even writes, "I have to imagine myself as man and woman in one person having intercourse with myself" (Schreber 1903, 282). Schreber provided a grandiose explanation when he writes that he feels he is becoming a woman to create a new mankind (Schreber 1903, 114–15, 124, 289, 293).

On another occasion, Schreber mentions that unmanning was forced upon him (Schreber 1903, 54). Curiously, he reports that this process was not one act but something that took years, if not decades (Schreber 1903, 225, 289).

Schreber also reports that in certain circumstances, he felt that his "breast gives the impression of a pretty well-developed female bosom" (Schreber 1903, 279). He claims that everyone who would watch him naked in front of the mirror would have that same impression. He concedes, however, that he still had hairs on his chest and that his nipples were still small. Interestingly, Schreber claims that people would not immediately see that he is a woman. They would have to look for 10 to 15 minutes (Schreber 1903, 279–80).

Schreber even claims that twice he had female genitals and felt in his body the quickening associated in women with the sign of having a baby. Still, Schreber hints at the fact that the idea of him being a female is connected with his imagination when he writes that when lying in bed he claims he could give himself the impression that his body had "female breasts and a female sexual organ" (Schreber 1903, 233). The imaginary dimension of Schreber feeling that he is becoming a woman is confirmed when he writes that he felt it necessary to shave off his mustache to support the idea that he was a woman, which he imagined at least at night. This is also confirmed when he writes that he is "*subjectively* certain" that his body "shows such organs as only occur in the female body" (Schreber 1903, 277). Women do not have to give themselves the impression that they have breasts, and women are not just having subjective certainty that they have breasts. Woman do not limit their idea of being a woman to the night. Women relate to their bodies as having breasts as a fact of life, day and night. The ambivalent relationship to his own sexuality is explicitly stated by Daniel Schreber himself when he writes that he has to imagine that he is "man and woman in one person having intercourse with himself" (Schreber 1903, 282).

Daniel Schreber also connects the feelings of voluptuousness to both sexual and anal experiences, as when he reports that he experienced, during his second mental breakdown, unusually strong feelings of voluptuousness when he went to the bathroom to produce the "liberation from the pressure of feces present in the guts" (Schreber 1903, 227). Daniel Schreber writes as if, for him, the anal and phallic phase in his sexual development and experience are overlapping.

The idea that Schreber was becoming a woman was used by Freud to argue that Schreber was not at ease with his sexuality. Freud hypothesized that Schreber was uneasy about his homosexual feelings, particularly his homosexual feelings for his doctor, Flechsig.

Lack of Ability to Think on His Own

At some point, Daniel Schreber explains the fact or the feeling that he was becoming a woman by the idea that foreign forces must have implanted this thought in his mind. He gave as argument the fact that the idea that he was becoming a woman was totally alien to him (Schreber 1903, 37). Schreber was hereby confessing that he was not able to think on his own. He felt that someone or something could implant ideas in his mind. This feature developed into an explanation for his production of a full-blown delusional system as being thoughts implanted in his mind.

This confession by Schreber that foreign forces could implant ideas in his mind was used by Lacan to argue that Schreber was deficient in his psychological development and did not reach the stage where he could feel that he could think for himself. Lacan argued that Schreber did not benefit from the positive consequences of the Oedipal transformation, i.e., the paternal metaphor that separates the child from the fusion with the mother and thereby invites and allows the child to speak and act in his or her own name. Schreber's explanation for feeling that he was becoming a woman thus presented a second deficiency in his psyche (Lacan 2006, 445–89).

Elements of Paranoia

Schreber's autobiography provides evidence of a third character trait, i.e., that he developed paranoid ideas about Dr. Flechsig. In an elaborate delusional story, Schreber concludes that Dr. Flechsig tried to commit soul murder on him. Schreber connects this attempted soul murder with the beginning of his second mental illness (Schreber 1903, 22–23).

Another indication of Schreber's paranoid relationship to Dr. Flechsig was Schreber's explanation for the fact that he had no children and that in the Schreber family there were no neurologists, whereas Dr. Flechsig was a neurologist. To be a neurologist was, in Schreber's opinion, to be a member of a holy profession, because it was a profession dealing with nerves, which Schreber saw as God's instrument for providing energy to the world. Schreber attributed both the fact that he had no children and that he and his forefathers were not neurologists to a conspiracy between Flechsig and God (Schreber 1903, 26–27). This last point lets us see how Schreber saw his relationship with Flechsig within a broad cosmological perspective where Flechsig was seen as having been able to mobilize God for his nasty plans.

Grandiosity

Schreber's grandiosity is made evident by both the explanation he gives for ultimately accepting that he was becoming a woman and the one he gives for his feelings toward Dr. Flechsig.

Schreber, at first, resisted the idea of becoming a woman (Schreber 1903, 57) but later embraced it by means of the grandiose idea that he had to become a woman to marry God for the purpose of creating a new mankind where he would then be the national saint (Schreber 1903, 114–15, 124, 282, 289, 293).

Schreber also reveals a kind of grandiosity when disclosing his competitive relationship with Dr. Flechsig. Thus, when Schreber comments on the so-called "white lies" used by Dr. Flechsig to reassure his patients, Schreber accepted that doctors might sometimes use "white lies" to reassure their patients; however, Schreber argues that Flechsig should have realized soon that "white lies" were inappropriate with him because he was a "human being of high intellect, of uncommon keenness of understanding and acute powers of observation" (Schreber 1903, 35).

The competitive spirit with Dr. Flechsig also reveals Schreber's grandiosity when Schreber comments on Dr. Flechsig's habit of praising Schreber by saying that he was the "greatest seer of spirits of all centuries." Schreber reports that he objected to this kind of praise by saying that it should at least have been the "greatest seer of spirits of all millennia" (Schreber 1903, 77).

Schreber also believed that his fame would surpass thousands of other people who were more intelligent than he was. Finally, there is the conclusion of his *Memoirs*, where he first reports the suffering his mental illness bestowed on him: He lost his profession, his marriage went bad, he experienced all kinds of pain in his body. He then claims this could only be compared to the suffering of Jesus Christ, including his crucifixion (Schreber 1903, 293). Daniel Schreber dealt with his psychological pain by thinking of himself as Jesus Christ.

Problems with Experience of Time

A fifth phenomenon that is worth noticing is the fact that Schreber had a kind of floating conception of time that extended to his vision of death.

When retelling the story of his life, Schreber mentions the period from mid-March to the end of May 1894. About that period he makes the comment, "Assuming always that it was really a matter of a few earthly months only and not of centuries" (Schreber 1903, 63). Thus, Daniel Schreber is confessing that, for him, three months were the same as centuries.

Then, at another time, when Schreber read something that looked like his own obituary, he interpreted this as a hint that he was condemned never to return to human society (Schreber 1903, 81). He does comment that he did not know if this was but a hallucination. Normal people know whether they are dead or alive, whether time is still ahead for them or not. Normal people also know that three months is not the same as centuries.

Problems with Body Experience

A sixth curious element in the self-experience of Daniel Schreber is the abnormal way in which he experienced his body. We learn from child psychology that a child first experiences himself as body parts: a mouth to eat, a stomach that can feel hungry, and a bottom that needs to be cleaned. Lacan teaches us that, at six months of age, in the mirror stage, children acquire the experience of a unified body image (Lacan 2006, 75–81). Daniel Schreber seemed either not to have achieved or to have lost that mirror stage acquisition because he reports not being able to feel that he had a body robustly containing all its parts.

Here are some examples that demonstrate that Schreber lacked the experience of a solid unified body. He reports that he once had another heart and that a "lung-worm" was frequently inserted in his lungs. He sometimes felt that his lungs were almost completely eaten up. He specifies that as a consequence of the disappearance of his lungs, the diaphragm of his lungs was pushed upward, close to his larynx. Hence, he felt that he had to regain his lungs with each breath. Schreber also felt that his ribs were sometimes broken, which he calls the "compression-of-the-chest miracle" (Schreber 1903, 159).

Next, Schreber felt that he had an inferior stomach, which he called a "Jew's stomach" (Schreber 1903, 151–52). Furthermore, he felt that his stomach was often taken away when he was eating. The food then fell into his abdominal cavity and thighs. He also felt that his gullet and intestines were regularly torn away. He reported that he ate his pharynx several times. Moreover, he felt that putrid matter was thrown into his abdomen, which he felt would make him rot alive and cause rotten smell to escape from his mouth (Schreber 1903, 153–54).

Daniel Schreber also thought that the fluid in his spinal cord was pumped out by little men, one of which was identified as "little Flechsig." As proof, he gives the fact that when he walked in the garden, he saw little clouds escape his mouth, which he identified as his pumped out spinal fluid (Schreber 1903, 154).

Daniel Schreber also felt that nerves were pulled from his head, which caused an unpleasant feeling in his head. He thought the bone of his skull was partially pulverized. Furthermore, little devils walked around on his head to check the destruction on his head (Schreber 1903, 154).

Daniel Schreber reported further that the muscles of his fingers were paralyzed so that playing piano became difficult (Schreber 1903, 155). He felt that some damage had been done to his kneecaps so that he could not walk in the garden or the corridors (Schreber 1903, 158).

Daniel Schreber thought his eyes were closed against his will so as to deprive him of visual impressions. This was done by little men who pulled his eyelids over his eyes. These little men also messed with his brain, and Schreber refers to this operation by using the word "head-compressing-machine." To perform this task, they entered Schreber's skull and slipped into the middle of his brain, where they compressed his head into the form of a pear by means of turning screws they put in his brain (Schreber 1903, 156–59).

Finally, Schreber mentions miracles directed against his skeleton, in particular his foot bones and his lower vertebrae. The last kind of attack Schreber refers to as the "coccyx miracle" (Schreber 1903, 160). It made it painful for him to sit or even lay down.

These examples show that Schreber was experiencing his body as a collection of parts that could be taken away, damaged, or even eaten up. Schreber lacked the psychic experience that his body was a solid unit.

Problems with Perception

A seventh curious phenomenon in the psychology of Daniel Schreber is the fact that Schreber showed signs that he was defective in his perceptive capabilities. From Kant we learned that perception consists of several steps (Kant 1929, 84–85). First, there is the reception of sensual impressions. These sensual impressions are, then, transformed into objects by the application to those sense impressions of the categories of the mind. Thereby, the mind gives those objects definitive characteristics, like the faces I see at my dinner table are the faces of my children. There are four of them. That is all of my children. Or, I look and see only three faces and conclude that not all of my children are present and I can worry about where that missing child is.

I can also dream and, when I'm awake, ask the question if the dream, that I am appointed as secretary of education, is true or false. Perception leads to facing real facts and real objects. This is different from dreaming that leads to nonexisting fantasies. Daniel Schreber shows that he lost the ability to distinguish between fantasies and real perceptions. Thus, when he had sense impressions of people, he was not able to feel that they were real people. Rather, he felt that they are "fleetingly-improvised-men" (Schreber 1903, 117–22, 168, 409). Schreber defines "fleetingly-improvised-men" as not existing (Schreber 1903, 409). Thus, his sense perception led to the construction of a less-than-real world. Schreber explicitly writes, "The human forms I saw during the journey and on the platform in Dresden I took to be 'fleetingly-improvised-men' produced by miracle. I did not pay any particular attention to them, because even then I was tired of all miracles" (Schreber 1903, 409). Here, Schreber is clearly reporting that he was not able or not willing to transform perception of human forms into the affirmation that they are real human beings.

Problems with Language

An eighth curious part of Daniel Schreber's psychology is his reported experience of language. First, there is the way God and his delusional voices use language. Daniel Schreber reports that God spoke to him in a basic language that did not follow the general rules of language, i.e., that there is a definitive connection between a word and some meaning (de Saussure 1959). When I speak English and utter the sound connected with the word *chair*, I must accept that that sound refers to a generally accepted meaning in English language, i.e., an object to sit on. I cannot decide that I personally use the sound connected with the word *chair* to mean a "book on Hegel." Daniel Schreber tells us that in the basic language, the word *reward* does not mean "reward" but its reverse, "punishment"; poison means food; juice means venom; unholy means holy; nontested souls were called "tested souls." Schreber also created such curious new words as "not-thinking-of-any-thought" or "musical-not-thinking-of-any-thought" (Schreber 1903, 169). The first artificial word refers to his experience that playing piano allowed him to forget his depressing thoughts, whereas the second artificial word refers to the attempt to deprive him of the power to forget his bad thoughts.

An additional curious experience with language was the "writing-down-system." Daniel Schreber reports that all his thoughts, all the sentences he spoke, all of what he did, all the people he was in contact with, and all of what he possessed was written down (Schreber 1903, 119). Schreber testified that he suffered much mental anguish from this "writing-down-system." This clinical symptom of Daniel Schreber might have a connection with a practice in the Schreber family. Indeed, father Schreber himself proposed and defended a kind of "writing-down-system" in which families were advised to have a so-called punishment board. That board was supposed to be hung in the children's room. On that board, every bad behavior was written down. At the end of each month, the entire family would gather, and either praise or blame would be given to the children (Schatzman 1973, 35–36).

Daniel Schreber reports an additional unusual experience with language, i.e., that the voices he heard spoke to him in a system of "not-finishing-a-sentence" (Schreber 1903, 217). The sentences were about him, and he needed to finish the sentences as the voices wanted him to finish them. One example of an unfinished sentence, spoken by the voices, is, "Now I shall." Schreber felt compelled to finish the sentence not as he wanted but as the voices wanted: "Now I shall resign myself to being stupid" (Schreber 1903, 217–18). If we remember that Schreber thought he was the greatest seer of spirits of all centuries (Schreber 1903, 77), then we can see that Schreber was forced to self-describe himself falsely under the pressure of others. Thus, Schreber reports that he felt like a young child looking to his mother when asked a question about himself, for example, Do you go already to school? or Do you like playing with a ball? This inability to describe himself gives us the hint that Schreber stopped developing emotionally or at some point in his life regressed back to the psychological development and attitudes of a child. Freud and Lacan will help us understand how far the regression went.

A last characteristic aspect of Schreber's unusual relationship to language was the idea that in Schreber's hallucinatory world, human beings lost their separate entity to such an extent that everyone who was in contact with Schreber's nerves understood all the languages that he himself understood. Schreber gives as explanation the claim that those people were partaking in his thoughts and concluded that they understood Greek when he himself was reading Greek (Schreber 1903, 50n8).

Problems Related to Imaginary View of the Cosmos

An additional interesting fact is the phenomenon that Daniel Schreber situates his personal experience within the broader context of a fantasized cosmology. Schreber believed that the possibility for human activity is to be attributed to the energy that is present in their nerves. That energy comes from God who is pure nerves. Human beings have nerves, which need to be purified by God. The unfortunate fact is that Flechsig, through his specialty as a psychiatrist, i.e., a nerve specialist, had the power to interfere with the natural way the nerves provide energy. In particular, Schreber believed that Dr. Flechsig used his power to damage Schreber. This is the paranoid dimension of Daniel Schreber's mind.

As Daniel Schreber believed in some kind of permanence of the nerves, including the human nerves, Schreber created a place for afterlife: the forecourts of heaven. There, human being were to rest after a process of purification. This forecourt of heaven is the anterior realms of God. The posterior realms are the home of both the upper and lower God. The first was called Ormuzd and the second Ariman.

In his delusions, Schreber found a way to make a connection between the beginning of his second mental illness and something fateful that happened to God. In that delusional story, Schreber also indirectly mentions the fact, which provoked his dissatisfaction with the life he was having, i.e., having no children. In that story, Schreber refers to himself as having no children as the result of a conspiracy between Dr. Flechsig and the anterior realms of God. Schreber writes,

> This "miraculous structure" has recently suffered a rent intimately connected with my personal fate. . . . I want to say by way of introduction that the leading roles in the genesis of this development, the first beginnings of which go back perhaps as far as the eighteenth century, were played on the one hand by the names of Flechsig and Schreber (probably not specifying any individual member of these families) and on the other hand the concept of soul murder. (Schreber 1903, 22)

Schreber then connects the idea of soul murder to the person of his own doctor, Flechsig, when he writes,

> The voices which talk to me have daily stressed ever since the beginning of my contact with God (mid-March 1984) the fact that the crisis that broke in the realms of God was caused by somebody having *committed soul murder*; at first Flechsig was named as the instigator of soul murder, but of recent times in an attempt to reverse the facts I myself have been "presented" as the one who had committed soul murder. I therefore conclude that at one time something had happened between perhaps earlier generations of the Flechsig and Schreber families which amounted to soul murder; in the same way as through further developments, at the time when my nervous illness seemed almost incurable, I gained the conviction that soul murder had been attempted on me by somebody, albeit unsuccessfully. (Schreber 1903, 23)

Schreber then concludes,

> One can imagine that in this way something like a conspiracy may have arisen between such a person and the elements of the anterior realms of God to the detriment of the Schreber race, perhaps in the direction of denying them offspring [Daniel Schreber had no children because of multiple miscarriages of his wife] or possibly only denying them choice of those professions, which would lead to closer relations with God, such as that of a nerve specialist. (Schreber 1903, 26–27)

The Presence of Some Sense of Reality in Daniel Schreber

We get an important insight into Schreber's psychology by looking at the arguments he presents for his release from the asylum against the judgement of his doctor. His doctor had testified that Schreber had delusions and hallucinations in which he believed with unshakable certainty and which for him were a sufficient motive to make his decisions (Schreber 1903, 430–31). The implication was that Schreber should remain in the asylum. Schreber responded to this argument by saying that he indeed had unshakable certainty in what the court referred to as his delusions; however, Schreber contradicted the doctor's report on the second point and claimed that his so-called delusions were exclusively concerned with a kind of second world, the world of God or the world beyond this world. Schreber then compared himself again to Jesus Christ, claiming that like Jesus, he could say, "My Kingdom is not of this world" (Schreber 1903, 431). Hence, Schreber, in front of the court, concluded that his so-called delusional ideas "*can* therefore *never in any way influence my behaviour* in any worldly matter" (Schreber 1903, 431). Consequently, his delusions should not be used as an argument for the claim that his delusions made him an irresponsible person.

In court, a specific argument had been made about the consequences of Schreber believing that he was a woman and that he needed some female jewelry to better give the impression that he was a woman. The fact was that, in Schreber's Germany, the husband had full responsibility for finances. The argument was then made that Schreber would spend the family fortune on the female jewelry he needed for living out his delusion of being a woman.

Schreber responded that in his case, the female jewelry he bought was cheap and not costlier than what other men spend for their own pleasure, for example, on smoking (Schreber 1903, 432–33). Schreber won the argument, and the court set him free on December 20, 1902 (Weber 1988, xxi). Still, the delusional world played an important role in the life of Daniel Schreber. Both Freud and Lacan will argue that the delusional world was used by Schreber to provide for him a world in which important desires, which were not satisfied in his life, were imaginarily satisfied. Freud and Lacan had a different opinion about the kind of unsatisfied desires at work in pushing Daniel Schreber to create for himself an illusionary world that could serve as an alternative to the unsatisfying real world.

LACAN'S THEORETICAL CONTRIBUTION TO UNDERSTANDING THE CASE OF DANIEL PAUL SCHREBER

Lacan's Theory of the Mirror Stage

Lacan's theory of the mirror stage is an attempt to answer the question, Why is it that the paranoid attacks his own ideal in the image of someone else? This question, as Muller and Richardson mention in their commentary on Lacan's *Écrits* (Muller and Richardson 1982), was an important problem for Lacan as early as his doctoral thesis (Lacan 1932).

Lacan's answer makes use of two ideas. The first idea is that the human subject's emotional life must be radically transformed and that several times. These transformations occur because a number of frustrations are encountered—the process of weaning, the intrusion of siblings into the affective relationship with one's parents, and finally the Oedipus complex. Each one of these frustrations forces the subject to undergo an emotional transformation that makes her accept more deeply the otherness of others.

According to this theory, the absence of one or more of these transformations damages the extent to which the subject can relate to the other as other. Thus, the paranoiac can be understood to be a subject relating to another as if that other were part of the self.

The second idea Lacan needed to formulate his answer concerns the function of images or ideals: The human child does not experience her own unity until she sees that unity in the Gestalt of another human being or the Gestalt of her own mirror image. Lacan claims that the human child becomes an "ego" only by means of this other: the mirror image. This theory explains Lacan's fondness for Rimbaud's aphorism "'I' is 'another,'" which for Lacan means "I" is based on an "image borrowed from another."

Having seen the structural importance of the theory of the mirror stage in Lacan's thought, we can now look more closely at the theory of the mirror stage itself.

Lacan's theory is an attempt to integrate several facts—scientific and cultural—and make them intellectually understandable. The first scientific fact is this remarkable difference between a human baby and a baby chimpanzee: The chimpanzee, at the age of about six to eight months, has a manifestly greater problem-solving ability than the human baby. But the chimpanzee cannot grasp the meaning of the mirror image, while the human baby can. The chimpanzee tries to look behind the mirror to establish the reality of the image. When the chimpanzee establishes that nothing corresponds to the image, she loses interest in it. She is, therefore, unable to recognize herself in the mirror. The human baby, on the contrary, shows great interest, even excitement, regarding her image in the mirror; therefore, Lacan, following others, concludes that the infant is able to recognize herself in the mirror image. Furthermore, Lacan stresses that the recognition of the self in the mirror image has, for the human baby, a significant emotional meaning: There is a "flutter of jubilant activity" (Lacan 2006, 76 [94]). Typical for the human baby, therefore, is not her problem-solving ability, but her relation to her image.

The second scientific datum to be incorporated into the mirror stage theory is the fact that, for certain animals, seeing the Gestalt of their own species members has physiological consequences. An example is provided by L. Harrison Matthews's study "Visual Stimulation and Ovulation in Pigeons" (1938–1939), which proves that the "stimulus which causes ovulation in the pigeon is a visual one" (Matthews 1938–1939, 558). A prior study by Harper had shown that "two female pigeons when confined together may both take to laying eggs" (Matthews 1938–1939, 557), proving that the act of mating is not necessary for ovulation. Matthews's experiment then examined whether the necessary stimulus was visual, auditory, olfactory, or tactile, or a combination of the four stimuli. He shows that ovulation occurs in female pigeons separated from either male or female pigeons by a sheet of glass or even in a pigeon confined alone with a mirror, but this does not occur in a pigeon that is in the same room with other birds but cannot see herself or other pigeons (Matthews 1938–1939, 554). Matthews compares his results with those of two other researchers:

> The visual stimulation here shown to exist in pigeons when confined with a single companion, or merely a mirror image, is carried to a higher level in those birds which nest in colonies. Fraser Darling (1938) showed that a definite minimum number of pairs is a requisite in any breeding colony of certain species of birds that nest gregariously, in order to produce the threshold stimulus for ovulation. The importance of visual stimulation has also been demonstrated in pigeons by Patel (1936). (Matthews 1938–1939, 559–60)

Lacan also mentions a study by Chauvin, which summarizes five years of research on the desert locust. As has been known since Uvarov, this locust can appear in a gregarious form and a solitary form. The two differ in behavior, color, metabolic activity (oxygen and food intake), and physiology. Yet, a transition from the solitary to the gregarious form is possible if the nymphs of a solitary locust are in contact with members of their own species during the early phases of their development. The age and sex of these other members is not relevant; however, they must be of the same or neighboring species. If they are members of a more distant species, the transformation does not occur. According to Chauvin, the contact must be visual, tactile, or by means of the locust's antennae. The mechanism of transformation of nymphs of a solitary locust into a gregarious locust explains the sporadic outbreak of the migratory locust.

Although Chauvin's study is more detailed, the study by Matthews provides more explicit support for the Lacanian thesis that seeing is the faculty that bridges the psychological and the physiological. Matthews's study confirms such a thesis for pigeons, but Chauvin's study of locusts, while it includes seeing as a transformation mechanism, does not exclude the sense of touch or the function of the antennae from this privileged position of bridge between psychology and physiology.

The third scientific fact to be incorporated into Lacan's theory of the mirror stage is transitivism in young children. Lacan evokes this phenomenon when he writes, "A child who beats another child says that he himself was beaten; a child who sees another child fall, cries" (Lacan 2006, 92 [113]). The essence of the phenomenon is that young children identify so much with one another that they cannot distinguish between themselves and other children, and, therefore, ascribe to the other child what they themselves do to that child and ascribe to themselves what is done to another.

The fourth fact to be incorporated into Lacan's theory of the mirror stage is the human fascination with dismemberment of the body, a fact from cultural history. According to Lacan, this fascination is present in such phenomena as "tattooing, incision, and circumcision." It is also present in dreams about "castration, mutilation, dismemberment, dislocation, evisceration, devouring, bursting open of the body," and in the "cruel refinement of the weapons" humans have forged. Finally, it has been immortalized in the paintings of Hieronymus Bosch (Lacan 2006, 85–86 [105]).

The fifth and last scientific fact concerns the so-called prematurity of human birth. Lacan writes, "The anatomical incompleteness" of the human brain results in "signs of uneasiness and motor uncoordination of the neonatal months" (Lacan 2006, 78 [96]). He also approvingly quotes the label given by embryologists to this phenomenon: fetalization.

Lacan relates these facts to one another partly on an intentionally philosophical level. Thus, in his opening paragraph he writes of his mirror stage theory that it is an "experience that leads us to oppose any philosophy directly issuing from the Cogito" (Lacan 2006, 75 [93]). Subsequently, he talks about his theory as an "ontological structure of the human world" (Lacan 2006, 76 [94]) and a "temporal dialectic that decisively projects the formation of the individual into history," which leads to an "alienating identity that will mark his entire mental development with its rigid structure" (Lacan 2006, 78 [97]). Finally, Lacan attacks Sartre's theory of negativity as incompatible with his theory of the mirror stage because Sartre still believes in the "self-sufficiency of consciousness, which, being one of its premises, ties the illusion of autonomy in which it puts its faith to the ego's constitutive misrecognitions" (Lacan 2006, 80 [99]).

Lacan thus presents his view of the human as an explicit antithesis to that of both Descartes and Sartre. He implicitly appeals to the Hegelian model when he attributes to the mirror stage the function of projecting the formation of the individual into history—that model being the master–slave dialectic, where Hegel explains why humans are necessarily history-making. Before Hegel, both Fichte and Schelling solved this problem by postulating at the dawn of humankind two human races, one rational and the other barbarous. Neither of these races had history; only their union made history and society possible. Hegel's analysis of the master-and-slave dialectic does not require the hypothesis of two human races, for it presents the inequality between humans as emerging from within the human himself or herself. The will to overcome this inequality then provides, for Hegel, the driving force for the making of history.

The history-creating possibility of this passage in Hegel's *Phenomenology of the Spirit* did not escape Alexandre Kojève, the forceful commentator who introduced Hegel to a generation of French intellectuals, one of whom was Lacan. Kojève writes,

> If man is nothing but his becoming, if his human existence in space is his existence in time or as time, if the revealed human reality is nothing but universal history, that history must be the history of the interaction between Mastery and Slavery: the historical "dialectic" is the "dialectic" of Master and Slave. (Kojève 1969, 9)

The aforementioned philosophical claims and many explicit references to Hegel (e.g., Lacan 2006, 80 [99], 98–100 [120–23]) show both that Lacan is consciously creating a philosophical anthropology in his theory of the mirror stage and that he is dependent upon Hegel's dialectic of self-consciousness for his theoretical effort. The originality of Lacan's contribution lies in his attempt to tie Hegelian dialectical moves of the human subject, which resulted from a speculative understanding of history, to concrete scientific facts. This part of Lacan's effort puts his philosophical anthropology in radical opposition to the overall intent of Hegel's system.

The five facts that Lacan incorporates in his theory of the mirror stage are not, as we saw, all from the same scientific domain. Furthermore, some function as negative and others as positive facts. Fetalization and dismemberment function as negative facts. Fetalization is to be overcome, and fantasies of dismemberment remind us that we can fall back to some undesirable state even though we might have overcome fetalization. Seeing, on the other hand, functions as the sense, which can help one overcome these negative facts. But, how can seeing overcome these negative facts? Here it is important to stress that the five facts do not all belong to the same scientific domain.

Fetalization is an anatomico-physiological fact, whereas the fantasy of dismemberment is a psychological fact. Nevertheless, Lacan makes the fantasy of dismemberment function as a reminder that our bodily unity is a psychological achievement. He thus needs a transition between the two domains of the anatomico-physiological and the psychological, and this is provided by the psychological function of seeing.

To these two domains of the physiological and the psychological Lacan must add the ontological domain, because he gives an ontological interpretation to some of the five facts he will incorporate in his theory of the mirror stage. Lacan interprets the fetalization of the human baby as constituting the person as lack, and therefore as to be in the sense of having to become; however, such an interpretation of a physiological fact is transposing by definition that fact into another domain, the domain of ontology of personhood. This will require that the fact, which will remedy the fetalization—seeing—will itself receive an ontological interpretation. For Lacan, seeing produces an image capable of filling the lack that the human is, and which will therefore almost imprison her by determining unconsciously the direction of her becoming. Human essence, therefore, is not inside the self, as was suggested by the classic concept of the soul; human essence is, on the contrary, located in something outside of the self: the image that will guide a person's becoming. I am therefore another. If this is Lacan's ontological vision of the human, then transitivism might become self-evident. It is the psychological manifestation of the ontological status of the human being.

The validity of Lacan's theory of the mirror stage will thus depend to a great extent upon the validity of the two ontological moves he makes. There is, first, the claim that the fetalization of the human infant constitutes the human as lack. Second, there is the claim that the idea that the mirror image is so central to the self that another (one's mirror image) becomes the master of one's own destiny.

The second move shows a Hegelian influence, as we have seen. The first move shows a Heideggerian influence in that the human is seen as to be or as ecstatic, which Lacan summarizes by his statement that the human is lack; however, these two ontological moves are neatly woven together by Lacan and are capable of sharing a view of humans in which they are radically dependent upon one another.

LACAN'S THEORY OF "PATERNAL METAPHOR" AS IT RELATES TO SCHREBER'S DELUSIONS AND HALLUCINATIONS

The Problem of Hallucination

In the *Comprehensive Textbook of Psychiatry* (Freedman 1975a) we find the following definition of hallucination: "A hallucination is the apparent perception of an external object when no corresponding real object exists—that is, an internal psychological event is mistakenly attributed to an external source. A dream is a simple example of a hallucination in normal experience."[2]

In the glossary of the same textbook we find essentially the same definition with other words: "*Hallucination*. A false perception without a concrete stimulus. It can be induced by emotional and by organic factors, such as drugs and alcohol. Common hallucinations involve sights or sounds, although any of the senses may be involved."[3]

This view of hallucination is a phenomenologically false description even though it is a classic psychiatric description and corresponds with the common sense understanding of hallucination.

When a claim is made from one philosophical tradition, in this case, the phenomenological one, that a view defended by common sense and a specialized field of knowledge, in this case psychiatry, is false, then arguments need to be presented.

A first argument against the aforementioned definition of hallucination can be developed from a consideration of Binswanger's view of schizophrenia, provided one accepts that there is a family resemblance between the concepts of hallucination and delusion.[4] Binswanger tells us that the central problem of schizophrenia is the problem of delusion and, more specifically, the delusion of persecution.[5] For him, delusion is interpreted as the most profound and serious capitulation of the subject, because in it the schizophrenic allows himself to become the plaything and victim of foreign powers.[6] Binswanger's view, however, encounters a fatal objection in the generally recognized fact that delusional schizophrenics, especially the acutely delusional ones, can anticipate a less pessimistic future than the nondelusional ones.[7] Defining delusion as giving up contact with reality and granting that its presence in a schizophrenic might be a criterion of hope forces us to state minimally that there must be more to delusion than giving up contact with reality. The definition of delusion as belief without grounding in reality is incomplete. This incompleteness problematically allows for the following false theorem about schizophrenia as formulated by Binswanger: Delusion is the final phase of the schizophrenic illness.

A second argument can be developed starting from a case description by De Waelhens. He writes,

> Another girl pretends to give birth each week to several children. Reacting to this story . . . I remarked in an indifferent tone that she must spend a fortune in expenses for gynecologists and baptisms! I received this surprising response, which gets to the bottom of the problem of delusion: "You are deceiving me, you always believed what I told you and now you no longer believe me."[8]

I propose that the reaction of the patient is not understandable if one defines hallucination (and for that matter delusion) as perception without sense-data (or as belief without warrant in reality). This definition makes of a hallucination or of delusion a failing (false) performance. Now in his reply, De Waelhens treats the delusion of the patient as a real instance of belief. He does so by pointing to logical consequences that pertain to real facts, in this case, that there are costs associated with births. De Waelhens's reply tactfully avoids pointing to a possible failure in the patient's thinking (human beings cannot give birth each week to several children) and might, therefore, be expected to elicit gratitude. Of course, the patient could, consciously or unconsciously, disregard this gesture of goodwill in De Waelhens's reply. But, the patient does not disregard De Waelhens's question, nor does she show gratitude for it. Instead, she is incensed.

Why would someone be incensed if another person attempts to overlook a failure in your thinking or perception? One solution is to acknowledge that hallucination or delusion is not a failure but something different, something that has a function of its own and thus, for the patient, a positive meaning. De Waelhens does not define hallucination and delusion as instances of failed perception but as instances of *belief*. This belief is characterized by two functions. "First . . . it fulfills an unsatisfied and generally narcissistic desire."[9] Second, it is the beginning of a kind of reinvestment in objects. The objects invested in will not be the objects of the patient's perception. Rather, they will be objects created by his own narcissistic feeling of omnipotence.[10] This last characteristic makes hallucination and delusion distinct from perception. Thus, to treat a hallucination (delusion) as a perception is to denigrate it and deny its essential function.

The argument that hallucination (delusion) is not a failed perception but some different kind of human activity is confirmed in the writing of one of the most famous psychiatric patients, Judge Schreber. After the court sentenced him to permanent commitment to an asylum and rejected his lawyer's appeal, Judge Schreber appealed again in person. His main argument rested on the clarification of the nature of hallucination and delusion. The argument was successful in that the court lifted the order and let Schreber free.

Schreber's argument is an attack upon the medical testimony, which was crucial for the prior legal decision to keep Schreber in an asylum. That testimony reads as follows: "The most important moment in judging the capacity of the patient to look after his affairs is and remains the fact that everything which objectively seen appears as delusions and hallucinations is for him (a) unshakable certainty and (b) adequate motive for action."[11] Schreber's argument against the medical testimony reads as follows:

> I have to confirm the first part (a) of this statement, namely that my so-called delusional system is unshakable certainty, with the same decisive "yes" as I have to counter the second part (b), namely that my delusions are adequate motive for action, with the strongest possible "no." I could even say with Jesus

> Christ: "My kingdom is not of this world"; my so-called delusions are concerned solely with God and the beyond; they *can* therefore *never* in any way influence my behavior in any worldly matter, if I may use this expression—apart from the whim already mentioned, which is also meant to impress God.[12]

Thus, Schreber explicitly claims that he locates hallucinations (delusions) and perception in two different worlds. If one treats hallucinations (delusions) as failed perceptions (false beliefs) one can construct a convincing argument for committing someone to an asylum. Schreber's contention is that placing someone under tutelage for hallucinations (delusions) is unacceptable because hallucinations (delusions) are separate, in his case, from the world that the law regulates. Hallucinations (delusions) should, therefore, be looked upon as activities in their own right, not just as failed perception or false constructions.

Freud and the Positive Approach to Hallucination

Freud's understanding of hallucinations and delusions can be illustrated by his analysis of the *Memoirs* of Judge Schreber. Freud's thesis is simple: Schreber experienced a "feminine (that is, a passive homosexual) wishful phantasy, which took as its object the figure of his doctor. An intense resistance to this phantasy arose on the part of Schreber's personality."[13] But the repressed homosexual tendency returns in the form of a projection upon the other, while allowing Schreber some unconscious (i.e., homosexual) satisfaction. The hallucination (delusion) thus has the double task of denying homosexuality *and* allowing homosexual satisfaction. Inasmuch as Schreber's delusions succeed in performing these two tasks, Schreber is able to liberate himself from his internal contradictions and relate again to the world and thus function more fully in it. Schreber even succeeded in presenting arguments that moved the court to release him from institutional commitment, something Schreber's lawyer had not been able to do.

Freud does more than give such a general interpretation of this case. He finds a technique by which he can use his general thesis to describe the genesis of a variety of delusions out of one underlying psychic conflict. That technique consists of presenting the delusional system as an intelligent and thus intelligible *whole*, the parts of which can be generated from the different ways in which the sentence "I (a man) love another (man)" can be denied. Of course, this raises a puzzling philosophical question: In the production of this delusional system, who thinks? Let us return, however, to Freud's magnificent pedagogical trick and see in what ways the aforementioned given sentence can be denied.

1. The first method of denying the sentence "I (a man) love another (man)" is to deny the verb and claim that instead of love there is hate between the ego and another. Because the repressed unconscious material returns as a projection, it is the other who hates the ego. This gives rise to the delusion of persecution (Freud 1911–1913, 63). In turn, the hate perceived emanating from the other allows the ego to be preoccupied with the other and thus satisfy itself, while at the same time hiding homosexual interest in the other.
2. The second method of denying the sentence is to deny that the love is between the ego and the object but is instead with a third. This mechanism of projection requires that it is the third who initiates love; it is this which gives rise to erotomania (Freud 1911–1913, 63). Homosexuality is satisfied in a hidden way inasmuch as, for example, Schreber, a male, is loved by a male God. The homosexual aspect is hidden by the delusional requirement that Schreber has to become a female. Freud points out that Schreber's acceptance of having to become a female marks a turning point for the better in his illness. Delusion (hallucination) is, thus, here claimed to be the method of partial recovery.
3. The third method of denying the sentence is to deny the subject: There is love, but it is between others. This gives rise to the delusion of jealousy (Freud 1911–1913, 64). One might argue that Schreber's delusion that Flechsig wanted, with the help of God, to prevent Schreber from becoming a neurologist (a nerve doctor) is an indication of Schreber's jealousy.
4. A fourth and last possible method of denying the sentence is to reject the entire sentence and claim that there is no love occurring at all, and hence that there is no relation between ego and object; however, according to Freud, the libido must invest itself somewhere. To claim that there is no investment can only mean that there is no investment in others. Thus, when the ego becomes the only object of investment, this results in aggrandizement (overvaluation of the love object). In this case, aggrandizement results in megalomania (Freud 1911–1913, 65). In Schreber, megalomania takes the form of Schreber's believing that he must help in recreating mankind by becoming the wife of God.

Freud is able to derive several other consequences from this last method of denying the sentence. Withdrawing all emotional investment from others means that others cease to exist emotionally for Schreber (Freud 1911–1913, 75). They can therefore be thought of as dead or fleetingly improvised. But, if there is no emotional investment in objects, then Schreber himself is open to nothing; he is emotionally dead, too. Even in his recovery, he will be but a shadow of his prior self. Freud goes one step further in his analysis of

Schreber's *Memoirs*. He argues that Flechsig, Schreber's doctor, stands for an older brother of Schreber, and that God (as well as the sun) stand for Schreber's father (Freud 1911–1913, 47). Clearly, Freud was able to make sense of an entire series of symptoms by the simple technique of proposing that Schreber wanted to deny in every possible way the sentence expressing his unacceptable homosexuality.

Let us look at the results of Freud's technique. You might remember the enumeration of the delusional (hallucinatory) symptoms of Judge Schreber. One follows the other. The surprising and innumerable symptoms of Schreber create the impression of an *open-ended series*. By means of his pedagogical trick, Freud made the symptoms of Schreber a *closed series*, a series of four distinctly different kinds of symptoms. No other kinds of symptoms are imaginable if Freud is correct in his thesis that the cause of Schreber's illness was repressed homosexuality.

But, Schreber mentioned several other kinds of symptoms that cannot be classified in one of the four kinds that Freud proposed. Two kinds of symptoms, in particular, are to be noticed. First, there is the curious phenomenon of God speaking a transformed (and antiquated) German and the fact that the voices speak in half-sentences. Let us call these symptoms the linguistic curiosities. Second, there are the series of hallucinations (delusions) concerning the body experience, whereby Schreber feels himself deprived of or losing certain body parts, or complains about special pains in parts of his body. Let us call these symptoms problems of body integrity. These unexplained kinds of symptoms will allow Lacan an opening for returning to the case of Schreber.

Lacan, Schreber, and the Idea of Paternal Metaphor

Lacan makes several steps in his study of Schreber. First, he accuses the psychiatric profession of having remained the prisoner of an eighteenth- and nineteenth-century epistemology. In such an epistemology, there was a predominance of faculty psychology whereby one considered as separate the different faculties of reason, sense-perception, willing, and feeling.[14] Furthermore, no great attention was paid to affect in its contribution to perception. Finally, both the empiricist and the rationalist tradition conceived correctly that the unity of the object was created by the subject. The empiricist attributed the creation of the unity of the object to the unification of associations by the subject. The rationalists attributed the unity of the object to the constituting activities of the subject. Both traditions naively believed that this unifying function remained an *unchangeable capability in the human subject.*[15]

Within this naïve epistemology, hallucination (delusion) could, therefore, in principle not be understood in terms of the subject's constituting or associative activities. It therefore could only be explained as the malfunctioning of the perception of the sense-data. Furthermore, the capability of properly perceiving sense-data was understood as having contact with reality—reality being understood as external to the subject and intersubjectively guaranteed. Thus, De Waelhens quotes a psychiatrist as replying to his patient, "You see, my friend, all this is not serious, all this is not true, let us get back to the real."[16]

It is here that Lacan makes use of a basic insight of phenomenological epistemology: To a different *noema* must correspond a different *noesis*. Or, in the language of Lacan, if there is a manifest difference between a hallucination (delusion) and a normal *perceptum* then we should not assume that the *percipiens* (or perceiver) is the same in both. Lacan then uses an example that is meant to attack the definition of hallucination as the absence of sense-data.

Let us use an example of our own. Let us imagine a situation in which the same sense-data are presented, let us say the sentence of an immigrant professor: "Hegel's dialectic is a new form of epistemology." Amplifying Lacan's example, let us suppose that there are in the audience two kinds of students. Some are philosophy students, who will overlook the foreign accent and intonation, and write down in some not too distorted form the idea communicated by the sentence. Other students are students in linguistics and will therefore overlook the idea expressed in the sentence but will write down in phonetic signs or even musical notes the distortions in pronunciation brought about by the foreign accent and intonation. In both cases, the same sense-data were presented, but because the intentionality of both groups was different, the same sense-data will be heard in two different forms[17] and thus the two groups of students will take different notes.

Similarly, the difference between hallucination and perception should be understood in terms of the difference of intentionality that results from differences in the personality structure of the normal and the psychotic person. This general epistemological requirement allows Lacan to formulate the project of relating the structure of the psychotic subject to the specific hallucinations (delusions) this subject produces. In this project, he will both follow Freud and explicitly correct him.

Lacan's second step is to execute the phenomenological requirement of relating the psychotic symptoms (the *perceptum*) to the structure of the personality (i.e., the *percipiens*) to explain the symptoms.

First, Lacan summarizes a clinical case of his own. The case concerns a girl who is offended because the lover of a neighbor had called her "Sow!" The girl offered this as an example of an insult to which both she and her mother were subjected. Lacan calls the mother and the daughter a couple with shared delusions. The daughter has left her husband and her in-laws because she was convinced that "these peasants . . . [were going] to cut her—the good-for-nothing city girl—into pieces."[18] Upon being informed about the insult of being called "Sow," Lacan asks the girl a question, which might seem mysterious to an outsider: "What had you said the moment before?" The literal translation of the French is even more astonishing: "What words could have been spoken in you the moment before?"[19] The girl replied that she had, in effect, murmured, "I've just been to the pork butcher's." But, to the further question asking to whom these words were addressed, the patient was not certain. She was not certain whether it had been to herself, her mother, or her neighbor's lover.

This gives Lacan the opportunity to make several remarks. First, the "I" of "I've just been to the pork butcher's" is, in the mind of the patient, not fixed. In linguistic "I" is a so-called "shifter" whose meaning is only fixed if the context is fixed (Jakobson and Halle 1956). In this case, the context does not seem fixed.

We now come to Lacan's second remark. The context becomes fixed when she hears in a hallucinatory (delusional) way the word *sow*. The implication is that in the word *sow* is a label she has given herself, she who experiences herself as a fragmented body, which according to Lacan is the unavoidable way of understanding oneself if one maintains a dual relationship with one's mother. We know, from her paranoid fear that her in-laws will cut her into pieces, that indeed she has a phantasy of a fragmented body.

Third, Lacan remarks that the depths of this girl's tragedy are revealed by words, which emerge in the form of a strophe (pork butcher's) and an antistrophe ("Sow!"), separated by a pause. I take this to mean that for Lacan, the patient is not in a position to deliver a straightforward description of herself. Instead, and here we come to Lacan's essential claim, "We also touch here upon the effect that every signifier has, once it is perceived, of arousing in the *percipiens* an assent composed of the awakening of the hidden duplicity of the second by the manifest ambiguity of the first."[20] And this, according to Lacan, usually occurs in the "form of a broken chain." We are now in a position to understand Lacan's summary of the self-understanding of the patient who does not understand to whom is addressed the "I" and "I've just been to the pork butcher's" until she hallucinates that another calls her "Sow." The summary reads as follows:

> After a pause, this uncertainty came to an end with the apposition of the word "sow," itself too loaded with invective to follow the oscillation isochronically. Thus, the discourse came to realize its intention as rejection in hallucination. In the place where the unspeakable object is rejected in the real, a word makes itself heard, so that, coming in the place of that which has no name, it was unable to follow the intention of the subject without detaching itself from it by the dash preceding the reply: Opposing its disparaging antistrophe to the cursing of the strophe thus restored to the patient with the index of the I.[21]

Thus, in the two-page summary of the case of his patient, Lacan has drawn attention to the two kinds of symptoms in Schreber that Freud does not incorporate in his closed series of symptoms: the hallucination of the fragmented body and the curious usage of language, when it is tied up with hallucination or delusion. Lacan will take the curious usage of language by a psychotic (Judge Schreber) as the starting point for introducing his concept of the paternal metaphor. It might therefore be appropriate to present Muller and Richardson's summary of Lacan's view of the function of language in the hallucination of his patient:

> Much more goes into the constitution of the hallucination here than the projective activity of the "unifying subject." . . . Some elemental pattern gives structure to the discourse, determines its antiphonal format, correlates the signifiers of the strophe (pork butcher's) and antistrophe ("Sow!"), etc.—and all this goes on *independently* of the conscious, speaking subject.[22]

In a second move, Lacan turns to the case of Schreber. He turns to that case with a specific theoretical framework for dealing with mental illness.[23] That framework includes Lacan's insistence upon the importance of signifiers or even letters. Muller and Richardson lucidly formulate that aspect of Lacan's theory as follows: "We take this to mean that symptoms experienced on the level of the conscious subject are to be relieved by discerning their place as signifiers within the structures of the discourse of the Other."[24] We are therefore not surprised that Lacan focuses his attention on Schreber's speech and his bizarre theories concerning the language he hears. This is a domain that Freud did not include in his own interpretation of Schreber's case.

The first curious aspect of Schreber's theory about the language of his auditory hallucination is his claim to a so-called basic language, a "somewhat archaic but always rigorous German" spoken by God. This basic language is full of euphemisms about which Schreber is informed in his hallucination.[25]

Lacan stresses the fact that in part of the *Memoirs*, Schreber claims that these messages about the code are "borne by beings,"[26] that "divine rays . . . are simply the joining together of the words (paroles) that they support" or that the "nature of the rays is that they must speak." Lacan finds in it a confirmation of his own theoretical vision and writes about Schreber's "basic language" that, "There is the relation here of the system to its own constitution as signifier" or "What is involved here, in fact, is an effect of the signifier." Lacan then mentions that it is precisely when the voices repeat purely repetitively expressions of the basic language that they take account of the "conception-of-signifiers." I take Lacan to mean that when the voices utter signifiers as pure signifiers, as a collection of letters and not as expressions of some signified, that it is precisely then that the voices take account the "conception-of-souls," that is, understand the nature of human beings. Lacan refers to this as "code phenomena" or "messages on the code."

The second curious aspect of Schreber's auditory hallucination concerns the content of the messages. Schreber hears voices pronouncing unfinished sentences. Thus, he hears, for instance, "Now I will . . . myself . . ." or "As for you, you ought to . . ." or "I will certainly." Schreber knows that the sentences have to be completed as follows: 1) "resign myself to being stupid"; 2) "be exposed . . . as denying God, as given to voluptuous excesses, not to mention other things"; or 3) "think about that first."[27] About this aspect of Schreber's auditory hallucination Lacan stresses that what Schreber hears is restricted to index-terms of shifters and ends before the real message is given. In Lacan's words, the message is "reduced to what, in the code, indicates the message."[28] Again Lacan sees in this aspect of Schreber's auditory hallucination another proof of his thesis that the "signifier . . . structures the subject."[29]

What I find fascinating about this second aspect of Schreber's auditory hallucination is that he feels obligated to finish these unfinished sentences lest he be annihilated.[30] Indeed, Schreber believes that the unfinished sentences are tests given by God to see if he can withdraw his rays from Schreber, which would be fatal for Schreber.[31] Furthermore, I find it worthwhile to draw attention to the fact that the completed sentences are not about such insignificant topics as the color of the leaves or the weight of a chair. Rather, the completed sentences are a form of self-description.

Finally, Schreber is not free to choose how to complete the unfinished sentences but rather must complete the sentences as the voices intended. And most interestingly, the sentences so finished describe Schreber, in several instances, in a way that is upsetting to Schreber because they are contrary to his self-conception. Thus, while Schreber is convinced of his great intelligence, he is forced to complete the first sentence as, "Now I will myself face the fact that I am an idiot." This is, of course, quite different from what Schreber freely writes about himself. Hence, to explain why the white lies told to him by Professor Flechsig were ineffective, Schreber describes himself as a "human being of high intellect, of uncommon keenness of understanding and acute powers of observation";[32] on another occasion, Schreber corrects a compliment made by Flechsig's soul that he, Schreber, was the "greatest seer of spirits of all centuries" by retorting that "one ought at least to speak of the greatest seer of all *millennia*."[33]

Stressing these three points moves us away from the Lacanian thesis of the "predominance of the signifier"[34] and calls attention to the position of Schreber as an actor in the drama that produced his psychosis. This will allow us to follow the Lacanian theory of psychosis and still remain true to the fundamental insight of phenomenology: the explanation of a noema requires the identification of the noesis that created the noema.

In a third move, Lacan now tries to give a theoretical explanation of the cause of psychosis. He claims that he will do so within a Freudian framework. Lacan identifies rather rapidly five themes he considers essential to Freudianism:

"the equivalence Freud maintains of the imaginary function of the phallus in the two sexes"
"the castration complex considered to be a normative phase of the subject's assumption of his own sex"
"the myth of the killing of the father rendered necessary by the constitutive presence of the Oedipus complex in every personal history"
"the splitting brought about in love life by the instance, indeed the repetitive instance, and its object that is always to be refound as unique"
"the fundamentally dissident nature of Freud's notion of the drive, the theoretical disjunction between the tendency, its direction, and its object"[35]

Of course, Lacan's faithfulness to Freud does not mean that he will abandon his own insight of the essentially linguistic nature of the unconscious process. He will maintain that Freud himself had that intuition but that it needed further articulation.

Lacan reconstructs Schreber's failure as a linguistic failure, that is, a failure to enter into the symbolic order. Success or failure in entering into the symbolic order depends upon the paternal metaphor taking hold or not taking hold of the child. More completely, Lacan argues that normal development requires the paternal metaphor to take hold of the child and that in such a way that metonymy becomes meaningful. Thus, Lacan requires us to think that in the psychotic person, the two crucial characteristics of language, according to Jakobson, are deficient (Jakobson and Halle 1956). This is the specific way in which one can, theoretically, claim that psychosis is some kind of linguistic failure.

Let us now see how Lacan presents his linguistic theory of psychosis. Lacan affirms that the child situates itself as the complement to the mother. In his own terminology, the child situates itself as being what the mother lacks. It imagines itself to be the object of desire of the mother.[36] It does so whether it is a baby boy or a baby girl. This is consistent with earlier psychoanalytic literature, given that Freud relabeled the pre-Oedipal genital stage as the phallic phase.[37] The baby is said to think of itself as the phallus of the mother. Lacan calls this the "imaginary phallus."[38] It is not difficult to talk about this in phenomenologically acceptable ways. Indeed, to think of the child as conceiving of itself imaginarily as the phallus of the mother means that the child will create itself as wanting to be that which it thinks the mother lacks. Somehow the child's intentionality is involved in the alienation of its own wants. I believe that this is the meaning of the messages of Schreber's voices.

Let us analyze the different elements of the message of the voices. First, Schreber feels obligated to finish the sentences that define him. He feels that if he does not do so he might be annihilated. This corresponds to the situation that the baby imagines itself to be in. It needs to define itself; it needs to project itself as being something, otherwise it is nothing. Second, Schreber tells us that the entire process of finishing the sentences starts not as his own initiative, but as the initiative of another, the voices. Furthermore, the voices present him with an incomplete sentence that must be completed as they intend and desire. Again, this is similar to the child who defines its wants according to the way it thinks its mother wants or needs it to be.

Third, the way Schreber has to define himself is not the way he really wants to be. Similarly, the way the child feels it has to define itself according to the wishes of the mother cannot be conceived as what the child really wants to be: free and autonomous. I therefore take the symptom of sentence-finishing to be an indication that Schreber, at some deep level, has not overcome the alienation that is typical for the symbiotic relation built between mother and child in early infancy.

Lacan's way of talking about this reconstructed period of the life of the child is, in important ways, different from the preceding account. Muller and Richardson summarize Lacan's views as follows: "For the phallus is not a physical organ in this conception, but rather an image that functions as the signifier of desire, playing a role for the subject insofar as he is entirely conditioned by the intrusion of the signifier."[39] In such a formulation the question is, How do we conceive of such an intrusion? Who does the intruding? Is the infant totally passive or is it actively accepting the intrusion? Without the idea of a subject actively accepting the signifier, a basic rule of phenomenology would be violated. It would be difficult to imagine how such a signifier would have any impact on the infant at all.

One more aspect in the symbiotic relation between mother and child should be stressed. The child experiences the mother–child unit as a kind of absolute totality. From the point of view of the child, the mother—from whom the child does not feel separated—has a fullness, a completeness that one could metaphorically describe as omnipotence. The child thus assigns itself and the mother a greater value than they each in fact have. Let us try to present this graphically (see figure 0.1).

M stands for mother. C stands for child. The + sign next to the child indicates the illusionary value that the child in imagination attributes it itself, i.e., that it is the complement, the phallus of the mother. The + sign next to the mother indicates the illusionary value that the child attributes to its mother, i.e., that she has a fullness, an omnipotence she does not have. The circle around M-C indicates that from the point of view of the child, there is an

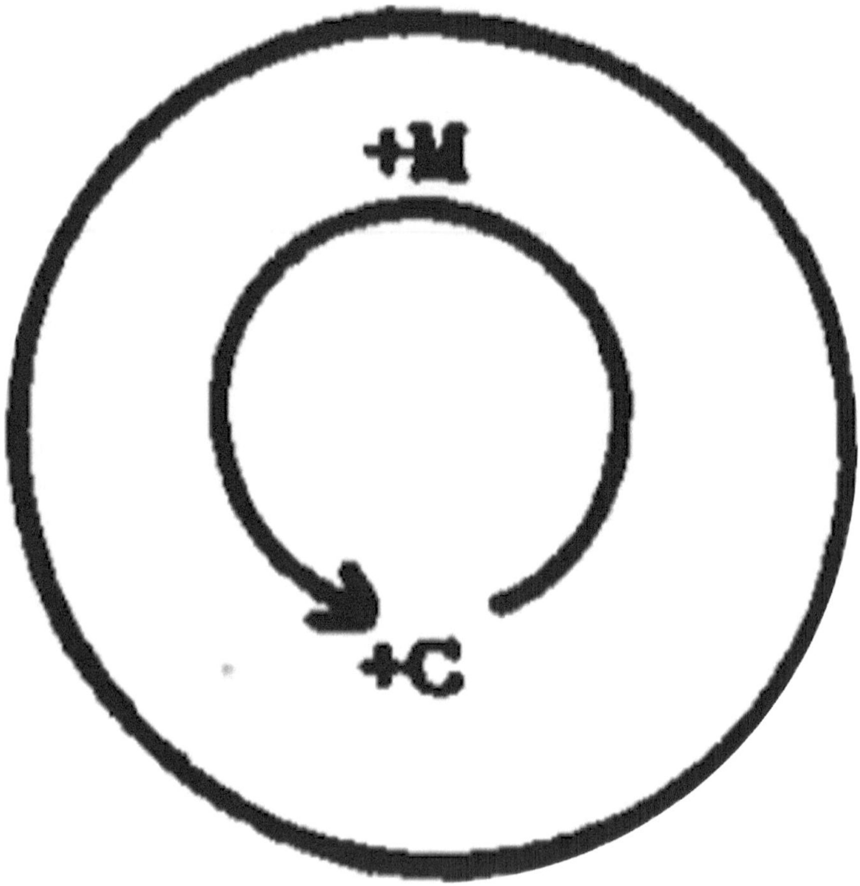

Figure 0.1. The symbiotic relationship between mother and child.

attempt to make the mother its sole relevant other. The child will therefore tend to exclude as significant all others but the mother. The arrow starting from the child going to the mother and pointing to the child again indicates that the child defines himself, has some kind of intentionality; however, the self-definition takes its clue from the mother. The child can therefore be said to allow itself to be defined by another (its mother), provided that we interpret the word *allow* in the strong sense of "actively participate, actively aim at."

Of course, plenty of mysteries remain. Why is the phallus used as the symbol of the complementarity of mother and child? Why not a cosmic image like as day-night or moon? Why not use the image of complementary tools, for example, hammer-nail or screw-screwdriver? If a body part must function as an image of complementarity, why is it that the preferred image is the one of the phallus? Even if the phallus is not the same as the physical organ of the penis, it is still the case that there is a privileged connection between phallus and penis. Indeed, the erect penis is the preferred representation of the phallus. But if we accept the argument that a bodily image is the preferred image for all early self-definitions—and Merleau-Ponty's phenomenology provides ample evidence for such a view—there still remains the question as to why the chosen image (the phallus) must be so tied up with sexuality. Could not other body parts, for instance, the tongue, the mouth, and the nose, do equally well in representing the complementarity of mother and child? According to the testimony of psychoanalysts, the universal image of the mother–child complementarity is the phallus. Philosophically, we are here in the presence of a reported fact.

For Lacan, psychosis will develop if the child does not correct the illusory vision of the self-developed in the symbiotic relation. That correction consists of a process that involves the imaginary phallus. The imaginary phallus is treated as a product, a signifier. Given that the child created its illusory conception of itself by defining itself from the point of view of the mother, any correction will have to start from a perceived change in the mother's relation to the child. That change can occur if, in the imaginary world of the child, a trace is discerned that puts into question for the child the meaning it gives to the signifier phallus, with which it has imaginarily identified.[40] Lacan continues to present this process very much as a purely linguistic process. I prefer to understand this process as an act of the subject, which results in linguistic processes, rather than a linguistic process that produces a subject. I therefore agree with De Waelhens's statement on Lacan: "[The failure of the metaphor of the Name-of-the-Father] can be traced to each one of the authors of the drama separately, or on the contrary, to several of them, indeed to all of them."[41]

But, let us first present Lacan's view. A logical reconstruction of the event "paternal metaphor" contains three steps. First, there is the mother and the child. Between them there is something called "désire de la mère," which means both "desire for the mother from the point of view of the child" and "desire inhabiting the mother."

Second, we now look at what the child does. The child interprets (imaginarily) the desire inhabiting the mother. That interpretation is an image, a signifier (S). In fact, Lacan holds that the child interprets the desire inhabiting the other as her desiring the child as her complement, as the mother's imaginary phallus. This is the signified (s), which for the child is tied to the signifier (S), which is the image the child forms of the desires inhabiting the mother. Of course, there are consequences when one defines one's life project as becoming the desired object of another. One problem is that one must enslave oneself to become what one thinks the other wants.

The third step in the logical reconstruction consists of the new signifier Lacan calls the "Name-of-the-Father." Lacan stresses that it is not the real father, but rather the symbolic father, which he calls the dead father, thereby alluding to two Freudian themes: the murder of the primal father and the imaginary will, presumably present in every child, to kill the father in the Oedipus complex. From the point of view of the child, that signifier arrives from nowhere and destroys the sense of self and the meaning system the child had built. That new signifier (S2) destroys because it appears as a totally new signifier of the desire inhabiting the mother and, as such, competes directly with the (S1) that the child imaginarily created of the mother's desire.

The child now faces two competing signifiers for the same signified reality: the desire inhabiting the mother. Either the child accepts the new signifier or does not. If it does not, the conditions are created for a possible psychosis.[42] If the child accepts the new signifier, then the first signifier has to disappear. The disappearance, however, takes on a special form: The first signifier is not erased; rather it is repressed, it disappears into the unconscious. Graphically, Lacan presents that by putting a bar (/) through (S1). Before (S2) arrived on the scene, the child had self-identity. The first signifier (S1) produced an explicitly signified (s), an explicit self-identity. The new signifier of the desire inhabiting the mother annuls and absorbs the first signifier. As it is in the nature of a signifier to signify, it is unavoidable that (S2) signifies something. Whatever that something may be, it will have to be different than what (S1) signified. That difference is what hits the child.

The introduction of (S2) puts the meaning of the child's life in question.[43] It leaves the child wondering how to situate itself as desire for the desire of another. The acceptance of (S2) destroys the possibility for the child to receive the message that it is the phallus of the mother. This destruction Lacan calls symbolic castration. Notice that everything turns around the destruction of the first signified (S1) by the arrival of (S2). That destruction occurs because of the acceptance of a new, competing signifier. That new signifier is such that it does not give a fixed, determined outcome to the question of the child: who am I, who am I supposed to be? Lacan refers to this entire third step as the paternal metaphor. It is a metaphor because the entire process can be understood as resulting from (S2) suppressing (S1), as is the case with a metaphor. Instead of referring to my friend as John (S1), I can, in a moment of exasperation, call him a "chicken" (S2). In doing so, I create a new meaning, a new signified: the idea "coward." This, in short, is Lacan's linguistic theory of the paternal metaphor.

I wish to turn now to the question of how the signifier, "Name-of-the-Father," is introduced in the universe of the child. I will use that question to propose a phenomenologically more acceptable way of talking about the paternal metaphor. The easiest way to imagine how the paternal metaphor might be introduced into the child's world is to imagine that it is mediated by the mother showing respect for the Name-of-the-Father. Lacan foresees that interpretation when he writes, "People will say that they are emphasizing the bond of love and respect by which the mother does or does not situate the father in his ideal place."[44] Such an interpretation must face the possible objection that the mother of Judge Schreber had some, if not a great deal of, respect for the father of Judge Schreber, as we can conclude from the testimony of Judge Schreber's sister, Anna. She wrote, "Father discussed with our mother everything and anything; she took part in all his ideas, plans and projects, and she read the galley proofs of his writings with him, and was his faithful, close companion in everything."[45]

One could also raise questions about the validity of such a view from a general philosophical point of view. This interpretation of the paternal metaphor would put the burden of saving the child from psychosis solely on the shoulders of the mother. It would also put the blame for the cause of psychosis solely upon the mother.[46] One could naively respond that a child is a child of both parents. Or, in more abstract, Hegelian language, one could say that the children need to find their identity in the unity of the will created by both parents.[47] This is the objection I formulated in the introduction to De Waelhens's book *Schizophrenia*. That objection is repeated by clinical psychologist M. Guy Thompson in his *The Death of Desire*.[48] And A. Vergote, drawing the theoretical conclusions of empirical research about the images of parental figures, writes,

> It is striking that judge is the only factor that characterizes the mother figure of the schizophrenics . . . the absence of the father results just as much from the desire of the mother to eliminate him from the family triangle. Doing this, she imposes herself on the child with an authority that contradicts her availability.[49]

This text obviously supports the idea that the contribution of the mother for the paternal metaphor is crucial; however, Vergote has a second reflection when commenting on the role of the father. In that text, he supports our thesis that the father, too, is at stake in the paternal metaphor. He writes,

> The law-authority set is . . . absent in the paternal figure of the schizophrenics. The primary factor is composed of two opposing dimensions, one expressing the idea of decision, a more concrete term than law-authority, and the other containing the idea of availability. The father here is therefore not really the symbolic father. . . . The physical presence of a nourishing and protecting father cannot sufficiently compensate for that which he ought to be symbolically.[50]

However, we can find in Lacan a half-page warning against this interpretation. The warning attacks the previous interpretation from two sides. From the side of the mother the warning is as follows:

> But what I do wish to stress is that we should concern ourselves not only with the way in which the mother accommodates the father as a person, but also with the importance she attributes to his speech—in a word, to his authority—in other words, with the place that she reserves for the Name-of the-Father in the promulgation of the law.

From the side of the father, and presumably with the father of Judge Schreber in mind, the warning reads as such:

> Further still, the father's relation to this law must be considered in its own right, for one will find in it the reason for the paradox whereby devastating effects of the paternal figure are found with particular frequency in cases where the father really functions as a legislator or boasts that he does—whether he is, in fact, one of the people who makes the laws or presents himself as a pillar of faith, as a paragon of integrity and devotion, as virtuous or as a virtuoso, as serving a charitable cause whatever the object or lack thereof that is at stake, as serving the nation or birth rate, safety or salubrity, legacy or law, the pure, the lowest of the low, or the empire. These are all ideals that provide him with all too many opportunities to seem to be at fault, to fall short, and even to be fraudulent—in short, to exclude the Name-of-the-Father from its position in the signifier.

The warning from the side of the father is stressed, again, from the point of view of the child:

> This result can be obtained with still less, and no one who practices child analysis will deny that children see right through hypocritical behavior, so much so that it can be devastating to them. But who articulates that the lie thus perceived implies a reference to the constituting function of speech?[51]

These warnings of Lacan allow us to return to De Waelhens's statement that the paternal metaphor can fail because of all three actors. De Waelhens's abstract claim is confirmed by the theoretical interpretation that Vergote gives to his empirical research about parental figures previously quoted. But clearly this line of reasoning allows for articulating the active contribution of the three actors, and it allows us to talk about the paternal metaphor as a product and not as an actor. I claim that this makes the Lacanian theory of the paternal metaphor compatible with the fundamental rule of phenomenology.

Let us start with an illustration. A 3- or 4-year-old boy was regularly picked up by his mother from preschool at noon. Each day when mother and son arrived home, the mother would ask the boy to tell his father that it was time for lunch. Almost on a daily basis, the boy would tell his mother when walking home with her that he would not call his father for lunch that day. The boy never executed his threat of not telling his father that it was lunchtime. Instead, he would storm up the steps halfway and then shout to his father that it was time for lunch. Then, he would immediately run back to the kitchen and regularly report to his mother that daddy did not want to come. Two minutes later, the father would appear, and lunch would proceed.

One day the mother could not pick up the boy, and the father picked him up instead. The son refused to come with the father. After the father talked to the child and the teacher, the son agreed to come with the father, who told the son that it was okay to express his preference to have his mother pick him up; however, the father stressed that if he, the father, came to pick him up, it was not okay for him to make a scene and refuse to come home with his father. The mother explicitly confirmed this. Eight days later, on that same lunch table, the boy declared that he would become a professor, the profession of his father. Eight days or so after the pronouncement, the boy declared that he would become a policeman. Two weeks or so later, he declared that he would become a bicyclist. I take this to be an illustration of a paternal metaphor that established itself in the boy.

Let us indicate that intentionality, from the point of view of the boy, is not absent. The boy clearly establishes an intimacy with the mother and attempts to exclude the father. The boy is invited by the mother to include the father in everyday activities, including the one activity where the boy tries to exclude the father. Thus, the boy is confronted by the mother with her respect for the father. However important respect for the real father is, there is something different at stake, according to Lacan, in the paternal metaphor. There must be respect for the symbolic father, for the word of the father. In the reported case, we see this respect for the word of the father at the moment when the father formulates and explains in words to the son the rule (the law) as to what constitutes proper behavior. This rule is repeated in the presence of the child to the mother and is confirmed by her.

That is, however, not sufficient. It would not explain why Judge Schreber was a psychotic, notwithstanding the testimony of a daughter that the mother and the father discussed everything together and that the mother proofread the manuscripts of the father. Two further conditions are to be fulfilled and are present in our example.

The first condition is that the father must relate to the law as something that *transcends* him, not as something that he arbitrarily invents. The father must make the law also binding on his own will.[52] In this case, the father referred to a social rule or what is *socially proper behavior*: If someone other than your mother picks you up, you can express preference for your mother, but you still have to come home. It is a rule that facilitates social life and trumps dictatorial demands from a child. It is a condition that one can find expressed in Lacan, when he writes, "The father's relation to this law must be considered in its own right."[53]

The second condition that must be fulfilled is that the respect for the word of the father by the mother must be consonant with her own acceptance of the law that she respects in the word of the father. This was the case in our example inasmuch as the mother had, day after day, asked the child to call the father for lunch even when the child was saying constantly that he was not going to do it. I did not find this idea in Lacan. It is, however, the main idea of a work of Maud Mannoni, who explicitly acknowledges her debt to Lacan. In her work *L'Enfant Arriéré et Sa Mère*, Mannoni develops the thesis that the developmentally delayed child often must fill the mother's nonaccepted lack. She summarizes the insights, gained from her clinical cases, as follows: "What will become of mother, if she does not have the retardation of her child to keep her going (i.e., what will fill the emptiness in the life of such a mother, if psychological or sociological intervention remedies in some way the retardation and thereby takes away what gave meaning to the life of the mother)?"[54]

Of course, this only gives the conditions for the paternal metaphor. Ultimately, the child has to accept the challenge and confront the conditions presented to him. To put it this way is to inquire about the intentionalities that are present in the child. It is to ask for a description of the paternal metaphor that conforms with a fundamental rule of phenomenology. Originally, the child forms an illusory identity of itself by thinking itself to be the complement of the mother—or, in more technical psychoanalytic language, the child thinks itself to be the phallus of the mother. Accepting the paternal metaphor means that the child accepts that, not he, but the father, has phallic power.

If the Oedipus complex were restricted to these moments, then the Oedipus complex would result in nothing but the dislocation of the child from the place that it occupied imaginarily. This is what psychoanalytic theory calls castration and what Lacan calls symbolic castration. Of course, if the self-conception of the child is challenged, then the child must be at a loss as to who it is, as to how it has to think about itself, how it can satisfy its felt need for love or, to use Lacanian terminology, its felt need to be the object of desire of another. The child must therefore face questions about itself. In summary, the mother's respect for the Name-of-the-Father causes the child to question itself. I take this to be the referent of Lacan's puzzling statement: "A [here the Name-of-the-Father], the locus from which the question of his existence may arise for him."[55]

In our example, the boy solves that question by identifying with the father and saying that he will become a professor. In psychoanalytic terms, the boy has accepted an ego ideal that he knows he is not but hopes and intends to become. I take the metaphoric move of the Oedipus complex to consist of the move made by the child whereby he accepts deprivation of an original but illusory identity and conquers a new identity. Even though this is a new identity, the child must create a kind of continuity for itself and therefore feel that it is both the same and not the same as before. I take this to be the essence of any metaphoric move. Indeed, a metaphor involves identifying something that is at the same time similar and dissimilar. I further take this metaphoric move at the level of one's identity to be the foundation for anyone's capability for creating and understanding metaphors. I take the metaphoric move at the level of the Oedipus complex to establish a permanent capacity in the person. Thus, when, in later life, the individual is forced to redefine himself, he has at the emotional level the capability of letting go of an ego ideal and being able to accept another one, in the way advised by the Stoics.

My interpretation of the paternal metaphor as resting upon the moves made by the child itself rather than resting upon the changed meaning of the phallus at the level of the unconscious is consistent with a crucial implication of Lacan's theory. Indeed, Lacan argues that psychotic breakdown occurs when a figure called "A-father" appears in the erotized field of the patient. The concept "A-father" is a technical term defined by Lacan as someone who "situate[s] himself in a tertiary position in any relationship that has as its base the imaginary couple a-a'—that is, ego-object or ideal-reality—involving the subject in the field of erotized aggression that it induces."[56] In the case of Schreber, Flechsig became the "A-father."

There was a subjective reason why Schreber, at that moment, was looking for "A-father." In his *Memoirs*, Judge Schreber tells us that he realized that he would not be able to have children and that this realization was one of the most painful realizations of his life. Furthermore, Judge Schreber was appointed by the king as presiding judge in the second-highest court of the land, a court where many sitting judges were 20 years his senior. In these circumstances, Judge Schreber felt obliged to work extremely hard to prove that he was worthy of the appointment; in fact, he overworked himself. There were, therefore, two aspects of his self-conception that Schreber realized were not going to be fulfilled. The difficulty I see is whether we should consider the two failures as deficiencies of Schreber's ideal ego or his ego ideal. In any case, a gap opens in the ideal of Schreber. I take Lacan to mean that psychologically, Schreber is in need of something, of someone to fill that gap.

There was an objective reason why Schreber looked at Flechsig as his "A-father." Flechsig had successfully treated him during a previous mental breakdown and had a great reputation. Furthermore, Schreber's wife had enormous affection for Flechsig.

My interpretation of Schreber's psychotic breakdown is that Schreber never acquired the emotional capability to replace one ideal with another. I identify this capability as a crucial metaphorical possibility of the emotional life. Of course, if the emotional life has not integrated the metaphorical move, metonymy also is not possible. In the example of the boy, it is clear that the substitution of the wish to become a professor with the wish to become a policeman, and then later with the wish to become a bicyclist, is only possible if the boy had accepted that he had to become someone. Successful integration of the Oedipus complex thus provides the subjective foundation for two aspects of language that Jakobson understands to be fundamental: metaphor and metonymy (Jakobson and Halle 1956).

One last word about the paternal metaphor. According to Lacan, the absence of the paternal metaphor will necessarily tear the subject apart imaginarily. In his theory of the mirror stage, Lacan had argued for the thesis that there is a psychic act that is responsible for our sense of bodily unity. The absence of the paternal metaphor, inasmuch as it makes imaginary castration unavoidable, thus will produce the loss of the sense of bodily unity. In this way, Lacan's paternal metaphor accounts for the two major phenomena in Schreber's symptomatology that Freud's theory did not account for.[57]

NOTES

1. The pages refer to the pages in the German original.
2. *Comprehensive Textbook of Psychiatry*, Freedman 1975a, b, 807.
3. Freedman 1975, 2588.
4. Both delusion and hallucination concern a subject's belief in things that are held to be false by the community. A delusion is more elaborate. A hallucination is more concrete and involves the claim of seeing something when it is not present. A delusion often has as an element a hallucination. Thus, as part of his delusion, Schreber believed that he saw his chest transforming into female breasts. I offer this example of the connection between delusion and hallucination even though psychiatrists refuse to call this phenomenon a hallucination and require the claim of seeing, for instance, a lion before using the concept hallucination. To further my point, I might have to argue that hallucination is a polar concept whose essential meaning applies to an entire series of phenomena.
5. De Waelhens 1972, summarizing Binswanger without giving references. It is technically more correct to talk about delusion of persecution (Freedman 1975). Thus, I corrected the references to Binswanger's ideas accordingly.
6. De Waelhens 1972.
7. De Waelhens 1972.
8. De Waelhens 1972, 221–22.
9. De Waelhens 1972, 222.
10. De Waelhens 1972, 222.
11. Schreber 1903, 431.
12. Schreber 1903, 301–2.
13. Rothgeb 1973, 240.
14. Lacan 2006; Muller and Richardson 1982.
15. De Waelhens 1972, 115. "In the nineteenth century it was thought that this function of unification . . . remained unchanged, whatever 'alterations in identity' may otherwise have taken place in the perceiving subject."
16. De Waelhens 1972, 221.
17. Lacan 2006.
18. Lacan 2006, 448 [535].

19. Lacan 2006, 448 [534]. "Nous [. . .] lui demandâmes tout uniment ce qui en elle-même avait pu se proférer l'instant avant."

20. Lacan 2006, 449 [536].

21. Lacan 2006, 448–49 [535].

22. Muller and Richardson 1982, 200–201. The idea that more is going on in the hallucinating subject than that subject is consciously aware of is argued for by Lacan in his comments on the auditory hallucination of Schreber (Lacan 2006, 447 [533]). This passage is commented on by De Waelhens 1972, 115–16. The major point of Lacan's comments is that signifiers and speech have a curious power in the hallucinations of Schreber. Thus, the voices are ineluctable. The message is not what it appears. Voices will be heard for the duration of the real message, even though they are accompanied by murmurs unrelated to the signifying chain and of different duration. Finally, the patient must pose as the voice who speaks and the one who listens before replying, which leads to ambiguities of meaning in the utterances. A phenomenon not mentioned by Lacan could be added—that is, the curious fact that hallucinating patients are not amazed to experience that others do not hear their "voices"; they do not even expect them to hear their "voices." What I will stress in Schreber's auditory hallucinations is not so much the autonomous power of signifiers as the power of some "other" on Schreber and the way he is forced to identify himself.

23. Muller and Richardson 1982, 196, write, "Though its [the essay on the case of Schreber, (chapter 6)] composition follows that of 'The Agency of the letter in the unconscious' (chapter 5), its thought represents a slightly earlier level of development." I interpret this to mean that the theoretical framework is quite similar in both chapters and that we therefore can find in chapter 5 an indication of the importance of letters in Lacan's early theory.

24. Muller and Richardson 1982, 209. The more obscure text of Lacan himself is quoted on p. 208 and immediately precedes Muller and Richardson's summary.

25. Schreber learns that in that basic language, reward means punishment, poison means food, juice means venom, tasting means purification, and "concerning Him Who Is and shall be" means God (Schreber 1903, 13–14).

26. For this and the quotations following in this paragraph: Lacan 2006, 450–51 [538–39], referring to Schreber 1903, 130.

27. Lacan 2006, 452 [539–40]; Schreber 1903, 217.

28. Lacan 2006, 452 [540].

29. Lacan 2006, 452 [540].

30. Bergeron 2002, 73: "The treatment must sever the psychotic from his or her imaginary relationship with that other being who dictates every action."

31. Schreber 1903, 206, 216.

32. Schreber 1903, 35.

33. Schreber 1903, 77.

34. Lacan 2006, 452 [540].

35. Lacan 2006, 455 [543–44].

36. Lacan 2006, 462–63 [554]: "The whole problem of the perversions consists in conceiving how the child, in his relation to the mother, a relation constituted in analysis not by his vital dependence on her, but by his dependence on her love, that is to say, by the desire for her desire, identifies himself with the imaginary object of this desire in so far as the mother herself symbolizes it in the phallus."

37. Freud 1905, 199–200.

38. Nobus 2000, 41: "A mother loves her child [. . .] because she uses the child to cover up her symbolic lack of enjoyment and to obtain supplementary satisfaction in a carefree and selfish way."

39. Muller and Richardson 1982, 211.

40. Lacan 2006, 464 [557]: "The signification of the phallus, I have said, must be evoked in the subject's imaginary by the paternal metaphor."

41. De Waelhens 1978, 127.

42. Lacan 2006, 479 [575]: "It is in an accident in this register and in what takes place in it, namely, the foreclosure of the Name-of-the-Father in the place of the Other, and in the failure

of the paternal metaphor, that I designate the defect that gives psychosis its essential condition, and the structure that separates it from neurosis."

43. Lacan 2006, 459 [549]: "A [here the Name-of-the-Father], the locus from which the question of his existence may arise for him."

44. Lacan 2006, 482 [579].

45. Schatzman 1973, 13, quoting Niederland 1974.

46. That is the point of view that I took myself in *Saying "No,"* 70–78.

47. Hegel 1967b, 163: "The ethical aspect of marriage consists in the parties' consciousness of this unity as their substantive aim, and so in their love, trust, and common sharing of their entire existence as individuals." Also 158, 161, 167, 173.

48. De Waelhens 1978, 20–22; Thompson 1985, 109–12.

49. Vergote 1980, 189.

50. Vergote 1980, 194–95.

51. Lacan 2006, 482–83 [579] for the three quotations.

52. Vergote puts it this way: "The father does not draw his authority from himself lest he render arbitrary and consequently destroy his function." Vergote and Tamayo 1980, 197. Lopez, in "The Oedipus Complex" (6) connects the symbolic function of the father to his accepting his own mortality: "What the father offers through the mediation of his name, of the Law, of his authority, of his role as a referent, is a right to inherit these gifts in order to pass them unto others. In so doing, the father announces the acceptance of his own death."

53. Lacan 2006, 482 [579].

54. Mannoni 1964, 173: "Que va devenir maman, si elle n'a plus la débilité de l'enfant pour la soutenir?"

55. Lacan 2006, 459 [549]; Muller and Richardson 1982, 208.

56. Lacan 2006, 481 [577].

57. J-A Miller argues that in the case of the absence of the signifier the "Name-of-the-Father," the "alterity of the Other" cannot be grounded (Miller 1994, 79). M. Alcorn 2002 formulates it as follows: "[The] logic [of racism] operates not according to the logic of the symbolic, as Lacan defined the term, but according to the real and the drives, in what Lacanians term the *jouissance* of the body" (107).

Part I

Psychosocial and Linguistic Complexity of Human Beings as a Basis to Understand Schizophrenia and Psychosis

Chapter One

Toward a Philosophy of Psychosis

Studies on infantile psychosis have given us remarkable results.[1] If one combines these studies with those on the psychic development of the child, it becomes possible to construct a comprehensive theory of psychosis. This theory also clarifies the structural development of a human being before it assumes the status of subject in the Oedipus conflict. Our theory of psychosis is thus also an attempt to construct a philosophy of the presubject or an etiology of subjectivity. I have found the elements for my theory of psychosis in the works of Piera Aulagnier, Jacques Lacan, René Spitz, and Maud Mannoni, as well as in a psychological encyclopedia.

LACAN'S THEORY OF THE MIRROR STAGE COMPLEMENTED BY SPITZ'S OBSERVATIONS

In his article on the mirror stage,[2] Lacan observes that, by the age of six months, the infant can recognize his or her image in the mirror. Moreover, she reacts to this recognition with a series of jubilant movements. The interpretation of this behavior tells us that at this age the infant can use perception to identify with her body; however, perception is only one of the factors. The observations of Spitz show us that the quality of the mothering figure's desire is also involved.[3]

Spitz has reported that children who suffer from hospitalism fear the approach of anyone who has not come to feed them. Children in these circumstances regularly produce negative cephalogyric motions. The greatest difference between normal children and children who suffer from hospitalism is that the former were the object of their mother's desire, while the latter were surrounded only by the scientific knowledge of doctors and nurses. If one wishes, one can see here the mutuality of desires even at a time when one of the desires, i.e., the child's, does not have the status of full subjectivity.

SPITZ AND THE EIGHT-MONTHS ANXIETY

Spitz observed a kind of anxiety in the child, which he has called the anxiety of eight months, two months after the child's jubilation of the mirror stage. At this age, the child shows signs of anxiety at the approach of anyone other than his mother (or mothering figure). Why anxiety? In addition, why the distinction between the mother and other human beings?

It seems to me that during the two months that separate the moment of jubilation and the eight-month anxiety, the child becomes conscious of the alienation that is hidden in the identification with the body. In fact, once the human being assumes her body as her own, there is a dimension of the self that escapes her.[4] Although the child is now the master of her movements, she does not know the result of her actions as others see them. Having assumed her body, the child can start wondering how she looks in the eyes of the others.[5] At the same time, this shows that the alienation of eight months can never be eliminated; the child must confront it.

AULAGNIER AND SPECIAL ASPECTS OF THE MOTHER–CHILD RELATIONSHIP

Since there is a special relation between child and mother, namely a symbiotic relation, the child never fears alienation from its mother. Indeed, the relation between the child and its mother is not necessarily mediated by the look; it is enacted more directly on the level of desire. It is here that Aulagnier's study clarifies matters for us. For Aulagnier, there is a difference between not only the normal and psychotic child, but also their respective mothers, particularly in the structure of their desires. From the time of conception, the mother of a normal child creates in her imagination an independent corporeal infant.

The mother of the future psychotic child speaks retrospectively of the infant during pregnancy as something that is just a part of her own body. Such a mother is not prepared to imagine the autonomy of her child. The difference between the two types of desire becomes clear with the birth of the child. The mother of a future psychotic tends to see the birth as a loss, whereas the other sees it as a stage in the life of the child. The first mourns the birth, while the latter knows to give meaning to it. Gynecologists report this distinct difference in behavior between the two kinds of mothers.

During the first months of life, the baby is "conscious" of herself only as a partial body in relation to her mother: particularly as a mouth in relation to a breast. The idea that the body is only seen as a partial one is not new. It was studied, for instance, by M. Klein, E. Erikson, and P. Aulagnier. Thus, the assumption of her body at six months gives the child a greater autonomy and a possibility to live without direct relation to her mother's body; however, one sees the difference once more at the age of eight months. Anxious due to the alienation felt because of the approach of others, the child must find help to surmount her alienation. The child of a normal mother finds this help in the imaginary desire of the mother, who, since the child's conception, has desired the child as an autonomous body. The child of a mother of a psychotic child has never desired the child as an autonomous being. Rather, Aulagnier shows that this kind of mother fears such autonomy and denies it to the child. In this way, Aulagnier argues that the alienation of a future psychotic child is facilitated by the structure of the mother's desire. Whereas the normal child finds support in the mother, the future psychotic finds a denial. It is at the alienating structure indicated by the eight-month anxiety that the psychic evolution of the psychotic encounters its greatest difficulty.

THE PERIOD OF NEGATIVISM OR "NO-SAYING"

There is a period of negativism in the development of the infant typically during the period from 15 months to two years of age. Psychologists have verified that the child directs her negativism more typically toward the mother than toward the father. The refusals at this period are not rational.[6] Indeed, when a mother asks her child, "Do you want a candy?" the child's refusal does not mean that she does not want the candy. If the parent leaves the candy near the child and goes away, the child will begin to eat the candy.

I had the opportunity to observe the following scene. At a Sunday afternoon dinner, a mother was going to serve cake. First, she asked the youngest child (two years old) if he wanted a piece, and he refused. This situation (question-refusal) was repeated three times. After the third refusal, the child took his mother's hand and kissed it. The cake was then served to the other guests at the table. A small piece of cake remained. After about 10 minutes, the mother asked the guests, and not the child, who was sitting directly next to her, if anyone wanted the rest of the cake. Before anyone could answer, the child said that he would like a piece.

Thus, in the period of negativism, no-saying does not seem to have the function of a rational refusal. No-saying is a refusal for the sake of showing one's own will, a refusal for the simple sake of refusing. In other words, no-saying is a refusal to show that one is autonomous, independent. The self-referencing emphasis of such refusals during this developmental stage helps facilitate the child's liberation from her symbiotic relationship with the mother. In this way, one can see that the no-saying prepares the Oedipal conflict, in which a person other than the mother and child is involved. Additionally, by his negativism, the child shows himself and his mother that he no longer needs the imaginary support of his mother to surmount the fundamental alienation revealed in the eight-month anxiety. In its negativism, the child assumes himself as a point of reference; however, he is not yet a subject, since he does not yet have his own identity. He uses refusals to begin the process of identity formation. It is still necessary for him to pass through the Oedipal tragedy to become a subject and acquire his own identity. In the meantime, he has conquered his autonomy. He is at least a presubject.

It is exactly this acquisition of autonomy, this realized ability to refer to oneself as it is carried out in the "no" and the refusal, that is lacking in the psychotic. One only has to read Mannoni's book *The Backward Child and His Mother* to be convinced of this. This same lack can explain some strange features of psychotic language. Since the psychotic does not feel empowered to embrace himself as a point of reference or a point of view, he will have difficulty in using the personal pronouns "I" and "you," which have only a referential meaning.[7] Or, the psychotic will tell you the following upon being asked what a fork is: "You see, for me, a fork is either wood and steel, and it is the use made of it by others that makes me understand its utility, or sometimes it is something that pricks, that penetrates, but then the word fork does not have for me the meaning it has for others."[8] Or, in reply to a question, supposed to evoke a personal response, the psychotic may reply with almost belligerent repetitions of successive negations of his earlier statements.[9]

CONCLUSION

In neurosis, one sees a person alienated from the image he has of himself and who asks himself who he is. In psychosis, one sees a person who is not only incapable of choosing an identity, but also unable to choose himself as point of reference. Thus, one can repeat with Rimbaud that at the heart of the "I" one finds the other, that "I am another" since I am constituted by the support of the other. In addition, since in the psychotic it is not the psychotic but rather another person who has the key for the "I," there is the likelihood, and often the guarantee, of supreme alienation. The psychotic thus feels condemned by others.

NOTES

1. Aulagnier 1964; Lacan 2006, 445–88; Maud Mannoni 1972; Mishler and Waxler 1966.
2. Lacan 2006, 75–81 [93–100].
3. Spitz 1957.

4. I describe the child as having a phantom ego during his stage, between the mirror stage and the pre-Oedipal period. See Ver Eecke 1984, 57, footnote.

5. Jean-Paul Sartre's analysis of the look expresses this alienating dimension in intersubjectivity well. Sartre 1966, especially the section on the look (part III, chapter 1, IV).

6. Spitz 1957; Erikson 1959.

7. In one of his case presentations, Dr. Green, in Paris, asked one patient, "Does your father love you?" The patient answered, "No, I do not love him."

8. Aulagnier 1964, 58.

9. Bleuler 1950, 191–98.

Chapter Two

The Subjective Experience of the Person with Schizophrenia

In this chapter, I make use of the writings of Louis Sass (Sass 2003; 2004). Contrary to the claims of psychiatry, Sass argues that the alogia of schizophrenic patients is not indicative of a lack of intellectual functioning. Rather, so claims Sass, alogia is a paralysis caused by hyperactivity of the schizophrenic mind. Sass uses Wittgenstein to connect the hyperactivity of the schizophrenic mind to his deficient psychic connection with his body. Sass's perceptive description of the schizophrenic's experience prepares the way for the demonstration that the schizophrenic's hyperactivity is a reaction to two defective developmental tasks.[1]

PSYCHIATRY VERSUS PHENOMENOLOGY ON SCHIZOPHRENIA: THE THESIS OF HYPERREFLEXIVITY

In his book *The Paradoxes of Delusion*, Sass attempts to comprehend both empathically and conceptually one of the most cryptic symptoms of schizophrenia—the delusion. In opposition to Karl Jaspers's view that, "The nature of [schizophrenia] . . . we are so far unable to describe, let alone formulate into a concept," Sass avers that a phenomenological or hermeneutic investigation into schizophrenic delusions, specifically, and, more generally, the subjective world of the schizophrenic patient, is to be better understood through careful description rather than explanation (Sass 1995, 6). He therefore sets out to conduct a subtler, phenomenologically oriented investigation of delusions by engaging with patients and performing a more exegetic reading of their autobiographical accounts.

Sass uses the thought of Ludwig Wittgenstein to help understand the delusions of schizophrenics, in particular that of Daniel Paul Schreber.[2] Wittgenstein argues that all human beings, and philosophers, in particular, share a proclivity for detachment from body, world, and community in favor of a more rationalistic and metaphysical approach to epistemological issues leading to alienation. Sass claims that this particular tendency of hypercerebralization has a great deal in common with the symptoms displayed by Schreber; however, in both cases, this matter of overintellectualization is not an ostensible operation we readily *see* in an individual.

Sass sets out to criticize the current and longstanding predilection psychiatrists and clinical psychologists share in prescribing cursory diagnoses of schizophrenia based primarily on etiology and causation. Two of the current and most pervasive criteria for diagnosing an individual as schizophrenic are the standards "poor reality-testing" and a theory of the patient regressing, cognitively, to a level of "primary process thinking," that brand of "thinking" most often ascribed to infants.

Poor reality-testing offers a kind of barometric measure on how well a patient is able to discern between her delusions and the actual, objective world the rest of us experience. There is a dangerous implication here, however, that in "some crucial sense, patients have the same subjective experience of living in the same kind of common-sense world as the rest of us—it is just that they are in error, a fact apparent from the standpoint of the external observer" (Sass 1994, 18). Furthermore, the notion of poor reality-testing carries with it a tacit implication that an objectively inaccurate perception or belief is taken, by the patient, as real.

But as Sass encounters in myriad accounts by individuals diagnosed as schizophrenics, their delusions are not accompanied by emotional states appropriate to their contents. In countless verbal and written accounts, schizophrenic patients suggest or even claim to be conscious of the inappropriate nature of their cognitive responses to emotional stimuli. Sass believes that some schizophrenics possess a rather acute sense of what would be considered their objective or actual circumstances in the world, and, as a result, they possess, too, a disconcerting insight into the otherness of the delusional world they also inhabit.

Rather than confusing the real world and their delusional world, schizophrenics often seem to live in two parallel but separate dimensions—one they subscribe to as we do and one erected and fortified by hallucinations and delusions of their own conception. The schizophrenic occupies two discrete ontological experiences of his world, then; one, experienced as objective, is perceived in the putative fashion, and the other, more subjective, is felt by the patient to exist only "in the mind's eye." As one schizophrenic coyly puts it, "In my world I am omnipotent; in yours I practice diplomacy" (Sass 1995, 49). Obviously, this level of intellection and "double-bookkeeping" does not correspond to psychiatry's understanding of schizophrenics as 1) victims of poor reality-testing and 2) regressive to states of mental sophistication correlative with that of an infant.

Sass is particularly critical of the poor reality-testing formula in light of Schreber's insights into his own delusions. Schreber suggests and even, at times, vehemently maintains that his delusions are not literally true but do possess a strange "subjectivized" quality—that is, as being in some sense the product of his own consciousness rather than as enjoying an independent or objective existence, which is precisely what the poor reality-testing formula implies.

Schreber shaves off his mustache, for example, to support his delusion of being a female—"a mustache would naturally have been an insurmountable obstacle for this illusion" (Sass 1995, 26). Here we get the sense that Schreber does not have a diminished capacity for judging the real world from the world in his own mind. Rather, it would appear that both worlds cohabit his mind and that there is yet a tertiary force in this psychic triumvirate: Schreber's meta-awareness of his subsisting in this double world, in a way that normal people do not.

When Schreber describes a delusional belief about himself, he uses such language as "I am represented as" rather than "I am" or "I was." Such modes of expression suggest that Schreber's delusional experiences "retain for him what might be called a 'coefficient of subjectivity,' as if whatever is experienced has an aura that labels it not as reality but as only an experience"—a kind of supra-reality to which the rest of the world is not privy (Sass 1995, 27). Talking about Schreber, Sass writes,

> "When the rays approach," writes Schreber, referring to the strange, scrutinizing entities—rays—which constitute an important center of consciousness in his delusional world, "my breast gives the *impression* of a pretty well-developed female bosom." And an observer, he states, "would get the undoubted *impression* of a female trunk. . . . All this naturally only in my imagination, but in a manner that the rays get the impression that these objects and phenomena really exist." (Sass 1995, 25–27)

Schreber's delusions are volitional on some level, that is, he is complicit in the maintenance of his own schizophrenic condition—nurturing, as we can divine from his language—the delusions that, for whatever reason, bring him peace.

The second standard criterion psychiatrists and clinical psychologists enlist for diagnosing patients as schizophrenic is a mental regression to primary process thinking, a developmental stage characterized as more infantile and subject to the predominance of the patient's recalcitrant id.

Sass maintains that schizophrenics' "experiences of delusional and subjectivized reality seem to be embedded in a form of consciousness that is hyperacute, hyper-self-conscious, and highly detached, qualities not at all characteristic of early stages of cognitive-emotional development" (Sass 1995, 40). Consider two examples from Schreber, quoted by Sass, which show Schreber's self-awareness: "Earlier I stated the contrary opinion. This is because these matters, by their very nature, make any absolutely final opinion impossible; hence I vacillate even now" (Sass 1995, 76) or "To make myself at least somewhat comprehensible I shall have to speak much in images and similes, which may at times be only approximately correct" (Sass 1995, 28, cf. 7).

Sass reminds us that psychoanalysis regards the infant's world as being pervaded by an intensity, a dynamism, and a mystical sense of emotional involvement. The infant considers the breast not as separate from itself, but rather as part of "itself" (there being at the outset no sense of "self," no sense of where one person or object leaves off and another begins); experience takes the form of a continuum, not of discrete, separate entities. The schizophrenic experiences that Sass examines are not characterized by a mystical "union and emotional involvement, but a profound disengagement from reality and detachment from the ordinary, communal life with others" (Sass 1995, 14).

> The parallels between Wittgenstein and Schreber reveal . . . something akin to Wittgenstein's notion of a disease of the intellect, born at the highest pitches of self-consciousness and alienation. Madness, in this view, is the endpoint of the trajectory consciousness follows when it separates from the body and the passions, and from the social and practical world, and turns in upon itself; it is what might be called the mind's perverse self-apotheosis. (Sass 1995, 12)

The idea that the mind of the schizophrenic suffers a detachment from others calls to mind, of course, the malaise of the modern age, which suffered, at least as evidenced through its art, a cerebralization of instinct and the body not unlike the cases we find in schizophrenic patients. In both cases, there is a profound inability to experience the body as such.

Sass combats both the notion of poor reality-testing and the idea of infantile regression as means of diagnosing schizophrenia because both lead to grave misinterpretations of the psychic world of the patient, thereby reinforcing these criteria as accurate and appropriate means for characterizing the schizophrenic experience.

If we accept the poor reality-testing formula, we are maintaining that the schizophrenic lives, actually, in the same world that we live in—and that her judgment is merely skewed in terms of her understanding of this shared objective world. In fact, the world of the schizophrenic, according to Sass, is infinitely more complex than our modes of understanding (i.e., the poor reality-testing formula) suggest. A danger, then, lies in the probability of diagnosticians using the aforementioned standards complacently, relying too heavily on their mendacious—or, at the very least, incomplete—representations and implications of the schizophrenic psyche. These deleterious misperceptions, then, become deeply entrenched in our ways of thinking about and treating schizophrenics, both clinically and socially.

> Notions such as poor reality-testing and the theory of infantile regression become immune to criticism the more often they are put into practice and their misappropriations go undetected. One gets the sense that an understanding of and desire to treat the schizophrenic is supplanted in clinical practice by the analyst's or psychiatrist's own desire to diagnose. Wittgenstein's reflections allow us to recover the sense of puzzlement, even wonder, that such phenomena [delusions] ought to arouse—and then to move beyond this to another level of understanding, one that can help us make some sense of the delusional world without slighting its subtleties or its paradoxes. (Sass 1995, xi)

We are confronted with the problem of psychologists and diagnosticians misinterpreting and therefore mistreating schizophrenics they find to be—in accord with Jaspers's notion of inexplicable otherness—just like us, only developmentally deficient; however, in a fundamental way, schizophrenics are not just like us.

We have, then, the binary responsibility of acknowledging the otherness of the schizophrenic and stretching our capacity for empathy. Sass argues that we must alter our own rationalist criteria to better understand the schizophrenic's form of life. Once we have stretched our own capacity for imaginative empathy, says Sass, borrowing an idea from Wittgenstein, we will be able to connect with that other, who, once we make a connection, will be, likewise, validated. To employ a rigid set of criteria or, in the other extreme, a protean definition of what "schizophrenia" is to adumbrate all patients within the rubric of a set theory of symptoms is to do a great injustice to our means of understanding these people, empathically—acknowledging them, in fact, as people.

Wittgenstein himself complained of the seemingly inexorable tendency to reify experiences in the course of philosophical analysis—to treat as "things" entities that by their very nature are not "things." "Wittgenstein is famous for likening much of traditional philosophy, with its irrepressible urge toward metaphysical speculation, to a kind of disease—even to a mental illness in need of therapy" (Sass 1995, 8).

Sass agrees with this conception of the epistemological tendency in the human subject. As previously mentioned, Sass uses a superb phenomenological approach in examining the experiences and accounts of schizophrenic patients using the thoughts that fueled Ludwig Wittgenstein's philosophical fervor. Sass contends,

> It is significant that the schizophrenic-type world so closely fits the description of solipsism—the illusory doctrine which, for Wittgenstein, is the quintessential example of the philosophical illness, that tendency to overvalue and reify abstract, contemplative thought and to lose contact with the true sources of wisdom that are to be found in a life of engagement and activity. (Sass 1995, 117)

We must remember that Wittgenstein is often less concerned with specific doctrines than certain tendencies of the mind, tendencies he recognized in both himself and others. "In Wittgenstein's view, to insist on the truism of solipsism is to engage in a form of life that is self-deceptive, futile, and ultimately absurd" (Sass 1995, 117).

For the solipsist who is struck by the profound and irrefutable centrality of his own experience, it seems ludicrous that anyone else might share in this experience and awareness. Consequently, the more obsessed the solipsist becomes with his own experience, the more unlikely it will seem to him that any other person can understand anything like this—and the more others come to seem unbridgeable, autonomous, and other, alienating and alienated, and perhaps not really conscious beings at all.

Schizophrenic delusions often have less to do with believing in what is not true, Sass tells us, than disbelieving in what is. Again, as was the tendency of many modern artists, schizophrenics come to view those around them, both things and people, as simulacra and, in turn, come to view themselves similarly. According to one schizophrenic, "I was, myself, a lifeless image" (Sass 1995, 45). Schreber, too, viewed "others" as mere simulacra: "Accordingly I did not know whether to take the streets of Leipzig through which I traveled as only theatre props. . . . At Dresden Station, it is true, I saw a fair number of people who *gave the impression* of being railway passengers" (Sass 1995, 33, italics added).

This alienated, detached form of life begets further alienation, until one is unable to communicate with others—others, one imagines, who presumably do not *really* exist. And here communication becomes implausible. As one patient put it, "Everything seems to slip away into impressions. . . . For what is, is, and yet what seems to be is always changing and drifting away into thought and ideas, rather than actualities" (Sass 1995, 49). In addition, another patient complained, "Even the sea disappointed me a little by its artificiality" (Sass 1995, 23). Schizophrenics succumb to the "natural" delusion that the activity of communication between two people is ultimately feckless and "true" understanding—as though this metaphysical misnomer actually existed as an object we could examine and agree upon—is painfully untenable.

The futility of expressing oneself, reaching out to others, and being reached becomes overwhelming and, indeed, debilitating. The danger here is not the despair that results from such acute insight into one's aloneness in the world, as existentialists of the modern era might claim. According to both Wittgenstein and Sass, the danger lies in investing in the delusion at all—the *delusion* of solipsism. "In what frame of mind must one be," asks Wittgenstein, "in order to feel profoundly struck with the truth of notions such as that 'the world is my world' or that 'only I feel real pain' or 'really see (or hear)'? Or, what is the sort of experience of the world to which this doctrine might correspond, out of which it is likely to arise?" (Sass 1995, 34).

The obsession human beings share in "determining" what, by all appearances, is relative, fluid, and dynamic in the world and within human beings, themselves, and their forms of life leads us into all sorts of philosophical and psychological quandaries. Just as any one of us may be "tempted to seek the meaning, intent, or cause that seems, like some Platonic or noumenal essence, to lie behind the merely phenomenal world one directly experiences," so, too, our psychiatric practitioners, philosophers, and schizophrenic patients fall prey to this delusion (Sass 1995, 106).

According to schizophrenic patient Jonathan Lang, "withdrawal from sensori-motor activity" into what he called the "ideological level" of abstract thought was the central feature of his own psychotic state (Sass 1994, 44). In addition, Schreber tells us that he felt as though he was "being continually forced to trace the causal relation of every happening, every feeling, every idea" (Sass 1995, 120). Interestingly—and perhaps this is why Sass gives so much attention to his account, in particular—Schreber possessed a Wittgensteinian sense of the absurdity and futility of his constant questioning and deducing, and he assiduously sought ways of palliating the tension that resulted when he did *not* account, intellectually, for every picayune observation of himself and his environs. Accordingly,

> These reifications or concretizations may actually indicate not a lack but an exaggeration of reflective distance and self-consciousness: Psychological processes and ideas the normal person would experience only tacitly or abstractly are focused on and thereby transformed into phenomena having some of the qualities of actual physical objects existing separate from the self. The experience of many schizophrenic patients involves not an overwhelming by but a detachment from normal forms of emotion and desire, not a loss but an exacerbation of various forms of self-conscious awareness. (Sass 1995, 95)

NEGATIVE SYMPTOMS IN SCHIZOPHRENIA: THE CASE OF ALOGIA

In his paper "'Negative Symptoms,' Schizophrenia, and the Self" (Sass 2003), Sass applies his insights from his book *The Paradoxes of Delusion* to what psychiatry calls the "negative" symptoms of schizophrenics.[3] Where psychiatry understands these negative symptoms as some kind of diminished functioning, Sass argues that at least some of the observed behavior, for example, alogia, is, on the contrary, the result of hyperactivity, in particular hyperreflexivity. Such hyperreflexivity then paralyzes normal human behavior. To make his point, Sass again uses careful phenomenological observation. In doing so, Sass allows us to see something of the tragic dimension of the schizophrenic subject hidden behind the innocuous description "negative symptom."

As a good phenomenologist, Sass discovered rich material to make his point. He uses Antonin Artaud's description of his difficulties with the simple act of saying "it is cold":

> If it is cold I can still say that it is cold, but there are times when I am incapable of saying it: This is a fact, for there is in me something damaged from the emotional point of view, and if someone asked me why I could not say it, I would answer that my inner feeling on this slight and neutral point did not correspond to the three simple little words I would have to pronounce ["it is cold"]. And this lack of correspondence, therefore, between a physiological sensation and its emotional response in the first place and next its intellectual response—insofar as it is possible to summarize and synthesize in general terms this series of swift, almost instantaneous operations which give rise to the truism *it is cold*—this lack of correspondence, since it does not select its subjects or spare me in any way, culminates, as it spreads, in the colossal troubles which correspond perfectly, alas, to the loss of personality. (Artaud 1976, 294–95)

Artaud correctly points out in this text that saying, "It is cold," is the result of a process consisting of three steps: There is an objective reality, which produces a physiological sensation; there is an emotional reaction (burr . . .); one says that it is cold.

For people, these three steps occur in a *continuum*: First, we are affected by the cold; second, we react bodily to that cold by shivering, that is, we *experience* the cold; and third, we describe the experienced situation by saying, "It is cold." The continuum consists of the fact that the "I" that says, "It is cold," is fused with the body that shivers. One could almost say, "I am so fused with my body that it says for me, 'It's cold,' or better, I let myself say, 'It is cold.'"

For Artaud the situation is different. Instead of a continuum from one step to the next, the process falls apart. Artaud can be physiologically affected by the cold, but his emotional reaction to the cold is not "burr," which would make him say, "It is cold." Rather Artaud's emotional reaction is—as Artaud himself claims—something else.

Let us call the "burr . . ." reaction making me say, "It is cold," X. Let us call Artaud's emotional reaction, which is different, the Y reaction. Artaud's Y reaction consists of two moments:

1. Awareness of the strangeness of the emotional reaction to the cold.
2. Transformation of the expression, "It is cold," from a sentence that expresses a meaning (i.e., a signified) to a sentence that consists of signifiers, "Three simple little words I would have to pronounce."

Artaud himself describes this double dimension of the Y reaction as a "lack of correspondence, therefore, between a physiological sensation and its emotional response in the first place and next its intellectual response" (Artaud 1976, 295).

While, for us, our embodied self almost automatically makes steps two and three in the process of feeling cold, the embodied self of Artaud creates for Artaud a discontinuity. Still, Artaud is similar enough to us to realize that his embodied self *should do for him* what it does for us. He writes that he is sometimes "incapable of saying it [that it is cold]: . . . In me something [is] damaged from the emotional point of view, . . . [there is a] lack of correspondence" (Artaud 1976, 294).

Let us use Husserl's concept of "passive synthesis" for referring to the activity that smoothly combines the three steps, since that combining activity occurs in us almost automatically. It is almost as if it is done for us, by our embodied self. After this "passive synthesis" is done for us, we might initiate a philosophical act of reflection and say, "Wow, how smoothly did this all happen! How can I distinguish between what happened to me and what I did?"

According to Artaud, this passive synthesis breaks down in him from time to time; however, he remains aware that this synthesis should have occurred. Thus, where we need a decision to start the process of reflecting philosophically on what happened, Artaud has an existential reason to start such a philosophical reflection. Indeed, Artaud senses that result X, which includes a passive synthesis, should have taken place. But he feels that Y has taken place and that the Y event or experience is a failure.

Consciousness is nonthematically present in its embodied activity, regardless of whether that activity is experienced as a success or a failure. When the embodied activity succeeds, there is normally no existential reason to thematize the conscious presence to our embodied activity unless one is in a program to improve one's embodied performance (athletics) or one is a philosopher. If one's embodied activity fails, there is an existential reason to thematize our conscious presence: One then starts to reflect almost naturally.

In the example of Artaud, his situation leads to his inability to say, "It is cold." There is no observable activity where one could expect activity. Sass correctly points out that behaviorists mistakenly conclude that in this situation—exemplifying typical schizophrenic behavior—one is in the presence of a negative symptom: diminished activity, diminished speaking (alogia). Sass perceptively argues that there are all kinds of intentional activity that go on behind the failure to say, "It is cold." In particular, there is hyperreflectivity. Unfortunately, these activities does not lead to a single "passive synthesis" X.

The problem of Artaud's inability to say, "It is cold," typifies a schizophrenic problem of alogia in general. In that case, one can claim that schizophrenics experience the fact that passive synthesis does not take place. Thus, a normal continuous form of embodied acts fails to materialize.

One form of therapy for schizophrenia is social rehabilitation. One accepts the inability of the schizophrenic to perform normal tasks. One, therefore, does not address the fundamental deficiency of failing passive syntheses. Rather, a normal task is subdivided in parts, and the patient is trained to do the part. Sass raises the interesting question of whether such an approach does not reinforce the disappearance of passive syntheses.

TOWARD A STRUCTURAL AND DEEPER UNDERSTANDING OF SCHIZOPHRENICS

Pointing to the hyperreflectivity hidden behind the negative symptoms is a great phenomenological achievement. It reveals the subjective world behind an objective observation. It reveals the noeses responsible for the noemas, called "negative symptoms." For Lacan, the essence of schizophrenia is a radical failure in the constitution of the subject.[4] Lacan pointed out the radical failure of the function of language in the schizophrenic because of the failure of the "paternal metaphor." Consequently, everyday words lose their metaphorical meaning and are reduced to their literal dimension.

Let me give an example reported by Sigmund Freud from his student Tausk (De Waelhens 1978, 11–12; Freud 1911–1913, 197–99). A girl was engaged to a boy who later dropped her. She had a hard time dealing with that disappointment but ultimately said of her boyfriend that he was a deceitful person. She used the Austrian German expression *Augenverdreher*. The literal translation of the word is, "twister of eyes." The metaphorical meaning of the expression as understood in its everyday usage was "deceitful person," that is, someone who has the capability of drawing the eyes of others to his or her good characteristics, while drawing them away from bad ones. Two weeks later, the girl complained to her doctor that she could not see straight. The metaphorical meaning of the word was reduced to its literal meaning. This literal meaning was then used as an instruction to create a bodily conversion: She could not see straight because her eyes had been twisted.

A Belgian analyst reported a second example. A girl entered the office and cried terribly. The analyst asked why she cried. The patient gave as her reason the fact that she had no hands. In response to the analyst's questioning why she thought she had no hands, the patient told him that her father had said so that morning, because he had told his daughter that she was "handicapped." The Dutch expression is "gehandikapt," where "kapt" is the past participle of "kappen," *to cut*. In Dutch the word *gehandikapt* means normally—that is, metaphorically—*disadvantaged*. The metaphorical meaning is created from the literal expression "my hands are tied" or stronger, "my hands are cut." The girl had taken the metaphorical meaning literally. She was therefore crying about the fact that, in truth, her father's words meant that she had lost her hands, that she was without hands. Both examples illustrate the cases of patients who show a disturbance in their symbolic structure.

Post-Lacanians, building upon Lacan, argue that in schizophrenia there is also a profound disturbance in the schizophrenic's relation to his own body (Vergote 1998, 237; Moyaert 1998). This is called a disturbance in the imagery. The mirror stage function has failed. At six months, the child jubilates in front of the mirror. That joy is interpreted as indicating that the child recognizes itself as a totality, whereas before it experienced itself in body parts. It now knows itself to be the object of love by the other and can now love itself. The mirror stage demands that the child inhabit both its external form and its proprioceptive interiority, and furthermore that it makes a synthesis between the two. By means of that synthesis, it is ready to translate inner feelings into actions in the external world. The child prepares itself for passive syntheses. In schizophrenia, the basis for "passive synthesis," the mirror stage, failed.

Let us apply this to the passage of Artaud on his inability to say that it is cold. Artaud himself reports two failures. First, there is the strangeness of emotional reaction to cold, which makes it unavailable for translation into words for people in the world. Lacanians would call this a failure of the imaginary, a failure of embodiment. Second, there is the fact that the expression, "It is cold," is reduced to its materiality, its literalness, "Three simple words I would have to pronounce." Linguistic expressions lose their capability to refer to a signified, a meaning, because they are reduced to the materiality of the signifier, "three simple words."

CONCLUSION

Without the work of people like Sass,[5] we might be stuck with psychiatry's criteria for the definition and description of schizophrenics. Psychiatry characterizes people afflicted with schizophrenia as having poor reality-testing and regressing to primitive thought. Their negative symptoms are interpreted as evidence that they lack agency. Sass's work opens the curtain to the subjective world of the schizophrenic: They show hyperreflexivity resulting from a lack of psychic relations to their body. Once that subjective world is revealed, one can further explore the deeper structure of that subjective world. I did so with the help of Lacan, De Waelhens, and some post-Lacanians.

NOTES

1. For a publication by a psychoanalyst critical of Sass's work, see Robbins 1998.

2. Two books by Ludwig Wittgenstein are of particular relevance: Wittgenstein 1978 and 1981. A useful introduction to the world of Wittgenstein is Janik and Toulmin 1973. Sass is not alone in using the insights of Wittgenstein to clarify either psychoanalytic insights or the problems of schizophrenics. Two other important authors who did the same thing are Heaton 2000 and Davoine 1992.

3. Among the primary negative symptoms are the following: poverty of speech, sometimes called "alogia," i.e., a tendency to speak very little or not at all; affective flattening or blunting—manifest in unchanging facial expression, paucity of expressive gesture or verbal inflection, poor eye contact, and a general lack of social responsiveness; avolition and apathy—manifest in a lack or slowing of spontaneous activity, poor grooming and hygiene, and an "inability to initiate and persist in goal-directed activities" (APA 2000, 301); anhedonia—an apparent dearth of energy or motivation for work, recreation, socializing, or sexual activity, and an apparent inability to feel closeness or intimacy with other people; and a general inattentiveness to the social or practical world (Andreasen 1999; Sass 2003).

4. Lacan's early theory of schizophrenia is developed in Lacan 2006, chapter 21, and Lacan 1993. For secondary literature, see De Waelhens 1978; Fink 1996, 1997; Ver Eecke 1988.

5. For a list of additional authors willing to look at the subjective experience of the schizophrenic, see the bibliography of De Waelhens and Ver Eecke 2001. An excellent recent examination is the one by Robbins 2002.

Chapter Three

Philosophical Questions about the Theory of Psychosis in the Early Lacan

In his "On a Question Prior to Any Possible Treatment of Psychosis" (Lacan 2006, chapter 21), Lacan formulates his early theory of psychosis. He argues that psychosis results from the failed emergence of the "paternal metaphor" because of the foreclosure of one crucial signifier in the symbolic system: the "Name-of-the-Father." I will concentrate on asking what Lacan means by "paternal metaphor" and reflect on what the cause of that failure might be. I will then articulate the implications by considering degrees of success and failure in implementing the "paternal metaphor." I will end by considering different possible approaches for the treatment of psychosis.

THE CONCEPT OF "PATERNAL METAPHOR"

According to the early Lacan, the child is invited to create a "paternal metaphor" when he or she notices that the mother has an object of desire other than the child, usually, the father. This observation challenges the fantasy world of the child. The child had created a safe and secure world by imagining that the mother is omnipotent and the child is everything the mother could want. By noticing that the father is the object of the mother's desire, the child's world is shaken. If the mother desires the father, she must not already have everything she desires and the child must not be the "all" for the mother, as the child had fantasized. I interpret this latter realization as the cause of a deep narcissistic wound in the child;[1] however, a richer interpretation could be that the child realizes that the joint unit "mother–child" is not complete. The mother–child unit is missing something. What is it that is missing? Psychoanalysis has given a name to that missing element: the phallus. What this means is not necessarily clear, as Lacan devoted an article to its meaning (Lacan 2006, chapter 24).

The concept of the missing phallus is essential; it indicates that there is an invitation experienced by the child to go in search of this missing element. But to respond to the invitation, the child will have to accept a transformation of the structure of its libido and thus of the kind of jouissance for which it can hope. The child will also have to do hermeneutic work: It must exercise interpretive skill to identify what in the father functions as the mother-child unit's missing phallus. In Lacan's words, "The signification of the phallus . . . must be evoked in the subject's imaginary by the 'paternal metaphor'" (Lacan 2006, 464 [557]).

As I see it, this evocation invites the child to interpret. Indeed, by relying on the mother's signals, the child chooses a mark in the father as having phallic power. This mark, or signifier, then becomes the organizer of the awakened desire in the child. That signifier is the kernel of the ego ideal of the child. It invites the child to accept that it wants to be something that it is not—at least not yet. Consequently, the child shows patience, is willing to work, and starts taking the future as the crucial dimension of its experience of time. The child is now also able to insert itself in the metaphoric dimension of language.

FAILURE OF THE "PATERNAL METAPHOR"

In the aforementioned article "On a Question Prior to Any Possible Treatment of Psychosis," Lacan stresses one key causal factor in the potential failure of the "paternal metaphor." This failure often occurs when the signification of the phallus has not been evoked in the imaginary of the child. The one who can evoke the signification of the phallus in the imaginary of the child is the mother (maternal figure). If she does not evoke the signification of the phallus, then the power of the phallus is nonexistent for the child. Jean Laplanche and Jean-Bertrand Pontalis, in their *Hölderlin et la Question du Père*, show how the pain that Hölderlin's mother felt after the loss of her first husband, Hölderlin's father, was so great that to any question young Hölderlin asked about his father, the mother could answer only with silence. Hence, where the young Hölderlin was expecting the "Name-of-the-Father," the mother presented only a void. And the signifier that could provoke for the child the challenge of the "paternal metaphor" was made inoperative; it was foreclosed.

In her studies, Piera Aulagnier presents cases where the mother has no place in her unconscious for accepting the sexual origin of the child (Aulagnier 1964). Others (Bergeron 1990, 146) present families in which fathers have played insignificant roles for generations. I interpret these latter two kinds of cases as deeper forms of foreclosing the "Name-of-the-Father." These are not cases where the pain of the loss of the father is so big it cannot be spoken of or discussed. In these cases, the mothers exclude the fathers from crucial functions in family life.[2] Aulagnier's mothers unconsciously refuse to acknowledge the sexual origin of their children and hence imaginarily see themselves as the sole producers of their children. In the other cases, the mothers have no place for the father in the psychic life of the family. Psychoanalysts have seen in these three different cases expressions of foreclosure of the "Name-of-the-Father," leading to a failure in the emergence of the "paternal metaphor." As these are somewhat different cases providing different reasons for the foreclosure of the "Name-of-the-Father," I wonder if one can talk about different kinds of failures in the creation of the "paternal metaphor."

In his "On a Question Prior to Any Possible Treatment of Psychosis," Lacan hints at a totally different reason for the failure of the "paternal metaphor." It may fail, not because the mother did not evoke the significance of the phallus in the imaginary of the child, but because the father excludes the "'Name-of-the-Father' from its position in the signifier" (Lacan 2006, 483 [579]). As we saw in the introduction, Lacan gives a hint of the kind of father he has in mind (Lacan 2006, 482 [579]).

IMPLICATIONS INTRODUCED BY THE IDEA OF DEGREE OF SUCCESS OR FAILURE OF THE "PATERNAL METAPHOR"

In the early Lacan there are two distinct reasons for the failure of the "paternal metaphor." One resides in the mother and is described as a failure to evoke in the imaginary of the child the signification of the phallus. Another reason resides in the father, because he "excludes the 'Name-of-the-Father' from its position in the signifier." Furthermore, followers of Lacan point out three different ways in which the mother can fail to evoke the signification of the phallus. I imagine that these different reasons for the failure of the "paternal metaphor" give rise to different kinds of failure. In particular, I argue that lack of evoking the signification of the phallus in the imaginary has a more profound impact on the child than the case where that invocation is done but the father misrepresents the "Name-of-the-Father." This would naturally lead to the idea that there can be degrees of failure of the "paternal metaphor."

If we do not conceive the "paternal metaphor" in all or nothing terms, we can say not only that there are degrees of failure of the "paternal metaphor," but also degrees of success. To clarify this possibility, we need to turn to the economic point of view of the libido. Prior to the Oedipal crisis, the libido of the child in the mother–child unit is characterized as deeply narcissistic. In the language of the later Lacan, that libido is marked by jouissance. As a result of the success of the "paternal metaphor," the economy of the libido is transformed. Phallic jouissance predominates. In particular, the idea of the all-good, omnipotent mother, from whom no separation is undertaken, and from which total acceptance is expected at the price of fusion, is given up.

Instead, the identification with a mark in the father introduces a principle of radical separation from the mother; however, is it not possible that only part of the libido is so transformed? Can we not imagine that part of the libido still expects narcissistic grandiosity, narcissistic satisfaction, and non-phallic jouissance? Can people not secretly hope for grand success in their profession, without saying it or stating it all the time? We could imagine that there is a psychotic kernel in the libido of every person, a psychotic kernel that may be small or large in different people.

The "paternal metaphor" transforms the quality of the libido, and we accept that it might transform it more or less. Can we also not imagine that the "paternal metaphor" may transform the libido in some areas of life but not others? Thus, Schreber was not able to accept the law of sexual difference. He imagined himself being both male and female. He even imagined himself copulating with himself. On the other hand, Schreber seems to have been fully capable of maintaining or recovering his legal reasoning and all that this requires from the libido. For example, the law does not accept wishes instead of facts. Furthermore, the facts might be impressive, but they must fit the applicable law. Could we, therefore, suppose that there might be a plurality of "paternal metaphors" and a plurality of "Names-of-the-Father"? Applied to Schreber, one "Name-of-the-Father" would transform the libido with reference to sexual difference (absent in Schreber), and a second one would transform the libido so that the social law can be accepted (present in Schreber, who could accept the rules and laws of the legal profession).

IMPLICATIONS FOR THE TREATMENT OF PSYCHOSIS

Psychosis is not characterized by the absence of language. People afflicted with psychosis do use language, but their usage of language is defective. They cannot properly use pronouns. They cannot use metaphors. They use language in their delusions to satisfy their imaginary wishes.[3] How do we envision the treatment of people afflicted with psychosis in light of the early theory of Lacan?

Villemoes, a Scandinavian psychiatrist informed by Lacan's early theory of schizophrenia, provided a method of therapy based on enriching the schizophrenic's use of language (De Waelhens and Ver Eecke 2001, 109–21). Instead of permitting language to express merely imaginary fantasies, Villemoes helped the patient to use language to structure the world, in particular, the world of objects. He reported a series of indications of progress in language use by the schizophrenic. In turn, he noticed also how language started to give the patient new possibilities.

Villemoes starts his therapy by describing objects in the therapy room and then later in the room of the patient. Villemoes reports two important signs of progress. First, the patient is no longer startled when there are sensory changes in the room (e.g., when a piece of paper or a key falls). Second, in her room the patient starts to feel possessive about her belongings and for the first time starts organizing them.[4]

Villemoes then delegates the duty to end the session to the patient and requests that the patient describe the objects of her early infancy. He asks no questions about people but allows the patient to populate the world she describes using encounters with people. Villemoes reports as a further sign of progress the fact that the patient starts to walk more elegantly. Language starts having an effect on the bodily experience of the patient.

Another important sign of improvement is the patient's ability to empathize. Villemoes sees this as an indication that language allows the patient to empathize without losing herself in fusion.

Finally, Villemoes encourages the patient to identify symbolically with a signifier. A schizophrenic patient might believe that they are Napoleon, without feeling that they need to walk to Moscow. Such a patient has the libidinal structure of a pre-Oedipal child and is imprisoned in nonphallic jouissance. The aim of Villemoes is to let the patient say, for instance, "I am not a thief," and thereby imply that her friends steal, that she likes to steal, but that she is committed to abstaining from stealing. Villemoes reports that these patients then go through a deep mourning period in which they experience their past lives as lost because of a lack of symbolic identification.

The Gifric group in Quebec, under the leadership of Willy Apollon, also aims at restoring the subjectivity of the schizophrenic person (Apollon 1990; Apollon et al. 2008). Crucial to Apollon's strategy is asking the patient to recount their dreams. Dreaming is one way the unconscious deals with the real. At a certain point in the therapy, the patient is asked to make a choice between the story of the delusion and the articulation emerging from dream analysis. The practice has a 65% success rate, where "success" is defined as a patient being able to become a citizen, hold a job, and pay for her own expenses.

The later Lacan stated that the psychotic was unable to structure the real by using either the imaginary or the symbolic. The three orders were not held together. He then suggested that a repair could be attempted by a fourth order, which would provide a suppletion. Lacan connected that suppletion with the function of naming (Harari 2002; Lacan 1975–1976). Lacan realized that the function of naming might be an alternative way to escape psychosis, even if the "paternal metaphor" failed. He saw in James Joyce a successful example of such a strategy. Lacan called this strategy the jouissance of the *sinthome*. This strategy looks for successful or artful skills of the patient (the practical, as Ginette Michaud calls it), which embody the patient's jouissance.[5] What James Joyce did with words might have been crazy; however, Joyce experienced words as epiphanies and, furthermore, saw his activity as a means for making a name for himself. This is a radically alternative therapeutic goal than the two previously sketched ones.

CONCLUSION

In this chapter, I point out that Lacan attributes psychosis to the absence of the "paternal metaphor." Second, I stress that Lacan has described two totally different causes for the absence or failure of the "paternal metaphor." Third, I draw attention to the fact that the lack of respect for the "Name-of-the-Father" can take at least three different forms. Fourth, I point to the fact that Judge Schreber was able to be a judge while producing hallucinations and delusions about his sexuality. Does this indicate that the "paternal metaphor" can fail in part of a patient's life while the "paternal metaphor" is operative in another part of the patient's life? Fifth, do the studies of Bergeron indicate that the "paternal metaphor" can be present more or less? I end the chapter by presenting the method invented by Villemoes for treating people afflicted by schizophrenia, assuming that schizophrenia is an illness created by a deficient relationship to language, as defended by Lacan.

NOTES

1. See Leader 2011, 141: "Trying to think through what the mother is for the father and what the father is for the mother constitute a painful and critical time in childhood."
2. In the words of Leader 2011, 57: Normally, "parents become curious when, at a certain moment, their child elevates the father into some kind of hero. However ineffectual or feeble he may be in reality, he suddenly becomes a champion, capable of the most amazing feats of prowess and accomplishment." But mothers can destroy this push in the child to elevate the meaning of the father by talking condescendingly about the father or answering with silence about all questions about the dead father, as was the case with the mother of Hölderlin.
3. For examples of schizophrenic speech, see Rosenbaum and Sonne 1986.
4. For an explanation, see chapter 9 in this book or Ver Eecke 2002a.
5. Julia Kristeva (1989) points to several artists who used painting (Holbein) or writing (de Nerval, Dostoyevsky, and Duras) to sublimate their own tormented life. The cases of de Nerval and Dostoyevsky are the most telling. In his writings, Dostoyevsky discovered and elevated forgiveness as a lifesaving virtue. Kristeva writes that for Dostoyevsky, "between suffering and acting out, aesthetic activity constitutes forgiveness" (Kristeva 1989, 199). The aesthetic production of de Nerval was not able to sublimate his suffering enough to avoid his suicide.

Chapter Four

Paternal Metaphor and Ordinary Psychosis

In this chapter, I briefly summarize Lacan's theory of "paternal metaphor." I then present Vergote's critical corrections to Lacan's conception of schizophrenia. Finally, I ask the question as to how we need to conceive of the life of a person before and after the psychotic breakdown. Miller introduces the concept of ordinary psychosis to conceptualize the peculiar way of organizing life by a psychotic person before and after his breakdown. Miller gives three characteristics typical of ordinary psychosis.[1]

LACAN'S CONCEPT OF "PATERNAL METAPHOR"

In a pathbreaking article (Lacan 2006), Lacan argues that the hallucinations and delusions by Daniel Schreber could be explained by the absence of an important psychological step in his development. Lacan called the missing psychological step the "paternal metaphor."

Children at first relate to a maternal figure who takes care of them. They would not even survive without a maternal figure. But, as total dependence is unacceptable for a conscious being, children develop two fantasies to eliminate the feeling of total dependency. They imagine that their mother is perfect and omnipotent so that they can feel safe under her protection. Next, they imagine that they are everything their mother could want. So, they feel sure that their mother can and will take care of them.

When the children start being able to differentiate between people, they start noticing that their mother has an interest in someone who is not themselves. That discovery destroys their two original fantasies. A new signifier presents itself to the mind of the child, which Lacan calls the "Name-of-the-

Father." The child is then invited, or forced, to create a new life project. In that new life project, the respect for the "Name-of-the-Father" plays a crucial role. The child looks for the mark in the father that the child feels interests the mother. The child then takes this mark as the basis of its future life project. But the child knows it is not the father. The child is even aware that it has not yet achieved the mark it aims for. Hence, the child is able to live with a gap, the gap between what it is and what it aims at being.

Lacan stresses the fact that this child has changed its psychic structure. But the fact of being different but still remaining the same child is a fact captured by linguistic metaphors. Thus, when I say to someone, metaphorically, that he is a chicken, I mean at the same time that he is not a real chicken but is, nevertheless, like a chicken. Hence, Lacan refers to the structural change in children between ages three and six as a metaphoric move. As the introduction of the figure of the father is crucial for that metaphoric move, Lacan refers to the phenomenon described earlier as the effect of the incorporation of the "paternal metaphor."

In normal children, this gap remains tolerable and is used as a motivation for their behavior. A consequence of taking this gap as its motivation is a change in the psychic structure of the child, as previously described. Such children accept that they are not what they want to be. This negative feeling is mastered by making the future the crucial dimension of their time experience. Within their new time perspective, in which the future replaces the now as the most important aspect of time, these children develop a willingness to work. Society seems to know that because it demands that children go to school at about age six. An additional characteristic of this new psychic structure is that such children have less of a temper tantrum if they are refused something, for example, candy at the exit in a store. Such children are able to develop patience and accept a future promise as a satisfactory substitute for an immediate gratification.

The aforementioned project, referred to as the "paternal metaphor," can fail. Many factors can contribute to the failure of the "paternal metaphor." The mother might not show respect for the signifier "Name-of-the-Father," like Mrs. Schreber burning the unpublished manuscripts of her husband at his death. The father might not be up to the role of being a father with all the demands connected with being a father (Lacan 2006, 482–83 [579]). Or, the child might resist the invitation to change its position from someone who feels protected by the mother and thus attaches herself deeply to the mother. In all three cases, Lacan argues that the signifier "Name-of-the-Father" is being foreclosed in the psyche of the child (Lacan 2006, 481 [577]). This makes the child vulnerable to a psychotic breakdown if special stress is encountered. Lacan names that special stress the appearance of an "A-father." An "A-father" is someone who has an emotional place in the life of a person as a kind of maternal figure but then because of some specific action becomes a father figure.

According to Laplanche and Pontalis (1969), the concept of the "A-father" explains the psychotic breakdown of German poet Hölderlin. The great German poet Schiller played a kind of maternal protective role for the precocious Hölderlin.[2] He helped him publish his first poems, invited him to his weekly meetings with Goethe, and introduced him to a family where Hölderlin was able to give piano lessons and earn some money; however, it is reported that Hölderlin had the ambition of starting a new journal of poetry. When Hölderlin asked for support, Schiller was not enthusiastic and did not unconditionally support Hölderlin.

By taking this paternal role, Schiller became an "A-father." As a mother figure, he had a crucial place in the emotional life of Hölderlin. Hence, Hölderlin could not reject Schiller after he refused his help for the journal he dreamed about. Schiller changed his role for Hölderlin from a mother figure into a father figure; however, the psychic structure of Hölderlin was not able to deal with a father figure. At the same time, Hölderlin could not reject Schiller in his emotional life because Schiller was already deeply part of his emotional life. The reason Hölderlin could not deal with the new Schiller, who from a mother figure had become a father figure for Hölderlin, is, according to Lacan, the fact that Hölderlin's mother had not introduced the signifier of the "Name-of-the-Father." That signifier was foreclosed for Hölderlin's unconscious. Confronted with an "A-father," Hölderlin's unconscious was at a loss as to how to deal with this challenge. Hölderlin needed to fill the hole created in his unconscious structure by the appearance of an "A-father." The delusional system is an attempt to deal with that hole in the unconscious.

VERGOTE'S IDEAS

Vergote observed that people afflicted with schizophrenia do not only produce hallucinations and delusions. They also have a defective relationship to their body. We can make use of Lacan's theory of the mirror stage (Lacan 2006) and Spitz's research on hospitalism to reflect on that defective relationship to the body (Spitz 1945). In both cases, we discover a crucial contribution of the mother to the development of the child. The ability to love one's body, which then leads to the willingness to inhabit that body and experience it as one's own body, is dependent upon having experienced that someone else, the mother (or mother figure), loved you in your embodiment; however, if the maternal love necessary to lovingly relate to one's body is absent, the children might experience other people mainly in their negative roles of imposing limits, hurting them, and so forth. Such children then also develop a negative attitude or a nonengaging attitude toward other people. They can, therefore, be expected to have an awkward relationship with other people.

Vergote also points to a specific deficiency in the language used by people afflicted with schizophrenia. In his *Memoirs*, Schreber does not use metaphors (Vergote 1998, 242).[3] Vergote then makes the following remark: In order to create a metaphor, an individual must possess two series of signifiers, which differ substantially from one another. But, so Vergote argues, schizophrenics tend to construct a psychic "ego" in which the pleasure-body is excluded (Vergote 1998, 237). By doing so, the schizophrenic loses access to the signifiers of embodiment. This deprives the person afflicted with schizophrenia of the tools required to create and even understand metaphors. This is illustrated by a case already reported of a patient who told her therapist that she had no hands. Asked how she knew, the patient stated that her father had told her so. Her father had said that she was handicapped. In this case, the patient was not able to hear the metaphoric meaning of the words of her father. She was only able to understand the literal meaning of the word.

Vergote thus adds one more characteristic of people afflicted with schizophrenia or psychosis beyond the lack in the unconscious of the signifier "Name-of-the-Father," i.e., a defective relationship to their body. We can now ask the question as to what the psychic structure of a schizophrenic patient is before his breakdown and after he recovers. To answer that question, we can consult J. A. Miller.

J. A. MILLER ON THE ABSENCE OF THE "PATERNAL METAPHOR" AND ORDINARY PSYCHOSIS

The breakdown in the life of the psychotic person is one moment in his life. As is clear from the autobiography of Judge Schreber, a psychotic can have a life before the breakdown. Daniel Schreber was married and had a job. He also had a life after the breakdown. It is true that Schreber declares that after his breakdown he had a delusion that he would marry God and create a new mankind, where he would be the patron saint. Still, his daughter testified that he was a better father than her mother was a mother. Hence, aside from having a delusion, Judge Schreber was able to engage again in life.

For this curious combination where someone like Judge Schreber both engages again in life while maintaining a delusion, Miller created the concept of ordinary psychosis. Miller also argues that, before the breakdown, the life of a future psychotic must have been fragile given that an event, a figure—called by Lacan an "A-father"—could provoke a psychotic breakdown. Miller uses the same concept, ordinary psychosis, to name the structure of the life of the future psychotic before he has a breakdown. Theoretically, Miller justifies his claim by pointing out that both before and after the breakdown, the person suffering a psychotic breakdown must organize his life without the benefit of the signifier the "Name-of-the-Father." There is thus a "hidden psychosis" (Miller 2009, 154).[4]

But, how does the life of a person look like without having internalized the "Name-of-the-Father"? Miller starts by describing the life of the psychotic after the breakdown. In the absence of the "Name-of-the-Father," the psychotic who re-enters life must create a substitute. Miller calls it a "delusional metaphor" (Miller 2009, 152) or a "Compensatory Make-Believe of the Name-of-the-Father" abbreviated to a "CMB" (Miller 2009, 153; 2013, 41). This CMB allows for a "delusional symbolic order" (Miller 2009, 152).

Miller claims that something similar takes place in the life of the future psychotic before his breakdown. One possibility is for the psychotically structured person to overidentify with their job (Miller 2013, 42). This was the case with Judge Schreber, who was appointed by the king as presiding judge in the second-highest court of the land, a court where many sitting judges were 20 years his senior. In these circumstances, Judge Schreber felt obliged to work hard to prove that he was worthy of the appointment; in fact, he overworked himself.

Judge Schreber's life history can be used as proof that, both before and after a psychotic breakdown, a person lived a life that was not structured by a "paternal metaphor" but by a "compensatory make-believe of the Name-of-the-Father." Miller calls it a hidden psychosis, for which he created the technical name "ordinary psychosis" (Miller 2009, 154).

But what does the life of ordinary psychosis look like? Miller gives three characteristics, summarized as a "threefold externality" (Miller 2009, 155; 2013, 42). There is the social, the bodily, and the subjective externality.

The social externality can take two forms. The negative social externality consists of the person not being able to feel that he belongs to society because there is some mysterious helplessness that makes it so that he cannot assume a social function, that he cannot conquer a place for himself in society (Miller 2013, 42). The positive social externality consists of a person with an "overintense identification" with his job (Miller 2013, 42), who might become psychotic when he loses his job. Miller puts it this way: "The job meant much more than a job or a way of living. Having a job was a 'Name-of-the-Father'" (Miller 2013, 43).

The bodily externality is evident in an "infinite gap" that exists between the ordinary psychotic person and his body. The "Name-of-the-Father" alone is not enough for such a person to feel connected with his body. He needs additional tools, for example, jewelry-encrusted piercings (Miller 2013, 43).

Finally, there is his subjective externality. "The identification is not symbolic but real because it is without metaphor" (Miller 2013, 44). If the ordinary psychotic person feels bad about himself, he will go beyond feeling bad.

He will not wash himself and smell bad. He will not change clothes and even wear bad ones. He will show that he is waste. Or, if an ordinary psychotic person feels good about himself, he will go to an extreme kind of mannerism (Miller 2013, 44).

CONCLUSION

I have tried to explain how one has to interpret the meaning of Lacan's concept of "paternal metaphor." Much of what happens in the Oedipal drama transcends the child. In other words, insisting as I do that the child's intentionalities are involved in the Oedipal drama is something that also *happens* to the child; however, in my opinion this does not require us to say that consciousness made a choice to become mentally ill. Rather, it requires us to say only that the subject, with his intentionalities, must have been present in the drama out of which he emerged as he is. Such is the interpretation I present of "paternal metaphor." I do the same in my analysis of original psychosis, where I show that a person who can be diagnosed as having an original psychosis actively creates a substitute for the "paternal metaphor."

NOTES

1. For a book-length study of ordinary psychosis, see Redmond 2014.
2. For an impressive study on Hölderlin, making use of the life of this poet to illustrate Lacan's concept of "A-father," see Laplanche and Pontalis 1969. For a short article making use of facts revealed by the research of Lothane 1992 and Israël 1989, see Ver Eecke 1995, included in this book as chapter 12.
3. Others, like Villemoes, have pointed out that people afflicted with schizophrenia have difficulties with pronouns (Villemoes 2002, 646). Thus, when a schizophrenic person was asked if "he liked his parents," he answered, "No, they did not like me." For documentation for the curious usage of discourse language, see Rosenbaum and Sonne 1986.
4. For a different interpretation of the case of Schreber, see Lothane 1998.

Chapter Five

Theoretical and Therapeutic Implications of the Later Lacan's Complex Theory of Psychosis

In his article "On a Question Prior to Any Possible Treatment of Psychosis,"[1] Lacan defends a primary cause for psychosis but also mentions a second cause. The primary cause is the lack of reference to the "Name-of-the-Father" by the mother, which makes the genesis of the "paternal metaphor" difficult, if not impossible. The second cause, which Lacan reports almost as an afterthought, is the situation in which the mother does make reference to the "Name-of-the-Father," but the father presents himself in such a way that he, himself, seems to escape the law of signification.[2]

At the end of his life, Lacan introduced an alternative way to avoid the danger of schizophrenia or psychosis, i.e., to create a name for oneself by doing something that one is good at and that situates oneself in the human world. Lacan calls this skill a sinthome (Evans 1996, 188–90).[3]

I will reflect upon the consequences of these ideas for the therapy of people afflicted with schizophrenia (psychosis).

THE EARLY LACAN'S CONCEPTION OF THE ROLE OF THE FATHER

The ideas used by Lacan in his article "On a Question Prior to Any Possible Treatment of Psychosis" challenge the way in which object relations theory (Mitchell and Black 1995, 85–138) and attachment theory (Maine 2000) explain the cause of mental illness. Both of these theories present the mother as the crucial figure for understanding the healthy or deficient mental development of the child. On the other hand, Lacan, even early on in his career, argues that the schizophrenic (psychotic) structure of the personality of Judge Schreber must be understood to be the result of a failure in the role of the father (Lacan 2006, 464ff. [557ff.]). He goes even further and attributes the misery of Judge Schreber to a defective relationship with language, a defective relationship that itself follows from a failed relationship to his father or, more specifically, the "Name-of-the-Father" (Lacan 2006, 464 [557]). This double thesis challenges, first, the idea that the causes of schizophrenia are biological and genetic. Second, it challenges any theory that identifies a defective emotional relationship with the mother as the primary cause of schizophrenia (psychosis).

Unlike in other theories (e.g., those of F. Fromm-Reichmann), there is no explicit place in Lacan's theory for the schizophrenogenic mother.[4] Third, this double thesis locates the failure of someone like Judge Schreber in something other than emotions; it locates Schreber's deficient psychological structure in a failure to deal properly with the challenges inherent in the mastery of language.[5] Let us now look at Lacan's theory of early child development to understand fully these Lacanian claims.

THE EARLY DEVELOPMENT OF THE CHILD WITHIN LACANIAN THEORY

For Lacan, as for Winnicott, there is, psychologically, no such thing as a child (Winnicott 1965, 39n1); there is the "mother–child" pair, where the child needs a mother figure to even survive. This fact is, psychologically, made evident in the emotional attitude of the child toward the mother. The child smiles and appears self-confident in the arms of the mother. When the child is hurt or tired, she wants to be picked up by the mother. In tragic cases where the mother dies a few days after birth, the baby will sometimes refuse all food. In one such case, a baby would have died were it not for the ingenious advice of a psychoanalyst, who asked if there was still unwashed underwear of the mother. To the positive answer, the psychoanalyst replied, "Wrap the underwear around the milk bottle and see what happens." The baby accepted this bottle. Without some presence of the mother, the child would have died. Even the partial presence of the mother, i.e., the smell of the mother, satisfied the child enough to accept a bottle.

We can imagine that awareness of such total dependency on another creates great uncertainty, if not anxiety, in the baby. Such profound uncertainty and dependency is not promising for the psychological development of the child; however, a baby has a means of psychologically overcoming this feeling of total dependency: her imagination. The imagination creates a fantasy, which, in psychoanalytic terms, functions as a coping mechanism for the feeling of dependency. There are two elements in the baby's fantasy that are necessary for overcoming the feeling of dependency. The first element is the assurance that the person on whom the baby depends is reliable. Hence, the baby develops a fantasy of the omnipotent mother figure. Indeed, if the mother is omnipotent, then, whatever the baby needs can be provided by her. Additionally, the mother will be strong enough to defend the child against whatever danger she might face. From then onward, the baby relates not to its real mother, but an imagined, idealized mother.

The second element of the baby's fantasy is her certainty of the mother's intentions and desires. If the mother does not care for the baby, then the omnipotence the child sees in her is no guarantee that the baby will be taken care of. The second element of the baby's fantasy solves this challenge. The child imagines that she, the baby, is everything the mother could ever want. As long as the baby holds on to these two elements of its fantasy, she feels secure and expects that the (m)other will do everything the baby needs and wants.[6]

We can now imagine that the child experiences a challenge to her crucial fantasy when she starts to crawl or, even more, walk. These skills can enable the child to crawl or walk into a room where the mother is not present. This situation can of course be liberating, but it can also be scary if the child accidentally hurts herself in the other room. In such moments, the double fantasy of the child encourages and allows her to expect that the mother will be there instantly to liberate her from her pain.

However, the mother may not bring help as quickly as the child expects. In such a case, the experience of this new reality contradicts the child's expectations. For some time, the child will not feel ready to challenge the fantasy that the mother is omnipotent. Hence, the only way to make sense of the reality of not being helped immediately when in trouble is to wonder if the child is everything for the mother, that is, if it is totally lovable for the mother. At least this hypothesis gives the child an option. The child can now try to figure out what it is that the mother wants of the child and remold herself in accordance with these wants.

The child starts to experience the mother as other than the self and begins to wonder what the mother wants her to do, thus taking the desire of the (m)other as the basis of her own desires. Lacan's explanation of the linguistic symptoms of Schreber consists in finding a parallel between the structure of this phase of human development and the structure of Schreber's experience of the voices (Lacan 2006, 457ff. [547ff.]). Let us now turn to the case of Schreber.

FREUD AND LACAN ON JUDGE SCHREBER

The *Memoirs* of Judge Schreber give us insight into the inner experience of a person afflicted with schizophrenia (psychosis). In it, almost page after page, we find new symptoms or curious ideas, experiences, and imagined explanations of the world. I will select a few of these, along with Freud and Lacan's psychoanalytic interpretation of them.[7]

Judge Schreber thinks that his psychiatrist, Dr. Flechsig, tried to commit soul murder on him (chapter 2) [paranoia]. He also believes that God gave energy to the world and people using his nerves (chapter 1). Hence, Schreber calls neurology, the science of nerves, the holy profession (chapter 2). He believes that the Flechsig family conspired with God to deprive the Schreber family of access to the holy profession. Indeed, there were no neurologists in Schreber's family [jealousy].

Schreber reports that Dr. Flechsig told him white lies, as he does with other patients; however, Schreber comments condescendingly that these white lies were "hardly appropriate in my case, for he (Dr. Flechsig) must soon have realized that in me he was dealing with a human being of high intellect, of uncommon keenness of understanding and acute powers of observation" (Schreber 1988, 35) [narcissism, grandiosity].[8] Dr. Flechsig once praised Judge Schreber by saying that he was the "greatest seer of spirits of all centuries." Judge Schreber indignantly writes, "From a wider point of view . . . one ought at least to speak of the greatest seer of spirits of all millenia" (Schreber 1903, 77) [narcissism, grandiosity].

Schreber also confides that "anybody who sees me standing in front of a mirror with the upper part of my body naked would get the undoubted impression of a female trunk—especially when the illusion is strengthened by some female adornments" (Schreber 1903, 280). Schreber reports that at first "my whole sense of manliness and manly honour, my entire moral being, rose up against it (the attempt to unman him and make him into a woman)" (Schreber 1903, 57). Later in his *Memoirs*, Schreber writes, however, that he changed his mind by asking the following rhetorical question: "Who, faced with the choice of either becoming a demented human being in male habitus or a spirited woman, would not prefer the latter?" (Schreber 1903, 178). Toward the end of his *Memoirs*, he even writes, "I have to imagine myself as man and woman in one person having intercourse with myself" (Schreber 1903, 282).

Presumably, this transformation of Schreber had a grand purpose. Schreber would marry God and create a new mankind, where he would become the patron saint (Schreber 1903, 14–15) [lack of stable sexual identity combined with grandiosity].

Another symptom is Schreber's reaction upon reading his own obituary in the newspaper. He writes, "I took this as a hint that I could no longer count on any possibility of a return to human society" (Schreber 1903, 81) [confusion of life and death]. Schreber also describes many people, but, in particular, his wife, as "fleetingly improvised" (Schreber 1903, 117 ff) [lack of ability to transform sense data into a constant object].

Schreber talks early on in his *Memoirs* about his unmanning; however, he devotes an entire chapter to describing the many sexual and nonsexual changes he experienced in his body, for example, a temporary change of heart, violent attacks on his lungs, smashing of his ribs, and temporary removal of his stomach when he was eating (Schreber 1903, chapter 11) [lack of stable body experience].

Finally, Schreber mentions in many places the fact that in his world, words do not have the meaning they have for others. Thus, "not-thinking-of-any-thought" means "playing piano" (Schreber 1903, 169; also chapter 13). He devotes another entire chapter to one linguistic phenomenon: his experience of the voices he hears. These voices only utter the beginning of a sentence, which Schreber feels obliged to complete. If he does not complete these sentences, God will withdraw his rays from him and he will die. Schreber, furthermore, must complete the sentences as the voices wish. The tragedy for Schreber is that the sentences are about him, and the voices want him to say something contrary to what he believes to be true. Thus, the voices say, "Now I shall . . . ," and Schreber feels obliged to complete the sentence as follows: "Now I shall resign myself to being stupid" (Schreber 1903, 218) [forced self-alienation]. Schreber was thus compelled to say that he was stupid even though he was insulted when his own psychiatrist told him that he was the "greatest seer of spirits of all centuries"; Schreber, by contrast believed himself to be the greatest seer of spirits of "all millennia" (Schreber 1903, 77).

Freud viewed Judge Schreber's symptoms very differently from the way such biologically oriented psychiatrists as Kraepelin (De Waelhens and Ver Eecke 2001, 123–24) would have. Biologically oriented psychiatrists pay attention to details, particularly those that frequently reoccur. Their hope is that these details may indicate which part of the brain is defective. Instead, Freud looked at the totality of the symptoms and noticed that throughout time the story told by Judge Schreber changed.[9]

When Schreber created his final version of the world, he recovered enough to take steps to be released from the asylum (Schreber 1903, 361ff.). Schreber, a lawyer, first asked the preliminary question to the court as to whether his tutelage was temporary or permanent. He had hoped that the court would declare it to be temporary; he would then have asked for permission to go home. The court, however, declared the tutelage to be permanent. Schreber then made his second move. He asked his lawyer to request to rescind the tutelage. His lawyer lost this appeal. One argument used to put Schreber in an asylum against his will was based on German family law of that time. The specific charge against Schreber was that as paterfamilias, he had the right but also the duty to manage the family finances. As he was subject to delusions that encouraged him to buy jewelry, he was declared unfit to perform his duties as a paterfamilias.

In a lawyerly fashion, Schreber agreed to the fact that his delusions made jewelry buying a compulsive necessity, but he made the point that, in his case, the jewelry he felt compelled to buy was cheap. He further argued that the price of his jewelry was not more, but rather less, than other men spent on such recreations as smoking (Schreber 1903, 432–33). Furthermore, Schreber made the general argument that, although he unshakably believed in what others called his hallucinations, he never accepted them as a sufficient motive for action (Schreber 1903, 430–31). The court agreed with Schreber (Schreber 1903, 515). He went home, and his adopted daughter testified that Judge Schreber was a better father for her than his wife was a mother.

On the basis of these and other facts, Freud concluded that Schreber's delusions were not defects per se. Rather, they were a creative way of trying to solve an unsolvable problem in his life (Freud 1911–1913, 71). Freud's first task was to guess what the unsolvable problem was. An important and much talked about symptom in Schreber's delusional system was the idea that he was becoming a woman. This delusion showed that Schreber, a married man in his 50s, had not established a firm sexual identity. Freud goes further and claims that Schreber's lack of sexual identity had to do with the fear of his own homosexual feelings, in particular his feelings for his psychiatrist, Dr. Flechsig.[10] Freud then proceeds to show that Schreber's symptoms could be understood as the patient's attempts to deal with this, his central psychological problem.

To argue for this thesis, Freud uses a genial pedagogical trick. He transforms the concept of homosexuality into an equivalent sentence: "I (a man) love him (a man)" (Freud 1911, 63). Freud then articulates his patient's problem, as he believes Schreber experiences it. Freud felt that Schreber's central problem was his fear of his own homosexual feelings. Thus, Freud hypothesizes that a possible defense mechanism is to deny having such homosexual feelings. Freud also points out that if Schreber had homosexual libido, he had to find a way to satisfy that desire. It is logically impossible to both deny and justify homosexual feelings at the same time; however, Freud continues, what human beings cannot achieve in reality, because it is logically contradictory, they can achieve in imagination. Freud then proposes that Schreber's delusions and symptoms can be interpreted as an attempt to solve a problem in imagination that cannot be solved in reality.

Freud starts by pointing out that denying homosexuality can take four and only four forms once it is defined by the sentence, "I (a man) love him (a man)." Homosexuality can be denied by denying the verb, the object, or the subject of the sentence, or finally by denying the entire sentence (Freud 1911–1913, 63–65).

Let us start by analyzing the strategy of denying the verb (i.e., denying the presence of loving) in Schreber's delusion. A crucial element in Schreber's delusion was the conviction that his psychiatrist, Dr. Flechsig, was trying to commit soul murder. Insofar as Schreber was convinced of this element of his delusional system, he could convince himself and others that he hated (not loved) his psychiatrist (Freud 1911–1913, 63). Thus, the belief in Dr. Flechsig's intent to commit soul murder achieved the first of two goals: It presented a strong argument against homosexual feelings. This is the strategy of *paranoia*. Freud now had the challenge of showing that this delusion also helped Schreber achieve the second goal: justifying his homosexual interest in his psychiatrist. Freud points out that if one is convinced that someone is trying to commit soul murder, then one is justified in permanently keeping an eye on this person for purposes of self-defense. Indeed, it would be irresponsible not to watch out for such a potential murderer. The permanent interest by Schreber in Dr. Flechsig was thus justified under the mask of self-defense.

Freud identifies the strategy of denying the object as *erotomania*, the strategy of denying the subject as *jealousy* and the strategy of denying the entire sentence as *megalomania* (Freud 1911–1913, 63–65). Lacan marvels at Freud's explanation (Lacan 2006, 453 [541]); however, Lacan adds one crucial observation: Freud's theory predicts that there can be only four kinds of symptoms. Lacan points out that there are two more kinds of symptoms, which can be observed in the *Memoirs* of Schreber: linguistic phenomena (Lacan 2006, 449–52 [537–40]) and phenomena of bodily disintegration (De Waelhens and Ver Eecke 2001, 216–18; Lacan 2006, 471–73 [565–68]). This observation encouraged Lacan's search for a broader theory, which can incorporate these two additional kinds of symptoms.

But Lacan faced a choice as to which of the two symptoms not discussed by Freud he wanted to take as the primordial one. Lacan chose the linguistic symptoms as primordial and then derived the phenomena of bodily disintegration from the linguistic symptoms (Lacan 2006, 464–65 [557–58]). He then also had to deduce the four symptoms, which Freud already explained.

One way to understand Lacan's claim that Schreber's linguistic symptoms provide the key to understanding his mental illness as a whole is to analyze the structure of those linguistic symptoms: the voices Schreber claimed to hear. The next step is to make the typical psychoanalytic move (as Lacan does) and look to normal childhood development. If there is a phase in normal development that is similar in structure to the adult symptom, then the symptom can be understood as a fixation in normal development. The final question is why Schreber, as child, did not further develop (Lacan 2006, 457–62 [547–53]).

Let us take a closer look at the crucial linguistic symptom described by Schreber. Schreber reports that he heard voices. It is worth noting that the voices heard served as only one of the many linguistic symptoms revealed by Schreber.[11] As already mentioned, these voices only began sentences, which Schreber then felt he had to complete. If he did not, a parsimonious God would withdraw the remaining rays in him. God does not want to lose all the rays He invests in people; however, withdrawing His rays would mean Schreber's death. Furthermore, Schreber felt that he had to complete the sentences as the voices wished. Unfortunately, as previously mentioned, the sentences were about Schreber and were contrary to his beliefs about himself.

Thus, Schreber felt that he had to complete the half-sentence he heard: "Now, I shall . . ." with, "resign myself to being stupid" (chapter 16). Notice that the grandiose and narcissistic Schreber did not think that he was stupid. On the contrary, he believed he was extremely intelligent (story of white lies, chapter 4) and the greatest seer of all millennia (chapter 6). Schreber thus felt condemned to affirm, contrary to his own beliefs, that he possessed negative characteristics. In his obedience to the wishes of others (the voices), Schreber committed self-alienation. He affirmed things about himself that he did not believe to be true and were different from how he wanted to be. Lacan found and actually had to find this psychological structure of self-alienation in his view of child development, as shown in section two of this chapter.

The question now facing Lacan was, Why did this self-alienation, which is typical in the development of all children, lead to schizophrenia (psychosis) in the case of Schreber but not the majority of human beings? Lacan argues that for most children, a radical new experience invites them to change their subjective position to a position from which it is possible to avoid permanent self-alienation. He attributes the structural reason for the necessity of a sense of alienation to the original dual relation "mother–child," which characterizes the psychological world of the baby. Everything changes when the child is invited to, or forced to, psychologically, enter a triangular world. This happens when the child notices that the mother has an interest in a third person, who is often the father (Lacan 2006, 464–65 [557]). Such an experience challenges, as we saw in the introduction, both elements of the child's fundamental fantasy. A child may first react by denying or refusing this new experience.[12] But if the signs of triangulation are unmistakable, then the child needs to, subjectively, reposition herself. In a first move, the child must accept the narcissistic wound.

The child is less than she fantasized: She does not fulfill all of the mother's wants and desires. In other words, this wound occurs because the child is not the phallus that the mother wants. Or, in strict Lacanian terms, the child realizes that the phallus is elsewhere (Lacan 2006, 464–65 [557]);[13] however, children are resilient. They search for ways to recuperate some sense of self-worth. Children try to find out what it is in the father figure that is of such great interest to the mother using signals from the mother. A child will attempt to guess what mark in the father attracts the mother, identify with that mark, and thus transform their ideal ego into an ego ideal. They move from the imaginary to the symbolic (Lacan 2006, 462 [553]). Children hereby acquire a new subjective position.[14] Instead of expecting another (the mother) to do for them what they wish, the child, in her new subjective position, is willing to work to become like the father, whom she knows she is not. Children in this new subjective position accept that they are not what they want to be. They constitute themselves as split people, and they accept a gap between who they are and what they aspire to be. Instead of having tantrums when they do not get what they want, these children develop a willingness to work and show patience.

For Lacan, the new subjective position includes the foundation of all human law: the acceptance of the prohibition of incest. This prohibition refers to more than physical incest. It also includes the emotional fusion of the child with the mother figure. Indeed, in this new subjective position, the child moves away from the mother in two steps. First, the child passively experiences the narcissistic wound of realizing that she cannot satisfy all the desires of the mother. Second, the child actively searches for what is of such deep interest to the mother in the figure of the father. Furthermore, in identifying with this crucial mark in the father, the child uses the father as a building block for her identity. Hence, in a sense the mother is left behind.[15]

One could, however, argue that the search for the crucial mark in the father is guided by the child's original interest in the mother. Furthermore, the mother's signals of interest in the father are precisely what guide the child in search of the crucial mark in the father. Hence, the desire of the child is still tied to the mother. Importantly, however, the child learns from the mother that there is something life-giving outside the mother–child relationship. The world of incestuous feelings between mother and child is not all there is to life. The child is given an invitation to move out of her fused relationship with the mother. In a compact statement, psychoanalysis argues that the mother–child relationship is missing something crucial: phallic power. Thus, the child learns that the phallus is outside the dual unity mother–child.

One could present a second argument for the idea that identifying with a mark in the father does not leave the mother behind. That mark inspires the child to make the ties to the mother permanent. Indeed, so goes the argument: The child identifies with a mark in the father precisely because the child guesses that it is this mark that is so important for the mother that she abandons the child as the sole object of her interest. Identifying with the mark in the father can then be interpreted as an attempt to regain the loss of the mother, because the child is now the child plus the important mark of the father. I agree with this interpretation of Lacan's theory of the Oedipus complex.

Again, this interpretation itself provides evidence that something radically new is happening to the child within this new subjective position. Indeed, the child abandons her strategy of direct fusion with the mother. The child also abandons the illusion that she can remain passive, as the mother both knows what the child wants and will provide it. Instead, the child accepts the burden of having to become active. This activity has at least two important steps. First, the child accepts that she lacks something and thus needs to find something that will enrich her. (Lacan would state this more strongly, saying that the child has to become herself.)

What I am here calling "enrichment" is not just an adding on; it is a fundamental change.[16] To enrich herself, the child accepts that she must try to achieve or acquire something that she does not naturally or automatically have. More burdensome, the child must accept that there is a difference between who she is and what she wants to become. The child might work to acquire one mark (or aspect) of the father, but she somehow realizes that she is not currently like the father. This situation creates in the child a split between the current reality and the ideal that she desires. This split can be the source of a future depression (Vergote 2003) or the source for existential motivation for becoming someone. The emotional world of fusion, and thus of incestual feelings, is forever abandoned and left behind.

The argument that identifying with a mark of the father is nothing but an attempt to regain the love of the mother also offers evidence that this identification introduces a second radical change. To identify with a mark in the father, the child must perform hermeneutical work. The child must watch the mother's communication with the father to discern what is so valuable outside the mother–child relationship. The child has to interpret the family situation. Hermeneutical work is never certain, but the child must nevertheless commit to something. She must take a gamble with her life. Where the child holds on to certainties in the mother–child relationship, the child must accept uncertainty when identifying with a mark in the father. The respectful relationship between mother and father is, for the child, a warrant that her gamble of building her identity from a mark in the father has some hope of paying off. This is why divorces of parents revive in children the question of the worthiness of the gamble they made in creating their own identity, as demonstrated by the research of Judith Wallerstein et al.

Incestual attitudes are infused with certainty. A mother accused of an incestual relationship with her son demonstrated this with her testimony in court, saying, "But I know my son better than anybody else." Furthermore, in hermeneutical work, a person sees something stand for something else. The mark in the father has to do with the mother but is not literally the mother. The mark in the father is of significant interest to the mother, and hence acquiring that mark might make the child more interesting to the mother. As described, it is clear that the mark provides not certainty, but possibility; it is a signifier of a possibility. But through this signifier, through this mark, the way is open for connections with other signifiers. A child who identifies with the mark "firefighter" can see a connection with "fighter" and then with "boxing fights" or "fight to win in sports." Or the child could see connections between "fire" and "being fired up (being enthusiastic)" or "fire-engine."[17] These signifiers open the way to many possibilities of engaging oneself in the world.[18] Such diverse engagements with the world are indeed grounded in the original attempt to regain the attention of the mother, but they also open up the social world. Identifying with a mark in the father inserts the child in the world of signifiers. Consequently, the child accepts the mediating role of language in her relationship to the world, including her relationship with the mother. The infinite connections made available to the child by language play a disruptive role with incestual feelings. Fusion is destroyed permanently by the mediating function of language.

Lacan's concept of the "paternal metaphor" suggests one last important contribution to the child's psychological life: the incorporation of the father figure (Ver Eecke 1988, 1993). According to Lacan's reading, the Oedipus complex provides the psychological basis for metaphor and metonymy. A metaphor is a linguistic expression characterized by the fact that we do not mean what we say. Thus, when I say that a person is a "chicken," I do not mean that the person has feathers. I mean that the person is a coward and runs away at the first sign of danger, as, presumably, chickens do. A word used as a metaphor thus applies and does not apply to the object to which it refers. The double use of metaphors enables language to create new meanings. People afflicted with schizophrenia (psychosis) are known to have difficulty with metaphors.[19] They often interpret them literally, as in the case of the patient who claimed she did not have hands because her father had told her she was handicapped. She understood the metaphor of being mentally handicapped as literally having had her hands cut off.

Lacan's theory addressed the difficulty that psychotic people encounter with metaphors by explaining it as a failed confrontation with the Oedipus complex. Instead, the child remains in a pre-Oedipal position, which is a position in which the child creates a self-centered form of identity.[20] The child feels that she is everything an omnipotent mother could wish for. She can thus expect to get everything she wants and needs from the (m)other. One way to articulate that position is to say that the child's identity is its ideal ego. The Oedipal stage, which includes the child's identification with a mark in the father, is the transition from ideal ego to a new position.

This new position invites or forces the child to have patience, to work, and to accept that she is not what she wants to be. What this means for the child is a newfound appreciation for the future, an appreciation absent in the pre-Oedipal stage. Thus, the child radically changes her identity. Nevertheless, from the perspective of others, the child is the same child as before, say John Smith, born on July 23, 2012. The child remains the same, while also being radically changed. This is the definition of a metaphor; therefore, in the transition through the Oedipal challenge, the child has psychologically become a metaphor. It thereby also acquires the psychological requirements to understand and use linguistic metaphors. Even more, the child can replace one word by another and thereby create a metonymic series.

PUZZLING DIMENSIONS IN THE THEORY OF LACAN ABOUT THE FUNCTION OF THE FATHER

There are two interesting puzzles in Lacan's early theory of the function of the father. First, Lacan mentions a possible case in which the child would not be able to fully benefit from the triangular family structure even if the mother made adequate reference to the father figure. Lacan suggests that this might occur where the father presents himself as inappropriate. Lacan gives some hints as to what he means by "inappropriate" when he writes that "devastating effects of the paternal figure are found with particular frequency in cases where the father really functions as a legislator or boasts that he does" (Lacan 2006, 482–83 [579]). Lacan suggests that such fathers cause damage to their children because they "exclude the 'Name-of-the-Father' from its position in the signifier" (Lacan 2006, 483 [579]).[21] One plausible interpretation is that such fathers present themselves as imaginary figures rather than the carriers of a symbolic message. Lacan writes that such fathers would either not invite or not allow a child to make the effort of creating the basic signifier in their unconscious. This signifier is required to enter the symbolic system and thus the world of language.

The second puzzle regards well-known facts about people who are thrown into psychotic states following a breakdown episode. Usually, prior to the breakdown, these people functioned at least quasi-normally. Lacan argues that the reason for the breakdown is the appearance of an "A-father" in the emotional life of such a person (Lacan 2006, 479ff. [579ff.]). This figure at first exhibits maternal attributes. Thus, the great German poet Schiller protected and helped the precocious Hölderlin.[22] But it is reported that Hölderlin had the ambition of starting a new journal of poetry. When Hölderlin asked for support, Schiller was not enthusiastic and did not unconditionally support Hölderlin. It is also reported that Hölderlin fell in love with the ladies to whom he gave piano lessons. He imagined that the ladies would ask Schiller if he, Hölderlin, would be a worthy future partner. Schiller was, thereby, put into the position of judge; however, the psychic structure of Hölderlin had foreclosed the "Name-of-the-Father." Confronted with an "A-father,"

Hölderlin's unconscious was at a loss as to how to deal with this challenge. Hölderlin needed to fill the hole created in his unconscious structure by the appearance of an "A-father." The delusional system was an attempt to deal with that hole in the unconscious.

Returning to Schreber, we see that his delusions included many normal wishes that were transformed according to the grandiose demands of an ideal ego typical of the mother–child relationship. Like many people, Schreber looked for a promising partner. Few aim at marrying God. Many want children, but few hope to create a new mankind.

THERAPEUTIC IMPLICATIONS

What can one hope for in a therapeutic environment informed by Lacan's complex theory of psychosis? One approach is to help the patient by repairing the deficient psychic structure in the patient so she can reintegrate herself into society. Two psychoanalysts, Karon and Robbins, have written about their methods to achieve such a goal. Their insights were derived independently from Lacan's, but their method can be understood within a Lacanian framework.

I will examine the work of three therapists who developed a method for treating people afflicted with schizophrenia, which is explicitly derived from Lacan's theory: Palle Villemoes, Jean-Max Gaudelière, and Willy Apollon and his colleagues in the Gifric group in Montréal, Canada. Lastly, an alternative treatment approach may be derived from Lacan's more complex later thoughts about schizophrenia, in which no restructuring is aimed at. One tries to avoid the initial breakdown by encouraging the partial solution already present in the life of the patient.

Karon and Robbins are two non-Lacanian psychoanalysts who have reported the successful treatment of people afflicted with schizophrenia. Bertram Karon wrote a book on his method (Karon and VandenBos 1981). His goal consists of trying to understand the unacceptable feelings of the patient, label them, and strongly justify them. He argues that repressed feelings are not at the disposal of the subject. Feelings that are labeled and recognized become tolerable. The theoretical challenge from a Lacanian point of view is to understand how Karon's method is able to restore to the patient that which was originally not only repressed, but also foreclosed. Karon then moves to a second step. He imposes limits on possible actions on the basis of arguments that are part of the patients' psychic structure (Ver Eecke 2001, 2002). One point is clear in Karon's method: Karon works on both the imaginary (recognizing feelings) and the symbolic (imposing limits).

Robbins reported that a patient who was afflicted with psychosis and was speaking schizophrenese stated that when she speaks "schizophrenese" it is because she does not want to be understood. Therapy then consists of earning the trust and confidence of the patient so that the patient is willing and able to translate her schizophrenese into regular language. This translation gives the patient a choice between adhering to elements of the delusion or dealing with the painful demands of the Real (Robbins, 2002).[23] Robbins's method also first deals with the imaginary dimension of his patient (by letting the patient feel that she is understood) and second with the patient's confrontation with the pain of the symbolic (as he confronts her with the choice of a flight in delusion or the acceptance of the psychic pain of dealing with her life).

Let us now reflect on the work of three psychoanalysts who use methods explicitly derived from the theories of Lacan and report curing schizophrenia (psychosis), and who we mentioned earlier: Palle Villemoes, Jean-Max Gaudelière, and Willy Apollon and his colleagues in the Gifric group in Montréal, Canada.

Villemoes, following Lacan, believes that the person afflicted with psychosis has a defective relationship with language. He developed a method to give language traction for the patient. Villemoes's first phase is to describe the objects in the consulting room, then in the patient's own room. In the second phase, called the working phase, Villemoes invites the patient to describe the objects she can "see" in her first memories. Villemoes avoids asking about people, since they are the origin of psychic problems, but the patient is, nevertheless, allowed to talk about people as she sees fit. By encouraging the patient to describe all the objects from their earliest memory in life onward, the patient is given the opportunity to create a life story. Villemoes's ultimate goal is for the patient to be able to identify herself with a word (a signifier in Lacan's theory) and accept the implications of such an identification. When the patient creates a delusion and believes that she is Napoleon, she does not feel obliged to walk to Moscow. When the patient truly identifies with a word and its implications, and states, for instance, that she is not a thief, she might imply that her friends steal, that she has inclinations to steal, but she affirms that she tries to do her best not to steal (De Waelhens and Ver Eecke 2001, 109–22; Villemoes 2002). Villemoes thus aims at letting his patients become, in Lacan's terminology, speaking beings. Villemoes actually based his method on Lacan's theory.[24]

Gaudelière accepts Lacan's idea that the psychotic person cannot adequately overcome the narcissistic wound introduced by the triangulation of the early family experience and uses delusions to fill the hole created by that narcissistic wound. The psychotic person was also unsuccessful in the creation of the primary signifier around which the foundation of one's personal identity is built. Gaudelière uses two techniques with his patients: One identifies an object from the world of the patient's delusion. The second searches for a means of creating a grounding signifier. Both techniques aim at restoring the symbolic function in the schizophrenic.

Gaudelière had a patient who worked in Paris but was originally from Bruges in Belgium. His delusions were connected with Bruges and not Paris. The patient associated Bruges with death: suicides on the canals and the historical expression "Bruges la morte" (Bruges the dead one), which originated when the port closed after the North Sea receded. Thus, Gaudelière told the patient that there was an exposition in Bruges about Memling and that he could not go; would the patient make sure to bring Gaudelière a catalogue from the exposition? Gaudelière's theory is that if an object is taken away from the world of delusion in which the patient lives, then the patient will start to talk because the hole thus created needs to be filled (Gaudelière 1998).

Gaudelière's second technique, helping the patient create a primary signifier (Lacan's concept of creating a "paternal metaphor"),[25] is illustrated by the patient who forgot his pipe in the waiting room. In French, one says about a soldier who just died in the war, "Il a cassé sa pipe" (He broke his pipe). This metaphorical saying was well known to the patient. Gaudelière decided to use the linguistic expression connected to the patient's act of forgetting as the first signifier by which to let the patient organize his world symbolically. He told the patient: "You forgot your pipe, you did not break your pipe [i.e., you did not kill yourself]. You had a choice and you chose to forget, not to break your pipe" (Gaudelière 1998).

Willy Apollon and his colleagues in the Gifric group also aim at restoring the subjectivity of the schizophrenic person (Apollon et al. 1990, 2008). A crucial strategy involves asking patients to describe their dreams, which are then analyzed. Dreams are how the unconscious deals with what Lacanian theory calls the "Real" (Evans 1996, 159–61). Apollon sees four steps in the treatment of people afflicted with psychosis. First, helping the patient tell her personal history limits the influence of the death instinct (symbolic work). Second, the patient is helped to reconstruct the psychic body image (imaginary work). Third, the patient is assisted in reforming her experience of time. In particular, she needs help with the contradiction between her inner experience of time and her sense of time demanded by social projects. It is the change in experience of time demanded from a child in the Oedipal experience. Finally, the patient needs help to reconstruct her expectations of the social world (Apollon 1990, 79). At some point in the therapy, the patient is asked to make a choice between the story of the delusion or the articulation of the patient's subjectivity as it emerges from dream analysis.

A second approach to the treatment of people afflicted with psychosis can be developed from the later Lacan's ideas on psychosis. Lacan pointed out that psychosis emerges after an "A-father" appears in the emotional life of the patient. It therefore follows that a person can have a psychotic structure that nonetheless allows them to remain integrated in social life. Two techniques can be developed making use of the Lacanian idea of breakdown.

A first technique can be inferred from looking at a patient, Josephine, described by Ginette Michaud. Josephine had a psychotic psychic structure, but she also had an aunt who was able to help her create a life for herself. She lived with her aunt and had the same profession as her aunt, who helped her in her profession. Just as Schiller did for the young Hölderlin, the aunt occupied a maternal, protective function for the patient. This maternal function changed into that of the "A-father" at the moment when the aunt said to the patient, "Clearly, you cannot do this!" (Michaud 2004, 203). The goal of treatment at this point is to avoid the transformation of the aunt into an "A-father."

A second technique derived from Lacan's idea of the psychotic breakdown considers and uses the way the patient managed her own life before the breakdown. This technique may also be used for those patients with a psychotic personality structure to avoid an eventual breakdown from happening. An example of this latter possibility can be drawn out of Lacan's reflections about James Joyce, who managed to develop no psychotic breakdown, although he is attributed a psychotic personality structure. In Lacan's terminology, Joyce had not successfully incorporated into his personality the "paternal metaphor." Instead of accepting the "Name-of-the-Father," Joyce aimed at creating a name for himself. Creating a name for oneself has a narcissistic and grandiose dimension. In Joyce's case, he intended to write works of art, where mankind would need at least two to three hundred years to understand what he meant.

Thus, a "Joycean" therapy would consist of finding skills that the patient can use in a narcissistic and grandiose way, such that she feels she can make a name for herself there where she has not identified with the "Name-of-the-Father." Michaud calls such a therapy the search for the "practicable" in the psychotic person. Lacan's son-in-law, Jacques Alain Miller, has created the name "ordinary psychosis" for people who lack the "paternal metaphor" but are attempting to create a name for themselves by means of some skillful activity (Miller 1999; Vanderveken 2009). Lacan names such skillful activities in people with a psychotic structure a "sinthome" (Lacan 2005; Harari 2002).

CONCLUSION

In this chapter, we summarize Lacan's views on the conditions that create in a human being the deficient psychological structures that make a person vulnerable to a schizophrenic breakdown. We also point out that an "A-father" (i.e., a maternal figure who at some point exercises a paternal prohibition) is necessary to provoke such a schizophrenic breakdown. Prior to and after the psychotic breakdown, such a person is argued to have a deficient psychic structure, labeled "ordinary psychosis" by J.-A. Miller. We discuss the methods used by several therapists who have successfully treated people afflicted with schizophrenia or psychosis.

NOTES

1. Lacan 2006, chapter 21. Two other important publications are Seminar III on the psychoses, published roughly at the same time and the much later Seminar XXIII on Joyce and the sinthome. Seminar XXIII focuses on the question of how someone like James Joyce, who seems to have a psychotic structure, is able to make a life for himself. For summary of the ideas of the later Lacan, see Soler 2014, chapter 15 and 16.

2. Lacan 2006, 482 [579]: "Further still, the father's relation to this law must be considered in its own right, for one will find in it the reason for the paradox whereby devastating effects of the paternal figure are found with particular frequency in cases where the father really functions as a legislator or boasts that he does—whether he is, in fact, one of the people who makes the laws or presents himself as a pillar of faith, as a paragon of integrity or devotion, as virtuous or a virtuoso, as serving a charitable cause whatever the object or lack thereof that is at stake, as serving the nation or birth rate, safety or salubrity, legacy or law, the pure, the lowest of the low, or the empire. These are all ideals that provide him with all too many opportunities to seem to be at fault, to fall short, and even to be fraudulent—in short, to exclude the 'Name-of-the-Father' from its position in the signifier."

3. See Demoulin 2009.

4. Schizophrenogenic is a concept referring to the original theoreticians of the psychological origin of schizophrenia where the argument was that it was the result of deficient mothering. One could, by implication, give a secondary place to this concept in Lacanian theory by pointing out that the primary cause of psychosis in the early theory of Lacan is the failure of the "paternal metaphor," which is sometimes due to the mother's failure to respect the "Name-of-the-Father." Still, for Lacan, the main failure is a deficiency of the triangular relationship in the family structure (Lacan 2006, 464 [557]). For a balanced and sophisticated view on the topic of "schizophrenogenic," see Karon 2018, chapter four.

5. It has been known for some time that people afflicted with schizophrenia have difficulty with metaphors and thus have difficulty with proverbs (Fort 1990). It is also known that such people have difficulty with pronouns.

6. An illustration of the veracity of this element in the child's fantasy world is the statement of a colleague who reported, 10 years after her divorce, that, as she now sees it, the main reason she divorced her husband was that she felt he could not guess what she wanted.

7. For a more detailed list of Daniel Schreber's symptoms, see the introduction of this book.

8. Pages refer to the German original edition.

9. Originally, Schreber reported that he resisted the idea of becoming a woman with all his manly honor (Schreber 1903, 36–37, 57, 176). Later, he reported that he accepted his transformation as a kind of common-sense compromise (Schreber 1903, 177–79). He even enthusiastically embraced the idea and gave a variety of reasons for accepting his womanhood (chapter 21). One reason given was that he would be able to marry God and create a new mankind (Schreber 1903, 114, 289, 293), where Schreber would become the patron saint (Schreber 1903, 115).

10. See Freud 1911–1913, 37ff. Also, in the Schreber household, the feelings for Dr. Flechsig were somewhat intense, as Schreber himself testifies: "My wife felt even more sincere gratitude and worshipped Professor Flechsig as the man who had restored her husband to her; for this reason she kept his picture on her desk for many years" (Schreber 1988, 36).

11. For further examples of the linguistic oddities in Schreber's world, see Schreber 1903, chapters 4, 12, 15, and 17.

12. Lacan, as does Freud, refers to three forms of refusing to deal with an unacceptable experience: Verneinung (denial), Verleugnung (disavowal), and Verwerfung (foreclosure). At

this point in the text, I make use of the idea of denial, because I am describing a successful Oedipal situation. Disavowal involves the mother making a reference to the father in a degrading, ridiculizing way. In foreclosure, the mother is said to have made no meaningful reference to the father (Lacan 2006, 465 [558], also chapters 15 and 16, and appendix I; for the concept of "disavowal," see Evans 1996, 43–44).

13. Elsewhere in the double sense of being somewhere other than in the child and somewhere other than in the unit "mother-child."

14. On schema R the subject changes from position "m" (me) (imaginary) to position "I" (ego-ideal) (symbolic) (Lacan 2006, 462 [553]).

15. Lacan makes use of the homophony one hears in French between "Name-of-the-Father" (Nom-du-Père) and "No-of-the-Father" (Non-du-Père) (Evans 1996, 119). Hence, as Laplanche and Pontalis point out, for Lacan there is an essential connection between wish and law, which includes the prohibition of incest (Laplanche and Pontalis 1988, 286).

16. Lacan does this in his famous article "On a Question Prior to Any Possible Treatment of Psychosis" (Lacan 2006, chapter 21).

17. For classic examples of studies of chains of signifiers in a particular person, see Freud 1901, chapters 1–2; Richardson 1983; Peraldi 1987. The latter two give examples illustrating and/or even explicitly referring to Lacan.

18. In the same way, the initial introduction of the phallus provides new kinds of choices for the child to make, i.e., shoes to fill. The shoe fulfillment analogy is interesting, since Lacan describes the role of the phallus here as "lack" (Lacan 2004, 38–39). Some argue that a better translation of "manque" would be "void." Lacan actually uses the two concepts (Lacan 2004, 26: "Il (le désir) est en apparence indéfini, parce que le manque, participant toujours de quelque vide . . .).

19. Langdon and Coltheart 2004. See also Mitchley et al. 1998 and Herold et al. 2002, both cited in Mo et al. 2008.

20. In my view, "Oedipal" is not a fixed time point (like "metaphase" in the cell cycle); rather, it is a period of time, like anaphase.

21. For the full quotation, see Lacan 2006, 482–83 [579].

22. For an impressive study on Hölderlin making use of the life of this poet to illustrate Lacan's concept of "A-father," see Laplanche and Pontalis, 1969. For a short article making use of facts revealed by the research of Lothane 1992 and Israël 1989, see Ver Eecke 1995, included in this book as chapter 12.

23. In Evans 1996, 159, we find the following definition of the Real: "The real emerges as that which is outside language and inassimilable to symbolization." See also Lacan 2006, 388 [464].

24. For a fuller explanation of Villemoes's method, see chapter 14.

25. For a full explanation of Lacan's concept of "paternal metaphor," see introduction and chapter 4.

Chapter Six

A Post-Lacanian View on Schizophrenia

In this chapter, I present De Waelhens's summary of Lacan's theory. I point out that we can discover in De Waelhens the idea that, according to Lacan, schizophrenia can be caused by two factors. I address this contradiction and present a solution, which is then illustrated by the case of Robert.

DE WAELHENS'S PRESENTATION OF LACAN'S THEORY OF SCHIZOPHRENIA

In his book *La Psychose*, De Waelhens provides a clear, book-length presentation of Lacan's early conceptualization of schizophrenia and psychosis.[1] De Waelhens situates his attempt to understand psychosis within the context of nineteenth- and twentieth-century psychiatric and philosophical movements. He points out that these philosophical movements were struggling to overcome the Cartesian dualist view of human nature. The two parts are the rational consciousness or the mind and an object-like body. De Waelhens draws from the discoveries of the schools of phenomenology (Husserl and Merleau-Ponty) and existentialism (Heidegger and Sartre) to argue that consciousness is only able to perform its many functions provided one condition is fulfilled: It must make use of many things that serve as background, while also forgetting and even repressing that background. Thus, to perceive a chair or read a book, I must use my eyes, but the eyes must remain in the background of my consciousness. If the background unexpectedly asserts itself (e.g., because I feel a sudden and sharp pain in my eyes), my consciousness ceases to be able to perform the simple function of seeing a chair or reading a book.

De Waelhens then looks at psychoanalysis and, in particular, the work of Lacan to explore whether there is an even deeper kind of background operating in human consciousness.[2] De Waelhens discovered the world of the unconscious and child development. Deeply influenced by both Hegel and Heidegger, De Waelhens began to stress the importance of language for human consciousness. From that point onward, as Paul Ricoeur observed, De Waelhens devoted progressively more space in his books to the problem of language. According to De Waelhens, language creates a distance between consciousness and its objects. This distance enables consciousness to experience objects in a vicarious—i.e., distanced—way that enables consciousness to articulate the experience of the objects; however, creating distance is not easy if one is dealing with fantasized or longed-for objects. De Waelhens thus articulates in two steps a new and much deeper horizon present and hidden in the working of consciousness.

The first step consists of analyzing the mother–child relationship, which allows a child to assume its body through a form of narcissistic merging and fusing, and then mirroring, with the mother (Lacan's mirror stage theory). For Lacan, this dimension gives rise to the imaginary dimension of psychic life.

The second step consists of analyzing the contribution made by the Oedipal experience. For De Waelhens, following Freud and Lacan, the Oedipal experience introduces a narcissistic wound, which is sutured by an identification with a mark (signifier) in the father. Such an identification is not a literal identification; it is a metaphoric identification. A child identifies with the father while knowing that she is not the father. Hence, for Lacan, the Oedipal triangle allows the child to make use of the metaphoric possibilities of language. The failure to acquire such metaphoric capabilities leads people suffering from schizophrenia to become prisoners of the literal meaning of linguistic metaphors, as was the case with a previously mentioned case of a patient who cried in her therapist's office because she was convinced that she had no hands. Pressed for evidence, she reported that her father had said that morning that she was handicapped. Lacan refers to the world of language as the "symbolic order," as it requires the Oedipal structuring.[3]

More than the early Lacan, De Waelhens stressed the contribution of failures in the mother–child relationship prior to the Oedipus complex to the advent of schizophrenia and psychosis. Still, like Lacan, De Waelhens located schizophrenia in a failure of the symbolic order (the "paternal metaphor") to correct the excesses of the imaginary. It is one thing to dream, as Judge Schreber did, that it must be nice to be a woman succumbing to intercourse. It is another thing to start thinking that one is becoming a woman. It is one thing to want to be divinely important. It is another thing to believe that God has asked you to marry Him to create a new mankind where you will become the Patron Saint, as Schreber believed. Having studied psychoanalysis, De

Waelhens was able to teach his philosophical colleagues that the background for the proper functioning of consciousness included the world of the unconscious.

Because De Waelhens stressed more than Lacan the function of the mother–child relationship in the origin of schizophrenia, his presentation appears contradictory. I will first present the apparent contradiction and then show how that contradiction opens the path for a more complete post-Lacanian theory. Let me summarize my strategy.

De Waelhens follows Lacan in arguing that the normal way for a child to correct its illusionary vision of others and itself—and thus avoid schizophrenia—is for the mother to show respect for a third, normally the father. That third—the father—need not be physically present. Indeed, he need not even be alive; therefore, Lacan summarized his view using a formula that requires the mother to show respect for the "Name-of-the-Father." Such respect by the mother gives a double message to the child. It shows the child that the mother is not omnipotent and shows the child that it is not the only object of the mother's desires. After first trying to destroy the message of the mother by either interrupting the communication between mother and father or wishing that the father be gone (or dead), the child then moves toward a more constructive solution. The child unconsciously selects a mark in the father with which to identify (a process called "paternal metaphor") in the hope of thereby maintaining some of the esteem of the mother. That mark is the signifier that, from then onward, will unconsciously organize the desire of the child. Lacan considered the failure of this process—foreclosure of the "Name-of-the-Father" or failure in the "paternal metaphor"—to be the cause of schizophrenia.

De Waelhens also makes use of the work of Aulagnier, a student of Lacan, to argue that the mother's relation to the child can make it difficult or even impossible to let the child have access to the symbolic order. This happens with mothers who unconsciously deny the sexual origin of their children and hence unconsciously believe that they are the sole creators of their children. Such mothers tend to relate to their children more as organs of themselves than independent beings. Such mothers do not perform the labor of the imagination that would allow them to experience the child as both their production and other than themselves. The absence of the introduction to otherness is, then, interpreted by De Waelhens as an impediment to introducing the otherness imposed by the Oedipal triangle and the acceptance of otherness required by language and the symbolic order.

Post-Lacanian authors (Antoine Vergote, Paul Moyaert, Jozef Corveleyn, etc.) argue explicitly that the cause of schizophrenia is not only a failure of the "paternal metaphor" (or a deficiency in the symbolic order), but also a failure in the imaginary, i.e., a failure in the psychic relation to the body.[4] As the imaginary failure is structurally deeper and temporally earlier than the symbolic failure, it follows theoretically that interventions at the symbolic level will be ineffective if not grafted to an intervention at the imaginary level.[5]

In this chapter, I analyze the case of Robert, presented by Rosaline Lefort in Lacan's first seminar, to prove that deeply emotionally disturbed patients not only have a deficient relation to language and the symbolic, but also to their body image (and thus to the imaginary). I use the work of such experienced therapists as Searles and Karon to show that effective treatment of people suffering from schizophrenia requires dealing with the dual dimension of the imaginary and the symbolic. This conclusion is a correction of Lacan's early theory on psychosis. I make reference to a book (De Waelhens and Ver Eecke 2001, 85–94), where I show that such diverse practitioners as Karon/VandenBos, Silver/Fromm-Reichmann, Davoine/Gaudelière, Pankow, Benedetti, and Muller report successful interventions that follow the golden rule defended earlier: A symbolic intervention can only be successful if it follows work done at the imaginary level. Still, as I mention in the conclusion, Lacan's insistence upon the importance of language and the symbolic remains a permanent achievement in theorizing about the life world of people suffering from schizophrenia.

AN APPARENT INCONSISTENCY IN DE WAELHENS'S PRESENTATION OF THE CAUSE OF SCHIZOPHRENIA

One can find in De Waelhens two versions of a psychological causal explanation of schizophrenia. The first causal explanation is derived from a student of Lacan: Piera Aulagnier (De Waelhens and Ver Eecke 2001, 154ff.). De Waelhens presents his explanation as a variant of the theory of the schizophrenogenic mother; however, he adds a correction. Schizophrenia must be understood as the result of a failure in a triangular structure in which each of the three angles (maternal figure, paternal figure, and child) can play a role (De Waelhens and Ver Eecke 2001, 224ff.). Compared with some Anglo-American variants, the causal explanation by De Waelhens has two unique features: It focuses on the desire (as opposed to the behavior) of the mother, and it begins its analysis of the influence of the maternal figure from the period of pregnancy (and not just from the period after birth).

The study highlights a number of observations regarding mothers of normal children. There is the narcissistic investment of the pregnant woman in her pregnancy and the transformation of that narcissistic involvement into expectation of a future child by the work of the imagination. There is the unconscious acceptance of the sexual origin of the child; the rather quick overcoming of postpartum depression; the delicate balance of feeling of oneness-in-otherness with the baby; and the support provided by the mother for the child as it learns to live with its body, even its paining body.

According to the report of Aulagnier, mothers of children suffering from schizophrenia tend to be deficient in the work of imagination that transforms the narcissistic involvement into expectation of the future child (Aulagnier 1964, 55). They also unconsciously repress the sexual origin of the child (Aulagnier 1964, 54–55) and imagine themselves as the sole creator of the child. Furthermore, they often have a harder time overcoming postpartum depression and show a disturbance in the delicate balance of the feeling of oneness-in-otherness with their children (for a confirmation of many elements of this report see two case studies in Karon and VandenBos 1981, 329–53). Since the child needs to deal with the paradox of experiencing her own body as other from the mother but still desirable by the mother, this latter disturbance can result in a child's difficulty inhabiting her own body.

One strain of thought in this explanation—which De Waelhens can legitimately use to diminish the apparent contradiction of having two different causal explanations—is the claim that the mother represses the sexual origin of the child. This can lead to the mother having difficulty recognizing the otherness of the child. Consequently, the mother does not do the necessary imaginary work to provide a desirable balance in her feeling of oneness-in-otherness with the baby. Using Lacanian language, De Waelhens summarizes this situation as pointing to the "mother's incapacity to construct a corporeal signifier," which "must result in a 'massive castration' of the future subject. . . . The foreclosure of the 'Name-of-the-Father' has here its point of origin" (De Waelhens 1978, 64).

Thus, one strain of thought, using a deficient "maternal function" as the explanation for schizophrenia, claims that the maternal figure helps to lay the groundwork for a failure in the paternal function. This explanation thus has a connection with the second explanation—that schizophrenia results from a failure in the paternal function. That second causal explanation, presented by De Waelhens, is derived directly from Lacan; more specifically, it is derived from Lacan's interpretation of Judge Schreber. The explanation starts by accepting that the child has a symbiotic relation with her mother. In that relation, the child creates an imaginary and illusionary solution to its problem of dependence upon others for survival. That illusion can be conceptualized as the child's attempt to situate herself in a maternal space characterized by the possibility of fusion with the mother. If the fusion is not total, the child still imagines that she is the sole object of an omnipotent mother's desire.

Lacanian theory argues that the normal way for a child to correct the illusionary vision of self and others is for the mother to show respect for a third, normally the father. That third—the father—need not be physically present; he need not even be alive. Thus, Lacan summarizes his views by saying that the mother must show respect for the "Name-of-the-Father."

Such respect by the mother gives a double message to the child. It shows the child that the mother is not omnipotent and that the child is not the only object of the mother's desires. After first trying to destroy the message of the mother by either interrupting communication between mother and father or wishing the father to be gone (or dead), the child moves in the direction of a more constructive solution. The child borrows the insignia of the father and carries them as regalia (glasses, hat, shoes) before selecting unconsciously a mark in the father with which to identify in the hope of thereby reappropriating some of the esteem of the mother. That mark is the signifier, which, from then onward, will unconsciously organize the desire of the child.

Of the many consequences that result, two are important enough to mention explicitly. First, by selecting and identifying with a signifier—which corresponds to the Freudian Oedipus complex—the child substitutes mediation for immediacy. Indeed, the child, in the post-Oedipal period, unconsciously aims at maintaining the esteem of the mother not by being directly present to the mother, but by incorporating something for which the child guesses that the mother has great affection: some mark in the father. Second, this move unites similarity and difference. Before the child was situated as the object of the mother's desire. Now the child wants to be like the father, who is respected by the mother. Still, the child feels she is the same child in both positions. Lacan called that move—which synthesizes similarity and difference—the "paternal metaphor." The absence of such a move is considered the structural cause of schizophrenia, which is expected to erupt if the proper occasion presents itself. Lacan conceptualizes that occasion as the appearance of an "A-father" figure in the emotional life of the patient (De Waelhens and Ver Eecke 2001, 220–22; Lacan 2006, 481 [577]; Laplanche and Pontalis 1969, 125).

ADDRESSING THE APPARENT INCONSISTENCY

De Waelhens sensed the problem lurking within his dual causal explanation of schizophrenia. In a special section entitled "The Relative Role of the Mother and Father in Psychosis," he writes, "Could we not be reproached for having located the origin of psychosis both in the child's relationship to the mother and in his relationship to the father?" (De Waelhens 1978, 137). De Waelhens answers his own rhetorical question by arguing that the two causes are not separate; they reinforce one another and thus become part of a single, more general cause. The schizophrenogenic mother omits the work of the imagination during pregnancy and thereby does not create a chain of signifiers into which the child will be introduced. If the child has not been introduced to the world of signifiers, then it cannot effectively internalize a paternal signifier, for the child has remained alien to the world of signifiers. On the other hand, if the father is a "caricatural personage" (De Waelhens 1978, 138), how can the mother show respect for him and introduce him to the child?

Thus, De Waelhens presents the overall cause to be both a defective maternal and a defective paternal role. The maternal role (among other things) contributes to creating the basis of self-esteem via fusion and mirroring. The paternal role (among other things) contributes to introducing a sense of finitude, limit, separateness, and law;[6] therefore, a person suffering from schizophrenia seems to be in need of help from two contradictory directions. But how can one claim that a patient needs fusion and separation at the same time, for instance? This claim is a paradox only if one has a static view of human development in which one sees one or the other element missing. It is not a paradox if one has a dynamic view of human development in which one postulates the need for the simultaneous healthy presence of both. This is similar to the view developed by Blatt when he argues that human beings need both the "development of satisfying interpersonal relationships and a well-differentiated sense of self" and that "these two developmental processes evolve in an interactive, reciprocally balanced, mutually facilitating fashion from birth through senescence" (Blatt 1995, 1012).

The view that both the maternal and the paternal function have been defective in people afflicted with schizophrenia goes a long way toward explaining the advice of many experienced and successful therapists.[7] Harold Searles, for example, argues that it is mandatory to

> foster the necessary emotional atmosphere in the sessions for the development of the contented, unthreatened emotional oneness, to which I refer by the term "therapeutic symbiosis"—a form of relatedness of the same quality as that which imbues the mother–infant relatedness in normal infancy and very early childhood. (Searles 1986, 598)

He also advocates for limit-setting as "one of the major dimensions of therapeutic technique in this work" (Searles 1986, 598).

Furthermore, Searles points to a dialectical connection between the two aforementioned requirements. In a passage that De Waelhens or Lacan could have written, Searles writes,

> The analyst is able firmly to set and maintain limits to the extent that he is aware of, and accepting of, his own individual limitations. But the very nature of the work with patients suffering from schizophrenia, who themselves have so much unresolved infantile omnipotent striving, is such as powerfully to evoke the analyst's unconscious fantasies of omnipotence. (Searles 1986, 601)

And, "An analyst who, for whatever unconscious reasons, cannot become able to live comfortably with the possibility that his patient may never become free from psychosis cannot, by the same token, foster the necessary . . . 'therapeutic symbiosis'" (Searles 1986, 598). Thus, the therapist who cannot control his own sense of omnipotence in healing people afflicted with schizophrenia will be incapable of not only setting the necessary limits to his patients (he will be defective in his paternal function), but also creating the necessary therapeutic symbiosis (he will be defective in his maternal function). In summary, a successful maternal function (e.g., therapeutic symbiosis) requires the incorporation of a paternal function (acceptance of finitude, limit-setting).

The previously mentioned reading of Searles allows me to make two points. The first point is a practical one: If effective therapy requires such contradictory capabilities, it is no wonder that Blatt can conclude that, "Significant differences exist in therapeutic efficacy among therapists, even the experienced and well-trained therapists in the TDCRP [Treatment of Depression Collaborative Research Program]" (Blatt et al. 1996, 1281–82). Indications are that a similar statement can be made for therapists of schizophrenia. Searles presents us a test, a criterion for effectiveness in psychotherapy. De Waelhens's theory, informed by Lacan, can provide a reason for why the criterion given by Searles is necessary.

My second point is theoretical: For the maternal function and the paternal function to be effective, feelings of grandiose omnipotence must be checked. When De Waelhens wrote his book, Lacan had articulated that requirement explicitly for the maternal function by insisting that a mother needs to acknowledge her own lack by showing respect for the "Name-of-the-Father." Lacan had not yet articulated the requirement so well for the paternal function. He did so later (Evans 1996, 64–65), writing that the father should be a symbolic father, that is, a subject himself submitted to the law and thus subject to finitude (death) and limitation, rather than an imaginary omnipotent father (Evans 1996; Lacan 1993).

BROADENING THE SEARCH FOR A SOLUTION TO THE DUAL CAUSAL THEORY

Since the original publication of the book by De Waelhens, several of Lacan's seminars have become available, and Lacan scholarship, too, has developed. Scholars and therapists using the ideas of Lacan have pointed out that, while Lacan's use of the "Name-of-the-Father" as the crucial element in the definition of psychosis and schizophrenia is an important conceptual achievement, Lacan's account still works with a *negative* definition (Calligaris 1991, 26; Vergote 1998, 227).

Vergote and several of his students at the University of Leuven have not only pointed out that Lacan's definition of schizophrenia, as foreclosure of the "Name-of-the-Father," is a negative definition, but also provided a positive definition. Thus, in a review of De Waelhens's book *La Psychose*, Vergote argues that De Waelhens, like Lacan, overemphasizes the ruptures that are necessary in the development of the child (including the rupture imposed by the "paternal metaphor") and neglects to analyze the "necessary presence, which precedes, supports, and maybe even helps to achieve the ruptures and upheavals in the constitution of the subject" (Vergote 1973, 781 [translation by WVE]). Vergote identifies presence, preceding the rupture, as one of the drives, as they either find representation or they do not. This model thus indicates that the Freudian economic point of view is the place where a more positive definition of schizophrenia should be sought (Vergote 1973, 783–85).

Ten years later, Vergote formulated his objection to De Waelhens and Lacan's views by claiming that understanding schizophrenia by means of a genetic constitution—including the idea of a "paternal metaphor"—is inadequate. Such a point of view, according to Vergote, does not permit one to understand why it is that the predominant experience of a person suffering from schizophrenia is not an anxiety-provoking experience of the body broken into parts. Rather, the schizophrenic experiences the body as in the process of breaking up under the influence of imaginary aggression that devours from the inside, corrupts and turns pleasure into pain, and tears a human being apart (Vergote 1984, 324).

Another 20 years later, Vergote reminded us that Freud made the distinction between the physiological body and the psychic body (Vergote 1994, 181). Vergote then pointed out that the skin, as physiological container of the body, is insufficient to protect the psychic self from invasion. That protection is provided by the creation of a psychic body image (Vergote 1994, 191). The body image is created through the interaction of parents and child in dealing with bodily needs, in the way the parents respond to, satisfy, or reject these needs (Vergote 1994, 188–89). Rudolf Bernet makes use of Schopenhauer to clarify the great challenge of human beings, that is, dealing as conscious beings with the demands of the body. To be effective, the energy of the body needs to find some representation to guide attempts at satisfaction. But no representation is a satisfactory translation of the demand for fulfillment of the original need. When the child does not succeed in connecting its bodily energy and needs with some form of representation, the energy races unbound and blindly. In a person suffering from schizophrenia, this creates the experience of a body falling apart (Bernet 1996, 76).

Paul Moyaert, in turn, points out that the Lacanian definition of schizophrenia as foreclosure of the "Name-of-the-Father" can only point to deficiencies. Such an understanding of schizophrenia does not allow us to comprehend what a person afflicted with schizophrenia is trying to do. Such a definition thus eliminates the dynamic point of view, which is essential in a psychoanalytic approach. Moyaert then points out that the drives without representation are experienced as a danger. He is thereby able to explain schizophrenic self-mutilation as an attempt to deal with the badness of the body because the drives of the body are experienced as the source of displeasure (Moyaert 1998, 142–45).

To provide a positive definition of schizophrenia, which complements Lacan's negative definition, Vergote and his students concentrate on the problem of finding representations for the demands of the body. If that search fails, then the body and its demands are experienced as dangerous. The human being will then be forced to fight its own embodiment. Thus, the dynamic point of view is reintroduced in the theory of schizophrenia. In Lacanian terms, one can say that Vergote and his students point to a deficiency other than the failure of the symbolic by the foreclosure of the "Name-of-the-Father." That other deficiency is one connected with the construction of a body image by creating representations for the drives. Lacan uses the concept of the imaginary to cover that domain. Schizophrenia can, therefore, be defined as a failure of both the symbolic and the imaginary.

However, one can find in Lacan's thoughts elements that go beyond his own negative definition. He identifies schizophrenia as the failure of the symbolic system to get hold of the imaginary (Fink 1997, 89), because both the symbolic and the imaginary are deficient. As a result of these deficiencies, the stitching of the symbolic to the imaginary and the creation of anchoring of meaning is defective. In Lacan's technical language, the person suffering from schizophrenia lacks "button ties"—also called "anchoring points" or "quilting points" (Fink 1997, 93–94; Moyaert 1993, 271). Consequently, the patient is confronted with the horror of the Real that can neither be imagined nor symbolized (Evans 1996, 77, 155).[8] This line of thought is, explicitly suggested by De Waelhens: The failure of the symbolic is also a failure of the imaginary; however, the solution suggested by De Waelhens can now be better articulated because recent theoretical developments have made us aware of the multiple failures that are possible in both the imaginary and the symbolic.

The possibility that the imaginary system may fail in many ways becomes obvious if one recalls that Lacan twice revised his mirror stage theory. In his original presentation, Lacan located the achievement of the child and the reason for her jubilation in the fact that she had now created a unified total body image instead of experiencing herself as body parts.

In his first revision, Lacan located the reason for the jubilation of the child in the child's discovery of the mother's narcissistic involvement with the child. The mother's involvement is noticeable in the child's search for the mother's eye when the child sees herself in the mirror. According to this reading, it is the mother's emotional involvement with the child that allows the child to invest emotionally in the child's own body (Fink 1997, 88; Simiu 1986, 3–27; Ver Eecke 1984, 70ff.).

In his second revision, Lacan endorses Rosaline Lefort's idea that the child needs to create not only a unified body image, but also a body image that performs the role of container to some contained (Lacan 1988a, 104). Lacan explicitly connects the idea of the body as container to a contained with his theory of the mirror stage by means of his famous flower vase metaphor: A concave mirror allows a person to see flowers that are outside of a vase as being within the vase (Lacan 1988a, 139). For a human being, the body image as container needs to have a place for needs, feelings, feces, urine, food and even pain. The baby's task of creating a body image as container requires the skilled help of a maternal figure.

Similarly, the multiple ways in which the symbolic system may fail can be better understood in light of later developments in Lacan's thought. Indeed, De Waelhens reconstructs Lacan's thesis on the basis of the article summarizing the seminar on psychosis. According to that summary, the major reason for the failure of the symbolic is that the mother shows no respect for the word (name) of the father (Lacan 2006, 482 [578]). It is true that Lacan there adds one paragraph about the deficiencies of the father himself, but it is almost presented as an afterthought (Lacan 2006, 482–83 [579]).

However, in the full seminar, Lacan stresses at length that the paternal function requires a symbolic father, not an imaginary father (Lacan 1993; Lacan 2006, 464–65 [556–57]). He defines an imaginary father as someone who "manifests himself simply in the order of strength and not in that of the pact" (Lacan 1993, 205). He describes the consequences of such a paternal figure as follows: "We are all familiar with cases of these delinquent or psychotic sons who proliferate in the shadow of a paternal personality of exceptional character, one of these social monsters referred to as venerable" (Lacan 1993, 204). Later on, Lacan conceptualizes this notion of the symbolic father as the "barred Other" (Evans 1996, 15). Thus, in light of the full development of Lacan's thought, we can argue that the father, too, can contribute to the failure of the symbolic order in a child. He can do so because he presents himself more as an imaginary, rather than a symbolic father.

Finally, the failure of the symbolic may not just be the result of a deficiency in the symbolic or the imaginary.[9] In some cases, it may also be attributed to the horror of the Real itself. This possibility arises because Lacan seems to accept two moments in the development of the child where language emerges. On the one hand, Lacan describes the result of the Oedipal complex as the establishment of the symbolic order and thus the creation of an effective signifier. On the other hand, he also comments on Freud's analysis of his grandchild, who, as an infant, did not cry when his mother left him because he had, first, created a transitional object (the spool) and then, second, replaced the spool by the words "fort-da" (away-here) (Lacan 2006,

262 [319]). Thus, by his dual theory of the origin of language, Lacan allows for the possibility that something might go wrong in the use of language (the symbolic) before the Oedipal period, at a time when the imaginary seems to dominate. Indeed, children may not succeed in using either transitional objects or words to deal with a departing mother, or they may do so in a radically defective way.

There may be multiple reasons for failures of the symbolic. Furthermore, these multiple reasons may exert their influence independently from or in addition to maternal and paternal influences. Two cases illustrate my claim. VandenBos presents a case in which a child's parents were going through a divorce, but the family physician also played a major role in creating the symptom. The boy was sent to the family doctor because he was quite "nervous" and was placed on mild tranquilizers. When the boy asked his doctor for explanations, he was told that he had bad nerves. To the boy's further questions, the doctor answered that nerves were like worms under the skin. The boy was sent to VandenBos because he was "compulsively splashing water on his face and soaking his hands . . . as many as 20 to 30 times a day. He would wake up in the middle of the night to do the same thing" (Karon and VandenBos 1981, 159). VandenBos discovered that the boy knew about worms from fishing. He knew that if they dried, they burst open. He was therefore afraid that his bad nerves were going to burst open. Hence, he tried to keep them wet. The nervousness changed into compulsive behavior because of the explanation given by an outsider (the family doctor) about the child's nervousness.

Lefort presents another case, that of Robert. Robert was grossly neglected by his mother (twice he was brought to the hospital in a state of acute wasting before he was a year old); however, a surgical team greatly contributed to the child's difficulties with developmental tasks because they administered an antrotomy at the age of five months without anesthetic, while simultaneously forcing a bottle of sweetened water into the boy's mouth to prevent him from crying. Lefort writes that she had the impression that the boy's horror "fantasies had become reality" (Lacan 1988a, 100). In the case presented by VandenBos, the family physician unwittingly helped create the horror of the Real by making a connection between the boy's nervousness and worms. In the case presented by Lefort, the encounter with life itself created too much of a horror (not being fed and being operated on without anesthetic).

As mentioned earlier, the later Lacan argued that psychosis is the reaction to a Real that cannot be signified by the imaginary or the symbolic. As the Real is horrifying, the lack of its mastery, by means of the power of signifying, leads to defensive strategies. In presenting psychosis as a reaction to a developmental failure on two levels, an opening is created for a more complex definition of schizophrenia. Indeed, a psychotic reaction is not a reaction to the failure of the symbolic alone, that is, a failure of the "paternal metaphor." It is a reaction to the joint failure of the imaginary and the symbolic. I will therefore articulate the connection and the difference between the functions of the imaginary and the symbolic.

Let me start by clarifying the imaginary as it is created in the mother–child relationship. The challenge in the mother–child relation is for the mother to introduce distance between herself and the child while creating a deep form of caring unity. The child's challenge is to use the gift of caring unity with the mother as the basis for accepting embodiment and the gift of distance offered by the mother as a method of separation from the mother.

The challenge of the symbolic is for both the mother and the father to introduce and make acceptable to the child the idea of finitude, which implies an acceptance of the child's place in the legitimate order of human beings. The painful dimension of this challenge is that the symbolic dislodges the child from its imagined place of privilege with the mother. This involves the experience of a narcissistic wound; however, it also results in the child discovering an identity and a direction for its desire. Both result from the child borrowing, through identification, a basic mark from the father. That identity is indicated by the name given to the child. But it is only significant if the child accepts that identity, which in turn means that the child has, in her unconscious, been marked and grounded in a central meaning-giving signifier.

The early Lacan called this meaning-giving signifier the "Name-of-the-Father." The later Lacan split the two moments involved in his original concept of the "Name-of-the-Father." He differentiated receiving a name from accepting the meaning associated with it (my name is John Smith, and I have the choice of honoring or dishonoring that name). Lacan continued to call the first moment the fundamental signifier, now also referred to as S1, and he called the second moment S2. The first moment is associated with the negative experience of alienation (my name is something different from the inner feeling of my selfhood and is imposed on me without my consent). The second moment is associated with separation (how I choose to individuate myself—as honoring or dishonoring my given name) (Fink 1996). This move allowed Lacan to connect his original idea—the "Name-of-the-Father" is the fundamental signifier—with a second idea—meaning consists in a chain of signifiers. S1 and S2 are seen to be the beginning of an infinite series of signifiers: S1, S2, S3, S4.

The case of Robert, presented by Rosaline Lefort, illustrates the claim that psychosis is not only the failure of the symbolic, but also the failure of the symbolic because of an already failed imaginary. In the case of Robert, we do not hear about the father. At the time of Robert's treatment, his mother was diagnosed as a paranoiac and confined (Lacan 1988a). His mother kept him with her, moving from house to house. She neglected his essential needs so much that at five months he arrived in a hospital with acute "hypertrophy and wasting." After an infection that necessitated an operation, he was isolated and "fed on a drip." At nine months, he was returned to his mother, only to come back to the hospital two months later, "again in a state of acute wasting" (Lacan 1988a, 91). Five months later, the mother legally abandoned the child. As a foster child, Robert changed residence 25 times before he was four years old. As indicated earlier, the therapist discovered that Robert had undergone an antrotomy at the age of five months without anesthetics. "Throughout the painful operation a bottle of sweetened water had been kept forced in his mouth" (Lacan 1988a, 100).

Some of Robert's symptoms were extreme lack of coordination in movement, hyperagitation, lack of coordinated speech (he would frequently utter screams and guttural, discordant laughter, and he yelled two words: miss and wolf), and uncoordinated prehensive activity. "[H]e would throw his arm out to take hold of an object and if he didn't reach it, he couldn't correct it, and had to start the movement all over again from the beginning" (Lacan 1988a, 92). He had convulsive fits of agitation without real convulsions that played a role "during each of the routine moments of his daily life—the pot, and above all the emptying of the pot, undressing, feeding" (Lacan 1988a, 92). "One evening, after going to bed, he tried to cut off his penis with a pair of plastic scissors, while standing on his bed in front of the other terrified children" (Lacan 1988a, 93).

> The business of undressing was for him the occasion for genuine crises, . . . one having lasted three hours, during which the staff described him as possessed. He howled, "Wolf!" running from one bedroom to the next, smearing the other children with feces that he found in the pots. It was only once he was tied up that he calmed down. (Lacan 1988a, 96)

Using the three categories of Lacan, Lefort writes of Robert,

> I had the impression [that] it was Robert's tragedy that all his oral-sadistic fantasies had been realised in the actual events of his life. His [horror] fantasies had become reality . . . the image that Robert had constructed of a starving, paranoiac, dangerous mother, who certainly attacked him. Then the separation, a bottle held by force, making him swallow his cries. The force-feedings with the tube, 25 moves in succession. (Lacan 1988a, 100)

Lefort continues, "I had the impression that this child had sunk under the real, that at the beginning of the treatment there was no symbolic function in him, still less an imaginary function." Lacan corrects Lefort by adding, "But he did have two words" (Lacan 1988a, 100). The treatment consisted of restoring the imaginary and the symbolic so that the horror of the Real diminished, if it did not disappear.

Lefort's effort at restoring the imaginary could be described almost completely in object-relations terminology. The body had to be accepted as a container with reference to milk, feces, and urine. Lefort remained present for Robert as a stable object even though he was aggressive and peed on her (Lacan 1988a). This, writes Lefort, helped Robert; but it only allowed him to create a bad self-image, as is evident from the following: "When I had to frustrate him—he ran to the window, opened it, and cried out—'Wolf! Wolf!' and seeing his own image in the glass, he hit it, crying out—'Wolf! Wolf!' That is the way Robert represented himself, he was the Wolf!" (Lacan 1988a, 95).

Then, in two phases, Robert reconstructed a good self-image using two forms of mirroring separated by a symbolic act. Robert first projected his bad image onto the therapist and separated himself from her. Lefort, the therapist,

> was made to swallow the bottle of dirty water and was on the receiving end of the aggressive pee. So, I was the Wolf! Robert separated himself from it during one session, by shutting me in the toilet, then, returned to the room where we had the sessions, all alone, climbed into the empty bed, and started to moan. He could not call me, yet I did have to come back, since I was the permanent person. I came back. Robert was stretched out, pathetic, his thumb now within an inch of his mouth. And, for the first time in a session, he held out his arms to me and let himself be consoled. (Lacan 1988a, 97)

Next Robert used a symbolic act in which he renamed himself. Lefort describes it as follows: "Robert, completely naked and facing me, collected up the water in his cupped hands, raised it to the level of his shoulders, and let it run the length of his body. He started afresh several times, and then he said to me, softly—'Robert, Robert'" (Lacan 1988a, 98). He then repeated the scene with milk. The separation of the good boy (Robert, not Wolf!) from the therapist was performed in another form of mirroring: "He first tried to differentiate himself from me by sharing with me. He gave me everything to eat, saying, while touching himself—'Robert, then touching me—not Robert.' I made great use of this in my interpretations to help him and me" (Lacan 1988a, 99).

We see that Robert's story is a case where there is not just a failure of the symbolic. It is a case where there is abuse of the symbolic—the patient calls himself Wolf instead of Robert—to structure an already deficient imaginary. Let us start with the deficient imaginary. Robert had not only failed at separating himself as a good object from a maternal figure, but also not yet established himself as a good object. Robert beat his own image and called it Wolf. He had created a bad self-image. But the creation of the bad self-image was an achievement of the therapy. Robert's self-image had no place for the things that go in and out of the body: milk, urine, feces. The milk and the bottle had been so connected with deprivation and pain that the imaginary assumption of his body must have become unacceptable.

The digestive body was, for Robert, one horror story. As reported by Lefort, digestive functions are used aggressively (the milk, the urine, and the feces). The symbolic order was then used by Robert to create some distance between himself and the digestive body that was unacceptable. He gave up his Christian name, "Robert," and called himself "Wolf," signifying his radical badness. Thus, the obvious failure in the symbolic order in which Robert did not call himself Robert but Wolf was more than a failure of the symbolic. It was, first of all, the failure to imaginarily inhabit his body, because that body was made the source of pain by others. And Robert needed to be a loved body for those others who had hurt him to be able to accept himself as embodied (Moyaert 1993, 267).

Lacanian theory does not require that physical pain be inflicted on the child to postulate that the child will fail in her imaginary effort to inhabit the body. It is crucial for the child to experience herself as lovable by others but in her own right. In a case presented by Karon, there is no indication that physical pain was inflicted upon the child—with one possible exception: The toilet training was completed early. There was evidence that the child was not treated as lovable in his own right. Indeed, while trying to praise the child, the mother proudly highlighted trivial achievements while neglecting real ones. Karon writes, "Consciously, she was attempting to impress people with the accomplishments of her son; unconsciously, she was convincing them of his worthlessness by presenting the worthless productions first and the worthwhile productions later or not at all" (Karon and VandenBos 1981, 340). Even though physically inflicted pain is not a necessary condition, in the case of Robert it was occurring within a context in which Robert experienced himself as worthless and unlovable. So, let us be clear, Lacanian theory does not make pain as such the cause of failure in the imaginary. It is the dialectic between the experience of pain and the experience that one is not lovable that creates difficulty in properly constructing a body image that the child can inhabit. A body that has been constructed as unlovable and painful requires distortions in the symbolic world. Sometimes these symbolic distortions are as visible as the imaginary distortions.

Robert's crucial use of one of the two words he knew—"wolf!"—is better explained by the Lacanian theory than the object relations theory. Robert lets go of his "bad" self by abandoning the self-given name "Wolf" and creates a "good" self-identity by publicly accepting his Christian name. Words and the symbolic organize the progress in the imaginary (see Lacan's comments on Melanie Klein's techniques in 1988a, 80–88; also Strauss 1987, 62).

CONCLUSION

In this chapter, we make use of the case of Robert to illustrate a theoretical point, made by Antoine Vergote. The cause for a schizophrenic personality is not just the absence of the "paternal metaphor," as Lacan seems to stress. There is at least a double cause. The absence of a good mother (or maternal figure) or the presence of an abusive one is an additional factor that can play a role in creating a defective psychic structure in a child, which can be called schizophrenic.

NOTES

1. De Waelhens's book *La Psychose* was originally published in French. The English translation was incorporated as part of De Waelhens and Ver Eecke 2001.
2. De Waelhens made use of the concepts of the imaginary and the symbolic developed in Lacan's early thinking. He did not use the later Lacan's thought, which stressed a third concept: the Real.
3. The close connection between the full use of language and the Oedipal structure is captured in the Lacanian concept of "paternal metaphor." Failure or foreclosure of the advent of the "paternal metaphor" is then seen as defining for psychotic personality structure.
4. See Soenen and Corveleyn 2003.
5. In part V, we will show that three therapists, Karon, Villemoes, and Prouty, who successfully treat persons afflicted with schizophrenia, obey this theoretical requirement in the way they treat their patients.
6. Lacan connects this role with the introduction of language (Fink 1996; Muller and Richardson 1982, 9ff.), while Freudians conceptualize it as the imposition of castration.
7. Successful interventions for people suffering from schizophrenia can therefore be assumed to be complex interventions that address both the imaginary and symbolic deficiencies of such people. The imaginary develops in relation to a maternal figure. The symbolic develops through the introduction of a third, normally the father. I explain the success of Karon's interventions with people suffering from schizophrenia by pointing to the double dimension of his interventions (Ver Eecke 2001; see also chapter 13 in this book). His interventions, first, repair an imaginary defect (e.g., by justifying a terrible feeling) and, second, introduce a symbolic distinction and prohibition (your murderous feeling is justified, but it is stupid to act upon it). In the first chapter of *Phenomenology and Lacan on Schizophrenia* (De Waelhens and Ver Eecke 2001, 82–94), I demonstrate that other therapists who report successes in treating people afflicted with schizophrenia, for example, Frieda Fromm-Reichmann, Harry Stack Sullivan, Harold Searles, Bertram Karon, Ann-Louise Silver, Y. Alanen, Gisela Pankow, Françoise Davoine, Jean-Max Gaudelière, Piera Aulagnier, Gaetano Benedetti, Isidro Vegh, Contardo Calligaris, and Willy Apollon, use similarly complex interventions.
8. Michael Robbins, a non-Lacanian, shows nicely that the language of a person suffering from schizophrenia—schizophrenese—is such that it sometimes intends to be a substitute for reality, not a way to signify that reality (Robbins 2002).
9. See Soler 2015, 201–15.

Part II

Hegel and Lacan on Mental Illness

Chapter Seven

Hegel as Lacan's Source for Necessity in Psychoanalytic Theory

Lacan intended to give psychoanalysis a scientific status by assigning some sort of *necessity* to phenomena that are central to the discipline. Two of Lacan's papers—the one on the mirror stage (Lacan 2006, chapter 5, 75–81 [93–100]) and the one on aggressiveness (Lacan 2006, 82–101 [101–24])—do indeed try to do just that. My thesis, however, is that such necessity does not come from psychoanalytic experience but from the Hegelian framework underlying these papers. I therefore propose to compare Lacan's theory of the mirror stage with the beginning statements of Hegel's discussion on the master–slave dialectic and Lacan's theory of aggressiveness with Hegel's discussion of the "Law of the Heart." I hope to show Lacan's dependence upon Hegel for providing the element of necessity required for the scientific status of his work, while at the same time drawing attention to the radical difference between Lacan and Hegel.

LACAN'S THEORY OF THE MIRROR STAGE AND HEGEL'S DIALECTIC OF LORDSHIP AND BONDAGE

In his article on the mirror stage, Jacques Lacan observes that, by the age of six months, the infant can recognize his or her image in the mirror (2006, 75–81 [93–100]). Moreover, she reacts to this recognition with a series of jubilant movements. The interpretation of this behavior tells us that at this age the infant identifies with her body. It also tells us that the identification with the image or the Gestalt of the own body allows the baby to overcome one of the consequences of the prematurity of birth of human babies, referred by Lacan as the fetalization of human beings at their birth. Lacan stresses the fact that perception, and thus seeing, has a crucial function for the assumption of the body. He makes use of Harrison's experiments on pigeons and Chauvin's on locusts to provide scientific evidence for his claim that seeing is crucial in the building of a self-conception.

However, perception is only one of the factors used to build a self-conception. The observations of Spitz show us that the quality of the mothering figure's desire is also involved. Spitz also reports that children who suffer from hospitalism fear the approach of anyone who has not come to feed them (Spitz 1965). Children in these circumstances regularly produce negative cephalogyric motions.

The greatest difference between normal children and children who suffer from hospitalism is that the former were the object of their mother's desire, while the latter were only surrounded by the scientific knowledge of doctors and nurses. If one wishes, one can see here an argument for the thesis of the mutuality of desires even at a time when one of the desires, that is, the child's, does not have the status of full subjectivity. The ontological claim of the mutuality of human desire is also the central thesis in Hegel, in particular in his passage in the *Phenomenology* of the master–slave dialectic (Hegel 1977, 111–19).

I want to concentrate on this ontological move because it is this move that provides Lacan's theory of the mirror stage with its overall unity. The basis of this ontological move in Lacan's theory of the mirror stage can be found in the beginning paragraphs of Hegel's master–slave dialectic of self-consciousness. I will quote these obscure passages and clarify them to make a comparison between Hegel and Lacan.

The beginning paragraph of "Lordship and Bondage" reads as follows: "Self-consciousness exists in and for itself when, and by the fact that, it so exists for another; that is, it exists only in being acknowledged" (Hegel 1977, 111). Here Hegel rejects atomistic individualism as a correct description of the becoming of self-consciousness. Becoming self-conscious is, according to Hegel, not a product of the activity or the will of an isolated individual. It is rather the *result* of an *intersubjective* relationship, of being acknowledged or recognized.

The second paragraph provides the arguments for the thesis stated in the first paragraph:

> Self-consciousness is faced by another self-consciousness; it has come *out of itself*. This has a twofold significance: First, it has lost itself, for it finds itself as an *other* being; secondly, in doing so it has superseded the other, for it does not see the other as an essential being, but in the other it sees its own self. (Hegel 1977, 111)

The paragraph starts with a phenomenological description and continues with a logical analysis of that description. With the statement, "Self-consciousness is faced by another self-consciousness; it has come *out of itself*," Hegel describes the fact of having before oneself another self-consciousness as involving an *act* whereby the first self-consciousness discovers in an external entity a quality of being that it has itself but that it was not yet consciously aware of. The first consciousness thereby *invests* in an external being qualities it has itself but is not yet fully aware of having. It is this *act of investment* that Hegel describes as the first consciousness "com[ing] *out of itself*."

The remainder of the paragraph is a logical analysis of this phenomenological description. Hegel points out that to "come out of" oneself to see another as a self-consciousness means two things. It means that the other is not constituted as *another* self-consciousness. The other is only constituted as a projection of the self-consciousness that the first consciousness has not yet become aware of in itself. In Hegel's words, the first self-consciousness "does not see the other as an essential being but in the other sees its own self." Hegel also points out that to "come out" means that the first does not know itself, but on the contrary, it has falsely discovered itself in another being and therefore has found itself as *another being*. As such, Hegel writes, the first consciousness "has lost its self."

The logical analysis of Hegel's phenomenological description points out that the full constitution of another being as self-consciousness will involve two steps. It will involve the step just described—that is, the constitution of the other as a self-consciousness. It will also, however, involve the constitution of that self-consciousness as a self-consciousness that is *other* than *one's own self*. Hegel's analysis seems to stress that it is *false to believe that the second step can be reached without the first step*. Both steps are necessary because the only way consciousness, at first, knows how to constitute another being as other than itself is to constitute it as an object. Only when the other has been constituted *first* as *another self-consciousness* can it afterward be constituted as a *self-consciousness* that is *other than one's own*.

> It must supersede this otherness of itself. This is the supersession of the first ambiguity and is therefore itself a second ambiguity. First, it must proceed to supersede the *other* independent being in order thereby to become certain of *itself* as the essential being; secondly, in so doing it proceeds to supersede its *own* self, for this other is itself.
>
> This ambiguous supersession of its ambiguous otherness is equally an ambiguous return *into itself*. For first, through the supersession, it receives back its own self, because by superseding *its* otherness, it again becomes equal to itself. But secondly, the other self-consciousness equally gives it back again to itself. For it saw itself in the other but supersedes this being of itself in the other and thus lets the other again go free. (Hegel 1977, 111)

These paragraphs elaborate upon the second step required for the full constitution of two self-consciousnesses. In the second paragraph we learned that on the way to constituting itself as a self-consciousness, the first consciousness constituted another being as a self-consciousness that it itself actually was. In doing so, the first self-consciousness did not constitute a *real other*, and it did not discover its own *self*. On the contrary, the first consciousness discovered itself *in and as* another self-consciousness. There is therefore otherness in the heart of self-consciousness; however, a self is not the otherness that it needs as a means to discover or constitute itself as a self-consciousness. Thus, to really become a self-consciousness, consciousness will have to *destroy that otherness in the heart of self-consciousness*. Only in this way can the first consciousness overcome the loss of self, discussed in the second paragraph.

In the process of constituting a real self-awareness by destroying the otherness in its own heart, consciousness differentiates between the self-consciousness it is and the self-consciousness the other is. It thereby sees the other as *other* rather than as *another self*.

These opening paragraphs of Hegel's "Lordship and Bondage" thus establish that the transition from consciousness to self-consciousness requires an *intermediate step* in which *a first consciousness discovers itself in another self-consciousness*. This intermediate step is alienating and must be overcome. Given the logical necessity of this intermediate step, we can now say that the ontological description of the process of becoming a self-consciousness *includes necessarily* a relation to another in whom I discover myself as a self-consciousness.

Lacan takes over the essence of Hegel's ontology of self-consciousness, while at the same time transforming it enough to be applicable to his observations, mentioned in the beginning of this chapter.[1] Like Hegel, Lacan maintains that the subject needs another to become a subject. Lacan, however, restates Hegel's ontology of self-consciousness as follows: At six months of age, the human subject gives itself objectivity and permanence by *seeing* itself in the Gestalt of another or even in the Gestalt of its own mirror image. It then invests this Gestalt libidinally, giving rise to the stage called *primary narcissism*.

In both cases, the *structure* of the ontological description of the self is the same. Lacan does not follow Hegel in stressing the *logical necessity* of an *intermediate step* in the transition from consciousness to self-consciousness. Nevertheless, the theory of the mirror stage is presented as a necessary part of the ontology of the human subject (Lacan 2006, 76 [94]). Lacan is therefore dependent upon the Hegelian analysis of self-consciousness to give the mirror stage its necessity.

Lacan's dependence upon Hegel is also obvious when one analyzes the relation of transitivism to the mirror stage. The latter theory points to the apprehension of the Gestalt of another's body as necessary for the human subject to be able to appropriate and unify its own body. It explains how the Gestalt of another is instrumental for the appropriation of one's own body. It therefore offers an explanation as to why one child starts making exactly the same gestures as another; however, this theory does not immediately explain why one child should cry when another child falls. To do so, one needs the Hegelian idea that consciousness "sees *its own self in* the other." In Lacan, one self relates to the Gestalt of another; in Hegel, however, a self relates to *another self because* the first self discovers itself in the other as *self-consciousness*. The latter intersubjective relation has a depth that allows us to understand why one child cries when another falls. Under Lacan's more restricted theory we would expect that when one child falls, the other child would fear that it too will fall, because this child's body experience is dominated by the Gestalt of the other. We expect such a child *to fear, not to cry*. Thus, notwithstanding the dependence of Lacan's theory of the mirror stage upon Hegel's dialectic of self-consciousness, we should not overlook the difference between Hegel's analysis and Lacan's theory.

A first difference between Hegel's dialectic of self-consciousness and Lacan's dialectic of the mirror stage concerns the status of the subject before it enters the dialectic. In Hegel, we have a consciousness that has discovered its own role in knowing the world. It lacks only the method needed to find out who it is. In Lacan, we have a subject who is ill at ease with herself, who is uncoordinated, who is anatomically incomplete, and who experiences her movements as turbulence (Lacan 2006, 76–77 [94–96]). By means of the mirror stage, the subject is offered an idealized unity that she does not have at that moment. By means of the Gestalt of another, Lacan's subject is not only *finding out* who she is, but also creating herself as what she is not yet but, in some sense, should become. What is hereby created, therefore, is not a self-consciousness, but rather an organizing matrix, a statue (Lacan 2006, 76 [95]), and this organizing matrix Lacan calls "I."

A second difference between the Hegelian dialectic and the Lacanian dialectic can be found in their results. In Hegel, the dialectic of self-consciousness leads consciousness to become aware of itself as the negative of objectivity. In a further moment of the dialectic, however, self-consciousness will become humble because of its fear of death. It is thereby willing to give a positive function to that which is other than itself—that is, objectivity (life, the body, etc.). Thus, the dialectic in Hegel allows consciousness to see what the dialectic is about because it is consciousness itself that is invited to give meaning to the other than the self. In Lacan, the dialectic of the mirror stage results in the creation of an idealized organizing matrix that the subject is not but that the subject projects itself as becoming. That Gestalt, that *idealized statue*, has a content, which the subject appropriates without a conscious justification. Contrary to Hegel's dialectic, the Lacanian dialectic of the mirror stage does not assign consciousness a crucial role in bringing about the dialectic move. Instead, Lacan has assigned this key role to the influence upon the child of the structural signifiers: the Gestalt of another and the "Name-of-the-Father." Lacan analyzes the idea of the "Name-of-the-Father" in his article on psychosis (Lacan 2006, 445–88 [531–83]).

A third difference between the Hegelian and Lacanian dialectics is their focus. In Hegel, the dialectic is the process whereby consciousness becomes aware of what it is and then affirms its discovery in reality. It discovers itself, first, as *negativity*. In Lacan, the dialectic is about the subject conquering its body as an exteriority. That body has a visual unity that the interior experience of the same body does not have. The mirror stage is therefore an instrument to synthesize the subject as *spatiality*.

These three differences in Lacan's emphasis are dictated by Lacan's concern with the scientific facts previously mentioned—in particular, the physiological consequences of seeing the image of one's own Gestalt or the Gestalt of members of one's species and the fetalization phenomenon. The differences locate the Lacanian dialectic more at the bodily level than at the conscious level. The Lacanian dialectic also implies that in the mirror stage, a statue—which is a form of content the subject does not consciously understand—gets hold of the subject. Inasmuch as Lacan claims that the synthesis achieved in the mirror stage is a foundation, a basis for further syntheses (or identifications), Lacan's theory presents us with a view of the human being in which an unconscious, alien identity is the basis of any further psychological development. Within such a framework, the Hegelian dream of conscious self-possession is radically impossible.

There is another possible point of comparison between Hegel and Lacan by looking at the function of aggressiveness Lacan hints at in his paper (Lacan 2006, 80 [99]). This aggressiveness could be related to the life-and-death struggle described in Hegel's dialectic of self-consciousness. Lacan makes this problem the object of a separate article, however, and I shall also devote a separate discussion to this theme.

LACAN'S THEORY OF AGGRESSIVENESS AND HEGEL'S PASSAGE ON THE "LAW OF THE HEART"

I wish to argue briefly that the aggressiveness present in the life-and-death struggle between the two consciousnesses, who will become the master and the slave, can illustrate only one of the forms of aggressiveness that Lacan's theory deals with. I believe that the passage on the "Law of the Heart" illustrates Lacan's main point of his theory of aggressiveness.

The main point of Lacan's theory of aggressiveness is that aggressiveness is a defensive strategy used when the loss of an ideal threatens the unity of the self. This is related to the theory of the mirror stage, in which an idealized image provides the subject with a unity that it does not have in fact but that it gives itself by means of an idealized project.

The aggressiveness involved in the master–slave dialectic is not defensive or repressive. On the contrary, the life-and-death struggle has a positive function. It is the only way by which the two consciousnesses can prove the truth of their feelings that as consciousnesses they are not tied to objectivity. Moreover, the life-and-death struggle in Hegel's dialectic is an attack on the other, which involves a risk of the self, rendering it a progressive and not a regressive move at this point of the *Phenomenology*. The attack on the other seems consonant with Lacan; however, a careful study of Hegel's text demonstrates that Hegel does not interpret the attack of a consciousness on another consciousness in the Lacanian sense. The purpose of the struggle is *not* to destroy the self in the other (one's ideal in the image of someone else) but to destroy the otherness in the other self. It is the otherness in the other self that is attacked in the master–slave dialectic and not the *self* in the other.[2]

The master–slave dialectic can, however, be a useful point of comparison with respect to a second, although less important, form of aggressiveness talked about by Lacan. In the first part of his essay, Lacan mentions the aggressiveness exercised by the person serving as model or image for the subject of the mirror stage. Lacan's strategy at this point of the essay seems to be to draw attention to the fact that the relation between the subject and her image has a link with aggressiveness from the beginning. According to that *quick* hint of Lacan's (Lacan 2006, 84–85 [103–5]), the subject has not tied herself down to an image purely spontaneously but because of the threat of the model itself. The idea that threat is essential if education is to be effective, or if a person is to be able to live up to the standards of an ideal, is an idea cherished by Hegel. Hegel writes in his *Philosophy of Right*,

> Similarly, the right of the parents over the wishes of their children is determined by the object in view—discipline and education. The punishment of children does not aim at justice as such; the aim is more subjective and moral in character, i.e., to deter them from exercising a freedom still in the toils of nature and to lift the universal into their consciousness and will. (Hegel 1967b, 117)

The necessary fear of a model is expressed as part of a systematic analysis of consciousness' experience of itself at the end of the passage on the master–slave dialectic, where Hegel writes, "Without the discipline of service and obedience, fear remains at the formal stage, and does not extend to the known real world of existence" (Hegel 1977, 119).

Thus, the fear of death is not productive of a further development of consciousness unless the *threat of the master* uses that fear to impose on the slave the discipline required to fulfill her commands. It is in trying to fulfill these commands that the slave deals with her own desires. She is forced to work and develop skills. And, about work, Hegel writes, "Work, on the other hand, is desire held in check, fleetingness staved off; in other words, work forms and shapes the thing" (Hegel 1977, 118). The slave can achieve such a constructive mastery of her own desires only by means of a *threat* by another. Furthermore, we know that this other (the master) functions as the "ideal ego" for the slave.[3] Lacan's reference to the "severe parent" or the "image of the Punisher" can, therefore, be taken to be more than a reference to a fact; it can be taken, by means of the Hegelian dialectic, to be a reference to a *necessity for consciousness*.[4]

The passage on the "Law of the Heart," which can clarify the other, more important aspect of Lacan's theory of aggressiveness, is part of the third great movement in the *Phenomenology*. The first movement describes the enrichment of consciousness when it relates to objects. Consciousness discovers that it cannot know the objects by sense impressions alone; it needs to use words (perception) and thoughts (scientific understanding). The second movement describes the advent of consciousness encountering another consciousness and thereby becoming self-consciousness. As we have seen, Hegel believes that the crucial concern of two consciousnesses meeting one another is not knowledge but recognition; it is possible to interpret the movement describing the advent of self-consciousness as the description of the different strategies that self-consciousness can adopt to gain recognition.

The third movement describes the experience of an enriched self-consciousness. It is a self-consciousness that has become certain of itself and is therefore not directly or immediately concerned with recognition. It is a self-consciousness that has discovered that it possesses reason. It is a self-consciousness that trusts that in and through reason it can *know that which is other than itself*, it can *know the world*.

At first, such a rational self-consciousness is puzzled by the objective world. It learns, however, that knowledge of the outside world is uninformative when it comes to the secret most dear to it—that is, itself. Rational self-consciousness therefore begins actively relating self-consciousness to the outside world. The first method it uses relates self-consciousness' desire (pleasure) to the outside world. That outside world can be either the laws of nature or the rules of social etiquette. Both appear to consciousness as an external imposition, but given that self-consciousness is rational, consciousness itself should have provided the norm of all rules, rather than having them imposed from without.

Out of this experience emerges the sentimentalism of the Romantic movement, which takes the principle of human reason as the norm for societal arrangements. The principle of reason is that, by thinking, I, as individual, have access to the universal rules by which nature and society ought to be structured. Applied to the social order, the principle of reason means that I as rational individual have access to these universal rules by means of my heart, which represents the heart of all humans. It is this move of *rational individual self-consciousness* that allows Hegel to explain by the same principle the emergence of natural science and the Romantic movement. Both are the result of the principle of subjectivity, which emerged, according to Hegel, as a central principle of modern times: consciousness takes itself to have the point of view from which to legislate the outside world. When the outside world is nature, the legislating takes the form of *description* by means of natural laws; when the outside world is the social order, the legislating takes the form of *prescription*.

Let us now look at the passage on the "Law of the Heart" and the function of aggressiveness in it. The experience that gives rise to the project of romantic sentimentalism is that the laws of nature or the rules of etiquette are a barrier to the enjoyment of self-consciousness. The project thus becomes opposition to these barriers on rational grounds or by means of a justification typical for modern times. *The barrier that I experience is assumed to be* a *barrier experienced by all.* I can thus project an alternative order that on the same principle *should be acceptable to all.* Thus, social reform can be experienced by the romantic person as a *reform for the "welfare of mankind"* (Hegel 1977, 222).

The problem with this project is that all reforms will involve the presentation of new rules that will appear as *new barriers*. Because of these new barriers, the romantic reformer must ultimately be angry unless she can experience them as *her* barriers and see that there are barriers that she finds rational. The angry reformer remains naive. If she takes a second approach to these barriers, she becomes a member of a social order (Hegel 1977, 224). She accepts that there must be rules in any social order and that such rules are sometimes a barrier to one's satisfaction. She is, however, at this point *capable only of accepting the rules that she herself is thinking*. Indeed, the purpose of the romantic reformer was not to put forth societal rules but to have societal rules that the heart of any human could identify with. This entire enterprise was built on the belief that it is possible to have *laws that are identical with the wishes of the heart*. And the romantic reformer takes the wishes of *her* heart to be normative for the wishes of *all* hearts.

The crucial turn in the dialectic of the law of the heart occurs when Hegel points out that other people find in the laws espoused by the romantic reformer not the law of *their* hearts but the law of *another* heart. Thus, remarks Hegel, the romantic reformer believes that something particular (the *law* of *her* heart) has universal validity, whereas others see the proposals of the romantic reformer for what they are: a *particular law imposed on them*. And just as the romantic reformer opposed societal law imposed on her, so the others oppose the proposal of the romantic reformer.

The romantic reformer thus faces two problems. First, she must be able to accept that there must be societal laws; however, even if she proposes laws, her heart does not feel comfortable with any law. Second, in attempting to reconcile herself with the *law* of *her* heart, she faces the problem that *others will reject her law for the same reasons that she started her romantic reforms*.

The fact that consciousness experiences societal laws as necessary but that this consciousness, as particular consciousness, finds societal laws in general worthy of rejection is, for Hegel, sufficient reason to conclude that we are faced here with a consciousness that is perverse. It is the craziness, the madness of consciousness. *How can consciousness deal with this, its own essential madness?* Hegel's answer is worth quoting:

> The heart-throb for the welfare of humanity therefore passes into the ravings of an insane self-conceit, into the fury of consciousness to preserve itself from destruction; and it does this by expelling from itself the perversion which it is itself, and by striving to look on it and express it as something else. It therefore speaks of the universal order as a perversion of the law of the heart and of its happiness, a perversion invented by fanatical priests, gluttonous despots, and their minions, who compensate themselves for their own degradation by degrading and oppressing others, a perversion which has led to the nameless misery of deluded humanity. (Hegel 1977, 226)

Consciousness is a perverted consciousness when it requires that societal rules be the direct expression of the wishes of the individual's heart. Hegel's dialectic shows that the perversion of such a consciousness is a *necessary* one. *Perverted consciousness defends itself against this experience of its own perversion by projecting it onto another.* It is in the other(s) that it attacks its own perversion.

At least three elements of Lacan's theory of aggressiveness remind us of Hegel's dialectic of the "Law of the Heart." First, just as Hegel presupposes that the romantic reformer is dominated by the will to reform social reality according to the wishes of her heart, so Lacan claims that the human being has a "mad passion . . . to stamp his image on reality" (Lacan 2006, 95 [116]).

In the rest of the text, Lacan goes so far as to say that the rational will, which *restricts* itself to rational transformation of the world, is related to that furious human passion to change the world to see the world give testimony to its own image. He calls that furious passion the "obscure foundation of the will's rational mediations" (Lacan 2006, 95 [116]).

Second, just as Hegel demonstrates that it is typical for the romantic reformer to situate herself in the societal reality in such a way that she and others are mortal enemies, so Lacan claims that a narcissistic identification with one's own image constitutes the human essentially as an aggressive competitor with other humans, particularly with brothers (Lacan 2006, 95 [117]). Lacan attaches great importance to this development of the human into aggressive competitor. He describes it in his theory as a *necessary moment.* He even gives it a status that rivals the importance of his theory of the mirror stage and Freud's Oedipus complex; he calls this moment the "intrusion complex." As early as his 1938 article on the family,[5] Lacan uses this element of his theory to elevate the fact of sibling rivalry from a *deplorable fact* into a *necessary moment* in the constitution of the self.

Third, just as Hegel describes the romantic reformer as attacking in the other her own perversion, so Lacan claims that the *aggressiveness* of the paranoiac has the dual purpose of projecting something unacceptable in her onto another and attacking it in that other. Indeed, he writes, "Thus, the two moments, when the subject negates himself and when he accuses the other, become indistinguishable; and we see here the paranoiac structure of the ego" (Lacan 2006, 93 [114]). To reinforce this view of the paranoiac, Lacan refers to Freud's study on Judge Schreber. In that study, Freud relates paranoia to homosexuality and claims that the paranoiac tries to *deny* the proposition "I (a man) *love him* (a man)" by denying either one of the elements of that sentence or the entire sentence. Furthermore, Freud points out that the paranoiac projects onto another her own denied action (Freud 1911, 63).

This similarity between Hegel and Lacan is not accidental. Lacan himself stresses the fact that his conception of paranoiac delusion is identical to the delusion of Hegel's misanthropic beautiful soul.[6] In that same passage, Lacan refers to Freud, too, thereby relating his own conclusion to crucial passages in two of his intellectual mentors.

> Thus the two moments, when the subject negates himself and when he accuses the other, become indistinguishable; and we see here the paranoiac structure of the ego that finds its analog in the fundamental negations highlighted by Freud in the three delusions: jealousy, erotomania, and interpretation. It is the very delusion of the misanthropic beautiful soul, casting out onto the world the disorder that constitutes his being. (Lacan 2006, 93 [114])

We should not, however, overlook the differences between Lacan and Hegel's views of aggressiveness. An obvious difference is that the two authors situate aggressiveness in different domains. Hegel locates the unavoidability of aggressiveness in the *social domain.*

Aggressiveness becomes unavoidable because the individual remains individualistic and requires that for any societal rule to be acceptable, it must conform to the wishes of her *own* heart.[7] Lacan, on the contrary, situates aggressiveness in the *spatial dimension* of a human being. For Lacan, my body as my subjective space is not available to me at the start. The act of appropriating my body, as my space, is done by means of a psychological act of identifying with an idealized image. Given that the subject is not this idealized image, Lacan claims that the bodily unity can be achieved only by means of imposing on others and the world that idealized self-image. This is the hidden aggressiveness mentioned by Lacan, which becomes open aggressiveness when that idealized image is threatened.

A second difference between Hegel and Lacan's views on aggressiveness is the way in which both see the solution to this aggressiveness. For Hegel, the solution comes when the individual is able to give up the individualistic point of view and identify with the point of view of the spirit (i.e., truth having a societal and objective point of view). Hegel defines this point of view as follows:

> [Spirit] is the *self* of actual consciousness to which it stands opposed, or rather which it opposes to itself as an objective, actual *world*, but a world which has completely lost the meaning for the self of something alien to it, just as the self has completely lost the meaning of a being-for-self separated from the world, whether dependent on it or not. (Hegel 1977, 263–64)

For Lacan, the solution lies in the Oedipus complex: "Oedipal identification is thus the identification by which the subject transcends the aggressiveness constitutive of the first subjective individuation" (Lacan 2006, 95 [117]). In the Oedipus complex, the subject creates an ego ideal on the basis of the image of the father. About the ego ideal, Lacan writes, "But what interests me here is what I shall refer to as the 'pacifying' function of the ego-ideal, the connection between its libidinal normativeness and a cultural normativeness, bound up since the dawn of history with the imago of the father" (Lacan 2006, 95 [117]).

Both differences indicate that Lacan takes a *more particularized* point of view than Hegel. For Hegel, the aggressiveness of the romantic reformer is connected with a lack of rationality in that consciousness. This form of aggressiveness is then also irrational. Once rationality has been broadened and reached the point of view of Spirit, then aggressiveness is rational in the specific sense that it is connected with *rational goals*. Thus, for Hegel the aggressiveness demanded by the state in the case of war is a rational form of aggressiveness because it subordinates individualistic and particularistic interests to the interest of the state, interpreted by Hegel as the universal. For Lacan, however, the problem of aggressiveness is connected with the very way in which the human must appropriate the spatiality of her being.

For Lacan, aggressiveness is therefore coextensive with the human appropriation of the self as a unified body.[8] According to Lacan's theory, aggressiveness must therefore be an omnipresent phenomenon for the individual as embodied subject. We find a confirmation of that in his reference to the aggressiveness present in all philanthropic activity (Lacan 2006, 80–81 [100], 85 [104–5]).

CONCLUSION

I have argued that the logical necessity that Lacan presents as part of his theory of the mirror stage and his theory of aggressiveness is dependent upon two separate moves in Hegel's *Phenomenology*. The theory of the mirror stage includes the thesis that something other than the self is necessary for the constitution of the self. The beginning pages of "Lordship and Bondage" establish that the transition from consciousness to self-consciousness requires an *intermediate step* in which a first consciousness discovers *itself* in *another self-consciousness*.

Lacan's theory of aggression includes the thesis that aggressiveness is an attack upon the self in another. Hegel's passages in the "Law of the Heart" present us with a consciousness (the romantic reformer) that, on the one hand, incorporates the modern principle that the individual has in reason *the* correct principle to discover the rules of reality and, on the other hand, emotionally identifies the wishes of its own heart with those of the hearts of others. This consciousness experiences itself as perverse because in executing its project, it necessarily does the opposite of what it intends. It can deal with this perversion because it identifies its own heart with the hearts of others. This identity is thus the origin of and the solution to its perversion. Indeed, it can condemn and attempt to destroy in the other what went wrong in its own heart. An attack upon the self in the other is therefore a possibility and a necessity, because consciousness is engaged with others in the world, while initially lacking the distinction between its own heart and the heart of others.

In this chapter, I also draw attention to some radical differences between Lacan's theories and the passages in Hegel. In the mirror stage, we are dealing not with another self, but with the Gestalt of another as constitutive of the self. In Lacan's theory of aggressiveness, we are not in the presence of a consciousness that lacks a distinction. We are in the presence of an embodied consciousness that can maintain its unity (including its bodily unity) only by means of an ideal, which it is not. It therefore needs to impose this ideal on others. Hence, in both cases, Lacan analyzes the bodily self rather than consciousness.

What, then, is the subject of Lacan? Even though he uses Hegelian moves in the explanation of his view of the subject, Lacan's subject is not a Hegelian consciousness. The importance given to the bodily element will allow Lacan to introduce in his concept of a subject the idea of radical finitude. He even has at his disposal Heidegger's philosophy to do so. Given the openness of Heidegger's philosophy to the crucial function of language, we now see how linguistics can be incorporated in Lacan's philosophical anthropology. It is this aspect of Lacan's theory of the subject that is masterfully explained by Richardson (1983a) in "Lacan and the Subject of Psychoanalysis"; however, by stressing almost exclusively the Heideggerian influence in Lacan, Richardson fails to present Lacan's subject as an emotional force that will, in its history, encounter radical frustration (weaning, intrusion, castration). This history has logical necessity, as De Waelhens's readings of Lacan have demonstrated (De Waelhens 1978, chapter 2, sects. III, IV). De Waelhens's reading is dependent on the early Lacan found in his article on the family. It is a reading of Lacan that is compatible with Lacan's own claim of a return to Freud, since it is in Freud that we find the idea of the subject as libido, with a normative development from autoeroticism through narcissism to heterosexuality. Too much stress on the Heideggerian influence in Lacan makes us lose sight of the developmental norms through which the Lacanian subject unfolds.

Finally, I should remark that the "Other" in Lacan is indeed different from Freud's "other scene," as Antoine Vergote so clearly demonstrates in "From Freud's 'Other Scene' to Lacan's 'Other'" (Vergote 1983). A crucial difference is the fact that Lacan's "Other" has a claim to truth that is more radical than Freud's "other scene." Lacan writes that the "Other" is the "locus from which the question of his existence may arise for him" (Lacan 2006, 459 [549]). It would be useful to pursue the Hegelian influence in Lacan's treatment of the concept of the "Other," given that Hegel himself locates the point of view of the truth in the subject's ability to see himself as a relation with the Other (the societal norms and truths) of the self (Hegel 1977).

NOTES

1. See also the introduction of this book, in the section entitled "Lacan's Theory of the Mirror Stage."

2. Hegel 1977, 114: "Its essential being is present to it in the form of an 'other,' it is outside of itself and must rid itself of its self-externality." And Hegel 1977, 111: "It must supersede this otherness of itself. . . . First, it must proceed to supersede the *other* independent being in order thereby to become certain of *itself* as the essential being."

3. "Servitude has the lord for its essential reality" (Hegel 1977, 117). "In the lord, the being-for-self is an 'other' for the bondsman, or is only *for* him [i.e., is not his own]" (Hegel 1977, 118).

4. Muller and Richardson see in this transition a big problem for Lacan (Muller and Richardson 1982, 46–47). But if one also situates Lacan's thought within Hegel's philosophy, the transition can be said to be there from the start, without having to be justified.

5. Lacan 1938, 840.8–11. For a brief English version of the main ideas of Lacan's "Intrusion complex," see De Waelhens 1978, 76–79, "The Sibling or the Incarnated Mirror-Image."

6. Lacan 2006, 345 [415], 140 [171–72]. "Misanthropic beautiful soul" is a metaphoric reference for consciousness as Hegel describes it in the "Law of the Heart." It should not be confused with the passage on the "Beautiful Soul" (Hegel 1977, 221–28, 383–409, respectively).

7. The individualistic point of view is overcome as soon as consciousness reaches the level of Spirit (Hegel 1977, 263). The passage of the "Law of the Heart" is one of the last passages before the one on Spirit.

8. Lacan 2006, 100 [123]: "The extent to which the fear of death . . . is psychologically subordinate to the narcissistic fear of harm to one's own body."

Chapter Eight

Hegel and Lacan on Paranoia and the Question of How to Avoid the Dangers Inherent in Ideas of Social Reform

In this chapter, I will analyze and compare a passage in Hegel's *Phenomenology* called "The Law of the Heart and the Frenzy of Self-Conceit" (Hegel 1977, 221–28) with Lacan's interpretation of paranoia as it appears in his doctoral dissertation (Lacan 1975).[1] My purpose is to better understand the origin and logic of paranoia.

HEGEL AND LACAN ON PARANOIA

Hegel's analysis concerns the heart's attitude toward the law and is aptly labeled by Howard Kainz as the analysis of the "Moral Sentimentalist" (Kainz 2008, 23–24).[2] This passage in Hegel's *Phenomenology* has three parts, not all of which are distinguished or even noticed by its many commentators.[3]

The first section sketches the hope that the human heart and the law can be reconciled. The second describes the disappointment about the failure of that reconciliation. The last section describes the desperate attempt to overcome that disappointment. Common-sense labels—some of which are used by Hegel himself—for these three moments in Hegel's analysis might be enlightening. The first moment, the hope, could be called the conviction of the Romantic reformer or the moral sentimentalist. The second moment, the disappointment of the heart in its inability to reconcile itself with the law, can be called craziness.[4] The third moment, the desperate attempt to overcome the heart's disappointment with the law, can be called paranoia.[5] Hegel's thesis, in my reconstruction, is that a sentimental attitude toward the problem that human law presents, leads, by way of disappointment, necessarily to paranoiac aggression.[6]

J. B. Baillie, the translator of the *Phenomenology*, claims that this entire passage is concerned with moral sentimentalism. He calls that attitude a mood of all times that appeared in Hegel's time as the Romantic School. The most important representative of this school was Rousseau, and the perfect literary example of it is Goethe's *Werther* (Hegel 1967a, 390). Jean Hyppolite, an important French commentator on Hegel, cites Schiller's *The Robbers* as a literary work of Hegel's time containing a literary representation of the ironic logic to which a Romantic reformer can be pushed. According to Hyppolite, Hegel did nothing more than articulate philosophically what Schiller represented artistically (Hyppolite 1946, 275, 277, 278).

Lacan's novel theory of paranoia can be reconstructed by reversing the logic of Hegel's passage the "Law of the Heart." Whereas Hegel starts with a utopian project, which causes a failure leading, in turn, to paranoiac aggression, Lacan starts with paranoiac aggression and goes back to a failure grounded in the need for a utopia. More concretely, Lacan explains the aggressive act of a paranoid person as the reaction to a previous failure. The paranoiac failed in the attempt to deal with unacceptable aggression by means of some project that would serve a utopian function. Without transition, Lacan puts forward the thesis that for these people, the father abused the law he presented to his children.

Thus, while Hegel starts with a naive conception of the law and ends with a paranoiac strategy, Lacan begins with a paranoiac patient and explains her behavior by the defective representation of the law by the father. For both Hegel and Lacan, the transition between the defective attitude toward the law and the paranoiac strategy is not direct. For both there is an in-between period: the disappointment. For Hegel, the disappointment is necessary. For Lacan, the disappointment by the paranoid personality, which leads to acting out, is not necessary. To avoid the disappointment and the acting out, it is necessary for society to provide a local community in which the utopian dreams of the paranoid personality are given a symbolic structure, for example, that the utopians' attempts are successfully implemented in the social reality. People are effectively helped and the moral dedication of the workers in the local community is effectively recognized and applauded. Thus, the local community needs to be a group that is both nice to work with and one that is morally effective in their attempts to better the lives of others.

Hegel's presentation can be reconstructed in compelling logical steps. His text also precedes Lacan's texts. Furthermore, there is direct dependence of Lacan upon Hegel. I will therefore present Hegel's analysis first.

In my applications, I question whether the psychic effort of the Romantic reformer does not also have a positive function. Indeed, the Romantic reformer creates certain psychic conditions that allow him or her to articulate and imagine a future in which aggression is used to transform society into a better place. Aggression is socialized. It is true that the transformation of the Romantic reformer into a paranoiac person increases the possibility of homicides; however, what happens if young people are not socially conditioned to create a future for themselves via idealist or utopian projects? We will consider the possibility that difficulties surrounding the creation of idealist projects might make aggression into a self-destructive force, leading to an increase in the number of suicides. We will also consider the cases of both egalitarian Sweden and China, with its one-child policy, thus noting that there are two forms of failure with regards to civilizing aggression: homicide and suicide. Lacan presented a suggestion to diminish homicides by paranoiac persons. We will infer that jealousy and fighting between siblings or young competitors (within reasonable norms) is one way to diminish suicide.

HEGEL'S ANALYSIS OF THE LAW

The Romantic Reformer's Presuppositions

For Hegel, the concept of law is important in understanding human affairs. The concept of law is even more important for understanding modern times because of the modern enthusiasm for science. Individuals are able to find themselves mysteriously linked to other individuals by the belief in a law of nature that is the same for everyone and that each individual can separately discover in its universal validity for all human beings. The human faculty responsible for individuals being able to discover what is universally valid is reason. The Romantic movement is a cultural movement of modern times. Hegel explains the Romantic attitude toward the social law with the same principles by which he understands the self-understanding of modern natural science. This is clear from the structure of the *Phenomenology*. Hegel places his analysis of the Romantic attitude just after his analysis of modern natural sciences, and both appear in the same chapter under the title "Reason."

The constitutive principle of reason is that I, as an individual, can think, and if by my thought I understand the essence of an object, then I can claim that I have understood all such instances and that my understanding is valid, not for me alone but for everyone else. That is the power of reason.[7]

Let us apply this insight to the case of the natural sciences. There it is undoubtedly true that if one individual understands that some water consists essentially and necessarily of H_2O, then that individual has the right to claim that all water must consist of H_2O. She furthermore has the right to claim that her personal insight is valid for all human beings.

It is Hegel's shrewd insight that some modern social movements can be explained by a similar claim about social life. Social life is regulated by rules and regulations. The claim of reason is that rules and regulations—in short, the law—need to conform to the exercise of reason in each individual. This claim implies two requirements. First, it requires that, insofar as they are reasonable, each individual is able to discover whether a rule, a regulation, or the law is to be accepted or rejected. "It knows that it has the universal of law immediately within itself, and because the law is immediately present in the being-for-self of consciousness, it is called the law of the heart" (Hegel 1977, 221). Second, it requires that what one individual considers desirable will also be experienced as desirable by all others. This implies the rejection of significant differences between reasonable individuals. Hegel will use this second implication to explain several turns in the Romantic reformer's fortunes.

Hegel has already used this second implication to explain the source of energy of the Romantic reformer. But before we can use the concept of law as understood in the natural sciences to explain modern social movements, we need to understand the difference between the function of law and reason in the natural sciences and social movements. In the natural sciences, human beings create a scientific law after first making observations. The newly created law respects the observations made. The Romantic attitude is not so much an attitude of observing the external world as it is an attitude that intends to use the external world for one's own self-realization (see Hegel 1977, 217–19, for Hegel's analysis of the origin of that aspect of the Romantic attitude). That change in attitude results in the law being experienced, in the first place, as opposing the personal wishes of the Romantic reformer (Hegel 1977, 221). The Romantic thus experiences the social reality as an alien, oppressive law. Pain is therefore the social reformer's primary experience of the law. This pain results from the movement of reason away from understanding toward self-realization. While the certainty of the existence of a natural law is a comfort to the natural scientist, the existence of social laws is, at first, experienced as a hindrance to a self-realizing consciousness. The social order—its rules, regulations, and laws—are experienced as restrictive (I cannot drive on the left side of the street. I cannot park where I want. I may not cross streets when the red light is on). Hegel describes the painful experience of the self-realizing consciousness as follows:

> This heart is confronted by a real world. . . . This reality is, therefore, on the one hand a law by which the particular individuality is oppressed, a violent ordering of the world which contradicts the law of the heart, and, on the other hand, a humanity suffering under that ordering, a humanity that does not follow the law of the heart but is subjected to an alien necessity. (Hegel 1977, 221)

This self-realizing consciousness, faced with such a hostile social world, could feel crushed; however, the self-realizing consciousness, as social reformer, gathers an enormous amount of energy from its identification with the position of reason. It benefits from the assumed likeness of all individuals in a similar position. If the social reality causes me pain, needless pain, then it is certainly causing pain to all individuals. The social reformer's own suffering under the law is immediately experienced as cosuffering, with a "humanity suffering under that ordering, a humanity which does not follow the law of the heart, but is subjected to an alien necessity" (Hegel 1977, 221).

When the Romantic reformer encounters a rule or a law that does not fit his own heart, he makes a project of transforming that reality, that law, because he is a self-realizing consciousness. In that project, he can also rely on a belief that is typical for reason: The transformation of the law according to the wishes of his heart will be an improvement on the law and be applauded by the hearts of all others [narcissistic motive]; therefore, his charge against the existing law and his attempt to change it is seen as a project that will improve the world for everyone. Consequently, when the Romantic reformer attempts to change the law into what her heart wishes it to be, she possesses the certainty that she will do a favor for her fellow human beings [moral motive].

Let us pay close attention to the possible sources of energy of the Romantic reformer. We can distinguish between a personal and a social motive. The personal motive emanates from the belief that the law is only justified if it is in agreement with the reformer's own wishes or, in Hegel's terminology, if the law is identical to the reformer's own heart. As Hegel says, "The law is a law of the *heart*" (Hegel 1977, 222) [justified selfishness or the right to pleasure motive]. Because of such a belief, the Romantic reformer must feel justified in rejecting any restriction, any pain experienced because of the law. The law simply has no right to cause pain. The Romantic reformer hereby possesses the justification to transform any pain imposed by the law into aggression against that law [sublimation of aggression]. As Hegel writes, "This individuality therefore directs its energies to getting rid of this necessity which contradicts the law of the heart, and also the suffering caused by it" (Hegel 1977, 222). This justification for using aggression to diminish pain rests on the difference between the use of reason in the natural science and in self-realization.

How a particular individual, for example, Rousseau, comes to feel that way about the law is a purely psychological problem not addressed by Hegel. How such an individual becomes the voice of his age, rather than a shunted outcast, is a question of cultural sociology or cultural philosophy for which there are implicit answers in Hegel but no explicit ones.

The social motive for the Romantic reformer is that she has the absolute psychological certainty that others feel the same about the law. Let us analyze the two points about which the Romantic reformer has absolute certainty. Here the identity between reason in natural sciences and reason in societal experience is fruitful. The first point is that I am equal to other human beings in having the absolute right to demand that the law cause no pain or that the law be identical to my wishes, to my heart, "its pleasure is at the same time the universal pleasure of all hearts" (Hegel 1977, 222). This certainty guarantees that the social reformer will not be alone in wanting to transform his pain into justified aggression [group support motive].

The second point is that the social reformer thinks that all others, having the same wishes she has, or metaphorically having hearts that are identical to her own, must object to the pain caused by the law in the social order for the same reason. Thus, the social reformer who takes the responsibility of changing the existing law that causes her and all others pain must feel that she takes charge of what she, but also the others, want [leadership motive]. She must therefore feel that she performs a desirable task for all others [altruistic motive]. The Romantic reformer must therefore see herself as a Robin Hood for all humanity "in promoting the welfare of mankind" (Hegel 1977, 222) [gratitude motive]. She thus sees before her a guaranteed narcissistic recognition [their own excellence]; "it is the earnestness of a high purpose which seeks its pleasure in displaying the excellence of its true nature" (Hegel 1977, 222). The romantic reformer is certain that her goodness, toward the whole of mankind, will inevitably be recognized by everyone.

The energy of the Romantic reformer can, thus, be deduced from her double certainty. She is certain that the law should be there for her pleasure, and she is also certain that her pleasure is equally the pleasure of others; "What it realizes is itself the law, and its pleasure is at the same time the universal pleasure of all hearts" (Hegel 1977, 222). This double certainty of the Romantic reformer is similar to the double claim of reason in the natural sciences: I personally can understand the natural laws, and my personal understanding is identical with and thus valid for the understanding of all others.

Transformation of the Law and Its Meaning: Disappointment in the Extreme

The Romantic Reformer's Experience of Making the Law Conform to Its Own Heart

The project of the Romantic reformer is to change the law, which is indifferent or even opposed to the heart of individuals into a law that conforms to her individual heart (and it is presumed that its heart is like the hearts of all individuals). The Romantic reformer must therefore propose a new ordinance, a new law that is to replace the old law. When the new proposal is enacted, it becomes law. But a characteristic of enacted law is that it is impersonal. An essential characteristic of the heart is that it insists on being treated for its own sake and in terms of its individuality. An objective way in which this difference manifests itself is that the law tends to be unchangeable, whereas the heart is alive and constantly changes its desires.

So, the successful Romantic reformer discovers that her intended project becomes something other than what she intended. She discovers that her very project, in succeeding, fails: "The law of the heart, through its very realization, ceases to be a law of the heart" (Hegel 1977, 223).[8] Nevertheless, something has been achieved. The new law is not equal to the old law. It cannot be treated as an alien law, which has to be changed. The new law is the product of the Romantic reformer and is thus her law. The romantic reformer has thus irrevocably gotten involved in the law; "what he brings about is merely the entanglement of himself in the actual ordinance, an entanglement in it, moreover, not as a superior power which is only alien to him, but one which is hostile" (Hegel 1977, 223). The Romantic reformer, because of her successful opposition to the old law, discovers that she is the originator of a new product (the new law), in which she cannot recognize herself. Worse, the Romantic reformer discovers that she is the originator of a product that has two characteristics. On the one hand, the new law is an essential aspiration of her consciousness. On the other hand, it is an unacceptable product. The Romantic reformer now experiences opposition not to an alien law, but to a law she created. The Romantic reformer thus finds herself opposed to her own essential identity as reformer and thus maker of law. In this way, the Romantic reformer becomes divided against herself.

The sole reason for this turn of events is the reformer's misunderstanding of the law. The Romantic reformer understands the legitimate function of the law to be nothing but the expression of the individual heart. It is, however, the function of the law to be universal and thus impersonal. The law allows for this misunderstanding because the law, in its universality, elevates some particular determination to law. The illusion of the Romantic reformer consists of the belief that the particular content is all there is in the law. The Romantic reformer does not understand that the particular content of the law is represented as universal and thus impersonal.

The Romantic Reformer's Experience of Her Expected Role as the Savior of Mankind

It is the reformer's hope that replacing the content of the law with a new content, borrowed from the personal wishes of the Romantic reformer herself, will lead to her reconciliation with the new law and also the reconciliation of all human beings with that same law. Thus, the Romantic reformer sees herself as an instrument of reconciliation for the law and all people.

The Romantic reformer's method does not address the form of law but only the content of the law. That oversight leads to her first negative experience. With reference to the content of the law, the Romantic reformer is certain that replacing the existing content with different and better content will solve the alienating function of the law. She further believes that all she needs to do is replace the current content of the law with content in line with her own heart's wishes. She believes this because she is subjectively convinced that there is no difference between her heart and the hearts of all other people; however, in making her preferences the law of the land, the Romantic reformer experiences opposition and dissatisfaction with this new law by many others. She thus discovers that she was mistaken in the belief that her wishes were universal. By making her personal preferences law, the Romantic reformer does not liberate other people. Rather, she imposes her wishes on them. The others now discover three reasons for opposing the Romantic reformer.

First, they might dislike the new law more than the old law and may therefore consider the new law worse than the old regime. Second, the others might accept the idea that the new law is an improvement. But if the others have the same conviction as the Romantic reformer, they cannot be satisfied with improvement. They must demand that the content of the law be identical with the wishes of their heart. The Romantic reformer chose the content of the new law based on her own preferences; others might have different preferences and may therefore want to see a slightly different content become law. Others might oppose the Romantic reformer because they see that she imposes her own preference on them: "Others do not find in this content the fulfillment of the law of their hearts, but rather that of someone else; and, precisely in accordance with the universal law that each shall find in what is law his own heart, they turn against the reality he set up, just as he turned against theirs" (Hegel 1977, 224).

Third, there might be a subtler reason for others' disappointment in the legal reform of the Romantic reformer. Even if others like the content of the new law as presented by the Romantic reformer, these others will experience the law-like form of the new law and therefore not experience any reconciliation with the new law. The new law will remain a law; the promise of reconciliation was always an impossible promise that necessarily disappoints.

I take Hegel to concentrate on the second reason for others to oppose the successful Romantic reformer. The Romantic reformer incorporates her preferences into the new law and naively expects that everyone else will feel reconciled with the new law, as she falsely believes that her heart is the norm for all hearts. "The deed is supposed to have immediately the status of a universal; that is to say, it is in truth something particular, and has merely the form of universality; the particular content of the heart as such is supposed to have the status of a universal" (Hegel 1977, 224).

The Romantic reformer actually believed that in imposing her preferences on others, she would be loved by them for bringing about the reconciliation with the law. Instead, the others are fully justified in opposing the Romantic reformer because she uses the force of the law to impose her preferences on them.

Two things now happen to the Romantic reformer. First, instead of a cold law that opposes her heart's desires, she now has to deal with warm bodies that oppose her reform movement. "Thus, just as the individual at first finds only the rigid law, now he finds the hearts of men themselves, opposed to his excellent intentions and detestable" (Hegel 1977, 224). Second, instead of being a messiah, she finds herself recast as an enemy of the people. "He finds [. . .] the hearts of men themselves opposed to his excellent intentions detestable" (Hegel 1977, 224). These two experiences alienate the Romantic reformer from other human beings. She is alienated from other human beings in as much as they are themselves entangled in the law.

Total Experience of the Romantic Reformer

The Romantic reformer becomes entangled in a contradictory experience of the law and is rejected by her cocitizens. This latter experience will force the Romantic reformer to become a lonely, isolated figure. Hegel seems to consider this experience to be a result and thus concentrates his analysis upon the contradictory experience of the law.

For Hegel, the law transcends the individual and thus demands from the individual a commitment, a surrender. The law as universal is an objective reality that is able to give existence to individual life. The Romantic reformer does not understand and is unable to accept the transcendence of the law. This deficiency in the Romantic reformer's understanding is responsible for her contradictory experience of the law and thus of herself.

On the one hand, the Romantic reformer feels and understands that the law is so important that she can make the enactment of a proper law the essence of her existence. On the other hand, the Romantic reformer does not understand the transcendence of the law and furthermore cannot tolerate the distance between the transcendent law and her heart. The Romantic reformer must therefore experience any law, even the law she enacted, as contrary to her deepest aspirations. The Romantic reformer is thus a consciousness that experiences the law as both its own essence and the denial of its essence.

The Romantic reformer has these two experiences in two distinct time periods. At first, time separates these two distinct experiences; however, consciousness is time consciousness. Time is therefore not capable of permanently separating the two contradictory experiences of the law.

When the Romantic reformer realizes that it aims at the law as its essence, while it considers any law necessarily as a denial of its essence, then the

Romantic reformer has the experience of its own essential contradiction. Hegel calls the experience of this essential contradiction alternatively perversion or craziness of this form of consciousness.

The Romantic Reformer's Attempt to Deal with Her Own Experienced Craziness

What is left for the Romantic reformer who experiences her own craziness? Such a consciousness needs to avoid its own self-destruction; however, as it is, in fact, crazy, it can succeed only by some process of denial. It must read its own craziness as something other than what it is.

The Romantic reformer is a consciousness that structurally sees no difference between itself and others. It is therefore natural that it discovers and projects its own perversion and craziness onto others.[9] This strategy allows the disappointed Romantic reformer to make sense of its secondary disappointment: the opposition by others to its social reform movement. It also allows her to express her opinion about the law. The disappointed social reformer now becomes a person who accuses her opponents of being perverts who use a perverted law for their own interests. In turn, this perverted law deprives millions of the happiness that a perfect law would be able to bring to the masses, who now suffer in misery.

The Romantic reformer hereby preserves in her own eyes her essential goodness and her narcissistic goal of being a savior to the suffering masses. Her goodness and the happiness of the masses still rest on her faulty understanding of the function of the law: Public law should be the expression of the wishes of individuals. Only now does the Romantic reformer need to replace her noble project of legal reform with paranoiac accusations against her opponents.

LACAN'S THEORY OF PARANOIA

Lacan was a psychiatrist. Let us therefore start with a definition of the paranoid position in a medical dictionary: "A mental disorder characterized by systematized delusions and the projection of personal conflicts, which are ascribed to the supposed hostility of others, sometimes progressing to disturbances of consciousness and aggressive acts believed to be performed in self-defense or as a mission."[10] This definition incorporates one step from Hegel's passage on the "Law of the Heart": The paranoiac, like the Romantic reformer at the end of the dialectic, accuses others of her own failure. Let us see how Lacan's analysis of the paranoiac introduces several additional steps, which we can find in Hegel's analysis of the "Law of the Heart," for example, the idea of a necessary disappointment resulting from a mistaken subjective belief in an identity with others.

Lacan's doctoral thesis includes a study of a paranoiac, Aimée, who Lacan observed for a year and a half (Lacan 1975, 151, 200–205). Aimée made a failed attack on a famous actress, Mrs. Z., and was subsequently jailed for that attack (Lacan 1975, 153–54). Aimée admired Mrs. Z. She also admired Sarah Bernhardt and Mrs. C, a writer (Lacan, 156, 164, 263). They were, in her opinion, successful women in a world dominated by males. For her they represented ideals that she tried to imitate. Aimée actually wrote two novels (Lacan, 177).[11]

Five months before the attack, for which she was subsequently jailed, a publisher rejected one of her manuscripts. Immediately thereafter, she had attacked an executive of the publishing company that issued the rejection (Lacan 1975, 156). She also filed a complaint with the police against that executive. Furthermore, she attributed to another author, P. B., powerful bad intentions. In his novels, she recognizes attacks and allusions to her (Lacan 1975).

Lacan also stresses the idealist reform projects of his patient. According to Aimée, her project of becoming a writer was motivated by pure dedication, pure altruistic motives, to make the world better (Lacan, 66)—as opposed to others, who made the world worse.[12] Lacan states that Aimée was animated by an "altruistic idealism" (Lacan 1975, 166). She wanted to create a world where the good reigned, that is, where there would be a "brotherhood between people and races" (Lacan 1975, 166). "It would be a place where children and women would reign. They would be dressed in white. It would mean the disappearance of wickedness on earth. There would not be war anymore. All people would be united. It would be beautiful" (Lacan 1975, 166). In her own words, Aimée states,

> I was devoted to an *ideal* [our italics], a sort of mission, the love for the human race to which I subordinated everything. I followed it with ever-increasing perseverance. I went so far as to detach myself from earthly things, and I turned all my suffering to the wrong that desolates the earth. (Lacan 1975, 177 [trans. Benvenuto and Kennedy 1986, 40–41])

In two steps, Lacan brings us to the point where Hegel started his analysis of the romantic reformer. Lacan will show us how the problem of Aimée consists in her inability to separate herself from her other-I, her alter-ego: her sister.

Lacan's first step is making a structural connection between the function of the ideals that those successful women (authors, actresses) played and the role Aimée's sister played for her (Lacan 1975, 253).[13] More precisely, Lacan argues that the sister became for Aimée a kind of prototype. Even though Aimée experienced many humiliating insults from her sister, that sister remained for Aimée an idealized model. This is shown by a number of facts.

First, there is the envy or the jealousy Aimée showed for both her sister and those successful women (Lacan 1975, 253). Second, there is the fact that Aimée tolerated having her sister, whose husband had died (Benvenuto and Kennedy 1986, 37), move in with her family eight months after Aimée's marriage. Her sister "took over the household duties, then took over Aimée's husband and tried to rear their child" (Benvenuto and Kennedy 1986, 37). Third, Aimée, talking to Lacan in the asylum, showed special interest in two people: her son and her sister.

Lacan refers to the fact that her sister moved in with her family and points out that Aimée did not resist this massive psychological intrusion. With reference to Lacan's ideas about family complexes, Aimée failed to deal with the intrusion complex—the function of the sibling (Lacan 2001, 36–45).

Lacan's second step consists of interpreting the unusual passivity of Aimée toward her sister. Aimée, according to Lacan, was not up to her own ideal. She did not resist her sister because she experienced her as the embodiment of her own ideals that she was not able to live up to.[14] Furthermore, in the interviews with Lacan, Aimée gave no indication that she was angry with her sister.

Lacan's theoretical move consists of showing how an exaggerated imaginary identification with the alter ego, the other who is the same, the sibling, inevitably leads to paranoia. Among siblings, one observes normally two moments: They imitate and they compete (Lacan 2001, 40–43). The moment of imitation indicates that the other sibling represents an ideal worth borrowing from. The first sibling is the ideal for the second. The competition, the rivalry between siblings, represents a totally different moment. It is a moment of separation from the other, who represents one's ideal, and also an awareness that such an idealizing imitation can be alienating (Lacan 2001, 43). Entering competition with another sibling means that the second sibling separates herself from the one in whom she located her ideal. She also affirms that her exterior image is not her whole self; however, doing so means that this sibling might discover that she is naked, that she is robbed of her ideal, which is located in the other sibling. It requires the competing sibling to face the uncertainty of not feeling who she is. She is then invited to start the process of individuation. Lack of competition with a sibling must therefore be interpreted as failure of individuation.

The sibling who failed to compete with the other siblings must experience competition as dangerous because it exposes her as naked, as worthless. As aggression is a crucial component of competition, that aggression becomes a danger. The noncompeting sibling has access to a temporary solution, but she also has a permanent problem. The temporary solution for the noncompeting sibling is to create a dual union with the sibling who represents her ideal—the ideal that she is unable to assume for herself. Thus, the first sibling becomes that which the second sibling lacks. To the second sibling, the first sibling is "more me than I am myself."

That line of thinking can explain the fact that Aimée allowed her sister to take over in her own family when she moved to Paris after the birth of her second child (Benvenuto and Kennedy 1986). In Aimée's mind, the sister must have been the perfect reassurance, since she represents the ideal that Aimée herself has not assumed. Aimée is not strong enough to do what she wishes to do. At the same time, she has the certainty that someone else, her sister, is able and worthy of doing what she cannot.

Even the temporary solution achieved by the dual union leaves one problem: The noncompeting sibling must fear her own aggression, because it separates and thus initiates individuation. Aggression must be repressed and thus goes underground.

The establishment of a dual union with a sibling and the repression of aggression to avoid the problem of individuation are neither permanent nor stable solutions. Aggression needs to find an object. Such an object cannot be an immediate love object (Benvenuto and Kennedy 1986, 41) because that would again pose the unsolvable problem of aggressive competition. Instead, the paranoiac starts a process of rationalizing by creating an illusionary utopian world without competition. The paranoiac envisions her happiness in such a world. In the meantime, the paranoiac will search for ideal models that are somewhat out of reach (actresses, authors). These she can either love or hate. She can try to imitate or hatefully accuse these models, or she may alternate between the two attitudes.

Lacan now speculates that if a paranoiac is integrated into a utopian society where there is mutual support and active improvement of the world, she sometimes can survive for the rest of her life, with a paranoid style. If the paranoiac does not have the benefit of a utopian, noncompetitive society, she will be confronted with her lack of individuation. Her lack of individuation consists of the fact that she endows others with her ideal. The others are, therefore, in her eyes entitled to invade her. She gives others unconscious permission to crush her. The others have that role because they possess the ideal that she herself lacks. This logic allows us to understand Aimée's hate–love relation toward her idols. As those idols represent her ideal, she will try to imitate them. She even writes two novels. When her manuscript is rejected, she is again confronted with the affirmation that she is not measuring up to the ideal that the others represent. She then attacks, first, the executive of the publishing house that rejected her manuscript and, later, one of the people she idealized (the actress, Mrs. Z.) (Lacan 1975, 153–54, 156).

Lacan's interpretation of the paranoiac does not relate paranoia to homosexuality. It is thus a different theory than Freud's (Lacan 1975, 261ff.). As proof for his theory, Lacan cites the clinical fact that a paranoiac tolerates rather well a homosexualized nearness of the same as other. Indeed, Aimée tolerates well the nearness of her sister. The presence of such another as same has even a salutary effect (Lacan 1975, 177). There is, of course, a generally recognized homosexual component in the paranoiac, which Lacan points to as being a consequence, not a cause, of the entire affair. The paranoiac experiences the principle of sexual difference as creating disorder in human relations; therefore, the paranoiac retreats to an asexual ego image. Rather than being an attempt to actually have homosexual relations with another, it's a denial of sexual difference.

Lacan has some comments about the role of the father, which are not fully related to his structural interpretation of the paranoiac. Lacan observes that the father is not absent in the psychic life of the paranoiac. Rather, the father is massively present. But in his massive presence, he is radically ambivalent. On the one hand, he is a helpful positive presence. On the other hand, he is a threatening destructive presence. The father is a positive presence in the psychic structure of the paranoiac—which is a structure that is pretty chaotic—as he is the only figure that is stable. He is also idealized as omnipotent. All other symbolic authority figures are considered hypocrites, corrupt, incompetent, power-hungry, and ridiculous. They demonstrate their incompetence in corruption, prostitution, and torturing of others. Notwithstanding his positive structuring presence, the paranoiac experiences the father as negative. He is considered a tyrant because in the name of the law, he abuses the law. In what sense does he abuse the law? He abuses the law in that he tries to impose on the child a law to which he himself does not submit. Thus, the child experiences the law imposed by the father as arbitrary. The defense that a child can develop against the imposition of such an arbitrary law is either to oppose and refuse that law or behave as a victim who executes blindly the orders that he or she does not understand.

When he introduces something of the Oedipal structure to explain the origin of paranoia, Lacan points to the function of the father in his role as mediator of the law. It's not immediately clear how that function is responsible for the failure of imaginary identification with the sibling. To make the connection, one would have to understand how the defective relation to the law explains one's deficient relation to others. Hegel's analysis of the romantic reformer does just that.

Hegel's analysis posits that a misunderstanding of the law is, at the same time, a misunderstanding of the relation between oneself and others. Hegel even makes the misunderstanding of the function of the law primordial. If one were to accept Hegel's analysis, then one would have to take the failed relation to the law as the crucial failure of the paranoiac. One would then have to deduce the failed relation with one's ideal, with siblings, and with sexuality as results.

CONCLUSION

Both Hegel and Lacan observed that the psychic structure of the paranoid person includes an inability to feel that other people are different. Both note that the paranoid person, at some point, has a utopian dream of transforming society for the better. They both also observe the explosion of aggression at some point in the paranoid person. Hegel, benefitting from Schiller's artistic description of Karl Moore, a paranoiac, is able to provide a dialectic connection between these different features in the life story of the paranoiac. Lacan is able to go a step further because he can explore the life of a real paranoiac by analyzing one point in her childhood.

Indeed, whereas children normally both identify (and thus idealize a sibling) and fight with siblings, Aimée, Lacan's paranoid patient, only identified with and idealized her sister. Lacan then points out that fighting with an idealized sibling is a risky business because it creates a separation of one's own ideal projected onto that sibling. In fighting an idealized sibling, so Lacan argues, the fighting sibling might find himself psychologically naked, that is, not enriched by an ideal. It is true that this experience of psychological nakedness then becomes an invitation to create one's own ideal, provided one can tolerate this psychological nakedness. The paranoiac was not able to face such a psychological nakedness and thus avoided and repressed the aggression that could cause it.

APPLICATIONS

Our study indicated a connection between creating ideas about idealistic reforms of society and paranoid aggression. This transformation of aggression into paranoia might lead to killing of other people and thus increased homicides. There is another path for aggression: suicide. Let us analyze the phenomenon of suicide rates in Sweden and China, as these cases relate to our study.

First, there has been a hypothesis that high suicide rates in Scandinavian countries, particularly Sweden, were related to the inability of young people to undertake the idealistic task of reforming society because society was already egalitarian and there was a generalized form of happiness. This hypothesis, or rather this attempt to smear egalitarian countries, contradicts the facts. The most recent World Health Organization statistic on suicides rates Sweden as number 59 (Wikipedia ranks Sweden as number 44). The statistics point to another fact: Countries with dictatorial regimes have higher suicide rates.[15] Thus, several of the 10 countries with the highest suicide rates have or had, until recently, a dictatorial or semidictatorial regime, or they have suffered or suffer from civil wars or colonial occupation. We could argue that in dictatorial societies, societies suffering from colonial occupation, or those undergoing civil strife, the flourishing of Romantic, utopian dreams in children and adolescents is much more difficult.

Let us start with Sweden. Swedish suicide rates have decreased, except for the population between 15 and 26 years of age.[16] This statistical fact gives me the opportunity to formulate a more precise hypothesis about Swedish suicide rates. Indeed, creating idealistic or Romantic reform ideas as a way to give oneself a place in the world is a task not so much for middle-aged or elderly people, but young people. Swedish young people need to find some way other than idealistic social reform combined with paranoia to deal with aggression. The diminished possibility for taking the path of romantic social reform combined with paranoia might explain two facts in Sweden. First, it can explain a substantially lower homicide statistic. Second, it can explain a higher suicide rate among its youth. Having a lower homicide statistic is a good thing. But what can be done in egalitarian societies to diminish the suicide statistics of young people? My article suggests two possibilities. First, discuss ideas, even idealistic ones, for improving society. Second, provide even young children with the opportunity to express aggression against siblings or other children in a civilized way. These two suggestions allow children and, thus, later adults to develop strategies to direct aggression away from the self and hopefully toward constructive tasks in society.

My second application concerns the high suicide rates among youth in China.[17] An often-cited explanation for these rates is the pressure to perform well in school; however, a top specialist on Chinese suicide connects the high rate of suicide among Chinese young people to the one-child policy (Caskie 2013; Shanshan 2007).[18] Lacan's theory might provide a plausible hypothesis for the connection between a rising suicide rate and the one-child policy. Lacan points out that children who have siblings are involved in a challenging and complicated interpersonal learning process (a process of which only children are deprived). They idealize the other sibling and thus imitate him or her. They also fight the sibling and are, thus, forced to give aggression a place in the building of their self-conception. This challenge allows a child with siblings to turn aggression outward. I therefore hypothesize that this normal challenge for children with siblings allows aggression to be turned outward and thus diminishes the likelihood of suicide.

Statistics quoted by Caskie, Yip Siu-fai, and Shanshan indicate that suicide rates have gone up in China since the one-child policy was enacted. If my hypothesis is correct, then my study suggests that families with one child should create an opportunity for their child to interact with other children in a way that is similar to sibling interaction. In particular, the interactions should allow the only child to develop idealization of and, also, jealousy toward some other children, thereby allowing only children to civilize aggression.

In my third application, I want to question whether all idealistic social reform needs to lead through disappointment to paranoia. There are many reform movements. I will concentrate on the one started by Ignatius of Loyola in the founding of the Jesuits *Summarium Constitutionum*. In that program we will find several important ideas that can help avoid the transition from idealist reformer to disappointment to paranoia (Roothaan *Summarium Constitutionum* #17).

First, Hegel's Romantic reformer had a personal mission, whereas the Jesuits are advised to make themselves instruments of the will of God. Second, the Romantic reformer aimed at a result, whereas the Jesuits aim at helping God, whose will is not known. Hence, Jesuits must accept the idea that what the Jesuits themselves aim at might not be the will of God. Third, the Jesuits have the ability to interpret the nonachievement of their goals as something other than disappointment. It can be experienced as the will of God. Hence, Jesuits need not feel that failure in their mission is a demonstration of their insanity in the way Hegel's Romantic reformer experienced her failure. Consequently, experiencing failure in their mission need not push Jesuits to paranoia. We can thus conclude that it is the narcissistic dimension of the Romantic reformer's efforts that produced a psychic process leading to disappointment and then to paranoia.

NOTES

1. For an explicit comparison of Hegel and Lacan's conception of madness, see the section entitled "Madness and Dissociability of the Human Soul" in Finkelde 2017, 140–47.

2. In his introduction to this passage, Baillie talks about the "Romantic school" and the "Romantic movement." He also uses the term "moral Sentimentalism" (Hegel 1967a, 390). Hyppolite talks about "Romantic individualism" (Hyppolite 1946, 276).

3. The German text does not explicitly provide a subdivision of the text. Neither does the French commentary by Hyppolite nor the two English translations of Baillie and Miller. Hyppolite's translation does, however, provide the three aforementioned subdivisions.

4. Hegel himself uses the expression "deranged" or the terms "madness" and "insane self-conceit" (Hegel 1977, 225–26).

5. Hegel does not use the term *paranoia*. He does use the expression "the rage of frantic self-conceit" or "fury of consciousness." He also often uses the term "perversion" to describe the state of consciousness at this point of the dialectic (Hegel 1977, 226ff.).

6. We find an interesting historical example in the figure of Leon Trotsky. Isaac Deutscher wrote a biography of Trotsky in three parts: *I. The Prophet Armed: 1879–1921*; *II. The Prophet Unarmed: 1921–1929*; and *III. The Prophet Outcast: 1929–1940*. The three parts of Trotsky's life, as suggested by the titles of the trilogy, compare in an intriguing way with Hegel's three-step path from aggressive Romantic reformer to necessary disappointment to person lost in paranoia.

7. Hegel expresses this idea speculatively as follows: "The idea of Reason [is] [. . .] the certainty that [consciousness] in its particular individuality, . . . has being absolutely *in itself*, or is all reality" (Hegel 1977, 138).

8. Terry Pinkard (1996, 212–13) provides a nice statement of the necessity for the Romantic reformer to translate his personal conviction into linguistic and therefore public acts of "declarations of conviction," i.e., into something objective. But, Pinkard does not articulate Hegel's idea that the transformation of the private conviction into something objective, particu-

larly a successful action such as the change of a societal law, is necessarily felt as a betrayal of the original conviction colored as it is by its grandiose aspects. Berthold-Bond (1995, 165–60) sees the kernel of the romantic reformer's craziness precisely in the necessary contradiction between the Romantic reformer's dream and the unavoidable contrary characteristics of his realized project. And, so does Robert Stern 2002, 121; J. Michael Stewart 2000, 253; Howard Kainz 1976, 121; Pierre-Jean Labarrière 1968, 172; J.-F. Marquet 2004, 200–201; and Robert C. Solomon 1983, 508. Not all commentators on this passage of Hegel, though, give full weight to this argument by Hegel. They rather stress the next disappointment encountered by the Romantic reformer: i.e., others oppose him while he expected approval and even praise. See Howard Kainz 2008, 23–24; H. S. Harris 1995, 55; Flay 1984, 141; Quentin Lauer 1976, 184; Terry Pinkard 2009, 141; John Russon 2004, 126 and 1997, 42–43; Philip Kain 2005, 104–5 and Jacob Loewenberg 1965, 158–62.

9. In his study on Kant, Hegel, and Lacan, Dominik Finkelde writes, "Christa Hackenesch points to the fact that Hegel does not understand madness as an illness of the body but rather as a Verrückung (displacement) between an individual form of consciousness and the historical universal" (Finkelde 2017, 285). See Hackenesch 2002, 40–43.

10. "Paranoia," *Dictionary.com*, https://www.dictionary.com/browse/paranoia (downloaded August 27, 2018).

11. We will not reflect on one aspect of the case of Aimée, i.e., the fact that Aimée was cured of her paranoid ideas 20 days after the attack and after having emotionally recognized (she even cried) that her attack was not justified (Lacan 1975, 164, 173, 249).

12. Lacan writes that Aimée wanted to "fulfill a great social mission" and dreamt of being an "idealistic reformer" (Lacan 1975, 159). Aimée also dreamt of having a function in the government so that she could direct reforms (Lacan, 167).

13. Lacan says that Aimée's sister became a prototype that Aimée also applied to literary women, actresses, and mondaine women.

14. See the many times that Aimée considers herself to be a bad mother (Lacan 1975, 163, 172, 252). Here is one quotation by Lacan of Aimée: "I feared much for the life of my son, wrote the sick person; if nothing were to happen now, it would happen later, because of me, I would be a criminal mother" (Lacan 1975, 163).

15. The countries with the highest suicide rates include the following: Lithuania (32 pro 100,000, released from the Soviet Union in 1990); the Russian Federation (30 pro 100,000, dictatorial regime); Guyana (30 pro 100,000, lingering effects of colonization); Belarus (28 pro 100,000, dictatorial regime); Democratic Republic of Korea (28 pro 100,000, separation from North Korea and, for some time, dictatorial leaders); Kazakstan (25 pro 100,000, Nazarbayev is by some described as a dictator, even if a forward-looking one); Ukraine (25 pro 100,000, political strife, semiwar); Suriname (25 pro 100,000, civil strife). "Suicide Rates Per 100,000 Population," *World Health Organization*, http://www.who.int/gho/mental_health/suicide_rates_crude/en/ (downloaded August 27, 2018).

16. Still, Sweden ranks number 51 for the suicide rate among people 15 to 19 years of age. "Suicides Increasing amongst Swedish Youth," *The Local*, November 26, 2018, https://www.thelocal.se/20181126/suicides-increasing-amongst-swedish-youth (downloaded August 27, 2018).

17. Overall, the suicide rate in China has declined sharply in the last two decades. Lily Kuo, "China's Suicide Rate Has Plummeted Because of Urbanization, but It May Be Climbing Again," *Quartz*, June 27, 2014, http://qz.com/227136/chinas-suicide-rate-has-plummeted-because-of-urbanization-but-it-may-be-climbing-again/ (downloaded August 27, 2018); "Back from the Edge: A Dramatic Decline in Suicides," *Economist*, June 28, 2014, http://www.economist.com/news/china/21605942-first-two-articles-chinas-suicide-rate-looks-effect-urbanisation-back (downloaded August 27, 2018).

18. Some experts say China's one-child policy could play a role in the rise of youth suicide. "Don't forget that many youngsters today have no siblings. . . . Many of them, unlike their parents, never really master the ability to deal with difficult interpersonal relationship problems," said Professor Paul Yip Siu-fai, director of the Center for Suicide Research and Prevention at the University of Hong Kong (Caskie 2013).

Part III

Psychosis and Schizophrenia Are Illnesses Marked by a Defective Relationship to Language

Chapter Nine

Phenomenology, Linguistic Intentionality, Affectivity, and Villemoes's New Therapy for Schizophrenics

PART I: PHENOMENOLOGY, LINGUISTIC INTENTIONALITY, AND HELPING THE MENTALLY ILL

Phenomenology is a discipline that attempts to avoid two forms of reductionism. It avoids the reduction of the mind to the brain by highlighting the many active intentionalities present in our everyday life. It also helps avoid a crude psychological reductionism that is inattentive to the many different forms of intentionality of which human beings are capable.[1] In this chapter, I pay particular attention to linguistic intentionality and its crucial role in the method of treating schizophrenics developed by Palle Villemoes, a Swedish psychiatrist.

Phenomenology and Linguistic Intentionality

In his essay "Words, Pictures, and Symbols," Robert Sokolowski points out that perception can give rise to two series of intentionalities. The first series consists of perception, remembering, imagination, and anticipation. The second series consists of perception, signification (using a word to refer to something), picturing, and indication (smoke is seen as an indication of fire). Perceptively, Sokolowski differentiates the two series by claiming that the first series is much more closely connected to sensibility than the second. The second series, claims Sokolowski, creates objects that are more intellectual and thus more closely allied with activities of the mind (Sokolowski 2000, 85–86).

I want to dwell on one form of intentionality that occurs in the second series: signification. Sokolowski calls this "signitive intention" (Sokolowski 2000, 78). He gives the following revealing example of an emerging signitive intention: One looks at a piece of paper covered with a seemingly meaningless collection of dots; slowly, the dots resolve into recognizable words, "The Burritt Hotel." Sokolowski points out that, compared with perception, signitive intention differs in at least three fundamental ways. First, perception refers to what is present *as* present. Signitive intention refers to the absent and can make it present in its absence. To be more specific, by reading the words "The Burritt Hotel," I know that I am not in the physical presence of that hotel. I am, however, present to the hotel in some way. Even if I am not physically present to the hotel, I can still be mentally present to it or make it mentally present to me. Signitive intention is thus a more mental intention than perception. As perception is present in animals whereas signitive intention is not, Sokolowski concludes that this form of intention is more characteristically human than perception (Sokolowski 2000, 86).

Second, perception consists of a fulfilled intention augmented by a number of empty intentions. The fulfilled intention in perception is understood to be a perspectival view that can be complemented by other perspectival views. When I see only the front of a desk, my awareness that it has sides and a back allows me to perceive it as a complete object. Sokolowski calls these latter forms of awareness "empty intentions." In perception, the cointended empty intentions are "continuous and ever changing" with the slightest change of the human body, of its head, or even of its eyes (79). On the other hand, a signitive intention makes the object present "all at once and as a whole" (Sokolowski 2000, 79). The words "The Burritt Hotel" refer to the hotel in its totality rather than in a perspectival way. The word, therefore, can be said to refer to the object at once. Signitive intention is discrete, not continuous in the way perception is. It is also more choppy and individuated than perception, which is smooth and gradual (Sokolowski 2000, 79).

Third, signitive intentions allow for the connection of the word used with other possible words, which can then be put into a syntactic statement. Thus, having referred to a hotel, I know that I can use other words to comprehend the intended object. If it is a hotel, it must have an entrance, it must have a reception area, it must have rooms with beds, etc. Thus, signitive intention prepares the way for linguistic reasoning (Sokolowski 2000, 79). Sokolowski therefore concludes that signitive intention is (potentially) a more rational intention.

Another phenomenologist, De Waelhens, has pointed out that the use of words has another characteristic worth describing. De Waelhens opens his own discussion with Freud's description of his one-and-half-year-old grandson (De Waelhens and Ver Eecke 2001, 143ff.; Freud 1920, 14–17). Freud assures us that his grandchild had normal and warm relations with his mother. Contrary to other children of his age, the child did not cry when his mother went away. He seemed to be able to either cover over or repress the pain that other children experience when they are separated from their mothers.

Freud observed that his grandchild had developed a game. He had a spool that he threw over the side of his crib and then pulled it back. While throwing it over the side of the crib, the boy would say "o," and when pulling the spool back the child would say "a." With the help of the mother, Freud interpreted the sounds "o" and "a" as meaning *fort* (gone) and *da* (here). Freud argued that the child first mentally substituted the spool for the mother and then actively played the game of the mother leaving and returning.

The spool here performs the function of what Winnicott's theory refers to as a "transitional object" (Winnicott 1991, 1–25). It is an affective substitute for the mother. But in making the spool a substitute for the mother, the child became the one who controlled the reappearance or disappearance of the mother. The child could play at making the mother reappear and disappear, and thus enjoy his mastery of the mother's fading. The joy of playing at the disappearance and reappearance of the mother could still be destroyed by the loss of the spool; however, in substituting the sounds "o" and "a," which stood for the words "gone" and "here," the child had definitively overcome the pain of experiencing the disappearance of the mother. Freud calls this one of the greatest developmental achievements of the child.

De Waelhens applies Freud's theoretical concept of primal repression to the description of his grandson (De Waelhens and Ver Eecke 2001, 143–67). Freud observed that repression created a curious situation. After an experience is repressed, consciousness does not have the ability to undo that repression because—as Freud observed—the repressed becomes entangled with other repressed phenomena and is thus held back by these connections. Such reasoning about repression creates a difficulty for Freudian theory that is similar to the one found in Aristotle's theoretical explanation of movement by prior movement. Both authors had to accept that the first phenomenon—be it the first movement or the first repression—had to be of a totally different kind. Before Aristotle knew the nature of the first movement, he had to accept that it was different from all other movements. Similarly, before Freud could know the nature of the first repression—called the primal or primary repression—he was forced to introduce the concept.[2]

De Waelhens points out that children are very attached to their mothers. Children cry when their mothers leave them. Successfully using a transitional object and then later successfully using words to deal with the disappearance of the mother is to be interpreted as the child succeeding in allowing the mother to disappear without experiencing the pain normally associated with the disappearance of the mother. De Waelhens connects the successful introduction of words to deal with the disappearance of the mother with the introduction of primal repression.

I will now connect De Waelhens's claims to the descriptions and analyses of Sokolowski. Sokolowski points out that perception has a sensible dimension and that the senses present us with a world we experience as something continuous. Signitive intentions, on the contrary, are choppy (De Waelhens and Ver Eecke 2001, 79). Signitive intentions present objects "all at once and as a whole" (De Waelhens and Ver Eecke 2001, 79). Using words to refer to a perceived reality does not leave the perceptual world untouched. Sokolowski implies that the use of words—signitive intentionality—chops and cuts up the perceived world. Instead of a continuous perceptual world, I now have a chopped-up world consisting of discrete objects: a table, a desk, etc. Furthermore, instead of perceptual objects consisting of empty intentions, I now possess mental objects in their totality.[3] The infinite richness of perceptual impressions is erased in favor of an abstract concept.

Commenting on Hegel, Kojève calls this function of the word the killing of the object in all its perceptual richness (Kojève 1969, 140). If words have a repressive capability with reference to the perceptual richness of the world, could not words also have a repressive potential with reference to affective attachments to the perceptual world? In particular, what should we make of the world of the child that includes its mother and its affective attachment to her: Couldn't the use of words to replace the mother indicate a comparable loss of the mother, as De Waelhens teaches us in his interpretation of Freud's concept of primal repression?

Sokolowski also points to a more positive function of the signitive intention in the use of words. Sokolowski calls it the "entrance into linguistic reasoning." Suppose I approach the Burritt Hotel from a side that lacks a door. I am thinking of the building in front of me as "The Burritt Hotel," and I know the meaning of the word *hotel* and that a hotel has an entrance. The word *hotel*, used in reference to the building in front of me, tells me that it has an entrance. So I know, despite not seeing it immediately, that the building I see has an entrance somewhere. A word and the possible connections with other words related to that object provide a guide for my behavior in the world of objects. As I am calling the building a "hotel," even if I do not see a door on the street side of the building, I am not paralyzed. I know there must be an entrance somewhere. Confidently, I walk around the building until I discover the entrance. Thus, the transformation of the experiential world of sense awareness into a linguistic world provides me with freedom because it provides a guide for action.

Signitive intentionality makes use of words; however, the use of words requires that we submit to all kinds of rules. First, there are the phonetic rules. One needs to make the effort to differentiate properly between such sounds as "r" and "l" or "t" and "th."[4] Second, one needs to accept as obligatory the arbitrary connection made in a particular culture between words and objects.

Two stories illustrate the presence of rules in the use of words and the psychological reactions that are possible to such rules. In the early years of our family life, we spoke Dutch at home while the children spoke English in pre-K. One morning, I asked my daughter to open "de venster," to which my daughter replied somewhat angrily, "This is not a 'venster,' it is a 'window.'" She felt that a rule had been broken. Later in our family life, when we had two children, I remember them coming to the breakfast table and, while pointing to the peanut butter jar, saying that it was jam. Then they would point to the jar of jam and say that it was peanut butter. While violating the rule of language, my children would burst into laughter. I could interpret their joy only as an enjoyment of violating the rules of social life in an area where the violation did not present a threat. Clearly, if speaking and signitive intentionality demands the submission to rules, shouldn't we suppose that children will need some help accepting the burden of submitting to these rules?

This is precisely what Husserl observes in his short essay "The Child: The First Empathy."[5] He writes, "Names first of all have the objective world as a presupposition. From its mother, its father, and so on, the child learns to understand the naming of those things to which they refer." Clearly, the statement by Husserl implies that naming makes no sense if there is not an objective world that is there to be named. Informed by Sokolowski, we can claim more. We can claim that naming implies that the sensible world is transformed in an objective world—that is, a world consisting of not only sense data, but also objects—separable entities with characteristics not revealed by our mere senses. In imitating the adult's act of naming, the child learns to use the mental objects of the naming intentionality and so learns to create the objective world presupposed in the adult's act of naming. The child thus borrows a form of intentionality it does not yet possess. We can therefore suppose that the child enriches its subjectivity and its sense of agency by using the borrowed form of signitive intentionality.

This line of reasoning leads to a puzzle, also noted by Husserl: "How does the child come to say 'I'?" Husserl generalizes this puzzle to include such questions as to how the child learns to understand personal pronouns and what have in the contemporary literature come to be known as indexicals.[6] As "I" means something different when used by the mother as opposed to when it is used by the child, the use of pronouns will only be possible if the child has established some form of distance between itself and its mother.

A New Treatment Method for Schizophrenics

The previous remarks allow us to better understand the therapeutic method developed by Swedish psychiatrist Palle Villemoes. It is well known that schizophrenics do not use pronouns properly (De Waelhens and Ver Eecke 2001, 207). Thus, when asked if their parents like them, schizophrenics will answer that no they (the patients) do not like them (the parents). As schizophrenics do not know how to use pronouns properly, Villemoes concludes that therapists should not treat schizophrenics as dialogue partners. They should not, for instance, position the patients in front of them. Rather, Villemoes puts the patients next to him, three feet apart and in the chair closest to the door.[7] He further argues that one should ask no questions of such patients, and when the patients ask questions, one should acknowledge the questions but not answer them. Instead, Villemoes describes the environment of the patient.

In contrast to the treatment of autistic patients who need to be taught the use of words, Villemoes emphasizes that schizophrenics need to be taught the use of the structural functions of language. The therapist should use genitives, prepositions, adverbs, adjectives, and conjunctions. The use of a structuring language transforms the world of the patients. As the insights of Sokolowski help us to understand, the use of language has a repressive function—it represses the richness and the captivating aspects of sense perception in favor of the mental present in linguistic intentionality.[8] One of the first positive consequences of Villemoes describing to his schizophrenic patients their own sensual world is that they cease to be startled by changes in the perceptual world. Two more changes emerge in the behavior of the schizophrenics: They start idolizing the therapist and rearranging the objects in their rooms.

Villemoes's interpretation of these three changes is sophisticated, but it sheds light on and is, in turn, clarified by Robert Sokolowski and Edmund Husserl's phenomenology of linguistic intentionality. One connection between the insights of Villemoes and Sokolowski is highlighted by the fact that work with schizophrenics in promoting linguistic intentionality requires great emotional effort. Sokolowski makes us aware that linguistic intentionality performs a repressive function with reference to the rich textuality of the perceptual world. Villemoes requires referring mental health workers to speak well of him and his method to referred patients. He thus actively promotes idolization. Furthermore, Villemoes tells us that he avoids antagonizing his patients. His advice includes not only the admonition that the therapist should not contradict what the patient says, but also the recommendations that the patient not be put in front of the therapist (an oppositional position) and that the therapist not ask questions of the patient.

One central problem emerges when one reflects on the method developed by Villemoes in relation to Sokolowski and Husserl's ideas about linguistic (signitive) intentionality. All three authors, in one way or another, are able to explain why acquiring linguistic (signitive) intentionality requires the help of another and why that help cannot be given without the patient (or the child) having a deep emotional attachment to the therapist (or the parent).

The basic reason for this requirement is that linguistic (signitive) intentionality is a new form of intentionality that provides the patient (or the child) with a new world where the rich and continuously sliding texture of the perceptual world is replaced by a world cut up into entities formed by linguistic units. This is a new intentional world wherein the connections between these cut-up units are suggested and articulated by linguistic operations (e.g., a hotel has an entrance, a table is something to put things on). This new world does not emerge spontaneously from sense impressions. Rather, the new world frequently reveals implausible connections. Thus, one of my children angrily rejected my question, "Did the doctor ask you to lie on her table?" "Dad," she replied, "you do not lie on a table!" After some explanation, she reconciled herself to the curious usage of the word *table*, which forbids that you sit on it at home but you are required to lie on it in a doctor's office. Only others, trusted others, can reliably introduce linguistic (signitive) intentionality and the new world it creates. But what about pronouns and indexicals? When talking to my child, I address her as "you." When referring to me, I say "I." How can one imagine that a child (or a patient) learns to say "I" when addressed as "you"?

A possible solution to this puzzle can be formulated along the following lines. For the child to learn that the world is not only a rich, textured perceptual world, but also a world cut up into pieces according to linguistic units, the child needs to accept the burden of seeing the world through the eyes of another. As pronouns (and indexicals) apply differently to me and to any other person, the use of pronouns cannot be learned by a person (be it child or patient) unless that person is able to cut herself off from others (including parents or therapist). In child development, we notice that the no-saying period precedes the acquisition of the use of pronouns (Ver Eecke 1984, 77–78). We should therefore expect that the successful therapy of Villemoes will introduce something equivalent to the no-saying of the child. Interestingly, we do find such a stage embodied in Villemoes's therapeutic technique.

I interpret the act of delegation of power, which in Villemoes's method marks the transition from the first phase to the second phase of treatment, as equivalent to the no-saying period of the child. Villemoes starts the second phase of his treatment—after enough of an idolization has been established—by taking off his watch before the session and then telling the patient that he—the therapist—has no watch and that therefore the patient is responsible for keeping time. From then onward, the patient has the last word in the session. The patient is given the power to cut, in this case to cut off the session, and thus seems to learn the power inherent in linguistic (signitive) intentionality.

In this second phase, Villemoes concentrates on describing historical scenes: the patient's kindergarten school, the road to kindergarten, etc. Three moments in this second phase are worth noting. The first is that the patient starts to make subtle and coordinated movements. It seems as if the patient develops a body schema. The second is that the patient begins to have empathy for other people. Patients start identifying with others without fearing that they will lose their own identity. Third, the patient starts making what Villemoes calls "symbolic identifications." A patient says, for instance, that she is not a thief. Such a statement is quite different from the statement of a mentally ill person claiming that he is Napoleon. In this last case, the patient does not feel obliged to march to Moscow. In the former case, however, the patient announces that she accepts the obligations implied by the words, "I am not a thief." In such a symbolic identification with a word, the patient becomes a subject.

Conclusion

Phenomenology provides a solid method for discovering and analyzing the rich varieties of human intentionality. In particular, both Husserl and Sokolowski emphasize the creative and puzzling dimensions of linguistic (signitive) intentionality. Villemoes's new treatment method for schizophrenic patients concentrates on the structuring effects that language performs for the human subject. Phenomenology thus plays and continues to play a crucial role in providing insights into the constructive treatment of mentally ill patients. The phenomenological approach to mental illness aims at more than symptom reduction; it aims at restoring or introducing new forms of intentionality that promote, create, or restore subjectivity.

PART II: THE AFFECTIVE DIMENSION IN LINGUISTIC INTENTIONALITY

BY RICHARD COBB-STEVENS

Professor Ver Eecke presents a concise summary of Robert Sokolowski's account of linguistic intentionality and makes some fresh and strikingly evocative suggestions about how that account may provide a philosophical basis for the treatment of mentally ill patients.[9] In what follows, I propose to consider three themes that are interwoven in this chapter:

1. language as mastery over presence and absence
2. personal pronouns and indexicals as keys to the development of the self
3. syntax as the manifestation of intelligence and responsible agency

In each instance, I shall call attention to the ways in which Ver Eecke's emphasis on the importance of the *affective* dimension of each of these human achievements adds a richness and depth to not only the clinical process of healing, but also the philosophical understanding of linguistic intentionality itself.

Words as Consolation for the Trauma of Absence

A fundamental tenet of twentieth-century philosophy is that philosophical questions are best approached through language. Husserl agreed with this conviction, but he also thought that linguistic analysis must be complemented by a detailed analysis of the relationship between linguistic articulations and perceptual discriminations. Like Aristotle, he was convinced that speech gives syntactical articulation and thus completion to the inarticulate but nonetheless meaningful insights of cognitive intuition, therefore, there is a continuity between intuitive and discursive *logos*. There is also a certain priority of seeing over speaking.

Loving parents and other caring adults introduce young children to the realm of meaning by encouraging them to imitate the phonemes and words of an established language used by the parents to refer to things, animals, and people in their environment. As Husserl points out, children could never succeed in taking these sounds as meaningful if they could not already discern their referents as identities presented, again and again, in a series of perspectival views that highlight different features of the same things.

In *Logical Investigations*, he observes that when we use words to refer to things, we identify them by way of their features. In short, our words express the contents of our perceptions. Of course, we make use of the network of meanings encoded in our dictionaries, but these meanings are ultimately derived from the contents of perceptions. Husserl thus essentially reaffirms Aristotle's account of the derivation of nouns and predicates from the "looks" (*eide*) of things. What presents itself to our intelligence when we perceive a particular thing is the "look" that it shares with a family of things. We grasp the "look" as a shape, or form, had by this particular thing and shared or shareable by other particulars (Husserl VI, #40–52; Aristotle, *On Interpretation*, 2b7–14, 16b25–26; *Metaphysics*, Z, 103 1b 6–7, 20–21). Husserl further suggests that children cannot get the point of linguistic references if they cannot already, in some inchoative way, appreciate particular things and their features as token instances of types. Indeed, how can they begin to take phonemes and words produced repeatedly by one adult, or by different adults having different tonalities and accents, as meaningful signs if they do not already have some understanding of the token-type relationship?

Even more remarkable than the ability to give linguistic expression to what we see is the ability to refer to things in their absence. Sokolowski points out that many readers of Husserl are at first skeptical of his claim that we truly intend what is absent. We are so accustomed to thinking of cognition in terms of the modern notion of mind as an enclosed theater of representations that we feel obliged to posit something *present* as the immediate target of our signitive intentions of *absent* things: e.g., an image, a concept, a sense impression, the word itself (Sokolowski 2000, 36); however, Husserl insists on our capacity to intend absent things themselves as identities across presence and absence. Signitive intentionality, he claims, is what constitutes us as rational beings who are not limited to a closed environment and can enjoy an openness to a world. Language thus reveals our transcending mode of being.

This is also the point of Freud's analysis of the *fort-da* game. Freud's grandson takes delight is this game because it provides him with control over the absence and presence of the spool and thus permits him to resolve symbolically the trauma of the occasional absence of his mother. More importantly, by alternately voicing the "o" and "a" sounds (baby talk for *fort* and *da*), in conjunction with the disappearance and reappearance of the spool/mother, the child learns to interrelate absence and presence meaningfully. The child no longer undergoes absence as annihilation and presence as overwhelming immediacy. Privation and presence are both transformed. Signified rather than merely undergone, they are transformed into intentionality.

Prof. Ver Eecke calls attention to De Waelhens's emphasis on the affective dimension of this discovery of the power of words. The price of this joyful discovery must be the repression of the immediacy and intimacy of uninterrupted presence. We must give up the object of desire to reclaim it as an object of cognition. Paul Ricoeur suggests that there is a similarity between Freud's analysis of this healthy repression and his account of the process of mourning the loss of a beloved person. As opposed to melancholia, which involves an unhealthy identification with the lost object of affection, mourning succeeds in "a giving up of brute presence and an intending in presence and absence" (Ricoeur 1970, 385). This comparison suggests the following question: Could the healing strategy developed by Dr. Villemoes also be of help to people suffering from melancholia?

In a recent lecture, Sokolowski developed the thesis that the "vowel dimension of the words is more associated with emotion and the syntactic structure is more associated with reason" (Sokolowski 2002, 30). He adds that vowels are especially linked to feelings, whereas consonants generally introduce intelligibility. Consonants clip the flow of sound and thus permit the formation of distinct and recognizable words.

I find this analysis particularly convincing because of an initial difficulty I encountered as an adult in learning French. Because of the smooth flow (elision) of French words into one another (e.g., "Je suis allé en ville ce matin"), the learner finds it difficult to break the flow of sound into distinct words. I remember the frustrating but intriguing experience of being able to grasp the feelings communicated by my professors and other interlocutors well before I could understand what they were talking about. The vowels were doing their job, but the consonants were not "hacking it" (so to speak). It might be said that this adult experience is somewhat akin to that had by the child engaged in the *fort-da* game. Of course, the adult already knows that words provide mastery over presence and absence, but while waiting for a new dawn of meaning, the adult can reexperience the consolation had in childhood at the first intimation of this power of language.

Repression and Indexicality

Husserl suggests that indexical reference is inherently egocentric. To think of something indexically (as "this," "mine," or "here") is to think of it in relation to oneself. Moreover, perception itself, inasmuch as it targets *this* particular as having some specific property or properties, is an indexical mode of experience. Perception presents *this* object as now, here, before me. It follows that perception necessarily entails a tacit awareness of subjective perspective on the part of the perceiver. Even definite descriptions used to identify particulars that are not sensibly present are never completely free of indexical components. Such descriptions tacitly depend on prior demonstrative identifications of particulars evoked by the descriptive terms (Zahavi 1999, 24–27).

The point is this: Indexicals cannot be adequately translated into exclusively objective terms because they make references from a particular position that is experienced by the speaker as a center of coordinates rather than a position locatable from some imagined centerless perspective. It follows that all types of reference that depend ultimately upon demonstrative reference must imply the ability of interlocutors to imagine themselves as enjoying the perspective of the original subject making the demonstrative reference. Husserl points out that to appreciate the indexical references of a speaker, I must be able to construe my "here" as his "there" and my "left" is his "right." Even when I attempt to conceive of the whole world, including myself and my interlocutor, from a neutral standpoint ("as if from nowhere," as Thomas Nagel puts it), I must acknowledge that I am the subject of this impersonal conception of the world that contains myself and others. The reference is still essentially indexical. I realize that the impersonal conception is attached to and developed from my original first-person perspective. This is not a trivial discovery, for it moves the sense of self-awareness to a higher level, which evokes a "strange sense that I am and am not the hub of the universe" (Nagel 1997, 64).

As Pascal pointed out, it is a source of not only wonder, but also anxiety that I can alternately make references from a first-person point of view and from the standpoint of a possessor of an objective conception of the world that contains myself. The ability to move with facility from one to another of these points of view is what permits us to engage in the pleasures of irony, humor, and philosophical contemplation of the human predicament; however, this same ability is also what makes us vulnerable to shame, guilt, and anxiety.

Given the complexity of the intellectual operations requisite for the transition from a first-person perspective, to a second-person (intersubjective) perspective, to a third-person (impersonal) perspective (all the while acknowledging that the intersubjective and impersonal perspectives ultimately remain nonetheless my perspectives), there is little wonder that some mentally ill people have difficulty in making these transitions. It seems to me that the genius of Villemoes's method of dealing with such patients lies in its slow and patient reconstruction of the steps involved in these transitions.

His method recreates the conditions of the patient's initial childhood learning experiences by first establishing a nonconfrontational climate of trust and even idolization, and then encouraging the patient to relearn from a first-person perspective the complex intellectual and affective maneuvers necessary for appreciating the perspectives of others. The patient must first rediscover the pleasures and consolations of naming things and articulating the relationships between things and their features, thereby solidifying the sense of self that emerges from the construction of a world from a mobile but continuously personal perspective.

Villemoes's technique of next allowing the patient control of the timepiece and thus the length of the session encourages the transition from an exclusively egocentric perspective to an emergent intersubjective perspective. A question occurs to me at this point: Does Villemoes have some similar strategy for encouraging a further expansion of the patient's perspective that might make possible a third-person point of view on the self and world? Is there a specific mode of repression requisite for the achievement of the impersonal point of view requisite for scientific inquiry and philosophical contemplation?

Syntax and Freedom

Sokolowski observes that people inhabit not only an environment, but also a "space of reasons" wherein they are able to deliberate and act in ways that determine who they will become. He also reminds us that access to the space of reasons requires a process of intellectual and affective maturation. All of the capacities we associate with the realm of rationality (freedom, contemplation, irony, and humor) are not innate faculties automatically shared equally among all human beings. These capacities have their source in the "ability to think in the medium of speech" (Sokolowski 2002, 29). They are more fully developed when the syntactical potential of that medium is more fully realized.

Husserl's theory of parts and wholes, and of the categorical structures of speech acts, pays off richly in this context. Husserl observed that categorial objects (states of affairs expressed by propositions) emerge as a result of intellectual articulations made possible by the syntactical power of language. The things and situations we perceive are, thus, brought into the field of rationality where connections form a logical network rather than a merely perceptual flow.

Sokolowski emphasizes that this elevation of perceived objects and situations into the realm of rationality does not subjectivize things in the world or convert them into mere constructs. Indeed, our syntactic operations make possible a "more complete and intersubjectively verifiable manifestation of things" (Sokolowski 2002, 29). The layering of levels of syntax make possible ever more nuanced displays of things and situations in the world, as, for example, in the sequential concatenation of parts within parts required by such operations as nominalization and quotation.

Sokolowski points out that syntax is also involved in the phenomenon of human laughter and the very phonemic structure of basic words. Vowels are associated more with elemental feelings and the moans and cries that express those feelings. Consonants are the first indications of rationality: They clip, fence in, and structure the vowels, thus creating phonemes and eventually words, and thus introducing the multifold variations that different languages bring to the task of articulation. I am reminded here of Hans-Georg Gadamer's evocative remark,

> Wherever language and men exist, there is not only a freedom from the pressure of the environment, but this freedom from habitat is also freedom in relation to the names that we give things, as stated in the profound account of *Genesis*, according to which Adam received from God the authority to name creatures. (Gadamer 1975, 402)

Husserl observes that categorial formings, since they are not part of the sensuous presentation of things, leave their objects sensuously unchanged. Even when we perform new categorial operations on earlier categorial articulations, we do not thereby tamper with the underlying perceptually given situation. When, for example, we nominalize an expressed state of affairs, thus making it part of a further state of affairs, the initial state of affairs remains as it was. It is changed in a purely formal way by being transformed into the subject of a new predication.

Sokolowski remarks that this marvelous transparency of categorial forms shows that they are something intellectual. Hence, we are free to carry out many kinds of categorical shaping, although we must maintain consistency and continuous respect for the underlying perceptual data. When we come to know the vocabulary and rules of grammar of our language well, we may even tinker with them for the sake of humor or irony. This is why Prof. Ver Eecke found the playful renaming of jars of peanut butter and jam by his children to be a sign of advanced intelligence rather than mere confusion. I am reminded here of Immanuel Kant's analysis of how certain aesthetic judgments relate to instances of beauty that by reason of their indeterminate character cannot be classified, i.e., brought under a concept or rule. The experience of such beauty elicits the free play of our faculties of imagination and understanding. Our delight in this free play, he suggests, is a discovery of a certain freedom.

Prof. Ver Eecke describes how, given the opportunity to engage in free categorial reconstruction of scenes from their childhood, Villemoes's patients began to make more coordinated movements, to rearrange objects in the present environment, and finally to achieve empathy with other people. The unstudied and yet purposive play of these categorial achievements are for them an introduction to the freedom that accompanies the exercise of rationality. It must be a source of great satisfaction for this doctor to witness these results. I am grateful to Wilfried Ver Eecke for introducing me to this moving and hopeful account of one doctor's efforts to heal.

NOTES

1. John Brough drew my attention to this double form of reductionism, which phenomenology exposed.
2. For a good, short summary of the problems connected with the concept of "primal repression," see Laplanche and Pontalis 1988, 333–34.
3. A similar view of the relation between sense data and words is developed by Hegel in his *Phenomenology* in the section entitled "Perception: Or the Thing and Deception," in Hegel 1977, 67–79.
4. For a classic study of the features defining phonemes, which also gives a hint of the great challenge involved in mastering the pronunciation of different phonemes, see Jakobson and Halle 1956, 1–51.
5. Manuscript of Husserl is referred to as Ms K III 11, pp. 7–11. Published (as appendix A) with an Italian translation (as appendix B) by Sancipriano 1965.
6. An indexical is, roughly speaking, a linguistic expression whose reference can shift from context to context. For example, the indexical "you" may refer to one person in one context and another person in another context. "Indexicals," *Stanford Encyclopedia f Philosophy*, September 14, 2001, https://plato.stanford.edu/entries/indexicals/ (downloaded January 11, 2018).

7. Aside from an article by Villemoes himself (Villemoes 2002), there are two English summaries of his therapeutic method: Edenius 1999, 166–76, and De Waelhens and Ver Eecke 2001, 109–17.

8. I am here substituting the term *linguistic intentionality* for Sokolowski's "signitive intentionality."

9. Richard Cobb-Stevens delivered part II as a comment to the main section of this chapter, which I presented as a talk to the American Philosophical Association in 2002. I thank him for his permission to include his comments in my book.

Chapter Ten

Self-Referencing in the Language of the Severely Mentally Ill

In this chapter, I make a connection between two phenomena. The first phenomenon is a curious linguistic symptom that is presented by people with schizophrenia. The second phenomenon is the generally observable way young children respond when asked a question.

TWO PHENOMENA WITH SIMILARITIES

Our first phenomenon is exemplified by the case of Judge Schreber, who had a schizophrenic breakdown and wrote his *Memoirs*, in which he describes his symptoms.[1] One symptom, among others, was the belief that he was becoming a woman[2] to marry God and create a new mankind.[3] He also showed many curiosities in his relationship to and his understanding of language. For example, he claims that different but similar sounding words ought to be, in some circumstances, treated as identical[4]—or that the language spoken by God had a "wealth of euphemisms."[5] He also reports hearing voices that began a sentence describing him. Judge Schreber then felt compelled to complete the sentence about him (Schreber 1903, 216ff.).

Our second phenomenon is a personal experience. When I travel by airplane, I often have to wait. When there are young children, I sometimes ask them a simple question, for example, "Are you already going to school?" or "Do you like to play?" Invariably I get the same response. The child turns to the mother and seems to expect that she will respond for the child. When mothers notice the interaction and see their child looking for her to respond, most mothers smile. Then the reaction of the mothers varies. Some mothers directly answer my question. Other mothers encourage their child to answer me, either saying, "You know," or providing the child with the answer and telling the child to tell it to me himself or herself.

These repeated examples of a child turning to their mother to answer a question to which they presumably know the answer indicates to me a profound puzzle about human consciousness. These examples show that consciousness is not naturally capable of describing in language what consciousness has experienced and thus knows. Consciousness wants a privileged other, the mother, to speak for it. Another is expected to speak for or guide the self. In developmental psychology, this phenomenon can be considered an example of "social referencing."[6]

PROJECT

In this chapter, I will demonstrate that the ability to articulate what one has experienced, what one knows, and who one is by using the first-person pronoun is a great achievement.[7] It follows that if the articulation, in the first person, is an important achievement, then it is quite possible that some human beings will not fully reach that ability.[8] I will further demonstrate that one way to understand some of the symptoms of a schizophrenic person is precisely to hypothesize that these patients are still in the psychological position in which they feel the need to let others describe for themselves how they experience the world and themselves. To prove my thesis, I rely on the *Memoirs* of Judge Schreber (see introduction).

One symptom of Judge Schreber was his belief that Dr. Flechsig, his principle medical doctor, wanted to commit soul murder on him (Schreber 1903, chapter II, 22–32). He also reported on his narcissistic grandiosity. Thus, he believed that he was becoming a woman to marry God so as to create a new mankind. Many of us want to marry a nice person, but it does not have to be a god. Many of us want children, but they do not have to become a new mankind.

Less grandiose, but still narcissistic, is Judge Schreber's report on his reaction to his observation that Dr. Flechsig often lied to his patients to make them feel better. Judge Schreber writes that Dr. Flechsig should have known that these white lies could not deceive an intelligent person like himself (Schreber 1903, 35). A further example of Judge Schreber's grandiosity was Schreber's confession that he was very disappointed when Dr. Flechsig told him—intending to give Judge Schreber a compliment—that Schreber was the best seer of all centuries. Schreber retorted that it should at least have been the best seer of all millennia (Schreber 1903, 77).

For our purposes, it is important to note that there were also linguistic disturbances in Judge Schreber's behavior. He claims that different words mean the same thing (Schreber 1903). Here we can refer to Jacques Lacan, a

French twentieth-century psychiatrist and psychoanalyst. Analyzing James Joyce, Lacan points out that he seemed to have a peculiar attitude toward words. Instead of using sounds merely to refer to something, Joyce seemed to pay special attention to the pleasure he took in the sounds of the words themselves. He experimented with words by slightly changing the sounds of the words to get extra pleasure.[9, 10] Joyce thereby violated a fundamental rule a speaker must accept to use language as an instrument of communication: The speaker has no choice in what sounds to use for a word. If one wants to talk about a chair, one must use exactly the sound corresponding to the word *chair*. One cannot say, "I want to talk about what others call a chair, but I like better the sound 'chais' or 'chis.'" If you want to use language to talk about a chair, you must pronounce the sound for chair as your community, as community, has agreed. Judge Schreber—or rather the birds in Schreber's mind—and also James Joyce violated that fundamental rule of communicative language.

With schizophrenics, we observe a second and subtler difficulty in the way they relate to language. We are all able to use metaphors while still being understood. By using a metaphor, we often succeed in getting our message across even better than if we'd just said what we meant literally. Thus, we could say to a friend who is afraid of doing the right thing that he lacks courage; however, we might be more forceful and tell our friend that he is a "chicken." In telling my friend that he is a "chicken," I do not mean to tell him that he is actually a "chicken"—that he has a beak or feathers. Curiously enough, by being told that he is a chicken, my friend gets the point.

Schizophrenic people cannot deal with metaphors. This is illustrated by a previously reported case in which a schizophrenic patient came to her therapist one day and said that she had no hands. "How do you know?" the therapist asked. "My father told me," responded the patient. "What did your father tell you?" inquired the therapist. The patient answered that her father had told her that she was "handicapped." Thus, this patient experienced the metaphoric description as a real description. For the schizophrenic person, language does not refer to the world or my experience of the world. Language is the same as the world. If people say that I am handicapped, then I have no hands.

A third linguistic symptom, as observed in Judge Schreber, was the fact that he heard voices. However, the voices only said half-sentences, like, "Now I shall . . ." (Schreber 1903, 217–18). Judge Schreber reports that he felt compelled to complete the sentences. If he did not, he had the delusion that God would think he was losing his energy, and God would not approve of this. Schreber thus feared that God would withdraw his energy from him, and he would thus die, if he did not complete the sentences.

However, Schreber was not just supposed to complete the sentences as it pleased him. Schreber had to complete the sentences as the voices wanted them to be completed. And in the aforementioned example, the voices wanted Schreber to say, "Now I shall resign myself to being stupid" (Schreber 1903, 218). If we compare that with Schreber's anger when his doctor called him the best seer of all centuries, claiming it should have been the best seer of all millennia, here we discover that the voices expect Schreber to self-describe himself as totally different than he believes himself—the expected self-description being much inferior to the one Schreber himself held to; however, in giving the voices such a power over his self-description, Schreber is in a curious situation. It is Judge Schreber, who, on penalty of death—as God will otherwise withdraw his energy for Schreber—is expected to say the completed sentence about himself. The content of the sentence he is expected to say is false and humiliating for him. But it is not the voices who say the humiliating sentence to Schreber; it is Schreber himself who is expected to say the humiliating sentence. Schreber is thus in a situation in which he must self-describe himself falsely and humiliatingly, thereby fulfilling the wishes of others. This is self-alienation, which has its origin in the power of social referencing.

Here we see that Judge Schreber is in this humiliating position because he is in the same psychological position of the children I describe in the beginning of this chapter. He, like the children, is unable to self-describe. Just as the children look to their mother when asked about themselves, Judge Schreber feels forced to depend on the voices to describe himself. This comparison allows me to hypothesize that the problem of the schizophrenic or the psychotic is that they are stuck in the same position as the child. The schizophrenic has not acquired the full development of the human mind. His or her development has stopped.

COMPARISON OF ONE SYMPTOM OF SCHIZOPHRENIA WITH ONE PHASE IN CHILD DEVELOPMENT

I will now reflect on the psychological structure of children. Human babies are totally dependent upon a mothering figure, much more so than other animal infants. Still, human babies have a nascent consciousness. And, for any conscious being, total dependence is dangerous and thus unacceptable. If I imagine being in an accident that would totally paralyze me, my first reaction is that I could pay someone to take care of me; however, babies have no money. When we, human beings, are confronted with a totally unacceptable situation and can do nothing about it, we start fantasizing. A student receiving a bad grade might fantasize that next time around she will study hard and get an A. Similarly, we are justified in assuming that a child who is in the unacceptable situation of total dependence upon another will need to find a solution in his or her fantasy.

There is evidence that the child creates two fantasies. The first fantasy is that the mother is omnipotent. One indication for this hypothesis is that teenagers do develop criticism of their parents; however, when a friend utters the exact same criticism of their parents, they are very upset. These teenagers show that they cannot tolerate any criticism of their parents. They feel the need to maintain that their parents are perfect. The fantasy that the mother (the parent) is perfect (omnipotent) guarantees that the mother (parent) can protect the child. If the mother is not perfect and not omnipotent, then the child is not safe. But the child is not certain whether the parent will care for him or her even if the parent is capable of doing so. This is where we hypothesize that the child needs to create a second fantasy. The child must imagine that she is everything the mother could wish for. If the child does create this fantasy, then she is certain that she will be cared for. Combined with the first fantasy, the child may be certain that she will be cared for efficiently. Children possessing these two fantasies will flourish.

However, when the child starts crawling and later walking, the child can get away from the mother. She can even get into the neighboring room. When she then falls and is hurt, the mother is not there immediately to help the child. But according to the child's two fantasies, the mother should be there immediately. The mother is omnipotent and should be motivated to help the child because of the child's fantasy that she is everything the mother could want. Consequently, the child must now develop a theory as to why the mother was not there immediately. To imagine that the mother is not omnipotent is too dangerous; therefore, we need to analyze the second fantasy.

The child can suppose that she is not everything the mother wants. For that hypothesis, the child has a possible remedy. The child can actively start to look for what the mother wants. The child can then try to become what she thinks the mother wants. And indeed, we can see that in families where a mother wants her child to always be neatly dressed and not help at the sink or splash water, after some time, the child does not often go to the sink to play with water. On the other hand, in a family where the mother shows great interest in having her child help with dishes even if the child splashes water, we see that after a while the child loves to go to the sink and clean dishes and splash water. Children look for what the mother wants them to do and be.[11]

We hypothesize that Judge Schreber was in the same emotional and psychological position as these children. Children do not originally have the ability to create their own desires. Children look to the mother to see what she wants from them. We can even go a step further. Mothers and parents often expect things from their children that the children do not want to do. It is true that sometimes the children protest, but oftentimes children surrender to the wishes of the parents and in this way become civilized. Having to look at what the other wants and forming yourself according to their wishes and expectations is a form of self-alienation. Even if it normally produces the beneficial result that the child becomes civilized, it nevertheless is a form of self-alienation.

As we mention earlier, Judge Schreber tells us in his *Memoirs* that he experienced the symptom of hearing voices telling him the first half of a sentence. Judge Schreber then had to complete that sentence according to the wishes of the voice; however, the content of the sentence was about him and was the opposite of what he wanted to say about himself (Schreber 1903, 216–17). This is a situation of self-alienation. We now understand that the psychic structure of the personality of the schizophrenic patient is a very human structure. A schizophrenic person has not fully accomplished the many steps a mind has to go through to be a mature human mind. One thing is clear: If the consciousness of a schizophrenic person is characterized by lack of maturity, it cannot be called a devilish structure, as was thought in Medieval Europe (Kemp and Williams 1987). Also, the schizophrenic person is not just someone who has a deformed brain. Rather, the schizophrenic person's psychic development has stopped. This is evidenced by a use of language that is more typically observed in young children. Thus, the schizophrenic has the same psychic structure we find in pre-Oedipal children.

At least two questions remain. The first question concerns the breakdown of the schizophrenic person. What is it that makes a childish psychic structure break down and give rise to a psychotic structure that includes the creation of delusions? We will not answer this question here.[12] But we will answer a second question: How is it that most of us grow out of this childish structure and develop the ability to speak, using the first-person pronoun, in an authentic way, whereas children and schizophrenic people define themselves by what others want?

The short answer to this second question is the Oedipus complex. After the no-saying period at about 15 months, the child starts to be able to differentiate emotionally between different adults. At that point, the child is able to realize that the mother has an interest in another person, mostly the father. That experience challenges the two basic fantasies of the child. If the mother has an interest in a third person, then the mother must be lacking something and must not be perfect; however, even if the mother is not perfect or does not have everything, why isn't the child enough for the mother? The child might try to negate the experience of seeing that the mother has an interest in a third.

When the child is unable to deny the mother's interest in the third, the child experiences a deep narcissistic wound. The child realizes that he or she is not everything to the mother. But children are resilient. Realizing that the father draws the interest of the mother, the child tries to figure out what it is in the father that is of such interest to the mother. Of the many things that the child sees in the father, he or she must choose a mark, in Lacanian terms, a signifier, that the child feels is of such interest to the mother that the mother prefers the father rather than the child. Having made this choice, the child then identifies with that chosen mark in the father and makes it the basis for his or her own identity. The child, however, knows that he or she does not yet possess the mark that is identified in the father. Hence, children at that age create a split in their own personality. They create an ideal for themselves but at the same time know that they have not reached that ideal. Hence, children at that age become willing to work, start developing patience, and make the future the most important dimension of time; however, one thing is certain: Children in that move identify an ideal for themselves. They are able to do what Judge Schreber and other schizophrenic patients are not able to do. They have learned to choose who they want to be. They can act on their own cognizance and can try to become who they want to be.

APPLICATION

Palle Villemoes developed a successful treatment method for schizophrenic people that includes the rule of not asking patients questions (Villemoes 2002, 647). Villemoes thus understood what we have been arguing for in this paper—that is, schizophrenic people have not yet developed the ability of self-description. The ability of self-description is the mark of human psychic maturity (Izcovich 2017, 140). Help for the psychotic person must take this deficiency into account and start at the place where they can be helped.

NOTES

1. We make use of the translation by Ida Macalpine and Richard A. Hunter of Schreber (1988), *Memoirs of My Nervous Illness*.

2. Schreber refers to his becoming a woman positively, negatively, and neutrally. Negatively, he refers to becoming a woman as "unmanning": (Schreber 1903, 293. See 54, 59, 94, 98, 127–28, 177, 219). Positively, Schreber refers to his status as being a woman by claiming that, "By divine fertilization offspring will issue from my lap" (Schreber 1903, 293). A similar claim is made in the footnote on page 4. (Also 124, 139, 177, 178.) Neutrally, Schreber simply references the experience of having female characteristics (Schreber 1903, 87, 139, 149, 178, 180, 196, 233, 274–82, 293).

3. Schreber 1903, 52, 127, 289, 293.

4. Schreber 1903, 210–12. Schreber gives as examples, among others: Santiago = Carthago; Chinesentum = Jesum Christum. Schreber is here pointing to a rule of unconscious association theorized about by Lacan when he argues that the unconscious makes connections based on metonymic similarity of words and not on logical connections between the ideas captured by the words. Schreber explains his attitude by the influence that miraculously created birds had on him. Interestingly, Schreber also states that the miraculously created birds "do not understand the *meaning* of the words" (Schreber 1988, 210). Schreber thus presents his birds as following the rules that later Lacan ascribes to the unconscious.

5. Schreber gives as examples "reward in the reverse sense for punishment, poison for food, juice for venom, unholy for holy, etc." (Schreber 1903, 13).

6. The definition of social referencing is as follows: "Social referencing refers to the process wherein infants use the affective displays of an adult to regulate their behaviors toward

the environmental objects, persons, and situations." Matthew J. Hertenstein, "Social Referencing," DePauw University, https://www.depauw.edu/learn/lab/publications/documents/infant%20development/2010_Infant_development_Social_referencing.pdf (downloaded January 13, 2018).

7. Benveniste 1971, chapters 20 and 21.

8. In the psychoanalytic literature, since Margaret Mahler, the ability to individuate is linked to the ability to separate and referred to as separation/individuation (Mahler, Pine, and Bergman 1975). In Spitz 1957, we find documentation that the great achievement of separation leads to the creation of the first clear univocal concept in the development of the child: the word "no."

9. Similarity in sounds had an emotional effect on the birds in Schreber's mind. Thus, Schreber writes that the similarity in words creates surprise in the birds and "makes them forget the rest of their mechanical phrases, and they suddenly pass over into *genuine* feeling" (Schreber 1903, 168).

10. Lacan 2006, 74–75. Lacan writes, "Joyce écrit l'anglais avec ces raffinements particuliers qui font que, la langue, anglaise en l'occasion, il la désarticule" (74). Lacan also gives examples used by James Joyce, for example, "eftsooneries" constructed from "after soon" (75). D. Tubridy, in his article "'In His Second Mouth Language': Joyce and Irish Poetry," refers to "Joyce's virtuouso [*sic*] linguistic performances." "In His Second Mouth Language: Joyce and Irish Poetry," *Credo*, http://search.credoreference.com/content/entry/wileycjaj/in_his_secondmouth_language_joyce_and_irish_poetry/0 (downloaded January 13, 2018).

11. Lacan states this explicitly when he claims that the desire of the child is originally the desire of the (m)other (Lacan 1981, Seminar XI, 235).

12. Lacan refers to the appearance of an "A-father" in the life of people with such a psychic structure as the cause of the psychotic breakdown (Lacan 2006, 481[577]). I understand this to mean that at one point the "A-father" occupied an emotional place that was maternal in nature. Then at some point this person took a stand that can be interpreted as a paternal function (e.g., impose a prohibition or apply a rule).

Part IV

Lacan's Concept of "Paternal Metaphor" Applied to Schreber and Hölderlin

Chapter Eleven

Reflections on the Concept of "Paternal Metaphor" at the Occasion of Lacan and Schatzman's Analyses of Schreber

For Lacan, psychosis is explainable by the foreclosure of the "paternal metaphor," by which Lacan means that the mother failed to show respect for the "Name-of-the-Father."[1] Consequently, the child was not invited or forced to restructure itself in a way already described by Freud. Niederland and Schatzman argue that Judge Schreber's symptoms can best be explained by the sadistic treatment of Schreber Jr. at the hands of his father.

In this chapter, I maintain the validity of Lacan's interpretation of the case of Daniel Paul Schreber, and I confront the challenge presented by Schatzman's book *Soul Murder*.

PART I: "PATERNAL METAPHOR" AND PHALLUS

In Webster's unabridged dictionary, the word phallus has three meanings: 1. A representation or image of the penis as the reproductive organ, worshipped as a symbol of generative power, as in the Dionysiac festivals of ancient Greece. 2. The penis or clitoris. 3. In psychoanalysis, the penis during the period of infantile sexuality. These three definitions juxtapose and thus confuse different levels of meaning. The confusion becomes evident when one sees that in definition two, phallus can be either the penis or the clitoris, whereas in definitions one and three, the phallus is exclusively the penis. Furthermore, in definition three, the phallus represents the penis only during the period of infantile sexuality. One might wonder what happens with the penis after infantile sexuality.

Another way of highlighting the confusion is to compare definitions one and two. In definition one, there is talk about a "representation or an image of the penis . . . worshipped as a symbol of generative power . . . in . . . festivals." "Phallus" is thus a concept that labels a product of the imagination, a psychic product: a representation. Furthermore, that psychic product, a product of the imagination, is worshipped because it is a symbol of generative power; however, generative power is both a male and a female attribute. This last remark puts forth the question of sexual equality or inequality at the level of imagination. In definition two, "phallus" refers to both male and female physical sex organs, but one of them, the clitoris, has no generative function, which was the central element in the psychic representation of definition one.

Many of the confusions can be clarified by introducing an explicit distinction between the psychic and the physical referent of the term *phallus*. Let us first draw attention to the complexity of the problem by quoting a footnote that Freud added in 1924, to his *Three Essays on the Theory of Sexuality*, originally published in 1905. Freud had described the phases of development of sexual organization and named them the oral, anal, and genital phases. In 1905, Freud wrote,

> The only difference [between infantile genital sexuality and the final form taken by sexual life after puberty] lies in the fact that in childhood the combination of the component instincts and their subordination under the primacy of the genitals have been effected only very incompletely or not at all.[2]

The footnote of 1924 reads,

> I myself modified this account by inserting a third phase in the development of childhood, subsequent to the two pregenital organizations. This phase, which already deserves to be described as genital, presents a sexual object and some degree of convergence of the sexual impulse upon that object; but it is differentiated from the final organization of sexual maturity in one essential respect. For it knows only one kind of genital: the male one. For that reason I have named it the "phallic" stage of organization. According to Abraham, it has a biological prototype in the embryo's undifferentiated genital disposition, which is the same in both sexes.[3]

Freud introduces the label "phallic phase" for what he used to call the genital phase with the argument that the child "knows only one kind of genital: the male one." The supposed knowledge of the child is different from the anatomical reality. Not satisfied with such a divergence, Freud quotes Abraham to the effect that in the embryo the "undifferentiated genital disposition . . . is the same in both sexes"; however, this reference to Abraham reduces the word *phallus* to a concept referring to an archaic state of affairs.

It thus tends to lose all validity. Indeed, one gets the impression that in the development from embryo to child, the genital anatomy has become differentiated, whereas the word *phallus* still holds on to an undifferentiated genital anatomy. Freud once again falls into the trap of taking the physical as the ultimate referent, whereas the real referent of "phallus" is a psychic representation.

One way to restore legitimacy to the word *phallus* is to see that human beings approach sexuality and sexual difference in at least three different ways. The first way, in our culture, is easiest to explain. It is the anatomical approach where such words as penis, vagina, and clitoris are used. A second and third way of talking about sexuality is more difficult to explain. It concerns sexuality as it takes on human meaning. Bruno Bettelheim, in his *Symbolic Wounds*, argues that preliterate man tried to master his fear and envy of woman by ritual circumcision or incision. In an article entitled "Phallus and Feminine Sexuality," Camille Laurin writes about the ancient Greeks and their veneration of the phallus:

> In this distant period, the erect phallus symbolized sovereign power, magically or supernaturally transcendent virility as opposed to the purely priapic variety of male power, the hope of resurrection and the force that can bring it about, the luminous principle that brooks neither shadows nor multiplicity and maintains the eternal spring of being. The ithyphallic gods Hermes and Osiris are the incarnation of this essential inspiration.[4]

Clearly, here we are dealing with the psychological meaning of sexuality. This domain includes both the concept of female penis envy[5] and the theory that an envious male tries to overcome his fear of inferiority by ritual incision or circumcision.[6] In Lacan's theory, the idea of an envious male recedes into the background. In that same psychological domain of meaning, Freud introduced some other surprising and astonishing ideas, for example, the fear of castration, the wish of the murder of the father, and the postulation of the killing of the primal father. Lacan's effort was to clarify the Freudian interpretation of the psychological meaning of sexuality by means of the philosophies of Georg Wilhelm Friedrich Hegel and Martin Heidegger, the anthropology of Claude Lévi-Strauss, and the linguistic theories of Ferdinand de Saussure and Roman Jakobson.[7] That effort resulted in the introduction of two distinct psychological meanings of sexual life—one that could be called imaginary and one that could be called symbolic.[8]

Two clinical vignettes further clarify these new Lacanian concepts. The first is an autobiographical account written by a psychoanalyst.[9] He writes that at the age of 18 months he suffered terribly from his father's sudden departure for the war. He had been particularly close to his father, who had taken almost maternal care of him during a grave illness. To console her son in his grief caused by his father's absence, his mother gave him a picture of the departed father, which the son piously kept in his bedroom, close to his bed. When the father returned from the war a year later, the child categorically refused to recognize the bearded, thin, and dirty man who appeared on the doorstep of the house as his father. The boy ran to his bedroom; took the picture, which he had kept there all that time; and ran to his mother screaming, "This is my father." The author writes that nothing has been able, not even his analysis, to make him accept that the man who returned from the war and lived with him and his mother was the same man in the picture. In this vignette, the imaginary father, who exhibited maternal qualities in his care of the sick child, dominated so much that a picture became an obstacle to the boy's acceptance of a flesh and blood father as his psychological father. What would have allowed the author to accept his father? What function of the father was the author refusing to acknowledge in adhering so closely to a picture, in adhering so closely to an imaginary father?

The second symbolic meaning is exemplified clearly in the case of Paul, reported by Julia Kristeva. Paul came to Kristeva after a hospitalization in St-Anne: "He was a man of sober appearance, precise in speech, and capable of telling his story in a skillful and charming way." But his words were a facade to cover up an "uncommon and almost incommunicable" drama in his life. Tragedy had struck Paul at age four, although Paul's focus on this tragedy was itself covering up a difficult early childhood. The tragedy involved "his father, a high official in the French colonial administration." He was "brutally tortured and murdered while his family watched" (Kristeva 1987, 13ff). I agree with Kristeva's comment that such an event by itself may be sufficient to destroy a life.

In the case of Paul, there was even more. A year before, at the age of three, Paul had discovered his mother, who he adored, with a lover. Kristeva mentions that Paul had an extraordinary close relation with his mother. "It bordered on identification . . . [and] was almost cannibalistic." The mother reacted to being found out violently, threatening, "If you say anything, I'll never speak to you again." Kristeva interprets this event as the mother's threat to "withdraw her love if . . . [the child chooses] a symbolic alliance with the father." At the heart of the prohibition of the symbolic alliance with the father is the mother's interdiction to speak. In giving in to the mother the son committed, according to Kristeva, the "first explicit murder of the father" (Kristeva 1987, 13ff); however, what father was murdered here? Not the father of flesh and blood; that occurred only a year later. Not the imaginary father, which involves a personal image created by the child that may even alienate him from the father of flesh and blood. To see which father was murdered in the case presented by Kristeva, we need to see that sexuality is connected with human commitment and compact. Sexuality as it is tied to a pact is what Lacan means when he speaks about the symbolic order. The father murdered by Paul is thus the symbolic father.

However, what is the symbolic order? For Lacan, that order is a human ordering and thus follows the laws of any human ordering. An entire school of French (Parisian) thinkers has opted to identify language as the model of human ordering and linguistics as the science par excellence of human affairs.[10] One idea that was generally accepted about language as an ordering system was that it works with binary oppositions, that is, with differences.[11] It remained for Lacan to give this idea a specific psychic dimension. Binary oppositions or differences require cuts.[12] They are the opposite of what Freud called the "oceanic feeling" typical of the infant's relation with the mother (Freud 1930, 64–65, 72) or the sense of limitless protection that is implied in the words "longing for" or "belonging." This oceanic feeling is what is aimed at by phantasies or images. For that dimension, Lacan reserves the concept of the imaginary. Clearly, from this point of view, the symbolic order presents itself as an ordering that will conflict with the imaginary. The symbolic order will impose frustration, privation, and castration.[13] Why should such an order that imposes all these negative consequences be accepted? The psychoanalytic answer (i.e., the Lacanian answer, which claims to be a conceptualization of the Freudian position) is that it is a way out of the impossible contradictions of the imaginary ordering.

PART II: "PATERNAL METAPHOR" AND PSYCHOSIS, OR THE TRANSITION FROM THE IMAGINARY TO THE SYMBOLIC

Lacan gives the most extensive presentation of his concept of "paternal metaphor" in "On a Question Prior to Any Possible Treatment of Psychosis."[14] I argue for a phenomenologically acceptable interpretation of Lacan's theory of "paternal metaphor" in "Phenomenology and 'Paternal Metaphor.'"[15] Let me present a summary of my reinterpretation of Lacan.

The child tries to solve its total dependency upon another, primarily the mother, by means of a false view of itself and that other. The technical Lacanian label for that false solution is the "imaginary order." Lacan connects the imaginary with the psychic development of the child by means of one of his most popular concepts: the mirror stage. In his first presentations, he grounded the mirror stage, and thus the imaginary order, in the biological fact of the premature birth of the human baby and thus the biological given of human dependency. Indeed, for Lacan, the "anatomical incompleteness" of the human brain in the newborn baby results in "signs of uneasiness and motor uncoordination of the neonatal months" (Lacan 2006, 78 [97]). Seeing herself in the mirror allows the baby to apprehend herself as a visual unity contrary to the fragmentation she is actually experiencing.[16]

In his "On My Antecedents," Lacan explicitly rejects the biological foundation of the mirror stage and accepts a kind of Heideggerian, and thus a philosophical, justification (Simiu 1986). The imaginary is a first and false response to the task of *having to be*. For Lacan, the correction to this false solution is the "paternal metaphor." This solution can be given a mechanical and purely linguistic reading: The imaginary phallus is replaced by a symbolic phallus in the unconscious of the child. As radically unconscious, this process happens to the child or it does not. If it does not, the child, while growing up, can witness the collapse of its false solution to the human condition. That collapse will occur in the form of an eruption of psychosis.

I object to this purely linguistic and mechanical interpretation. One must recognize that the child is an *active participant* in the process, even if the child *does not know the significance of its activity*. Whether one interprets the Oedipal structure as *forcing* the child, or rather as *inviting* the child to make the correction to its false solution, it is the child who *does the correcting*. It is the child who makes the moves—moves Lacan teaches us to call the "advent of the 'paternal metaphor.'" Of course, the child makes the moves only in response to a structure presented to her. One can therefore appropriately call the structure a necessary condition for the "paternal metaphor." Yet, that does not exclude the possibility—or even, from another point of view, the necessity—of allowing for the active participation of the child. That active participation of the child is captured in the Freudian terminology "ideal ego" and "ego ideal." Prior to the Oedipus complex, the child creates an ideal ego. It is narcissistic. In Lacanian terms, it is "imaginary." Because of the Oedipus complex, the child changes its ideal ego into an ego ideal. An ego ideal requires that the child accept distance, time, and thus the future as project. With this acceptance must come the acceptance of possible failure, and somehow the child must *do the accepting*.[17]

The question remains as to what is metaphorical in the correction that the child executes in this acceptance. Here, the difference between Lacan and my reinterpretation becomes clear. For Lacan, the metaphoric character of the "paternal metaphor" consists of adding to the imaginary interpretation of the phallus a new signification. The signifier phallus thus has two layers of meaning. According to Lacan, the new signification attached to the signifier phallus opens the way for the child to see symbolic, metaphoric meanings. Otherwise, the child is condemned to stay with the first layer of meaning, that is, the literal one. In summary, for Lacan, what is metaphorical is the fact that the signifier phallus has two layers of signification in the unconscious. According to my interpretation, "metaphorical" refers to the child's capacity to change its self-definition and accept that, notwithstanding its radical change in self-conception, it still can see itself as self-same. This move can be called metaphorical because it is the equivalent (at the psychological level) of the definition of metaphor: synthesis of identity and difference. This synthesis is naturally an *act of the child*.

Depending upon one's prior view, one might look at my reinterpretation as consistent with Lacan's view and thus as simply clarifying or specifying the general suggestions contained in Lacan's writings; however, one might look upon my interpretation as shifting the emphasis so much that it contradicts the general drift of Lacan's theory.

Since writing the paper on the psychological interpretation of the "paternal metaphor," I have discovered at least one possible objection to my reading. My interpretation requires that the child be able to feel itself to be identical to its prior self, even though it has accepted a radical change. It is possible that Lacan wanted to interpret the Oedipus complex as a radical cut, as a form of death that produces such a change in the personality of the child that it cannot feel any identity with its own prior self. The empirical observation of radical amnesia concerning the pre-Oedipal stage is evidence for such a lack of identity bridging the Oedipus complex. I concur that there is indeed a serious break, but I like to maintain that it is not a break that is so radical that no form of remembering and retrieval of the pre-Oedipal period can be said to occur.

PART III: "PATERNAL METAPHOR" AND THE FUNCTION OF THE FATHER

Joseph Lyons argues that because Lacan's theory of psychosis is built upon his concept of "paternal metaphor," it is invalidated by the argument presented by Schatzman in *Soul Murder*—an argument that is, in turn, based upon the research of William Niederland. The implied thesis of Schatzman, explicitly adopted by Lyons, is that the

> content of Schreber's hallucinations and delusions conforms perfectly to the known evidence concerning what his father did to him when he was a child. . . . Schreber's father was himself a nut. He was a small-time educator, [who] for his own nearly psychotic purposes . . . tortured his children with instruments of his own devising.[18]

I reject the explicit thesis of Lyons, the implicit thesis of Schatzman, and perhaps also that of Niederland.[19] Before offering the reasons for this rejection, I will summarize, in the most forceful and charitable way possible, Schatzman's argument.

Schatzman's explicit thesis is that there are "two sets of facts—the son's bizarre experiences as an adult and his father's techniques of educating children," and that the first set of facts is "an image or a transform" of the second set (Schatzman 1973, x).[20] He asserts that this thesis offers a better interpretation of Judge Daniel Paul Schreber's experiences than the interpretations of both the judge himself and his doctors. Schatzman thus explicitly rejects the interpretation given by Judge Schreber of his experiences as "supernatural revelations." He also rejects the doctors' interpretation of them as "symptoms of mental illness" (Schatzman 1973, xi). Schatzman warns us, however, that he will not focus "on why, but on how Judge Schreber came to feel persecuted; not on what caused his feelings, but on events that can be correlated with them" (Schatzman 1973, x–xi).

Correctly, Schatzman says about his effort, "I offer no polished model for understanding people called schizophrenics" (Schatzman 1973, 10). Unfortunately, Schatzman does not adhere to his own announced limits. Thus, immediately after announcing this methodological constraint, he claims that "his [Schreber's] father had taught him [Schreber] as a child patterns of operating upon his experience such that later on he felt forbidden to see that his strange relation to God was a reexperience of his childhood relation to his father." He furthermore accepts as true the thesis that "odd experiences and actions of some schizophrenics can be rendered intelligible as responses to maddening families" (Schatzman 1973, xi). Applying this thesis to the case of Judge Schreber, Schatzman writes, "I find it painful to imagine living with him [Judge Schreber's father] and terrifying to think of growing up in his household" (Schatzman 1973, 10).

In the chapter following this confessional remark, Schatzman presents two events that he considers terrifying for a developing child. One of those terrifying conditions is the fact that the father demands the child's total obedience, is willing to break the child's own will, and thinks that this is justified as a means to foster freedom in the child. Schatzman gives as evidence a number of quotations from the publications of Schreber Sr.

> Our entire effect on the direction of the child's will at this time will consist in accustoming it to absolute obedience, which has been in great part prepared for already by the applications of the principles laid down previously. . . . The thought should never even occur to the child that his will could be in control; rather should the habit of subordinating his will to the will of his parents or teachers be immutably implanted in him. . . . There is then joined to the feeling of law a feeling of impossibility of struggling against the law; a child's obedience, the basic condition for all further education, is thus solidly founded for the time to come. (Schatzman 1973, 17, quoting Schreber Sr.)

Or,

> The most generally necessary condition for the attainment of this goal is the *unconditional obedience* of the child. (Schatzman 1973, 18, quoting Schreber Sr.)

Or,

> If the child has been led in the first stage of development [before one year old] along the path towards habituation to unconscious obedience, so now [after one] is it timely and indispensable for the attainment of the noble aim of upbringing, that this habit should be gradually raised to an act of the free will, that obedience is conscious. The child should be trained . . . to noble independence and full strength of his own will. The transition is much facilitated by previous habituation. (Schatzman 1973, 18, quoting Schreber Sr.)

If signs of rebellion are obvious in the child, Schreber Sr. offers further advice:

> In the case of nearly every child, however, even the most well-brought-up, there are sometimes surprising manifestations of defiance or rebelliousness, although if the discipline has been good these should occur only rarely—a vestige of that *innate barbarity* that leads the developing *self-confidence* astray. This mostly happens towards the end of the second year. The child suddenly and often quite surprisingly refuses what until now he has most willingly given—his obedience. This could be caused by anything—the most important thing is that the disobedience should be *crushed* to the point of regaining complete submission, using corporal punishment if necessary. (Schatzman 1973, 19, quoting Schreber Sr.)

Schatzman concludes that obviously Judge Schreber's father must be "ruled by a wish to oppress, or a fear of not oppressing, children" (Schatzman 1973, 19, quoting Schreber Sr.).

The second terrible condition in Schreber's educational method, according to Schatzman, is the close connection that Schreber was able to establish between his authoritarianism and God. Schatzman offers as evidence a letter written by Judge Schreber's sister, Anna, as summarized and quoted by Niederland:

> She [Anna] describes in it in some detail how everything in the Schreber home was *Gottwärts gerichtet* (oriented towards God), how God was present in their childhood world at all times, not merely in their daily prayers, but in all their feeling, thinking, and doings. She concludes the letter with the words: "All this was finished with the sudden death of our beloved father." (Schatzman 1973, 13, quoting Niederland)

And Schatzman quotes Schreber Sr.:

> It is just as well that these youngsters learn to appreciate at an early stage that every human being is duty-bound to accept that everything that transcends the realm of his own power rests upon the dispensation of a Higher Hand. (Schatzman 1973, 14, quoting Schreber Sr.)

Schatzman is now ready to draw conclusions from these terrible educational methods, and he writes,

> If a child's father is his God, and if he learns that everything that transcends his own power rests upon God, then his father's power over him increases even more. I propose (as Freud did) that the author of the *Memoirs* transfigured the father of his childhood into the God of his "nervous illness." Throughout this book I display links between the father's probable behavior toward his son and the son's strange relations with God. (Schatzman 1973, 14)

And more generally, Schatzman concludes,

> Schreber's entire madness is an *image* of his father's war against his independence. He is never free of coercion by what he thinks are external spiritual powers. However, he never connects the coercion with his father. A reason why might be that his father [probably unawares{*sic*}] masked the source of control by defining the state of being controlled by parents as *self*-control. (Schatzman 1973, 20)

Contrary to Schatzman's claim that he is only going to describe Schreber's illness, not give an explanation of why he is ill, I see in the aforementioned material a clear attempt to give a reason, a why, for the mental illness of Judge Schreber. Schatzman himself must consider this material an explanation. He tries to make precise what he considers crucial in the following text:

> Dr. Schreber's [the father's] system implies a contradiction between where it trains a child to look for instructions and where it trains him to *think* he looks. It teaches the child to expect an external authority to instruct him ("the habit of subordinating his will to the will of his parents or teachers" must be "immutably implanted in him"), but also teaches him to see himself as "self-reliant" and "self-determined," i.e., as the origin of his instruction. (Schatzman 1973, 21)

Schatzman then continues,

> Certain experiences of the son in his "nervous illness" can be seen as an ingenious attempt to deal with the contradiction. God watches, dictates, or condemns his every move, all day, much as his father seems to have done. The son feels God and God's "rays" to be at once outside *and* inside himself. He sees them with his "*bodily eye*" when I keep my eyes open and with his "*mind's eye*" when my eyes are closed by miracles or when I close them voluntarily. (Schatzman 1973, 21)

This is too rationalist an explanation. One can agree that, in his hallucinations, Judge Schreber deals with the material of his childhood. It does not explain why that material creates the need to hallucinate to deal with that material. In fairness to Schatzman, one could say that he does give a reason: Schreber Sr.'s educational system has an internal contradiction. But such an argument overlooks two classical requirements of psychoanalytic explanation. It locates the cause of mental illness in the faculty capable of dealing with secondary processes (i.e., contradiction), rather than in the faculty dealing with the primary processes. Second, it locates the cause of mental illness exclusively in the relation between father and child rather than in the triangle father–mother–child. From a philosophical point of view, this argument requires that the consciousness of the child be necessarily identical with what is taught to that consciousness, or that a consciousness is incapable of seeing by itself and on its own strength the truth or falsity of a set of propositions.

The truth of Schatzman's explanation thus would require a conception of consciousness that makes it passive and devoid of native capabilities regarding the determination of truth; however, a view of truth that implies that consciousness cannot know the truth undermines the very definition of truth, insofar as any definition of truth requires a judgment and thus some conscious awareness. Thus, a view of truth that makes consciousness totally passive is performatively inconsistent.

Of course, systematically breaking a child's will must be debilitating. I am not disputing that Schatzman is right in designating this the area where something wrong is occurring. I am disputing the reason that Schatzman gives for why what is wrong is causing mental illness—that is, the presence of a contradiction in an educational approach.

That Schatzman's explanation of the cause of psychosis is too rationalistic is confirmed by two conjectures he makes with reference to the explicit thesis of the book—that is, that many of Judge Schreber's symptoms are transforms or images of actual childhood experiences.

Schatzman makes the first conjecture in connection with the so-called punishment board. This is what Schreber Sr. advises:

> In families . . . a quite effective means of education is a punishment board, which is to be stuck upon the wall of the children's room. Such a board would list the children's names and against them every committed misdeed: All ever so little signs of omission, all instances of insubordination, would be chalked up by a tick or by a remark. At the end of each month everybody would assemble for the hour of reckoning. According to what transpired, reproach or praise would be assigned. If one or other of the children had shown some recurring faults or weaknesses, particular mentions would be made of these. It is indeed surprising what moral effect such a board has on the children, even the less naughty and more indifferent ones. This is so, because the board is constantly in front of them, because every misdeed that has been committed remains as a sort of *permanent* visual warning in front of their eyes for a considerable period of time. By this method many otherwise necessary educa-

> tional steps, reminders, corrections, and punishments need not be applied and can be replaced in a far more efficient manner. (Schatzman 1973, 28–29)

One of the symptoms Judge Schreber suffered was the "writing-down-system." He wrote the following about this symptom in his *Memoirs*:

> Books or other notes are kept in which for years have been written down all my thoughts, all my necessaries, all the articles in my possession or around me, all persons with whom I come into contact, etc. . . . I presume that the writing down is done by creatures given human shape on distant celestial bodies . . . but lacking all intelligence; their hands are led automatically, as it were, by passing rays for the purpose of making them write down, so that later rays can again look at what has been written. (Schreber 1988, 119)

> The writing-down-system . . . became a mental torture, from which I suffered severely for years and to which I am only slowly getting a little accustomed; because of it, I had to endure trials of patience as they have probably never before had to be borne by a human being. (Schreber 1988, 122–23)

According to Schatzman, the writing-down-system is the "re-experiencing" of the punishment blackboard (Schatzman 1973, 29); however, contrary to his own stated methodological restrictions, he ventures beyond showing the similarity between elements of Schreber's childhood experience and elements of his symptomatology. Schatzman writes,

> The son changes their [the events] venue from his family of origin to a celestial context; his father's punishment board has become God's "writing-down-system." Why did he do it? Had he not replaced "my father himself" with "God Himself" as the source of the "system," he might have been seen as resentful but not, at least in this regard, as mad. . . . The son, probably still "habituated" and governed by his father's former responses to his "self-will" may have found it more forbidden to resent him than God. (Schatzman 1973, 29)

Clearly, this is a very rationalistic explanation in that it supposes that someone center is capable of overseeing everything. It is rationalistic also in that the crucial factor for Schatzman is seeing or understanding, while the vicissitudes of desire are pushed into the background.

Let us address the content of Schatzman's book that respects the limits he explicitly sets himself—that is, correlating two sets of data. On the one hand, there are the things that father Schreber does to his children. On the other hand, there are the symptoms described by the son in his *Memoirs*.

We can rescue from our previous discussion one such correlation. The childhood experience of the punishment board is presented in Judge Schreber's symptom called the "writing-down-system," which refers to his impression that all his thoughts are written down on distant celestial bodies.

A second example is found in the son's complaint concerning "miracles of heat and cold," which he claims are "daily enacted against him . . . always with the purpose of preventing the natural feeling of bodily well-being" (Schatzman 1973, 259, 33). Corresponding to the son's symptom is the father's theory, which he presumably put into practice, "starting about three months after birth cleansing of the infant's skin should be cold ablutions only . . . in order to physically toughen up the child" (34); "cold baths are the accepted rule after four or five years old" (Schatzman 1973, 34). In a PhD dissertation concerning Dr. Schreber, Alfons Ritter (1936) claims that the elder Schreber put his theory into practice because in the Schreber family there was one strict rule: One got up very early, did some gymnastics, bathed, and swam before starting work. Occasionally during the winter, the ice had to be broken first. Father Schreber even wrote a book: *The Cold-Water Healing Method.*

Schatzman further correlates Judge Schreber's assertion that little men were opening and closing his eyelids with his father's theory that recommends a number of practices for the health of the eyes, including the proper alternation between looking near and far, the spraying of the eyes with cool water, and repeated visual exercises.

Schatzman gives three further impressive correlations.[21] Still, correlation is not explanation, and symptoms must get their material or content from somewhere. Schatzman is in accord with psychoanalytic thinking when he traces the content of symptoms back to childhood; however, there were probably many children who received cold baths and got up early and swam in water, the ice of which had to be broken first.[22] Must we conclude that all those children had to produce the hallucinations that Judge Schreber produced as a method of appropriating those childhood experiences? Or can we imagine that some became capable of swimming in cold water, that others started to paint or write about water, and still others simply expressed or felt resentment toward their parents about the cold-water treatment? That treatment, as with all the other childhood experiences, may become material for hallucination if there is a sufficient cause for psychosis. The correlations that Schatzman presents do not exclude, but rather require, such an explanation.

It is true that Schatzman's work poses explicitly the question of the role of the father in the creation of psychosis. Another Lacanian concept, the concept of the barred subject, will allow us to specify that role. Indeed, for Lacan, the father who represents the law and is thus able to promote the "paternal metaphor" is himself a barred subject. Father Schreber is not a barred subject. He is an omnipotent father who presents himself as the law. He does not represent the law.[23]

Lacan's theory of the "paternal metaphor" gives us a conceptual map that is different from Schatzman's model for explaining psychosis. Lacan's theory explicitly widens the explanatory domain from the father–son relation to the triangle mother–father–son.[24] For Lacan, it makes a crucial difference whether the mother introduces or does not introduce the child to the "Name-of-the-Father."[25] Schatzman's account implies that the analysis of the father–son relation is sufficient to account for the psychosis of the son; however, Schatzman's work can be used to introduce a clarification in Lacan's theory. The correction is that even if the mother introduces the child to the figure of the father, the father might try *to be the law* rather than *represent the law*. In that case, the child is invited to make a false correction to its illusionary solution. How false that correction is and how it impacts the constitution of the subject is another question.[26]

CONCLUSION

Let us recapitulate the results of our study.

1. The concept of the phallus has an ambiguous relation with the physical dimension of sexuality. On the one hand, it would be false to separate the concept of phallus from all connection with sexuality and make of it a purely psychological category. The lesson of psychoanalysis is that the constitution of subjectivity as it is discussed by means of the concept of the phallus is, in an essential way, connected with the mystery of sexuality. On the other hand, the concept of the phallus is not an anatomical concept in that it overlooks the anatomical difference between the sexes. The concept of the phallus must, therefore, be understood as a psychological concept. It is a concept by which one locates oneself with reference to the desire of another. This raises the question of whether the phallus is the only possible psychological concept that could connect the constitution of the subject to sexuality in an essential way.
2. Schatzman's model, however intuitively appealing, has several shortcomings. It disregards two requirements of psychoanalytic explanation: It attempts to explain hallucination by means of the faculty proper for the secondary processes, and, because of this, Schatzman's model restricts the analysis of the cause of hallucination exclusively to the father–son relation, excluding the third, here, the mother. Schatzman's model makes the philosophical mistake of presupposing a consciousness (that of the child) that is unable to make judgments regarding truth by itself. But truth requires judgement, and thus Schatzman works with a conception of truth and consciousness that is performatively inconsistent.
3. The confrontation between Lacan and Schatzman has the advantage of forcing us to point to a cause of psychosis that has its origin in not

only what the mother does or does not do (referring or not to the "Name-of-the-Father"), but also what the father does or does not do. There is thus a function of the mother and the father. Lacan's theory, and especially its mathematical formulation (Lacan 2006), gives the impression that there is only one relevant function or role to be played: the role of the mother referring to the "Name-of-the-Father." Such a reading of Lacan makes his theory one among a group of theories attributing the cause of psychosis exclusively to the mother. It is important to correct such a one-sided theory whether the one-sidedness is the result of Lacan's theory itself or Lacan's failure to clearly delineate the different alternative interpretations of his theory and explicitly indicate which one he favored or which one is, simply, a misinterpretation. Of course, we would like to know more about the differences between the functions that the mother and father must normatively perform for the well-being of the child; however, this would lead us to the work of Vergote.[27]

NOTES

1. The crucial function of the concept of "paternal metaphor" in the theory of Lacan becomes evident when we note its connection to other crucial Lacanian concepts, for example, the phallus, the "Name-of-the-Father," foreclosure as the mechanism of psychosis, the imaginary, and the symbolic.
2. Freud 1905, *Three Essays on the Theory of Sexuality* (S.E. vol. 7), 199.
3. Freud 1905, *Three Essays on the Theory of Sexuality* (S.E. vol. 7), footnote 2, 199–200.
4. Laurin 1964, 15. Quoted from a translation of Laplanche and Pontalis 1988, 313.
5. For a good survey of the problem of penis envy, see Laplanche and Pontalis 1988, 302–4.
6. A summary of Bettelheim's thesis can be found in his book *Symbolic Wounds*, 1962, 18–23.
7. For an elucidation of the influences on Lacan's thought, see Muller and Richardson 1982, particularly the introduction, 1–25.
8. For a brief definition of these two terms, see Laplanche and Pontalis 1988, 218, 439–41.
9. Peraldi 1984, 41.
10. For an interesting survey of the breadth of the structuralist movement, see Ducrot and Wahl 1968.
11. Saussure 1959, 120: "Everything that has been said up to this point boils down to this: In language there are only differences. Even more important: A difference generally implies positive terms between which the difference is set up; but in language there are only differences *without positive terms*."
12. Cuts are required in psychoanalytic technique precisely when imaginary identifications want to establish that oceanic feeling. This is one way Lacanians defend the right and the duty of the analyst to cut the time of the analytic session.
13. Here Lacan can build on not only the Freudian term *castration*, but also the term *Versagung*, most often translated into English as "frustration." See "frustration" in Laplanche and Pontalis 1988, 175.
14. We build on the overview of the argument, a mapping of the text and explanatory notes for Lacan's essay available in Muller and Richardson 1982, and a philosophical digest of the arguments in chapter 4 of De Waelhens 1978. Also relevant is Allison et al. 1988.

15. Simon Silverman lecture, given at Duquesne University, Pittsburgh, 1988. Here incorporated in the introduction.

16. Lacan 2006, 78 [97]. See also Ver Eecke 1983, 114–26, here incorporated as chapter 7.

17. Giving the child an active role in the Oedipus complex might go a long way toward removing the validity of Sartre's objections to Freudian psychoanalysis as formulated in his "Existential Psychoanalysis" from his *Being and Nothingness* 1966, 682–704.

18. Silverman lectures, Duquesne University, 1988, "Commentaries and Discussions, VI Annual Symposium, 1988," 27.

19. My rejection of Lyons's (and Schatzman and Niederland's) thesis is not based upon a rejection of the historical facts presented by Niederland and used by Schatzman and Lyons. I reject the theoretical explanation of the facts as presented. For a correction of the historical facts as given by Niederland and Schatzman, see Israël 1989, and Lothane 1989 and 1992. I have not done the work to see if my reinterpretation of the concept of "paternal metaphor" can accommodate the facts about the life of Schreber as presented by Lothane. Lothane stresses the effect the roles of females (mother, aunt, and elder sister) had on Judge Schreber. My reliance on the work of Aulagnier, Mannoni, and Spitz forced me to give an important direct role to the mother in the explanation of schizophrenia. See Ver Eecke 1984, chapter 2, 45–84.

20. See also Schatzman 1973, 7.

21. First, in Judge Schreber's hallucination there is an "inability on the part of God to learn by experience." "A long time ago I formulated the idea that God cannot learn by experience" (Schatzman 1973, 24–25). Schatzman correlates this with the fact that "Dr. Schreber talks everywhere of parents changing children, not of parents learning from children. The channel of effects is one-way" (Schatzman 1973, 24). Second, there is "Dr. Schreber's method of teaching a baby self-denial [by setting] . . . up a hierarchy by which he applies his power upon the nurse to apply hers upon the baby. Only the baby is denied everything." Schatzman correlates this with the following hallucination of Judge Schreber: "In his 'nervous illness' many years later [he] experienced 'a hierarchy of powers in the realm of God.' He may have been re-experiencing the hierarchy of powers in the realm of his father" (Schatzman, 57–58). Thirdly, there is the symptom of Judge Schreber's stomach. He writes in his *Memoirs*, "For a time, the miracles were in preference directed against my stomach," and "I existed frequently without a stomach." Schatzman correlates this hallucination with the father's practice of specifying "in detail what children up to seven years should eat and drink at each meal, what they must never eat or drink, when they are and are not allowed to drink water, and how often and at what times meals should be." Schatzman interprets the father's habits as follows: "The father demands that a child disobey the child's natural desires to eat. The son may be re-experiencing his father's assaults against his appetite [when he hallucinates about his stomach]" (Schatzman, 58–59).

22. Actually, my father told us the story of how the soldiers in the Belgian army were to wash themselves with snow in the winter. It is true that the soldiers were not children.

23. Lacan 2006, 482–83 [579]: "Further still, the father's relation to this law must be considered in its own right, for one will find it in the reason for the paradox whereby devastating effects of the paternal figure are found with particular frequency in cases where the father really functions as a legislator or boasts that he does . . . all ideals that provide him with too many opportunities seem to be at fault, to fall short, and even to be fraudulent—in short, to exclude the 'Name-of-the-Father' from its position in the signifier."

24. In his theory of the "paternal metaphor," Lacan reduces the function of the mother to respecting or refusing to respect the "Name-of-the-Father." Spitz, Aulagnier, and Mannoni teach us that the relation of the mother to her own body and her own sexuality determines her relation to both her child and the "Name-of-the-Father." This theoretical insight creates an opening to incorporate the historical claims made by Lothane about the direct influence of female figures on Judge Schreber (Ver Eecke 1984, chapter 2, #6, 70–78).

25. Lacan 2006, 482 [579]: "But what I do want to stress is that we should concern ourselves not only with the way the mother accommodates the father as a person, but also with the importance she attributes to his speech—in a word, his authority—in other words, with the place she reserves for the 'Name-of-the-Father' in the promotion of the law."

26. Vergote (1976, 108) defends the thesis that for a boy, depression finds its origin in a defective role of the father. In the words of Vergote, "The father in question contradicted the symbolic function which is required of him, i.e., to represent the law."

27. See, for instance, Vergote and Tamayo 1980, 185–204.

Chapter Twelve

The Concept of "A-Father," or the Psychological Origin of Mental Breakdown in Schreber and Hölderlin

Lothane's writings on Schreber present us with new facts, but they also challenge many older interpretations of Schreber's illness. In this chapter, I use the new information provided about Schreber by Lothane to address one theoretical point about psychosis: the breakdown. I use a Lacanian framework to interpret the psychotic breakdown.

THE LACANIAN MODEL

Lacan, like most analysts, differentiates the cause from the occasion of the psychotic breakdown. He calls the cause of psychosis the "foreclosure of the 'Name-of-the-Father.'"[1] He calls the occasion for the psychotic breakdown the appearance of an "A-father" (Lacan 2006, 481 [577]). This summary of the Lacanian model needs explanation. Foreclosure of the "Name-of-the-Father" roughly means the absence of the Oedipal triangle. Absence of the Oedipal triangle is more than fear, hatred, or even rejection of the role of the father. When there is fear, hatred, or rejection, then the father has a negative role in the emotional life of a person. Foreclosure implies a deeper form of absence of the father's function. We can develop a sense of what foreclosure of the "Name-of-the-Father" means by consulting a work by Jean Laplanche and J. B. Pontalis, two students of Lacan.

LAPLANCHE AND PONTALIS ON HÖLDERLIN

Laplanche and Pontalis studied the German poet Hölderlin. Even though Hölderlin talks a lot about the function of the father in his poetic works, he mentions his real father very little in his voluminous and very personal (even confessional) correspondence (Laplanche and Pontalis 1969).[2] His father died when Hölderlin was two. He was financially much better off than his mother, which indicates a marriage of love, at least on the part of Hölderlin's father. The style of living maintained by the new couple was more affluent than simple middle-class style. Hölderlin's mother apparently enjoyed this; however, the sudden death of her husband seems to have left her bewildered and unable to deal with the loss. Her permanent sadness indicates that the death of her first husband left a lasting wound. The poet's mother remarried when he was four, but his stepfather (who he refers to as his "second father") passed away when he was only nine. In a letter to his mother the poet shows that he was aware of his mother's basic sadness and a similar tendency in himself; however, Hölderlin differentiates his own sadness from his mother's. He writes,

> But you are not the one who gave me the inclination towards sadness. . . . I know very well when this tendency started. It was with the death of my second father, whose affection is for me unforgettable. At that point I experienced myself with an incomprehensible pain as an orphan. I also witnessed your sadness and the tears that you shed every day. At that moment my soul took for the first time that grave turn which has not left me and which has become stronger over time. (Laplanche and Pontalis 1969, 88)

Laplanche and Pontalis view this testimony as evidence that Hölderlin was able to mourn the loss of his stepfather but unable to reach beyond the stepfather to his original father. As further proof, Laplanche and Pontalis point to the fact that Hölderlin's father was a lawyer trained in Tübingen, where Hölderlin himself was a student. His mother was the daughter of a chaplain. In his early years at Tübingen, Hölderlin wanted to abandon his theological studies in favor of law. Hölderlin was unable to decide for himself and gave in to the demands of his mother. With resentment, he wrote a year later, "If I am still in the convent, it is because my mother has requested it" (Laplanche and Pontalis 1969, 88).

At age 24, Hölderlin left his place of employment at Waltershausen to go to Jena, where he experienced financial hardship and emotional isolation; however, he seemed to have had a purpose. He writes, "I thus returned to Jena in peace with myself in order to be independent, which I now enjoy being for the first time" (Laplanche and Pontalis 1969, 31).

At age 25, he suddenly moved back home to Nürtingen after writing for advice from his mother. He had been offered a well-paid position as a private tutor. He asked for advice by saying, "I have often had the opportunity to convince myself how salutary it was for me to follow your maternal advice" (Laplanche and Pontalis 1969, 49). Laplanche and Pontalis conclude that Hölderlin here falls back into a symbiotic relation with his mother after having tried to establish his independence. This led to a hurried departure from Jena, which Hölderlin's acquaintances did not fully understand (Laplanche and Pontalis 1969).[3]

Laplanche and Pontalis find their diagnosis confirmed by Hölderlin's attitude toward Schiller. Schiller took a liking to Hölderlin and received the young poet almost daily. He introduced him to his friends and acquaintances, including Goethe. He published several of Hölderlin's poems and recommended his novel to the publishing house Cotta (Laplanche and Pontalis 1969). Hölderlin experienced Schiller as a (maternal) father figure. He wrote to his mother, "Schiller really takes care of me in a fatherly way, such that I had to confess to this great person that I did not know how I deserved the fact that he took such an interest in me" (Laplanche and Pontalis 1969, 41–42).

In another letter, Hölderlin writes, "Schiller overloads me with his friendship and a really paternal care" (Laplanche and Pontalis 1969, 41–42). That this treatment meant much to Hölderlin is clear from a letter written to Schiller after his departure from Jena. In that letter, he writes, "If I see you only once a month, that would enrich me for years" (Laplanche and Pontalis 1969, 51). The relation to Schiller also deeply hurt Hölderlin, however. He felt like nothing compared to Schiller. Thus, in two different letters he writes, "Because I wanted to be everything for you, I had to tell myself that I was nothing for you" (Laplanche and Pontalis 1969, 50). Speaking of when he was late with a contribution requested by Schiller, Hölderlin writes, "Maybe you will not want it [my contribution] if I can only send it later. I belong to you—even if it be as a *res nullius*—; and thus also the fruits that I create" (Laplanche and Pontalis 1969, 57).

Crucial, according to Laplanche and Pontalis, is the moment when Hölderlin requests help from his friends and Schiller for starting a journal. Schiller responds with a "measured and motivated refusal, accompanied by a warning against the adventurous character of Hölderlin's project" (Laplanche and Pontalis 1969, 84). Hölderlin's biographer Beck reports that Hölderlin's reaction was totally out of proportion and was followed by a letter to Schiller full of excessive gratitude. Laplanche concludes that the pathological center is gathered around Hölderlin's almost delirious image of Schiller (Laplanche and Pontalis 1969, 84).

The dual or symbiotic relation that Hölderlin maintained with his mother is repeated with Schiller, but something new emerges in that relation. That new dimension has fatal consequences for Hölderlin's psychic structure: It necessitates a psychotic breakdown. That new structure is what Lacan called the "A-father," and it provokes a breakdown because Hölderlin's unconscious had not been transformed by the introduction of the "Name-of-the-Father." Laplanche and Pontalis call the deficiency in Hölderlin's psychic structure, which made him unable to deal with the new element, the "absence of absence" (Laplanche and Pontalis 1969, 125). It is, in other words, Hölderlin's inability to introduce distance into his emotional relations.

LACAN'S HUNCHES ABOUT SCHREBER

Lacan attributes the foreclosure of the "Name-of-the-Father" in psychosis, in general—and in Schreber, in particular—to the absence of a move by the mother (De Waelhens 1978). In psychotics (Hölderlin, for instance), the child remains within the field of the mother's desire because the mother does not introduce the paternal function. Two paragraphs in Lacan's writings suggest the possibility that the father might be the cause of his child's psychosis: if the father is a "nobody" or a megalomaniac (Lacan 2006).

When we look to the facts of Judge Schreber's case, as we know them, it seems implausible that Judge Schreber's mother did not show respect for her husband and thus did not introduce the "Name-of-the-Father." Indeed, Judge Schreber's sisters testify that their mother not only read Schreber Sr.'s books, but also proofread them (Lothane 1992).

As to the appearance of an "A-father" as the occasion for the eruption of psychosis, we must make a distinction between the two moments necessary for the construction of the "A-father" function. First, Lacan points out that Flechsig must have been part of the imaginary field of Judge Schreber.[4] Indeed, Judge Schreber writes in his *Memoirs*,

> The main point was that I was eventually cured (after a prolonged convalescence), and therefore I had at the time no reason to be other than most grateful to Professor Flechsig. . . . My wife felt even more sincere gratitude and worshipped Professor Flechsig as the man who had restored her husband to her; for this reason she kept his picture on her desk for many years. (Schreber 1903, 36)

Second, Lacan points out that the positive identification with or admiration for Flechsig is transformed into an attitude that assigns Flechsig a different position, called the position of the third. As his sole evidence, Lacan submits the "face of Judge Flechsig, with its scientist's gravity (Mrs. Macalpine's book contains a photograph that shows him profiled against a colossal enlargement of a cerebral hemisphere)" (Schreber 1903, 220–21).

By that shift in position, Flechsig becomes for Judge Schreber an "A-father." Lacan finds a confirmation for his claim in the fact that in his *Memoirs*, Judge Schreber constructs a delusional genealogy of Flechsig by means of "Schreber's own ancestors—Gottfried, Gottlieb, Fürchtegott, and, above all, Daniel—which is handed down from father to son and whose meaning in Hebrew he gives" (Lacan 2006, 482 [483]).

Schatzman's thesis that Schreber Sr.'s sadism resulted in Judge Schreber's mental illness and Niederland's research supporting this theory present a profound challenge to the Lacanian reading of Schreber;[5] however, the research of Lothane may be able to reintroduce with more sophistication the Lacanian theory of psychosis.

LOTHANE'S RESEARCH

Let me start by stressing that Lacan's theory is a dual-stage theory. There is a cause and there is an occasion.

The Cause of Judge Schreber's Illness

First, Lothane's research reintroduces the possibility of the mother's contribution to the *cause* of her son's illness. Lothane reports that even if the mother read and proofread her husband's publications, she also burned several unpublished manuscripts after his death.[6] Thus, the reading and proofreading of manuscripts during the lifetime of her husband, at best, could have been an ambiguous form of respect.[7]

Second, Lothane argues strongly that Schreber Sr. was not sadistic and that he even had humane qualities. Lothane entertains the possibility that the "authoritarian upbringing of the father and the ethos and etiquette of the times" were responsible for the "rage that Schreber has repressed almost completely" (Lothane 1989, 251). Lothane argues that cruelty on the part of the father is not enough. He claims that at the root of impotent and repressed rage lies the profound conflict between rebellion and love" (Lothane 1989, 251). Lothane returns to Judge Schreber's relations to the women in his life to clarify this problem.

The Occasion for Judge Schreber's Breakdown

Lothane's research clarifies the changing position of Flechsig in the emotional life of Judge Schreber. Flechsig was one of the new neuropsychiatrists who believed in the somatic origin of mental illness. He also wanted to make a name for himself by making use of medication. Flechsig thought that he could best establish his reputation by demonstrating that he could produce quick improvements. He established a strict deadline of six months for stays in his hospital. After six months, patients who were not on their way to recovery were sent to the state hospital.

Three facts were different about the state hospital compared with Flechsig's hospital: One could be sent there for life; one could lose, even permanently, one's right over one's own person; and, at death, the law provided that the bodies of mentally ill patients in state hospitals be subjected to an autopsy to make the final diagnosis. This was based on the belief that mental illness was an illness with an anatomical or physiological cause and therefore only an autopsy after death could give a final report. Flechsig had several brains in fluid in his office.

Lothane makes it clear that Judge Schreber was aware of the six-month deadline and its threatening consequences. No patient, and certainly not one as intelligent as Judge Schreber, would be ignorant of the meaning of the brains exposed in Flechsig's office. Furthermore, Judge Schreber wrote on the title page of his *Memoirs* that there were "Postscripts" and an appendix, dealing with the question, "In what circumstances can a person considered insane be detained in an asylum against his declared will?"[8] (Schreber 1903, 30, 38–39). *Flechsig's six-month deadline must have changed his emotional significance for Judge Schreber.* Flechsig was now the man who could decide to terminate the free life of Judge Schreber.

Lothane links the beginning of Judge Schreber's paranoid delusion to his awareness that Flechsig's six-month deadline would be catastrophic for him.[9] According to Lothane, Judge Schreber experienced this six-month deadline and the change it brought about in his relations with Flechsig as a betrayal.[10] It might be argued that it was, in fact, a betrayal. For Lothane, the experience of Flechsig's betrayal (real or not) provoked Schreber's delusion.[11]

MY INTERPRETATION OF LOTHANE'S RESEARCH

Flexible Interpretation of Psychotic Breakdowns

One line of interpretation is that the breakdown of a future psychotic is already predetermined if the Oedipal structure failed. According to this interpretation, the patient already has a psychotic structure and is only waiting for an occasion to break down.[12] The occasion may be puberty, which makes new demands upon the psychic structure, or it may be more personal, as with Judge Schreber. Schreber was deeply pained by the fact that he would probably not become a father after the sixth stillbirth by his wife. He was also overworked before his breakdown.[13] Finally, he held a paternal job (chief judge) when he was possibly profoundly ambivalent about paternal functions. De Waelhens's interpretation of Lacan's theory accepts this line of argument. De Waelhens gives no causal role to the occasion for the breakdown (De Waelhens 1978).[14] By stressing the contribution of Schreber Sr.'s behavior to Judge Schreber's mental illness, Schatzman must be supposed to take the same position.[15]

A second line of argument sees the occasion for the breakdown as causally contributing to the psychotic moment. The occasion is understood to contribute so much to the psychotic breakdown that the breakdown could have been avoided if the occasion had not arisen. A strong reading of Lothane's discoveries could claim that Judge Schreber's illness would not have deteriorated into delusion without a new major disappointment: the deep betrayal of Judge Schreber by a trusted personal psychiatrist.

A third line of argument, which I endorse, sees a dynamic relation between the cause and the occasion of the psychotic breakdown. The healthier a person's psychic structure is, the more traumatic an occasion will need to be to cause a psychotic breakdown. It may be instructive to compare the cases of Hölderlin and Judge Schreber. Lacan claims that when a male figure with a maternal function shifts to a paternal role, the psychotic breakdown is occasioned. That male figure then becomes an "A-father." The male figures that performed the role of the "A-father" for Hölderlin and Schreber were Schiller and Flechsig, respectively. Both Hölderlin and Judge Schreber first had a positive emotional relation with these male figures. What was required for these maternal male figures to become "A-fathers"?

In the case of Hölderlin, it was sufficient that Schiller showed a slight disinclination for Hölderlin's *project*. In the case of Judge Schreber, it was necessary that there was a *deep professional betrayal by Flechsig*. The psychotic breakdown required a much more traumatic occasion in the case of Judge Schreber than in the case of Hölderlin. The conclusion that the psychotic structure was more deeply inscribed in the personality of Hölderlin than in that of Judge Schreber seems warranted. Hölderlin really only needed an occasion. For Judge Schreber, the occasion functioned as a *second cause*.

The Dual Level Theory of Psychosis

A clear separation of the cause and the occasion suggests two different tasks for the therapeutic professions. First, there is the question of the cause and the early discovery of its presence. Second, there is the question of the occasion of the breakdown. Here again, the comparison of Hölderlin and Judge Schreber may be useful.

For Hölderlin, it would be the great poet Schiller who became the "A-father" and thus the occasion for the breakdown. Originally, Hölderlin related to Schiller, and according to Laplanche, to Fichte also, as messianic figures. That should have been a warning. In Laplanche's reading, it was enough that Schiller showed some slight reservation about one of Hölderlin's projects for him to receive a new function in the emotional life of Hölderlin. By that slight reservation, he became an "A-father," provoking the psychotic breakdown. *The slight reservation of Schiller was rational. Hölderlin could not deal with rational attitudes of people who occupied a messianic role for him*. All that the therapeutic community could have done was detect the cause before the occasion provoked the psychotic breakdown.

For Judge Schreber, it is his therapist who became the "A-father." Flechsig's successful treatment of Judge Schreber's first illness gives the psychiatrist a positive place in the emotional life of the patient. There is no indication that Judge Schreber attributed a messianic function to Flechsig in the same exaggerated way Hölderlin did to Schiller. For the admired Flechsig to become the "A-father" in Judge Schreber's emotional life, more than a slight refusal by Flechsig of one of Schreber's projects was required. Lothane connects the origin of Judge Schreber's delusion to the approaching six-month deadline set by Flechsig. Instead of continued responsibility for Judge Schreber's recovery, Flechsig would ship him off to a state asylum, with the possibility of permanent hospitalization and a mandatory autopsy of his brain for the diagnosis of his illness. Lothane points out that Judge Schreber most likely experienced Flechsig's six-month deadline as a *professional betrayal*. Lothane depicts this professional betrayal more as a *cause* than an *occasion* for Judge Schreber's delusion. In my two-stage theory of psychosis, that would mean that the *occasion itself* has a *causal impact*. The occasion could not have its causal impact if there had not been an original cause, however. Lothane seems to allow for such an interpretation of his research. He accepts the idea that the original cause is the "rage that Schreber has repressed almost completely. This is Schreber's character, and here Niederland and Schatzman are right: This character has been shaped by the authoritarian upbringing of the father and the ethos and etiquette of the times" (Lothane 1989, 251).

The research by Lothane seen in light of the two-stage theory of psychotic breakdown suggests that the Oedipal structure can be more or less inscribed in a person. The more the Oedipal structure is inscribed, the more serious an occasion must be to provoke a breakdown. For Judge Schreber, the occasion certainly had to be more serious than for Hölderlin. That occasion was not just a distancing (Schiller vis-à-vis Hölderlin); it took the form of a betrayal of trust (Flechsig vis-à-vis Schreber). It is appropriate to distinguish between these two kinds of occasions for mental breakdown. The first (taking distance) is but an occasion. The second (betraying trust) is a secondary cause. The therapeutic professional can raise great hopes in the mentally ill person and is therefore in a position to provide the secondary cause for mental breakdown.

Are there currently situations in which therapists can be imagined to betray the patient professionally in a way that is similar to what Flechsig did to Judge Schreber? I believe that the Tarasoff rule *legally requires therapists to betray their patients*.[16] Dynamic therapy requires the promise of honesty from the patient.[17] In return, the therapist promises confidentiality. Freud makes it clear that any exception to the promise of absolute honesty will lead to therapeutic failure.[18] He mentions a patient who was allowed to use his duty to keep state secrets and whose analysis therefore failed.[19] What must we expect as a consequence of a therapist violating confidentiality?

My understanding of the dual theory of psychosis makes me anticipate that reporting of criminal intentions to the police by therapists and the interrogation or arrest of the patient must, in some cases, be the occasion for mental breakdown (interpreted either as acting out and committing a crime, or as psychotic breakdown) because it is a betrayal. The reason for my anticipation is that betrayal transforms a trusted therapist into an "A-father" for a patient in whom the Oedipal structure is weakly inscribed.

CONCLUSION

Lacan believes that a person with a psychotic structure need not necessarily have a psychotic breakdown. Such a person might show some curious characteristics, as J.-A. Miller has shown; however, these characteristics do not constitute schizophrenia or psychosis. For schizophrenia or psychosis to break out, an occasion or, stronger, a cause must be present. Lacan called this an "A-father" figure, defined as a maternal kind of figure who at some point presents the patient with a paternal action or intervention. Schiller played that double role in the case of Hölderlin.

NOTES

1. Lacan 2006, chapter 12, in particular 464ff. [557ff.]. For clarifying comments, see De Waelhens 1978, chapter 4, and Ver Eecke 1988 and 1993 (incorporated respectively as chapters 4 and 12 in this book).
2. Laplanche & Pontalis 1969, 44. All translations from this text are my own.
3. Laplanche and Pontalis 1969, 49: "It was sudden and made a return to Jena difficult."
4. Thus, Flechsig must have had great emotional significance for Schreber.
5. Schatzman 1973, 10: "I find it painful to imagine living with him [Judge Schreber's father] and terrifying to think of growing up in his household," or "Schreber's entire madness is an *image* of his father's war against his independence."
6. Reported by Lothane in oral communication. See also Israël 1989, 126. "Anna [Jung née Schreber, Z. L.] also told Richter (1935) [Richter, G.: Report of a visit at 14/3/1935. Typescript. (Leipzig). p. 353] something of the effect her father's death had: 'After his death her mother, in her grief, destroyed everything that reminded her of him.'"
7. Another line of thinking could lead to the same results as Lothane's discovery of the burning of unpublished manuscripts. Indeed, what is required for establishing the Oedipal triangle is that in the eyes of the child, there is a desire for the father in the mother. Reading the manuscripts of her husband did not mean that Judge Schreber's mother was involved with her own desire in the person of her husband. If anything, Lothane's discovery suggests the opposite.
8. Schreber 1903, 30, 38–39.
9. Lothane 1992, 237: "[T]he florid delusions did not appear until months after Schreber's second admission to Flechsig's."
10. Lothane 1992, 238: "The relation between Flechsig and Schreber ended on a sour note." Also, "As the sixth-month deadline approached, Schreber's continued dependency on these two

people [his wife, Sabine, and his doctor, Flechsig] was becoming progressively more problematic."

11. In a written communication, Lothane provides further evidence. Lothane received a letter from Devreese, another Schreber scholar, the contents of which Lothane describes as follows: "Around the time of the commencement of soul murder, that is March or April of 1894, a notice appeared in a newspaper saying that Mr. Seyffert had been appointed as a judge at the Oberlandesgericht, replacing Schreber. The implication here is that since at that time Schreber was still seeing Flechsig, it meant that Flechsig was consulted about the patient's diagnosis and prognosis, to cover the decision by the Ministry of Justice. It proves again that Schreber was right when he said a Komplott [conspiracy] was underway" (personal letter of January 11, 1995).

12. Miller (2009) created the name "ordinary psychosis" for this prepsychotic phase.

13. Some even suggest that Judge Schreber feared that syphilis was the cause of the stillbirths. This, in turn, may have caused feelings of guilt.

14. See also De Waelhens 1978, 22, 137.

15. Schatzman 1973, 7: "My study is an attempt to connect the mind of an adult, considered mad, to his father's behavior towards him as a child."

16. Arras and Rhoden 1989, 121: Dissenting Justice Clark wrote, "Overwhelming policy considerations weigh against imposing a duty on psychotherapists to warn a potential victim against harm. While offering virtually no benefit to society, such duty will frustrate psychiatric treatment, invade fundamental patient rights, and increase violence. The importance of psychiatric treatment and its need for confidentiality have been recognized by this court. . . . Assurance of confidentiality is important for three reasons." This opinion was overruled by the majority, as expressed by Justice Tobriner (Arras and Rhoden 1989, 117): "Plaintiffs can state a cause of action against defendant therapists for negligent failure to protect Tatiana." Justice Tobriner's opinion results from the following facts: "On October 27, 1969, Prosenjit Poddar killed Tatiana Tarasoff. Plaintiffs, Tatiana's parents, allege that two months earlier Poddar confided his intention to kill Tatiana to Dr. Lawrence Moore, a psychologist employed by the Cowell Memorial Hospital at the University of California at Berkeley. They allege that on Moore's request, the campus police briefly detained Poddar but released him when he appeared rational. They further claim that Dr. Harvey Powelson, Moore's superior, then directed that no further action be taken to detain Poddar. No one warned plaintiff of Tatiana's peril."

17. Thompson distinguishes sharply the difference between the process of free association and the moral promise of telling the truth (1994, 167–70).

18. For a book-length study about the ethical dimensions in psychoanalysis, see William W. Meissner 2003.

19. Freud 1958, 135–36, n. 1. Reprinted as "Further Recommendations in the Technique of Psychoanalysis," in Freud 1963, 148.

Part V

Lacanian Reflections on Successful Talk Therapies with People Afflicted with Schizophrenia and Psychosis

Chapter Thirteen

A Lacanian Interpretation of Karon's Psychoanalytic Treatment of People Afflicted with Schizophrenia

In this chapter, I use Lacan's theory to clarify the success of a number of techniques and interventions with schizophrenics, proposed by the therapists with Michigan State University's Psychotherapy Project. To do so, I first point to a deficit in Lacan's theory, which I describe by means of arguments presented by Jozef Corveleyn and Antoine Vergote. In comparing Lacan's theory and a successful American practice, I focus on a publication by Bertram P. Karon and Gary R. VandenBos, two of the important therapists connected to the Psychotherapy Project.[1] I focus on both Karon's general advice and his practical techniques, and I ask the question as to whether Lacanian theory, as corrected by Corveleyn and Vergote, can explain the success of Karon's approach.

LACAN'S THEORY

Lacan presents his early theory of schizophrenia and psychosis in his famous essay "On a Question Prior to Any Possible Treatment of Psychosis" (Lacan 2006, 445–88 [531–485]). In this essay, Lacan also presents a theory of psychoanalytic practice. In particular, Lacan developed his schema L to clarify the necessary positions the analyst must take up in therapy (Evans 1996, 168–70; Lacan 1993, 14; Lacan 2006, 458 [548ff.], 859 [904]).

The presentation of Lacan's early theory of schizophrenia is the result of his reflections on Schreber's *Memoirs* (Lacan 1993; Lacan 2006, 445–88

[531–485]). In these reflections, Lacan stresses the great insights of Freud, but he also points out Freud's theoretical shortcomings.

Freud explains Schreber's symptoms, hallucinations, and delirium in terms of his troubled and ambiguous sexual identity (Freud 1911, 62–63). Schreber fantasized that he was becoming a woman, was going to marry God, and was going to conceive children with God. These children would then populate a new kingdom. Freud assumed that Schreber's sexual identity was his fundamental psychological problem. He then tried to show that Schreber's dozens of symptoms and hallucinations were the means used by Schreber to deal with this fundamental problem. Freud used a pedagogical technique to make his argument. He defined Schreber's psychological problem with his sexual identity as his inability to accept his homosexuality. He then translated the concept of homosexuality into a proposition: "I (a man) love another (man)." Freud was then able to claim that Schreber's inability to accept his homosexuality could express itself as attempts to deny any of the three crucial parts of the previous sentence (the subject, the verb, or the object) or as an attempt to deny the entire sentence (Freud 1911, 63–66).

If Freud succeeded in his explanation, then he could claim that Schreber's dozens of symptoms and hallucinations were reducible to four strategies or four series of symptoms. Denial of the verb leads to a persecution complex or paranoia. Denial of the subject leads to a complex of jealousy. Denial of the object leads to erotomania. Denial of the entire sentence was interpreted by Freud to mean, "I love only myself" (Freud 1911–1913, 65). Such a psychological attitude leads to megalomania; devaluation of the world, people, and oneself; and even the belief by Schreber that he himself was dead.[2]

Freud points out that Schreber's symptoms, hallucinations, and deliriums needed to succeed in not only denying his homosexuality, but also allowing him to satisfy those same homosexual desires using some disguise. Paranoia succeeds in this double task by providing arguments for hating the other (which makes love impossible) and, at the same time, being constantly preoccupied with that other (he could try to murder me, and, thus, I must constantly keep an eye on him).

Lacan underlines that Freud does not include in his brilliant explanation two broad categories of Schreber's symptoms (Lacan 2006, 463–67 [555–60]). Schreber hallucinated that his body was not solidly integrated and that, for instance, his stomach was, from time to time, taken away, just when he started to eat. Schreber also had hallucinatory experiences about language. He claimed to hear voices that started sentences that they did not finish. He felt compelled to complete these sentences as the voices wished, even though the sentences expressed embarrassing and untrue ideas about him. Lacan had to decide which of these two unexplained symptoms he should take as the central symptom. He chose Schreber's symptomatic relations toward language (Lacan 2006, 463–66 [555–60]). Lacan then faced the challenge of explaining Schreber's hallucinations about his body and the four other series of symptoms explained by Freud's theory in terms of his defective relation to language. Lacan tried to do this in his seminar on psychosis.

I will clarify Lacan's theory using his analysis of Schreber's hallucinations of the voices. Schreber felt obliged to complete the half-finished sentences about him, as the voices intended, even if those sentences described Schreber in a way that diverged from his own self-conception. On the one hand, Schreber wrote that he had been indignant when his therapist called him the "greatest seer of spirits of all centuries" (because he was convinced that he was at least the "greatest seer of spirits of all millennia") (Schreber 1988, 88 [77]). On the other hand, he found himself compelled to complete the sentence, "Now I shall resign myself to being stupid" (Schreber 1903, 172 [218]).

Such a hallucination reveals the unconscious structure of Schreber's personality. He allows himself to *be defined by the desire of the other*. This situation normally occurs in the pre-Oedipal period of the psychic development of the child. The child tries to deal with the terror of their complete helplessness by imagining that the mother is omnipotent and wants nothing other than the child. When the child experiences a situation in which the mother is not there to satisfy their needs immediately, the child must wonder why that is the case. According to the child's illusionary vision of the world, the child must imagine that the mother does not immediately satisfy their needs because she has interests other than the child. The child feels that it is no longer everything for the mother. The obvious strategy for the child is to inquire as to what it is that the mother wishes and then transform itself into that which he or she thinks the mother wants. Such a strategy is self-alienating and similar to the one described by Schreber in his auditory hallucinations. Schreber thus seems to be stuck in his pre-Oedipal relations, or he has regressed back to them.

The question to be asked about Schreber, then, is what structure did he fail to achieve? According to Lacan, Schreber did not succeed in incorporating the structural role of the father, which would have allowed him to escape the illusionary and symbiotic relation with his mother (Lacan 2006, 464–65 [557]). By showing respect for the name (or the word) of the father, the mother gives a double message to her child. She shows that she is not omnipotent and that the child is not everything for her.

After having first refused these messages, the child normally accepts them and draws the unavoidable conclusions. The child resituates itself. Instead of fantasizing that it is everything for an omnipotent mother, the child searches for a mark in the father that the child feels interests the mother. By identifying with this mark, the child develops an ego ideal that gives direction to its desire. As the child realizes and accepts that it is not yet identical with its ego ideal, but that it can approach that ideal with patience and work, the future starts to replace the present as the most important dimension of time.

Lacan emphasizes that this resituation allows the child to acquire metaphorical capabilities. Lacan's clarification of this claim consists of reminding us that psychoanalysis expresses the child's illusory idea (that it is everything that the mother can want) as follows: The child imagines that it is the phallus of the mother. By accepting an ego-ideal, the child renounces this illusion. The child is satisfied with being but a "shadow" of the father, who is the real phallus of the mother. For Lacan this means that the child gives to the signifier "phallus" two significations: first, the omnipotent phallus and, second, the shadow phallus. Hereby, the child has created the unconscious conditions for the psychic capability of understanding metaphorical language. One signifier has two significations that are not quite the same but not quite different either.

Lacan attributes still another meaning to the acquisition of metaphorical capabilities. The child's acceptance of their status as only a shadow phallus means that the child has accepted castration and also the prohibition of psychic incest with the mother. When the child incorporates the structural consequences of the "paternal metaphor," the child does not need to alienate itself in the hope of remaining the omnipotent phallus of the mother. When the child fails to accept their status of shadow phallus, they will experience at some moment that they are not, in fact, the omnipotent phallus they hope to remain. This may happen when someone appears in the emotional life of the person as an "A-father" figure (Lacan 2006, 481 [577]).

According to Lacan, that experience produces the feeling that the psychic body image is disrupted. Thus, Lacan explains the two series of symptoms that are not explained by Freud's theory. Lacan borrows Freud's explanation of Schreber's homosexuality with one important change: When a child holds on to the idea that it is the omnipotent phallus of the mother, it is not possible to make distinctions or differences relevant. According to Lacan, Schreber was not so much an active homosexual as someone who had not accepted finitude and was therefore unable to incorporate the aspect of finitude connected with sexuality and sexual difference.

For Lacan, schizophrenia is defined as the absence of the "paternal metaphor" in the unconscious of the patient. The "paternal metaphor" gives a person access to the metaphorical dimension of language. It also installs castration and the prohibition of incest. In so far as language possesses a metaphorical dimension, it also contains a form of prohibition and limitation. The subject needs to accept being a "shadow phallus." Lacan clarifies the dimension of finitude connected with the structure of language by calling upon the structuralist analysis of language (Evans 1996, 182–84). The structuralists demonstrate that language functions on the basis of differences;

however, appealing to difference introduces finitude. To speak thus implies for Lacan the introduction of finitude.

But Schreber could speak. He could write. He wrote a refined literary biography. Interestingly, Corveleyn and Vergote demonstrate that Schreber's *Memoirs* show two deficiencies. Corveleyn points out that Schreber's literary work creates a story that does not succeed in realizing the purpose of normal speech. In his *Memoirs*, Schreber does not succeed in presenting himself as a person like other people, with characteristics that other people could also possess (Corveleyn 1998, 204). Schreber presents himself as a person who is anything but a normal person. He is a man who loves his wife but is also becoming a woman. Furthermore, he is becoming a woman not to marry another human being, but to marry God. He will have children, but not as other humans do. Rather, Schreber will conceive children with God, and those children will form a new mankind. As such, Schreber will play the exceptional role of the patron saint of the new mankind.

Even in his suffering, Schreber is aware that he is exceptional. He feels that his stomach is taken away while he is eating. His food then falls into his thighs. He thereupon comments that such an event in normal human beings would lead to the food starting to rot; however, Schreber believes he has an exceptional relation with God's rays; he believes that God's rays purify the food in him and thus God will not permit the food to rot. Finitude, which is normally imposed by language on any speaker, was not imposed on Schreber. The language of Schreber thus suffers a fundamental deficiency.

Vergote, in turn, also points out that Schreber's *Memoirs* are an exceptional literary work. Vergote too points out that this literary work shows an important deficiency but a different one than that pointed out by Corveleyn. In his *Memoirs*, Schreber does not use metaphors (Vergote 1998, 242). Vergote then makes the following remark: To create a metaphor, an individual must possess two series of signifiers that differ substantially from one another. Vergote hypothesizes that the absence of metaphorical language in Schreber can be explained by the absence of radically different signifiers. Vergote points out that people afflicted with schizophrenia often construct a psychic "ego" in which the pleasure-body is excluded (Vergote 1998, 237). Thus, the schizophrenic loses access to the signifiers of embodiment. When the body is excluded from the psychic "ego," the person has, by definition, not appropriated the body. According to Lacan's theory, this is a task to be performed during the mirror stage. When a person has not traversed the mirror stage properly, there is a failure in the imaginary.

The critical remarks of Corveleyn and Vergote allow us to see that the structural deficiencies of the schizophrenic are more complicated than Lacan originally thought.[3] The schizophrenic is someone who suffers from a failure in not only the symbolic, but also the imaginary.

If the imaginary is defective and if the symbolic does not work properly, can one then expect that a symbolic, linguistic intervention alone will be able to help the schizophrenic? The answer seems to be no, since Corveleyn points out that the language used by a schizophrenic person is not capable of making him accept the pain of finitude (Corveleyn 1998, 204). For example, a particular therapist treated a gravely ill psychotic patient in a hospital. The patient wanted to leave the hospital. The therapist explained to the patient that she was very ill and that leaving the hospital was therefore ill advised. The intervention of the therapist contained a prohibition and arguments in favor of the prohibition. It was thus mainly a symbolic intervention. The patient left the hospital. The words of the therapist had no effect on the patient. The symbolic was ineffective.

LACANIAN INTERPRETATION OF KARON'S APPROACH

Let us now look at the therapeutic intervention of Karon and his colleagues. Karon describes a patient who constantly had terrible nightmares about his stepmother (Karon and VandenBos 1981, 198). He asked Karon if the nightmare would cease if he left the therapist and went and killed his stepmother. A pure symbolic intervention would have pointed out that to murder someone is legally and morally not permitted, and should therefore not be done. It is likely that such a pure symbolic intervention would have been as inefficient as the prohibition to leave the hospital in the previous case. As I see it, Karon's therapeutic intervention consisted of, first, making an imaginary move and, second, giving a symbolic prohibition. Let me first describe Karon's intervention and then later analyze it.

The patient told Karon that every night he had the same nightmare, in which his stepmother was beating him with a stick. Even when he awakened, he felt the beatings of the stepmother. After this story, the patient asked what would happen if he were to leave the therapist and kill his stepmother? Would the nightmares then cease? (Karon & VandenBos 1981, 198)

Karon asked the patient if someone had told him that it would be wrong to kill his stepmother. After some hesitation, the patient conceded that no one had told him so. Karon replied that someone must have told him that it was wrong. Karon again asked who had told him that it was wrong to kill such a bitch? He added that the old witch deserved to die for what she had done to the patient. Later, Karon repeated that each time a person is hurt by someone, that person develops hate and even the feeling of wanting to kill the one harming him or her. But, declares Karon, this is healthy (Karon and VandenBos 1981, 198).

Karon clarifies this part of his intervention by insisting that he wanted to diminish the patient's guilt concerning his aggressivity (Karon and Vanden-

Bos 1981). Karon claims that such a patient unconsciously wants to be punished. He wants to be told that he may not hate his stepmother (or he may not kill her out of hate). Such advice would prove that he is bad and his stepmother good. Karon maintains here and elsewhere that it is a fundamental strategy of gravely mentally ill people to make themselves look bad to maintain the illusion that their own mother is good.

From this clinical vignette, it is clear that Karon aims his intervention at transforming the imaginary of his patient. He justifies to the patient the reasonableness of his negative feelings. He helps the patient let his body become a container for his feelings so that he can own them. He undermines the phantasmic dimension of the imaginary (guilt feelings), which makes the acceptance of those feelings difficult.

Karon makes the following phenomenological comments. After Karon asked the patient who had told him that it was wrong to kill his stepmother, the patient reacted with surprise. After Karon assured the patient that his stepmother deserved to be killed for what she had done to the patient, he reacted by telling stories about the cruelty of the stepmother during his childhood. Karon finally gives a last reason for the first phase of his intervention. He writes that truly murderous patients do not hate consciously. Presumably, Karon is convinced that recognized (and justified) hate does not lead to murder.

After the patient reveals the cruelty of his stepmother, Karon starts the second phase of his intervention. He tells the patient, "The only reason not to kill her is that you will be caught. If you are prepared to die for her, then you must feel that she is more important than you. That, I feel is stupid. (But notice, I did not say that it would be bad). It would be stupid to kill her, but you certainly should want to kill such a bitch" (Karon and VandenBos 1981, 198).

Karon himself explains that this second intervention is an attempt to let the patient make the distinction between thoughts that are justified and actions that should be avoided (Karon and VandenBos 1981). To make a distinction and make a prohibition acceptable is, in Lacanian terms, making it such that the symbolic has a grip on the personality. Karon tries to introduce the symbolic only after performing work at the imaginary level.

I wish to describe a second vignette in which Karon makes the same double move with an extremely mentally disturbed person. The patient was hearing voices and seemed to be suffering from bodily hallucinations. The patient declared that there was something wrong with his head and that he therefore needed an operation (Karon and VandenBos 1981). Karon started by saying, "Of course there is something wrong with your head, if you hear voices" (Karon and VandenBos 1981, 186). As before, Karon mirrors and justifies the patient's experience. Here, too, Karon makes a second intervention that consists of making the patient accept something with reference to his own actions. He says to the patient, "The only operation you need is to talk to someone about your problems and about the reasons why you hear voices. Are you interested?" (Karon and VandenBos 1981, 186). The "difficult" patient relaxes, smiles, and says, "That sounds like a good idea" (Karon and VandenBos 1981, 187).

Again, the first intervention consists of mirroring the experience of the patient, and the second intervention can be described as an effort to make the symbolic effective. This time, too, the symbolic intervention was effective because the intervention was connected with a previous imaginary intervention.

Let us now approach the theory of Lacan from another angle. Lacan describes the position of the analyst in schema L (Lacan 1993, 14; Lacan 2006, 458 [548f.]). The patient uses the analyst to project on him an image of himself or herself and thus creates some kind of fusion with the analyst. In this way, the patient can feel that the analyst understands him or her; however, such an exchange is a superficial kind of talk because deeper layers of meaning are not uncovered; they are often not even touched upon.

One could imagine that the author of the first chapter of *The Psychopathology of Everyday Life* (Freud 1901) could have said to his analyst that he tried to recall the name of the painter of the "four last things" in the cathedral in Orvieto. He could not, however, recall the name Signorelli, and instead of the correct name, two other names appeared: Botticelli and Boltrafio. As an excuse, the author could have offered the idea that his memory was not so good anymore. If the analyst then replied that he too had noticed that his memory was fading, the patient would have succeeded with his imaginary projection. Both the patient and the analyst would have agreed that to forget is mainly, if not exclusively, the result of the biological fact that older people forget more and more. Such a conclusion would have covered up the deeper meanings of the specific forgetting uncovered by Freud, who, in this case, was both the analyst and the patient.

In the treatment of the neurotic, it is mandatory that the therapist move away from the imaginary position in which the patient tries to capture the analyst. The analyst needs to move to a symbolic position by, for instance, asking the patient what happened just before the patient tried to recall the name of Signorelli. Such a question, which avoids imaginary identification, allows for the emergence of the many and unexpected meanings hidden behind this particular act of forgetting, described by Freud in his first chapter of the aforementioned book. Consequently, the patient appears as not only someone who forgets names because he is getting older, but also a person who is concerned about his professional failure because one of his patients committed suicide.

In Lacanian terms, this means that the patient revealed a dimension of his subjectivity that was hidden by his ego-structure. The patient reveals this new dimension in reaction to the fact that the analyst moved from an imaginary to a symbolic place. In his commentary on Lacan, Bruce Fink summarizes Lacan's intention with his theory of schema L as follows: In the early 1950s, Lacan saw the goal of analysis to be the breaking of the imaginary relation to confront directly the symbolic dimension. In this conception, the imaginary and the symbolic are radically opposed to one another. The only dimension that heals is the symbolic one (Fink 1997, 34–35).

Fink uses Schaetzel's patient, Roger Bronzehelmet, to apply schema L to the therapeutic relation with the psychotic. For Roger, the paternal function was so absent that he looked for a new father. He created a new name for himself, made of the letters of his first name and the family name of his therapist. He wrote this new name on a piece of paper and considered it his birth certificate. He hid this paper in a hole in the foundation of his family home and covered up the hole. He enjoyed this activity.

When Roger recounted a dream in which he was sitting in a golden cage with roses and being looked at by his analyst, the analyst left the imaginary position imposed on him and took up a symbolic one—he gave an interpretation of the dream: Is it that you see the world as if you are in a golden cage full of roses and admired by your analyst? (Fink 1997, 104). The patient reacted with a psychotic crisis. According to Fink, the symbolic position of the analyst demands that the patient search for a deeper subjective dimension in himself; however, this deeper subjective dimension does not exist in a psychotic patient. There is only a lack, a big hole (Fink 1997, 105). The patient tries to cover this with a delirium. Taking up a symbolic position with a psychotic patient is thus dangerous.

PRACTICAL INTERVENTIONS OF KARON

General Comments

The analysis of the successful interventions of Karon allows us to support three conclusions. First, we can conclude that it is important to make the distinction between the imaginary and the symbolic dimension of a therapeutic intervention even in non-Lacanian approaches. Second, it is incorrect to claim that one has to fight the imaginary dimension to reach the symbolic one. We learned that the therapist can effectively reach the symbolic dimension only if sufficient and effective work has been done first on the imaginary level. Third, it is possible for the therapist to perform a symbolic function, which is healing, under the condition that one first build a successful imaginary relation.

First, in the advice given by Karon, the distinction between the imaginary and the symbolic appears in the following form: Karon points out that the therapist must find a way of justifying to patients their own feelings. As mentioned in a previous vignette, Karon is prepared to accept and even justify feelings of murderous hate in his patients. He names the feelings, which allows the embodied subject to become a container for these feelings and thereby able to own them. Karon, however, also recommends making the distinction between feelings and actions. The therapist must find an argument that will both justify the patient's feelings and make the action suggested by the feelings unacceptable. The latter can be described in Lacanian terms as an attempt to let the symbolic intervene effectively. Such a symbolic intervention makes a distinction and prohibits some things.

Second, in much of his advice, Karon recommends that the therapist cooperate with the imaginary. Sometimes, he explicitly advises not fighting the imaginary. If the imaginary absolutely needs to be fought, then it should be done with an argument borrowed from the imaginary of the patient. Thus, Karon does not contradict the patient who says that there is something wrong with his head because he hears voices and thinks that he needs an operation. On the contrary, Karon says that there must be something wrong with his head. He even agrees with the patient that he needs an operation. Karon does not present his symbolic interpretation to fight the imaginary of the patient. On the contrary, he presents his symbolic intervention as the continuation of the imaginary. Karon says that the only operation that the patient needs is one in which he talks with someone about the reasons why someone hears voices. The difficult patient relaxes, smiles, and says that this is not such a bad idea (Karon and VandenBos 1981, 187).

In another example, Karon explicitly advises therapists not to contradict the patient. In this case, the patient tells the therapist that the voice he hears is the voice of God. Karon says that if the therapist replies that the voice heard is not the voice of God, this intervention can provoke a violent attack on the therapist. God represents all that is good. To say that the voice is not the voice of God is interpreted by the patient as an attempt by the therapist to deprive him of God. Crusades have been organized for lesser insults, so declares Karon. The only time one can directly challenge a patient about the voice of God is when the patient reports that such a voice demands something terrible. The therapist can then say that he does not believe that God demands such a thing, since God is all goodness and that He therefore cannot demand something terrible (Karon and VandenBos 1981, 184). Thus, also here, the symbolic intervention is made by an appeal to the hallucination itself.

Third, the advice of Karon demonstrates that symbolic interventions with severely mentally disturbed patients can be successful and need not provoke a crisis. Thus, after having listened to stories about the voice of God, Karon recommends that one say something like, "I wonder if your mother used to say . . . [whatever it is that 'God' said]" (Karon and VandenBos 1981, 184).

Karon's Advice for Treating Schizophrenics

Karon recommends that the therapist quickly establish contact with the patient, that he must reassure the patient that he will not allow another to kill him (Karon and VandenBos 1981), that he must talk to the patient in a way that conveys he is experienced as someone who gives, and that he needs to understand the problematic of the schizophrenic as oral and his sexual problematic as pre-Oedipal. I will interpret these recommendations as means to deal with a defective imaginary of the patient.

That Karon's views of schizophrenics are compatible with Lacan's is indicated when he reflects on the false thinking process of the schizophrenic. He makes use of Lidz's concept of "egocentric overinclusiveness," defined as the schizophrenic's habit of believing that everything that happens is related to them and also that they can influence all kinds of things over which they have no realistic control. Karon reinterprets Lidz's concept by arguing that the life of a schizophrenic patient is not so much "ego-centric" as "parent-centric." The deficits of the patients are those that are necessary to compensate for the deficits of the parents (Karon and VandenBos 1981, 127). He points out two difficulties that schizophrenics may encounter in their family of origin.

The first occurs when a family accepts and attempts to satisfy the distorted needs of one family member—often the mother. The second occurs when both parents have distorted child-rearing ideals and cannot come to an agreement about those ideals. Thus, the children need to internalize a parental dispute. In the first case, one may suppose that the father figure declines to impose the symbolic law. Karon gives the example of a patient who claims that his mother is crazy and makes him crazy to save herself (Karon and VandenBos 1981, 352). Karon even reports the confession of the mother: "I'm so busy now I don't have time to worry about myself, but when he [her mentally ill child] gets better I'll have a nervous breakdown" (Karon and VandenBos 1981, 352).[4] In the second case, one may suppose that the parental disagreement destroys the mutual respect required for the father to exercise a symbolic function.

Karon's general advice to the therapist is to provide a protective environment. He and other authors describe such an environment as a good maternal environment (Karon and VandenBos 1981, 145). Karon uses three methods to create a protective environment. The therapist must present himself or herself as a person who exists and can become an object of transference. Practically, Karon has the habit of offering the patient a cup of coffee. Such a gesture, says Karon, is an offer of oral satisfaction without interpretation and demands. Most of the patients refuse the coffee, as they are too distrustful; however, they feel good being able to reject the offer. The rejection must come from the patient, not the therapist.

The therapist can also create a protective environment by eliminating threats. Karon claims that schizophrenics feel terrorized; therefore, it is important for the therapist to reassure the patient, if possible in the first treatment session, that she will not allow anyone to murder the patient (Karon and VandenBos 1981, 52. 153). This reassurance must then be repeated in concrete interventions. Thus, when a patient told him that the "Athenian girls are laughing at me. They say their breasts are poisoned," Karon answered that he was stronger than the Athenian girls and his milk was not poisoned. The patient asked for a first and a second glass of milk, and showed no further fear of milk (Karon and VandenBos 1981, 342).

A last method whereby the therapist can create a protective environment is for the therapist to appear to the schizophrenic as a giving person, giving even when talking (Karon and VandenBos 1981, 165). The therapist must appear to be someone who gives, not someone who takes. He must also appear to be someone who does not punish or poison (Karon and VandenBos 1981, 165). As already mentioned, Karon recommends offering the patient a cup of coffee at the start of a session. This giving attitude must then continue during the treatment. Karon does this in the advice he gives to parents and particularly to mothers. Sometimes, mothers are afraid to be too kind with their children because they fear that family members will not approve or think it will spoil their children. In such cases, Karon tells the mother that there is a distinction between short-term and long-term consequences. To spoil children creates nuisances in the short term, which can easily be overcome in the long term; however, too much deprivation or too much strictness can have long-term negative consequences. Thus, Karon advises mothers that when they are in doubt, it is better to err in the direction of kindness (Karon and VandenBos 1981, 131).

For Karon, the creation of a protective environment for the schizophrenic patient is not a purpose in itself. It is a condition to do further work. The further work consists of the therapist mirroring to the patient the feelings he has and the situations in which he finds himself. We have already seen that Karon even accepts and justifies murderous hatred (Karon and VandenBos 1981, 198). Karon defends this strategy in general by arguing that anger, fear, sadness, or joy always have a reason and are therefore justified (Karon and VandenBos 1981, 188). Naturally, it is possible for the patient to feel ashamed or guilty about these feelings. It is also possible for the patient to misinterpret their feelings. Karon's method consists of guessing what feeling the patient is experiencing—anger or fear, for instance—and making those feelings acceptable. He makes fear or even terror acceptable by being protective and saying in the first session, if possible, that he will not permit anyone to kill his patient. He makes other feelings, for example, anger, acceptable by neutralizing guilt in connection with those feelings and demonstrating that those feelings are reasonable given the patient's circumstances ("The old bitch deserves to die, for what she did to you. [. . .] Any time anyone hurts you, you hate them, you want to kill them. And that's healthy") (Karon and VandenBos 1981, 198). Such interventions echo the theory of Lacan, who insists that the first task of the therapist consists of being a mirror. Playing the role of mirror for the patient results in the patient's slow acceptance of their feelings, which they could not accept initially. The feelings can thus be accepted as part of the self, as part of the bodily ego, and can be put in the bodily ego, just as the flowers that were originally outside a vase can be put in the vase by the mirror in Lacan's optic model (Evans 1996, 130–31; Lacan 1988b, 109).

Karon also gives advice on how to help patients understand why they are in the situation they are in. Here, too, Karon uses a kind of mirroring technique. Karon claims that patients often have no difficulty seeing that other people who are not family members are mean to them (Karon and VandenBos 1981, 168). These patients often think that people react that way to them because of their thoughts. They are not aware, continues Karon, that people react negatively because of their own bizarre behavior. Such patients do not answer questions, or they react in a funny way. Karon recommends that one draw the patient's attention to their own behavior and explain to the patient that not answering other people when they ask a question is experienced by other people as an insult or the behavior of a crazy person. Crazy behavior frightens people, and frightened people often react in a mean manner.

In this intervention, Karon explains the threatening attitude of other people—they are mean—as the natural consequence of a feeling that the patient is familiar with: They are afraid. Karon then connects the well-known feeling with those patient behaviors that provoke the well-known feeling in others. In turn, the experience of these well-known feelings by others results in unpleasant, unreasonable, or mean attitudes. Mirroring is, thus, used to transform a passively experienced threat by others into a natural process familiar to the patient—a process of which the patient is the original cause. Karon hereby gives the patient the opportunity to experience himself as an active player instead of someone who undergoes the situation passively. The strategy of mirroring is used to create subjective possibilities for the patient. The creation of subjective possibilities points to the fact that Karon does not forget his symbolic function, even if he applies mirroring strategies.

Karon's subsequent advice may be considered a specification of the theory of Lacan, unless one keeps in mind Lacan's theory of object *a* (Evans 1996, 124–26). According to Karon, some mirroring strategies with schizophrenics must be explicitly oral to be effective. He affirms that the problems of schizophrenics are basically oral in nature, because they develop during the relationship with the mother in the oral period. Like Erik Erikson, Karon maintains that problems are not so much problems with the oral zone as they are problems with the relationships developed during that period. Karon believes that what was fought out psychologically in the oral relations also emerges in anal and genital relations (Karon and VandenBos 1981, 75).

Karon gives a dramatic example of an oral mirroring strategy. The patient had already been in treatment for a long time. Few facts in his history could account for his situation. His stuttering had started in high school. The first sign of mental illness appeared in the army. He was diagnosed with a venereal disease, with symptoms in his mouth. The next day, he attacked a stranger and almost choked him. He was dismissed from the army and regularly admitted to the hospital, each time because he attacked a stranger. After each hospital admission, he was dismissed in reasonably quick order, only to be again admitted after again attacking another stranger. In those attacks, he choked his victims until they were unconscious. He then released them before they were dead. Karon slowly learned that his mother had punished this person as a child by putting a cloth around his neck and then choking him. Karon's interpretation was that this patient was trying to prove that his mother did not want to kill him. He proved that by playing the role of his mother and used strangers to play his own role (Karon and VandenBos 1981, 36–37). Karon learned a second fact about this patient: he had been raped at age eight by his alcoholic father (Karon and VandenBos 1981, 37).

Next, Karon discovered a third fact. The patient stuttered a lot. The stuttering of this patient was not a normal stuttering. In a therapeutic session, the patient stuttered and spoke a couple of Latin sentences. Karon suspected that the stuttering had a traumatic origin, and he asked himself how this uneducated man of Detroit knew Latin. To a subtly introduced question as to whether he had been an altar boy, the patient replied, "You swallow a snake, and then you stutter; you mustn't let anyone know about it" (Karon and VandenBos 1981, 38). Karon suspected that the patient possessed enormous feelings of guilt in connection with a forbidden deed symbolized by the image of the snake. Karon used a mirroring technique to let this patient accept a supposedly forbidden act. He took away the feelings of guilt by making the act acceptable. Karon even pointed out that his intervention was verbalized in oral terms even if it concerned a genital problematic. He said to the patient, "I know you sucked the priest's cock, and it's all right. Anybody as hungry as you were would have done the same thing" (Karon and VandenBos 1981, 38–39). The stuttering stopped. Every time it reappeared, it could be stopped by repeating the intervention: "I know what you did with the priest, and it's all right. Anyone as hungry as you were would have done the same thing" (Karon and VandenBos 1981, 39).

According to Karon, a schizophrenic patient can accept an interpretation more easily if it is an oral one. Karon explains this by pointing out that the fundamental problem of the schizophrenic is connected with problems of the oral period, for example, survival, relations with others, integrity of the body, and identity (Karon and VandenBos 1981, 85–86). An illustration of this claim is, according to Karon, the presence in schizophrenics of the "draining fantasy." The oral dimension of this fantasy refers to lack of the provision of milk. The anal dimension refers to strategies of toilet training that involve laxatives and enemas, and give the child the impression that it loses control of its inner body. The genital dimension takes different forms with males and females. Schizophrenic males fear becoming drained by sexual relations. Schizophrenic females create the hallucination that the penis is a vacuum cleaner (Karon and VandenBos 1981, 86–87).

A clinical illustration of such a draining fantasy with a male is the case of a 20-year-old man who had several psychotic breakdowns, each time caused by his wife's demand for sexual relations (Karon and VandenBos 1981, 87–88). The wife refused to use contraceptives and demanded that the man take two jobs while she remained without a job. The man felt inferior because he could not satisfy the so-called legitimate demands of his wife. Karon suspected that there was an oral draining fantasy hidden behind the inability to satisfy the demands of his wife.

Karon is also sensitive to the demands of the symbolic. He demonstrates this in several of his interventions. A first sign that Karon shows sensitivity for the requirements of what Lacan calls the "symbolic" is Karon's attitude toward mistakes made by the therapist. Karon recommends that, with schizophrenics, the therapist must interact even if they are not certain about their actions. Otherwise, one gives the impression of being reserved, and that makes it difficult for a schizophrenic to build a relation. When the therapist makes a mistake, it is good to discuss it with the patient. And if the therapist can make mistakes, so can the patient. It is a disadvantage to the patient if the therapist believes so much in their divine power that they, just as the parents of the patient, cannot be challenged. As a consequence, the patient's belief that a good person never makes a mistake is confirmed. From an infallible therapist a fallible patient learns that he is inferior (Karon and VandenBos 1981, 139). Karon's insight matches well the Lacanian idea that the symbolic creates a kind of lack that contradicts the narcissistic feelings of omnipotence. The condition for accepting this lack, according to Lacan and, presumably, also to Karon, is that the mother figure or the therapist present themselves to the child or the patient as finite subjects who recognize and accept their own shortcomings. Karon defends such a thesis in his practice without Lacanian theory. He finds this idea so important that he recommends introducing it early in the therapy; the therapist needs to say explicitly that making mistakes is a good thing (Karon and VandenBos 1981, 169).

Karon's attitude toward the confidentiality of the information provided in therapy is a second kind of intervention in which Karon pays attention to what Lacan calls the symbolic. Karon insists that one tell the patient that the patient is allowed to say anything he wishes but that no one has the right to know the thoughts of the patient. Even the therapist does not have that right, although the therapist may be able to help the patient. Karon then explains to the patient that he will provide no one with information about what the patient tells him. He will not even say whether the patient is his patient. He further specifies that he will do so even with the FBI and that the FBI has, in the past, respected his attitude. He furthermore points out to the patient that the FBI did not succeed in getting information about Ellsberg, not even by breaking into the office of Ellsberg's psychiatrist (Karon and VandenBos 1981, 171).

When forms have to be filled out for those who pay for the treatment of the patient, Karon discusses with the patient the information that will be provided. Karon finds it reasonable that such forms ask for a diagnosis, a prognosis, the proposed treatment, and whether the patient attends the sessions. The first time that such a form is requested, Karon shows it to the patient and discusses its content. When more detailed reports are requested, Karon always presents a draft to the patient. The patient can change parts of the report and is allowed to give or refuse his permission to send the report away. Karon concludes that he finds it important that the patient knows that the patient himself has the ultimate say about what happens with information about him.

From a Lacanian point of view, one can describe the strategy of Karon as a method of introducing a distinction between the patient and the therapist on the basis of a rule respected by the therapist: The thoughts of the patient legitimately belong to the patient and to him alone. By his way of handling confidentiality, Karon refuses to act practically as if he and his patient are one agent. He uses the symbolic order as a method to situate his patient as someone who has ultimate authority. One can imagine that this attitude in the therapist gives the patient the opportunity to develop a deeper form of subjectivity.

Karon's attitude toward sexuality is a third kind of intervention, which I interpret as a symbolic intervention. Karon claims that schizophrenics live in a pre-Oedipal experience of their sexuality. He maintains that schizophrenics unconsciously feel as if their body and their sexuality do not belong to them but rather to another, usually the mother figure (Karon and VandenBos 1981, 203). Thus, Karon continues, schizophrenics experience masturbation not as incest, but as treason. Karon therefore recommends that the therapist try to diminish the feelings of anxiety, guilt, and worthlessness. Karon suggests that the therapist must tell the patient that masturbation is neither harmful nor morally prohibited. Masturbation is something one does when one has nothing better to do; that almost everyone does it, even those who claim that it is sinful; that he, the therapist, approves of masturbation. Karon stresses that, to be effective, the verbal lifting of moral prohibitions must not be ambiguous or hesitant (Karon and VandenBos 1981, 203). It is important that the therapist tell the patients, in unambiguous terms, that they, and no one else, are the legitimate owners of their penis, vagina, and body. Consequently, they alone have the right to use their body (Karon and VandenBos 1981).

According to Karon, the therapist has the same task in connection with difficulties concerning the heterosexual relations of their patients. The therapist needs to tell the patients that having sexual intercourse is fun, that it is one of the pleasures of life. The patients need to be told that they may have sexual intercourse, if they find it pleasant. If they do not find it pleasant, then they do not need to have intercourse. Sexual intercourse is a matter to be decided by the two people involved and no one else. Karon adds that it is not permitted to hurt innocent people. If the couple does not want children, then they should take precautions, and rape, just as beating, is not permitted.

Karon's interventions regarding the sexuality of the schizophrenic patient can be interpreted in two different ways. According to Karon, the most important task of the therapist is to help patients accept their own sexuality. This task can be described as an attempt to use a mirroring technique so that the patients learn to place their sexuality in their own psychic ego image. This is work at the imaginary level. Karon then adds a symbolic dimension. He allows the patients to give a place to their sexuality in their own ego image by means of a rule: if it pleases you, then you are allowed to engage in sexual activity. If it does not give pleasure, then you are not obliged to engage in sexual activity. For heterosexual relations, Karon adds one more symbolic dimension. He tells patients that sexual intercourse should not hurt anyone. Precautions need to be taken not to produce unwanted children, and rape, just as any other form of violence, is not permitted. In this interpretation of Karon's intervention, we maintain that the symbolic intervention consists of giving a rule that both justifies and limits sexual activity. This rule is given only after a mirroring technique worked at the imaginary level.

It is possible to give another interpretation of Karon's intervention. One could argue that Karon's intervention is mainly a symbolic intervention because Karon proposes a symbolic rule that allows patients to separate themselves from an imaginary other (the mother figure who imaginarily has a claim on the sexuality of the patients). Karon's intervention then has the consequence that a rule is presented which makes the patients subjectively the proprietors of themselves, their body, and their sexuality. Karon then ties a second rule to the rule that gives property rights: use your property (your sexuality) in such a way that you do not hurt others (avoid unwanted children and do not rape).

CONCLUSION

I use Lacanian ideas, complemented by ideas of Corveleyn and Vergote, to explain Karon's successful interventions in the treatment of schizophrenics. I point out that Karon's practical interventions, first, address a deficiency of the patient in the imaginary by means of a kind of mirroring technique. Only after an intervention in the imaginary does Karon make a symbolic intervention. Sometimes it is clear when the intervention in the imaginary finishes and the symbolic intervention begins, as in the case of the patient having terrible nightmares. Justifying murderous feelings of rage is an intervention in the imaginary. To make a distinction between justified feelings and prohibited deeds, which can follow from those feelings, is making a symbolic intervention.

In other cases, it is more difficult to distinguish the imaginary from the symbolic intervention. This is the case when Karon helps his patients accept their sexuality—which involves imaginary work—using the idea that the patients are the proprietors of their bodies and sexual organs. In this way, Karon helps his patients to break away from an imaginary unity with the mother figure. It seems that the imaginary work, whereby the patients accept their own sexuality, is closely tied to the symbolic intervention, which allows the patient to separate themselves from another. It even seems as if the imaginary work is promoted by the symbolic intervention: the patients are helped by the symbolic idea that they are the proprietors of their own sexuality.

I have proved that symbolic interventions alone cannot help the schizophrenic. The symbolic, as Corveleyn demonstrates, is not able to do its normal work with the schizophrenic. I am convinced that successful therapies for schizophrenics need to treat the deficiencies of the imaginary before a symbolic intervention can be successful, as Vergote has already demonstrated theoretically. The practical interventions described or advised by Karon provide concrete proof of my thesis.

NOTES

1. Two other important therapists connected with the group are Gary VandenBos and Michael Teixeira.

2. For an extensive summary of Freud and Lacan's explanations of Schreber's hallucinations, see De Waelhens 1978, 97–139.

3. For an article critical of Lacan's idea of the "father's rule," see Scott 1989.

4. This phenomenology of the mother–child relation with some mentally ill children is almost identical with the description made of such cases by Maud Mannoni, a student of Lacan (Mannoni 1964, 68–69, 80, 109, 173). See also my commentary on Mannoni (Ver Eecke 1984, 70–75).

Chapter Fourteen

On Villemoes's Lacanian-Inspired Treatment Method of People Afflicted with Schizophrenia

Villemoes, a psychiatrist in Sweden and Denmark, developed a treatment for schizophrenia based upon Lacan's theory of schizophrenia[1] and De Waelhens's philosophical interpretation of it.[2] I will start by giving the theoretical foundations of Villemoes's method; I will then present his method and finish by reporting the results of some evaluative studies.

THEORETICAL FOUNDATIONS

Lacan's theory of schizophrenia starts from the observation that Freud's interpretation of Judge Schreber's *Memoirs* overlooks two important symptoms: the lack of a solid body image and Schreber's curious remarks about language (introduction of this book; Ver Eecke 1988, 100). Lacan identifies Schreber's curious reports about his use of language as his most basic schizophrenic deficit. Lacan argues, by means of an example concerning one of his own patients, that schizophrenics have difficulty using and understanding pronouns (Lacan 2006, 447–49 [534–35]). Lacan explains that the origin of this difficulty is the childhood fusion of the patient and mother or maternal figure. Lacan believes that such a fusion between mother and child is resolved by the child's response to the mother's reference to a third, that is, the father. If the child observes the mother's interest in the father, the child understands that he is not the sole object of the mother's wants and desires. In Freudian language, the child learns that it is not the phallus of the mother. Accepting that they are not the phallus of the mother is, according to Lacan, the equivalent of what Freud called castration. The child tries to overcome the experience of castration by identifying with some mark in the father that represents to the child phallic power (Lacan 2006, 464–65 [557]). In trying to become like the father, the child's fusion with the mother, or the fear of castration, is replaced by symbolic identification with a mark in the father (Izcovich 2017, chapter 13). To make that symbolic identification true, the child is willing to work and have patience. The child has created an ego-ideal.

De Waelhens, more so than Lacan, makes use of Freud's analysis of his grandchild to clarify Freud's concept of primal repression (De Waelhens and Ver Eecke 2001, 143–67). Freud introduced the concept of primal repression to explain one characteristic of repression: Patients are not able to undo a repression. Freud speculated that the repressed got entangled with other repressed material. Undoing a repression thus meant undoing all relations with the other repressed materials. Such an understanding of repression does not explain the first repression by its entanglement with other repressed material. Primal repression thus had to be explained differently.[3] Referring to Freud's analysis of his grandchild, De Waelhens believes that the child uses a spool to represent his mother and later—when the spool disappears—uses words to master his fear of the disappearing mother. By using the spool, and later words, the child is the master of the imaginary appearance or disappearance of the mother.

De Waelhens interprets the game of the child as the child transforming the figure of the mother. Whereas before, the mother was experienced as a figure who had to be present (without her, the child feared annihilation), now the child is capable of creating a mother figure who is capable of disappearing and also susceptible to rescue. De Waelhens interprets that transformation of the mother figure as primal repression. The child is now capable of letting go of the idea of a mother as necessarily present. This primal repression prepares the child to let go of the mother and search for a mark in the father, which will be the basis for the child's symbolic identification and thus its own identity.

VILLEMOES'S TREATMENT METHOD FOR SCHIZOPHRENICS

The treatment method developed by Villemoes can be explained by two of his observations. The first is that schizophrenics cannot properly use pronouns.[4] The second is that schizophrenic autism is not an indication of the construction of a defensive wall. Rather, it is the expression of a great fear of human dialogue due to the schizophrenic's tendency to fuse with other people.

The treatment plan has three phases.[5] The first phase helps the schizophrenic idolize the therapist and thus to create a bond. The second phase encourages the patient to develop historical narratives. The third phase attempts to end the therapy without a sense of loss from the point of view of the patient.

Villemoes makes a number of assumptions about the patient and the ideal role of the therapist. Villemoes asserts, as does De Waelhens, that the schizophrenic is not a dialogue partner. He therefore recommends avoiding face-to-face treatment. Rather, the patient should sit next to the therapist, three feet apart, and closest to the exit. The therapist should not use personal pronouns. Pronouns are isolating, and they put the patient on the spot (E-mail, June 24, 2000, 2).[6] The therapist should also not ask any direct questions. That too puts the patient on the spot. In Lacanian language, any question makes a demand upon the patient. Other theoreticians could point out that schizophrenic patients must experience the therapist as giving, since the patient is fixated on or has regressed to the oral stage (Karon and VandenBos 1981, 164–65). If questions need to be asked, one can say something like, "I wonder, if . . .?" Do not gainsay the patient (Karon and VandenBos 1981). The purpose of the first phase is to promote bonding and overcome autism, not create a separation that would be experienced as rejection.

According to Villemoes, the therapist must positively do three things. He must give the patient one and only explanation when asked about the reason for any of the therapeutic arrangements (time, length, frequency, sitting arrangement). That explanation is, "It has been prescribed from elsewhere" (Villemoes 2002, 647). Or, the therapist can say that the questions are legitimate and the therapist himself wonders about the same thing (Villemoes 2002). The second task of the therapist during this first phase is to describe sceneries in which the patient is the center. The first scenes described should be of the consultation room. Later, the therapist can introduce descriptions of the hall, the consultation room, the bedroom of the patient, and other rooms that the patient frequents—rooms not directly present to the senses of the patient when she is in the consulting room. The descriptions should use language as a structuring function. The therapist should use genitives, prepositions, conjunctions—even adverbs, adjectives, and subjunctives (e.g., the door of the house, the color of the bricks) (Villemoes 2002, 648).

Villemoes warns that this is a challenging task for the therapist. The therapist should therefore think beforehand what themes she will discuss. She should also expect to do most or all of the talking. The third task of the therapist is to present a specific attitude toward questions asked by the patient. The therapist should not answer the questions but admit the legitimacy of them (Villemoes 2002, 3).

The Lacanian explanation for the first task of the therapist, as I see it, is that the therapist must present himself as a finite subject, a subject submitted to a law, or, as Lacan calls it, a "barred subject." Like the finitude of the therapist, the idea of a third is introduced from the beginning of the therapy. This technique corresponds, at least partially, to the recommendation by Bertram Karon that the therapist introduce early in the therapy that the patient—and the therapist—can make mistakes and that this is good, because only people who do not do anything new make no mistakes (Karon and VandenBos 1981, 167, 169).

The Lacanian explanation for the second task of the therapist, in this first phase, is that there is a basic deficiency in the schizophrenic's relation to language.[7] Following Freud, I would stress that the schizophrenic develops an overinvestment in words and an underinvestment in the things themselves; therefore, one might think that it would be a good technique to let the patient relate words to things or even help the patient invest in the things by letting them feel, touch, smell, and taste things.

Villemoes takes a totally different approach. He encourages the therapist to introduce language as a structuring instrument capable of structuring the experienced environment. According to De Waelhens, language gives human beings distance from things and the world, such that a human being can experience the world (De Waelhens and Ver Eecke 2001, 145). Without language, human beings seem to be glued to the things in the world and thus cannot experience them. Borrowing ideas from phenomenologist Robert Sokolowski, one can say that speaking is a different form of intentionality than perceiving. The richness of sense data present in perception is partially lost in speaking (Sokolowski 2000, 79).[8] Speaking thus performs a repressive function toward the richness of sense data. At the same time, speaking allows human beings to make connections. Thus, if it is a hotel, it must have an entrance, a reception area, and bedrooms. It is thus for me a possible place to stay.

Villemoes reports that after a while, the patient starts seeing the environment as the therapist sees it (the patient starts to identify with the therapist or her voice). The patient will then react and make small comments. This indicates that the patient has at least partially adopted the role of an agent. In her reactions and comments, the patient shows that she accepts the structuring role provided by the therapist. The patient does not yet actively structure her environment, but she accepts the structuring result provided to her by the therapist. By identifying with the speech of the therapist, the patient passively accepts the structuring role that speech provides. This prepares the patient to become even more of an agent when she is introduced to narratives in the second phase of therapy.

Villemoes warns that the therapist should not focus upon people, because people create problems. If the patient herself brings up people, it is best to focus on such objective aspects of the people as their work, their car, or their holiday habits.

The third positive task of the therapist is to acknowledge the legitimacy of the patient's questions but not answer them. This attitude promotes the advent of the symbolic in two ways.[9] It encourages the patient to develop agency by nurturing wonder about the world. It also presents the therapist as someone who either lacks knowledge or encourages and tolerates wonder in the patient. In short, this attitude promotes otherness in the patient.

When the patient starts to assume the function of agency offered by the therapist's attitude and her description of sceneries using structured language, the patient will reciprocate by idolizing the therapist. Signs of idolization are as follows:

> The patient arrives on his own and in time; sits down in the waiting room; smiles and arises quickly when the therapist invites him in; looks at the therapist and seeks eye contact; becomes ingratiating; uses goodbye gestures when leaving; combs his hair; arranges his clothing; becomes sensitive to alterations in the room; agrees with the therapist in everything; uses the therapist's phrases on leaving. (Villemoes 2002, 649)

Villemoes argues that the patient has made the therapist a fetish. From Freud we know that a fetish is an object that permits a patient to organize and act in her world as a desiring subject.

When a patient calls the therapist to ask that the session take place on the current day rather than tomorrow or two days later, Villemoes argues that this indicates that the patient has eroticized the therapist. He argues that eroticization makes it more difficult to make the next step in therapy.

The second phase of the treatment encourages the development of historical narratives. This will require a higher form of agency than was reached in the first phase. Villemoes recommends that this phase be initiated at the appropriate time through an act of delegation by the therapist. The therapist may take off her watch before the session and tell the patient that from now on, the patient is responsible for keeping time and thus for ending the session. This delegation of responsibility guarantees that the patient will from then onward have the last word in every session. That delegation guarantees the autonomy of the patient and anticipates what Lacan calls the advent of the "paternal metaphor" (Villemoes 2002).

To prepare for the development of historical narratives, the therapist must shift from the description of actual scenes to historical ones, while still focusing on such factual matters as the patient's primary school, its location, and its structure. By moving to the past tense, the construction of the scenes is no longer a description of immediate sense impressions. The reconstruction of the past scenes must again be done by the structure of language: adverbs, adjectives, prepositions, and subjunctive and conjunctive verb forms. This work is hard for the patient. Slowly and with the shared interest of the therapist, a picture with sufficient detail can be reconstructed, which, in turn, has an effect: It creates fascination with what is lacking. It generates, as it were, blind spots about which the patient develops curiosity.

Reconstructing the past reveals several signs of growing agency in the patient. The signs come in sequence. Villemoes reports the following sequence. First, the patient starts making *subtle and coordinated movements*, which indicate that a functioning image of the body is taking hold of the patient (Villemoes 2002, 652). Later, the patient shows *signs of inspiration*. One thought (linguistically formulated) brings up another, and the patient shows signs of delight in these thought combinations. Still later, the patient starts *reflecting on facts* as if she is concerned with the *truth*, for example, "My brother was born in 1976—or was it 1977?—no I think it was 1976" (Villemoes 2002, 652). Still later, the patient makes associations: "That reminds me of . . . ; speaking of that" (Villemoes 2002, 652). Combining signifiers allows the creation of new meanings.

Next comes the modulation of speech and increased body language. Prosody, modulation of speech, and body language are efforts to empower the signifier so as to help the creation of the signifieds. This, in turn, leads the patient to show an interest in her environment (Villemoes 2002, 653). The patient asks the therapist if she should close the door when leaving the office. She wonders if another picture used to hang on the wall. Villemoes interprets these signs as evidence that the patient is structuring, by means of language, the objects around her into a world *for her*. The patient is no longer an object among objects. She is the structuring center; even more, she is the structuring agent.

Next, the patient develops the capacity for *empathy*. Before, sympathetic or empathic feelings led to fusion with the other person, so much so that many of the symptoms of psychotic patients (or children—as is well known in child psychiatry) are symptoms of others. Empathy is the ability to identify with another person without losing one's own identity. Consequently, the patient can put herself in the shoes of others and remain autonomous enough to make observations about the person empathized with (e.g., "It couldn't have been easy for mother to look after so many children.") (Villemoes 2002, 653).

Empathy prepares the patient for the next step, in which *people start to appear in the memories* of the patient. Before, people seldom emerged in the patient's memories, but now they emerge as centers of opinion. Schoolmates have names and characteristics. Family members are described as having a life of their own. Villemoes attributes this to the increased structuring role that language starts to play in his patients. Given Lacanian theory, it is unsurprising that the next step Villemoes observes in his patients is the creation of enough of a split that self-reflection becomes possible. Indeed, as Villemoes himself points out, self-reflection requires something less than full identity with oneself. A person must be able to look at herself from the "outside." Two forms of self-reflection (historical and contemporary) are observable, which allow Villemoes to postulate two forms of split in his patients. A historical self-reflection—I used to listen to my parents in every matter, nowadays I seldom do—implies a noncoincidence of the self with the self throughout time. A contemporary self-reflection—"I am not a shoplifter"—implies the awareness of an ideal and its opposite as possible identities and the emerging awareness of the person's own freedom in choosing to be one or the other (Villemoes 2002, 654).

Symbolic identification (I am not a shoplifter) leads to the next step in developing agency because the patient is now identifying or refusing to identify with a word, a signifier. Symbolic identification puts the patient in a historical context. Identifying oneself as "not a shoplifter" means that yesterday, last year, four years ago, I had the opportunity to steal, and even if my friend did it, I—the patient—did not. The descriptions of mere scenes are replaced by beginning narratives. Moreover, symbolic identification is quite different from imaginary identification. Mentally ill patients who claim to be Napoleon, Caesar, or Christ do not feel obliged to conquer Moscow, cross the Rubicon, or preach to the masses. Symbolic identification does however impose obligations. When those obligations have historically only been half fulfilled—or have not been fulfilled at all—then symbolic identification is defective or has failed completely. The telling of their poor and failed symbolic identifications makes the patients sad. Their past traumas become now—*nachträglich*—painful. Villemoes considers the sadness around the construction of historical narratives, guided by themes of symbolic identifications, a sign that castration takes place (Villemoes 2002, 654).

At this point, Villemoes believes that the patient is able to accept the dialectic demands of language as discourse. When she speaks, the patient looks at her interlocutor—like human beings normally do. The patient thereby signals that she understands that the value of her message depends upon the decision of another, and she is now willing to participate in negotiations with others for the creation of meaning (Villemoes 2002, 654).

From this point onward, Villemoes considers the patient's ego as structured and points to at least three signs of such structuring. First, the future becomes part of the present in that the future is not just a series of possibilities, but rather a requirement that the present needs to be structured such that a future becomes possible. The future begins today by the planning required to achieve the anticipated future. Second, all the possibilities open in the present cannot be realized. Priorities need to be established following the dictates of anticipation, which must already be planned. Third, whereas before other people were reduced to "something to count," now people, like schoolmates, appear with names and characteristics (Villemoes 2002, 653). They become alive.

Villemoes now starts the third and final phase of therapy. The agency of the patient has been increased by the collaboration between patient and therapist. The therapist provided structuring forms of language, and the patient accepted first passively and then actively (by means of identification and idolization) the help of the therapist. For the patient to become not just an agent but a semiautonomous agent, the idolization of the therapist must be broken. Otherwise, the patient will be forever tied to the therapist as an authoritative father figure. The process of ending the idolization of the therapist started already with a delegation of power to the patient (Villemoes 2002, 649–50). In that delegation of power, the therapist gives the patient the duty to end each therapy session. The next step in breaking the idolization of the therapist by the patient comes when the therapist introduces the third phase of the treatment, that is, preparing for termination of the treatment. The therapist says something like, "Therapy cannot go on forever." Normally the patient agrees. The therapist then enjoins the patient to choose a date for the last session. Putting the calendar in front of both, the therapist asks the patient to choose a date—say, between the 4th of May (about a month from the present date) and the 30th of June (Villemoes 2002, 655). The patient is encouraged to think it over. Normally, the patient chooses a date somewhere in the middle.

From this point onward, the therapist needs to give the power she received through the patient's identification and idolization of her back to the patient (Villemoes 2002). By taking less initiative and using less of her knowledge and professional insight in the sessions, the therapist allows the patient to start taking over more and more (Villemoes 2002). The challenge is for the therapist to master her own narcissism: to become a disappointment to her patient so that the patient can leave the therapist without feeling a loss. The felt loss should be only that of the therapist. If that is the case, then the "Name-of-the-Father" (phallic power) is correctly located in the structure of the patient and not in the power of the therapist (Villemoes 2002). If that is not the case, the patient will call back and ask to have another appointment. In this case, Villemoes recommends making the appointment to discuss the problem. In the session, the therapist should listen carefully and answer something like, "About that problem, I do not know too much," so that the patient is given back the power she invested in the therapist.

CONCLUSION

Villemoes makes an overall remark about his therapy. He argues that no effort is made to understand the symptoms of the patient. Efforts at understanding the symptoms of the patient are attempts to integrate the world of the patient into the world of the therapist. Instead, efforts should focus on letting language structure the patient and thereby promote agency in the patient (Villemoes 2002).

Report on Evaluative Studies

Several evaluative studies have been done of the ego structuring method pioneered by Villemoes. First, there are two TIPS scientific reports by the psychology department at the University of Umeå. TIPS Report nr. 49, by Annika Stencrantz and Britt Marie Malmgren (Stencrantz and Malmgren 1997), is a description of the ego structuring therapeutic process of the first four young psychotics treated in the therapeutic community of Norrgården in Härnösand. TIPS Report nr. 50, by Annika Stencrantz, compares the patients at Härnösand with those of another therapeutic community in Sweden. In the other therapeutic community, 264 to 900 hours of therapy were given, while in Härnösand 46 to 150 sessions were given, and the results were markedly better in the latter (Stencrantz 1998, 33–34).

Second, the study by Gunny Bertilsson and Eskil Berggren gives a quality assessment of the first 46 patients receiving ego structuring therapy at the psychiatry department in Skellefteå. The therapy took between 30 and 100 sessions, with two sessions a week lasting between six months and two years. In all of these cases, mental illness had become evident between the ages of five and 50. Many were thus chronic patients, and many were hard to help with other methods. A total of 38% were borderline patients, and 62% were psychotic (Bertilsson and Berggren 2000, 2).

Using medical reports and personal interviews, the authors provide the following statistics using five categories: 1) clear improvement; 2) improvement but less; 3) no change, not clear improvement; 4) worse; and 5) much worse. By adding the numbers for the different tests, I obtained the following numbers: clear improvement (35.1%); improvement but less (38%); and no change, not clear improvement (27%). None were worse or much worse. For the categories of "clear improvement" and "improvement but less" we thus have jointly 73%. This was considered a good result for the length of therapy and considering that the patients were chronic ones.

Third, there are the two studies by Bengt Göran Aronsson and Bo Edenius. Aronsson's study is TIPS Report nr. 51 of the psychology department, and Edenius's book is his published dissertation for the department of psychiatry. Both studies were completed at Umeå University in Sweden. The two studies examined about 24 patients at Norrgården therapeutic community who started their ego structuring therapy between 1986 and 1992 (and ended it in or before 1992) (Aronsson 1999, 16). The patients had received prior treatment and been given up by classical psychiatry; they were expected to become chronic, were on medication, and were receiving a disability pension (letter by Villemoes).

Of the 24 patients, 13 did not start or interrupted their treatment for reasons not related to the treatment.[10] The final pool thus consisted of 11 patients—10 diagnosed as psychotics, mostly schizophrenics, and one diagnosed as having personality disorder with drug abuse. The patients were evaluated retrospectively in 1992 (one to four years after patients were discharged) and 1996 (five to eight years after discharge) (Edenius 1999, 174).[11] In 1992, 50% of the patients were no longer diagnosed as psychotic. Medication was diminished by 50%, and two patients were without medication (Edenius 1999, 175). The cost per patient changed from 350,000 Swedish Crowns the year before the treatment to 30,000 Crowns in 1996 (Aronsson 1999, 21; Edenius 1999, 176). Individually, by 1996, six patients had experienced clear progress. The development of one was stunted in 1996, compared with 1992. Three patients had become worse, and one had committed suicide (Edenius 1999, 175). One puzzling fact in this group was that of the 11 patients who continued the treatment, eight were women and three were men.

NOTES

1. There are a number of other therapists who have developed treatment methods derived from Lacan's theory: Rosenbaum and Sonne 1986; the Gifric group, with a publication by Apollon et al. 1990; and Vanheule 2014, 2017. There are also non-Lacanian approaches to the treatment of people afflicted with psychosis: Silver and Cantor 1990; Moskowitz et al. 2008; Dorman 2003; Eigen 1986; Nuland 2003; and Murray 2001.

2. There are two English summaries of the therapeutic method developed by Palle Villemoes: Edenius 1999, 166–76, and De Waelhens and Ver Eecke 2001, 109–17.

3. For a good, short summary of the problems connected with the concept of "primal repression," see Laplanche and Pontalis 1988, 333–34.

4. For a case illustrating the misuse of pronouns, see Waugaman and Searles 1990, 99, 101. See footnote 3 in chapter 4.

5. Villemoes is able to train psychiatric nurses and claims to be able to treat schizophrenics in one to two years.

6. Villemoes 2000, e-mail, June 24, p. 2.

7. Vanheule 2017, 397, also points out that schizophrenic or psychotic patients have a deficient connection with language: "The Lacanian treatment of psychosis starts from the assumption that at the level of the unconscious, some themes cannot be addressed in a steady way. A lawful 'Name-of-the-Father' is missing. Therefore, alternative ways of naming or handling the issues that bear witness to foreclosure need to be invented" (Vanheule 2017, 397). But whereas Villemoes's method consists of strengthening the patient's everyday relationship to language, Vanheule makes use of the patient's tattoos as a kind of prelinguistic naming that then makes talk therapy possible.

8. One patient actually said that his senses reveal a very rich world; however, when he wants to talk about that rich world revealed by the senses, he loses much of that richness. Thus, this patient was deeply experiencing the loss involved in speaking. This patient then developed an interest in art, which allowed him to capture more of the sensual world.

9. For a definition of the Lacanian concept of the symbolic, see Laplanche and Pontalis 1988, 439–440, and Evans 1996, 201–3.

10. Eight patients did so in the beginning of the treatment because either they or their parents did not accept the treatment. Five interrupted the treatment in a later phase because of social conflicts resulting from a pregnancy (Aronsson 1999, 14).

11. The evaluation used interviews of patients, a questionnaire for the staff, DSM/III/R, medical reports, the Strauss–Carpenter scale, and a questionnaire about quality of life.

Chapter Fifteen

On Prouty's Successful Treatment Method for People Afflicted with Schizophrenia

Garry Prouty (Kreitmeyer and Prouty, 2003; Prouty 1994, 2003; Prouty et al. 2002) has developed a successful new method to treat people afflicted with schizophrenia that he has given the name "pre-therapy." Relying upon Lacan's early theory of schizophrenia, as corrected by Antoine Vergote and his students, I accept the thesis that people afflicted with schizophrenia have two different deficits. The healing of these two different deficits requires contradictory interventions. Prouty has creatively developed ways to provide such contradictory healing methods.

PROUTY'S APPROACH

By calling his method "pre-therapy," Prouty signals that his patients do not have the psychic development necessary for regular therapy. Prouty works with the assumption that human beings must acquire a certain state of complexity and that sometimes this acquisition fails. He thus works with a deficit model of mental illness. In particular, Prouty sees in his patients a deficiency with relation to language. This fits in with the ideas developed by Lacan.

I will argue, on the basis of ideas developed by Antoine Vergote, that Prouty's method assumes a second deficit in the development of schizophrenic people. Indeed, schizophrenic people also have a defective relation to their body. Thus, Judge Schreber felt that he was a man who was also becoming a woman (Schreber 1988, 75). In Lacanian theory, but also in Kleinian theory, the relation to the body is developed in the imaginary and primarily in relation to the maternal figure.

The ideas developed by Vergote suggest that the treatment of schizophrenic people will make contradictory demands upon the therapist. If schizophrenia is characterized by the absence of the "paternal metaphor," then one kind of correction is required. Indeed, the absence of the paternal function is connected with the absence of the Oedipal structures, and correcting the absence of the Oedipal structures requires the imposition of the narcissistic wound, which brings about the Oedipal restructuring. This is accomplished by imposing separation, distance, boundaries, and limits.

However, if the schizophrenic person also has a deficient relation to his body, then we are in the presence of a deficient imaginary dimension; however, the imaginary is connected with the construction of a psychic body created during the mirror stage, in which a lovingly admiring mother figure allows and encourages the child to accept and embrace its body. Thus, if there is a failure in the imaginary, the therapist would have to do work that resembles the work of a caring maternal figure.

We now have a theoretical question we can ask of Prouty: How does his method fulfill the requirements to deal with two totally different and even contradictory deficiencies in the schizophrenic person?

Comments made by Prouty indicate that he is aware of the linguistic deficiencies suffered by schizophrenic people. Indeed, Prouty conceptualizes hallucinations as being presymbols. Symbols refer to something else. A hallucination refers to itself and can thus be understood as an attempt at symbolizing an experience without succeeding (Prouty 1994, 72). Prouty even coins the term *preexpressive self* for referring to schizophrenic people. Prouty also treats patients afflicted with schizophrenia who are autistic or close to autistic. He is thus aware of serious deficiencies in language in schizophrenic people.

However, in the method he uses, he is not applying primarily paternal functions. In his own method, Prouty borrows insights from Carl Rogers's "client-centered therapy." For doing client-centered therapy, Rogers recommends two attitudes, which one could describe as maternal: an unconditional positive regard, defined as a "warm acceptance of each aspect of the client's experience," and empathy, defined as "sensing the client's private world as if it were your own" (Prouty 2003, 59). Prouty accepts both of these attitudes (which are very much maternal attitudes used to nurture children) as central for pretherapy.

Prouty also borrows a third attitude from Rogers: congruence. This attitude is defined as the "therapist being freely and deeply himself, with his actual experience being presented by his awareness of himself" (Prouty 2003, 59). I interpret this attitude as the attempt to split the person of the therapist into two aspects. First, the therapist must sympathize with the patient. Second, the therapist must remain herself. In remaining herself, the therapist provides the third, by whom the Oedipal triangle can be introduced when necessary. Prouty makes use of this idea, even though he himself does not stress it.

Most of Prouty's approaches are what I like to call "maternal functions." The five contact reflections are ways by which the therapist can help the patient develop a psychic body concept. Thus, in one example given by Prouty, the therapist reflects the environment (situational reflections) as it is bodily available to the patient and thereby validates the patient's sense of the body. "Thus the therapist says: I can hear the children playing. It is very cool here. I can hear people talking in the kitchen" (Prouty 2003, 64). The facial reflections allow patients to become aware of themselves as they are visible to others. Thus, the therapist says either, "You look sad," or more concretely, "There are tears in your eyes" (Prouty 2003, 62).

In word-for-word reflections, the therapist repeats the socially correct part of the spoken language of the patient. Thus, in a mumbled paragraph Prouty hears three words: ". . . run . . . three . . . paper . . ." He then, in his role as therapist, repeats the three articulated words (Prouty et al. 2002, 17). Prouty stresses that such reflections give the patient the "experience of being received as a human communicator" (Prouty et al. 2002, 17).

In body reflections, the therapist literally imitates the gestures of the patient or describes the body gestures in words. Sometimes the patient follows up the body reflection by the therapist with a revealing statement: Having put his arms on his head and having seen the reflection by the therapist, one patient said, "My head hurts me when my father speaks" (Prouty et al. 2002, 17). Finally, reiterative reflections are a way to hold on to previous contact methods.

However, it must be noted that a therapist, following Prouty's method, is not treating the patient as a dialogue partner. Thus, when one patient tells him, "My head hurts me when my father speaks" (Prouty 2003, 64), or "Priests are devils" (Prouty 2003, 65), or "My brothers can't forgive me" (Prouty 2003, 65), Prouty is not asking for any explanations. He simply repeats the statement to mirror it so that the patient can feel that his statement has been heard. At this point, language is not used as explanation or a tool of exploration. It is simply used as a method to reflect.

But Prouty (or his follower) *is* slowly introducing language. Thus, when doing situational reflections, Prouty does not limit himself to gestures. Instead, he uses words. When hearing noisy children, the therapist is not pointing to his ears. When feeling that it is cool, he does not just shiver. Prouty transforms the experienced world into a communicated world. The therapist says, "I can hear the children playing" or "It is very cool down here" (Prouty 2003, 64).

When making facial reflections, Prouty can say, "There are tears in your eyes," or he can say, "You look sad" (Prouty 2003, 64). To say that the patient is sad is to abandon descriptive language and introduce interpretative language. Still, Prouty does not push the interpretative function of language too far. He abstains from asking what any of the patient's statements mean. To say to a patient that she is sad helps her to experience her own body by providing a linguistic description. To ask a patient why it is that her head hurts when her father speaks is for the therapist to ask the patient to define herself. Wisely, Prouty knows that this is a task that would confront the patient with her inability to define herself. Prouty does not push for a self-identification, as it emerges in and through the Oedipal restructuring.

Let me report two other examples of how Prouty avoids putting his patient in an Oedipal position. Prouty refers approvingly to Pietrzak's method of using the first name of the patient, not the pronoun "you," in contact reflections. Using "you," writes Prouty might "be a little too intimate for clients for whom relationships may be threatening" (Prouty 2003, 32). Using instead the expression, "'John waved his arm' probably helped form the basic identity at a safe psychological distance" (Prouty 2003, 32).[1]

The second example Prouty uses to stress the need for the therapist to maintain distance is again borrowed from Pietrzak. She advises the use of "it" when referring to a hallucination. Using "it," writes Prouty, "provides semantic distance and a little more psychological safety in approaching the material" (Prouty 2003, 32).

I now turn explicitly to the paternal steps in Prouty's method. My first example of a paternal intervention is Prouty's comments regarding a nonresponsive client. Prouty writes that students often say that nothing is happening. Prouty argues that this is not true. Tiny things are happening, but students do not notice them. Prouty gives the following example:

> A client may be sitting close to a therapist. The therapist may reflect, "You are sitting close." This may make this particular client uncomfortable or frighten him. It could be important to capture this by reflecting, "You moved a little" or "You look a little anxious." These contacts may open more expression from the client. (Prouty 2003, 31)

In an effort to establish contact and warm rapport, Prouty is not avoiding the reflections about the patient who moves away from the therapist. On the contrary, Prouty suggests that labeling the act of separating is a good thing.

I now want to turn to the case of Laura. Here the two paternal functions of setting limits and creating distance come into full view. About Laura, Prouty writes, "Laura herself often wanted much more than she could carry through, so I had to be aware of her limits and reestablish them if necessary. To continuously maintain this balance was at the time the main issue of my working with her" (Prouty et al. 2002, 7). A page later, he writes,

> To verbalize her actions helped her to better recognize her competencies and her personal power. . . . The word "wait," for example, was particularly meaningful because it was so difficult for her to endure even a short moment of waiting. . . . In her relations with the staff, Laura became more open to language and could deal increasingly better with various situations in everyday life. (Prouty et al. 2002, 7–8)

Here Prouty points to a connection between limit-setting and the imposition of the difficult task of waiting, on the one hand, and the patient's opening up to language and her ability to deal better with everyday life, on the other. It looks as if Prouty's intuition correctly suggests therapeutically beneficial steps that are not maternal. Lacanian theory calls them paternal.

I believe that here we witness the great challenge of dealing with very regressed patients. Prouty himself gives us two more descriptions. He writes,

> Finally, I realized that I had to give her more time and space, and allow her more distance. This was what she really needed: more space to live. This was a cue and a new beginning. I had to find a different way to communicate with her, different from what had been tried before and what I had adopted: to go into her room and expect something from her. (Prouty et al. 2002, 5)

Prouty continues, "So I sat down in front of Laura's door. And for a long time I just sat there—on the edge between her world and the world of the group" (Prouty et al. 2002, 5).

Prouty gives this as an example of developing a contact boundary between therapist and client. Prouty adds, "What at first seemed to be just a stopgap—to sit at the doorstep and silently allow contact and proximity—turned out to be a real chance" (Prouty et al. 2002, 5). Finally, Prouty concludes,

> It was extremely difficult to give Laura enough space for her actions, and on the other hand, to set limits for her when the chaos within her became overwhelming. Then, I had to bring her back to her room, close the door, and keep contact there. It was a continuous shuttle between these two poles, where I had to adjust to her abrupt changes . . . I followed her with a goal in mind but had to make enormous sidesteps in all directions. (Prouty et al. 2002, 7)

It is clear that Prouty constantly keeps his pretherapy goal in mind: Establish and increase the contact with his patient. Prouty is clear in articulating his contact reflections. Here, a Lacanian inspiration is helpful, allowing us to see that the paternal functions of creating distance and limit-setting are also important for letting the patient move from a preexpressive self to a more expressive self.

CONCLUSION

I hope that I have been able to indicate that the successful treatment method developed by Prouty is successful because it deals with the dual deficiency of the schizophrenic personality: a deficient relation to the body and a deficient relation to language. The first deficiency can be remedied by mirroring, acts of fusion, and idealizing. Remedying the second deficiency requires the introduction of acts of separation, limit-setting, and a rich usage of language. In child development, the first function is more maternal, and the second is more paternal. Prouty's method deals with both.

NOTE

1. See chapter 10 of this book, "Self-Referencing in the Language of the Severely Mentally Ill."

Conclusion

Human beings are not determined, like animals; human beings are free. Still, human beings need building blocks for their growth. Two crucial building blocks are their ideal ego and their ego ideal. Both Hegel and psychoanalysis understand the importance of these two building blocks.

A close look at Hegel's analysis of the passage in the *Phenomenology* on the master–slave dialectic (Hegel 1977) provides the insight that the slave, at first, used identification with an idealized master as the basis for giving himself self-esteem. In the world of the slave, the only one who was considered as having infinite worthiness was the master. The slave then borrowed from the master his own dignity. The slave did not experience the role of the master as a dead-end street, as Hegel shows. For the slave, the master represented an ideal from which the slave wanted to borrow. The master became the ideal ego for the slave.[1]

However, we have seen that if the slave internalized the role of the master as his ideal ego, the slave was not able to value his own work. When the slaves started to value their own work and the skills they thereby acquired, as Frederick Douglass did in proudly enjoying his reputation as the best caulker in the area, they discovered an ego ideal. The ego ideal functions as a goal that a person is willing to work for, which is what Douglass did.

The difference between ideal ego and ego ideal is also present in psychoanalytic theory. Winnicott is a good author to study the concept of ideal ego. Lacan is a good author to study the concept of ego ideal.

For Winnicott, the ideal ego is the result of the interaction or even the fusion of the child with its mother or mother figure (Winnicott 1965); however, not all children have the benefit of what Winnicott calls a "good enough mother" (Winnicott 1990, 179). Spitz tells us how disastrous it is for children if the mother is absent or only present in a failing way.[2]

From Lacan we learn in the introduction of this book that the creation of the ego ideal is the result of the child noticing the respect of the mother for the "Name-of-the-Father." Indeed, in noticing the respect of the mother for the "Name-of-the-Father," the child is invited to give up its fusion with the mother and search for an own desirable ego ideal. But not all mothers show or are able to show respect for the child's father, as we saw in our analysis of the case of Hölderlin in part IV of this book. And not all fathers deserve the respect of the mother of their child, as Lacan points out (Lacan 2006). So, here, too, the child's path toward maturity can be made difficult. These are environmental challenges for a normal human growth process.

In this book, particularly in parts I, II, and III, I defend the idea that mental illness is not exclusively the result of genetic determinism. Instead, I argue that mental illness is a deficiency in the psychosocial and linguistic development of a human being.[3] I hereby defend a theory of serious mental illness that is the opposite of the position held by an important part of the psychiatric profession. As I also report in the introduction of this book, the official position of the psychiatric profession is expressed in *DSM-V*, where the following is stated: "There is a strong contribution for genetic factors in determining risk for schizophrenia" (American Psychological Association 2013, 103). This claim is contradicted by the following confession, also stated in *DSM-V*: "Most individuals who have been diagnosed with schizophrenia have no family history of psychosis" (American Psychological Association 2013, 101).[4] The claim that genetic factors are determining for schizophrenia is further weakened by another statement in *DSM-V*: "Currently, there are no radiological, laboratory, or psychometric tests for the disorder" (American Psychological Association 2013, 101). The view that the cause of schizophrenia is genetic or biological is thus no more than a belief.[5]

The belief that schizophrenia is genetic and thus a permanent condition is factually contradicted by the case of John F. Nash, a brilliant mathematician who recovered from schizophrenia.[6] It is also contradicted by the Vermont experience where a "flexible program of psychosocial rehabilitation" was developed (Harding 2002) and where 62% to 68% were found to be significantly improved [. . .] or to have completely recovered" even 30 years after their treatment (Harding 2002).[7] Courtenay M. Harding reports that, "Patients in the Vermont Longitudinal Study admitted that the most important ingredient in their improvement—and in some cases, their complete recovery—was hope, 'Someone believed in me, someone who told me I might have a chance to recover'" (Harding 2002, 672).[8] Whereas the genetic biological view of schizophrenia destroys hope for recovery, the psychosocial linguistic view of severe mental illness preserves hope. A deficit in psychosocial linguistic development can be remedied (Fort 1990). Having a "bad brain" is understood as being a permanent condemnation, needing medication for the rest of one's life.[9]

Let us now return to scientific evidence, mentioned in the introduction of this book, for the importance of the environment in the emergence of schizophrenia. Crucial is a study by Tienari et al.[10] Tienari looked for all the women who had been hospitalized for schizophrenia or paranoid psychosis. Next Tienari looked for any of these women who had given up children for adoption to nonfamily members in Finland (Tienari 1992). Tienari then evaluated the adopting families, dividing them between those judged to be healthy, those judged to be neurotic, those who had personality disorders, and those judged to have functional psychoses. Tienari reports that zero children of psychotic mothers developed a "functional psychosis" if the adoptive family was classified as "healthy" (Tienari 1992). Thus, Tienari's study clearly demonstrates that the environment is a crucial factor for a genetic predisposition to schizophrenia to be able to lead to an actual case of schizophrenia (Dean and Murray 2005).

I also mention in my introduction that there is factual evidence that proper use of talk therapy can be efficient in the treatment of schizophrenic people. In part of Finland where "Open Dialogue"—an approach relying almost exclusively on talking—is used as a method for dealing with schizophrenic patients, it was reported that 86% had returned to their studies or full-time job and that only 17% had relapsed during the first two years and 19% during the next three years.[11] The method of "Open Dialogue" is described as follows: "The focus is primarily on promoting dialogue and secondarily on promoting change in the patient or in the family. In dialogue patients and families increase their sense of agency in their own lives by discussing the patient's difficulties and problems" (Seikkula 2006, 216).

The Tienari study and the treatment method developed by Jaakko Seikkula and colleagues provide the empirical evidence for the two main ideas defended in this book. First, the environment plays an important role in causing the emergence of schizophrenia. Second, appropriate talk therapy can be effective for the treatment of schizophrenia and other psychotic illnesses.[12]

In the introduction and the first part of this book, I rely on the ideas of Lacan, mainly the early Lacan, to present a theory for the emergence of schizophrenia and other psychoses. In the last part of this book, I use Lacan's ideas to explain the success of three therapeutic approaches for the successful treatment of people afflicted with schizophrenia and other psychoses: Bertram Karon (an American psychologist), Palle Villemoes (a Danish psychiatrist working in Sweden), and Garry Prouty (an American psychologist). Crucial for my presentation is Lacan's article "On a Question Prior to Any Possible Treatment of Psychosis." Here, Lacan reinterprets Freud's analysis of Judge Schreber's *Memoirs*. Lacan rejects Freud's idea that fear of his homosexual feelings became the cause of Judge Schreber's mental illness. Instead, Lacan argues that Schreber's mental illness was the result of the psychic absence in Judge Schreber of the "paternal metaphor." According to Lacan, the "paternal metaphor" corrects the fantasies that the child develops in the period of fusion with the mother; however, what are the fantasies that need to be corrected and how do they come about?

A human baby, more than the offspring of other animals, is totally dependent upon a mother figure. Without a mother, a human baby would not survive. Consequently, so argues Winnicott, one cannot talk about a human baby by itself; one must see the human baby as a unit with its mother. But a human baby has a consciousness, and total dependency is not acceptable for consciousness. Still, the baby can do nothing about its dependency. When human beings are faced with a situation they do not want to be in but cannot change, they have recourse in their imagination. The human baby makes the total dependency upon its mother acceptable by creating two fantasies. First, it imagines that the mother is perfect and, thus, to some degree omnipotent. Hence, it can feel safe with the mother.[13]

Second, the child must feel that it is everything the mother could want. There is even a proverb describing this need of the child: The child must feel that it is the "apple of their mother's eye." These ideas are confirmed by the literature on attachment theory. Indeed, it is as an embodied being that a child is loved by its mother. Hence, one result of having a loving mother is that a child is able to make use of the love of its mother to lovingly inhabit its own body during what Lacan calls the mirror stage; however, lovingly inhabiting its own body means that the child does so by means of the two previously described imaginary fantasies. Thus, Lacan calls the psychic structure of a child from zero to about three years of age an imaginary structure.

But feeling that one is the center of the universe is not a characteristic that will allow the growing child to develop good relationships with peers and other people. Thus, it is logically necessary that the psychic structure that is beneficial in early childhood be radically transformed. This happens through the Oedipal challenge. When the child starts to observe that the mother has an interest in a third party (normally the father), the child experiences a challenge to his two fantasies. If the mother pays attention to a third person, it is because she does not have everything she needs or desires. Furthermore, if the mother relies on the father to complete her incompleteness, then the child feels that he is simply not enough to fill some emptiness in the life of the mother. The child is not, in fact, the "apple of their mother's eye." Thus, the child experiences a deep narcissistic wound. Nonetheless, children are resilient. The narcissistic wound is, for the child, an invitation to restructure itself and its psychic structure.

Here Lacan's interpretation of the Oedipus complex is useful. Lacan shows that an important result of the Oedipus complex is that the child becomes psychologically separated from the mother. In this, Lacan agrees with Freud; however, Lacan differs from Freud in that he pictures the child as creating a kind of self-separation. Indeed, following the reference of the mother toward the father, the child asks, "What is it about the father that is of such interest to the mother?" This hermeneutic search encourages the child to identify that "mark," or in Lacan's terminology, that signifier in the father that is so attractive to the mother. The child then identifies with that mark or that signifier in the father and makes it the basis of its own identity.

Still, the child knows that it, itself, is not the father, but it wants to become like the father. Thus, for a post-Oedipal child, the future becomes the most important dimension of time, whereas in the pre-Oedipal period it was the "now" that was the most important dimension of time.[14] Lacan calls the psychic structure of a child who has internalized a mark or a signifier of the father and takes the future as the essential dimension of time the symbolic structure of human beings. Lacan considers the linguistic dimension crucial for that symbolic structure.

In the early years, the basis of a child's identity is being the "apple of their mother's eye." After his Oedipal restructuring, the child takes a mark or a signifier of the father as the basis of his identity. The same child thus changes the basis of his identity and, as a result, takes on a new and different identity. Borrowing from the theory of language, Lacan refers to the fact that someone may become different while nonetheless remaining the same person as a "metaphoric process." Lacan actually calls this metaphoric process the "paternal metaphor" because of the central importance of the figure of the father for this restructuring of the child's psyche.

In the absence of the Oedipal challenge and the attendant radical restructuring described here, the child is deprived of the psychological basis for metaphoric moves. When such a child becomes an adult, they will lack a crucial strategy to deal with difficulties in life. Thus, if, as an adult, such a person is denied entrance to law school, she is unable to use a metaphoric move to resituate or reposition herself in life. A normal person could easily ask, "Why is it that I want to become a lawyer?" If she discovers that it is because lawyers make a lot of money, she may instead decide to become an antique car salesperson. If she discovers that she wants to become a lawyer because she likes to talk a lot, then she could become a teacher. In both cases, she sees that she could become something different that "feels" the same. She would be able to make a metaphorical move.

If this person had not undergone an Oedipal restructuring, she would be unable to make this metaphoric move. Thus, in the case where the absence of the Oedipal restructuring became the cause for a later schizophrenic or psychotic breakdown, such a person might interpret metaphors literally (e.g., the patient who was told that she was handicapped and therefore felt that she had no hands). This kind of defective relationship to language is addressed explicitly by the three therapists whose methods I discuss in the last part of this book: Bertram Karon, Palle Villemoes, and Garry Prouty.

In the last part of the book, part V, I analyze the methods of these three therapists. All three have developed successful methods for treating schizophrenic and psychotic patients. I explain their success by using Lacan's theory and stress that all three therapists accept that the schizophrenic person is incapable of self-organizing her role in the world. The schizophrenic needs help using language to relate to their body[15] and the world. All three therapists have different techniques to provide that help, but in each case, the help is psychosocial and linguistic. It does not rely exclusively on medication. If medication is used, it is only to suppress or diminish the symptoms and/or allow the patient to sleep.

Karon listens to and justifies the imaginary rages of his patients, even saying, "The old bitch (stepmother) deserves to die for what she did to you" (Karon and VandenBos, 1981, 198). Such a statement liberates the patient from his guilt of hating his stepmother, and he then reports all the abuses he suffered. Next, Karon introduces a symbolic prohibition in a form that the patient can accept, saying, "The only reason for not killing her is that you'll get caught. If you are willing to die in order to kill her, she must be more important than you are. That sounds stupid to me" (Karon and VandenBos, 1981, 198). When the patient went home, he did not kill his stepmother, and his nightmares about her disappeared.

Villemoes starts his session with a catatonic patient by sitting next to the patient with a desk in between them. The patient is allowed to sit closest to the door to avoid their fear of being controlled. Villemoes then starts to describe the objects in the room of the patient, thereby transforming the sense impressions, which dominate the psychic life of the schizophrenic person, into objects. Next, Villemoes describes the objects in the room or living space of the patient, elevating the patient to the guarantor of the truth as the patient and the therapist talk about things that only the patient knows. This process leads the patient to idolize the therapist.

When the idolization is established, Villemoes delegates the task of ending the sessions to the patient. Hence, the patient has the last word in each session. Villemoes then lets the patient remember and describe the sceneries in the patient's earliest memories without asking about people. The patient, at her own pace, introduces memories of relations to human beings. Slowly the patient describes how she has become the person she is now. Villemoes uses the patient's idolization of the therapist as the driving energy for the historical work that the patient needs to do. Villemoes sees this history writing as a replacement for the paternal third, who was psychologically absent in the life of the schizophrenic or psychotic patient. When there are no gaps or omissions in this historical self-description, Villemoes begins the final phase of his therapy: ending therapy without the patient losing what she has gained.[16]

Prouty establishes communication with catatonic patients by sitting in front of them and imitating their position and every gesture. If they sit in a half-lying position on their chair, so does Prouty. If they raise their arm, so does Prouty. In mirroring their posture, he impresses on the patient the feeling that they exist for the therapist. They experience an imaginary presence. Prouty's next step is to use language. When he notices a tear in the eye of the patient, he says, "There is a tear in your eye." At this point, the patient's behavior is still mirrored back but not in its objective form (by the therapist also producing a tear). Instead, it is mirrored back in a linguistic description of the patient's tear.

All three therapists develop a successful method to repair the psychological deficit in their schizophrenic or psychotic patients. Their success demonstrates that schizophrenia and psychosis are not diseases of the brain but result from a psychological deficiency in childhood development that can be remedied.

To finish, I like to repeat a quotation of Winnicott: "Psychoanalysis tends to show that the basis of mental health is not hereditary [. . .]; the basis for mental health is being actively laid down in the course of every infancy when the mother is good enough at her job, and in the span of every childhood that is being lived in a functioning family" (Winnicott 1990, 179).

In this book, I argue that Winnicott's idea of a "functioning family" includes the mother showing respect for the word of the father, which Lacan technically calls respect for the "Name-of-the-Father." For a child to develop as a psychologically healthy child, he needs the presence of a healthy triangle: mother–father–child. This triangle can be seen as mother figure, a third, and the child.

The idea of a third can be—according to the thoughts developed by Lacan later in his life—the fact that the mother points to something that the child is good at and the mother asking, "What do you hope to do with that in your life?" In this case, the mother puts between herself and her dreams for her child the fact that the child has some skill, something the child is good at. The child is then not just a means for the mother to fulfill her own dreams, like wishing that the child will become a lawyer like her father. In people afflicted with schizophrenia or psychosis, a "third" seems to have been absent in the development of their psyche, as seen in the case of Hölderlin (see chapter 12), and as Lacan argues was the case for Judge Schreber (see chapter 11). In therapy, that "third" is introduced as a verbal description of the behavior of the patient (Karon and Prouty) or the patient's history (Villemoes).

In the last part of this book, I show that Lacan's theory of schizophrenia and psychosis allows us to explain why the different treatment methods of three different therapists are all successful. All three therapy methods rely on a psychosocial and linguistic view of serious mental illness, which is the thesis of this book.

NOTES

1. Frederick Douglass testified that on Saturdays, the slaves would fight about whose master was the better one. Douglass writes, "They [the slaves] seemed to think that the greatness of their masters was transferable to themselves" (Douglass 1999, 20).

2. For a recent study about the importance of motherhood for young children, see Komisar 2017.

3. Making use of Schiller's novel *The Robbers*, Hegel was able to show that there was a logically unavoidable connection between a particular psychic outlook toward life and paranoia. Hegel demonstrates that if a person creates a plan that is too utopian for one's life, a painful disappointment for such a person is unavoidable. This disappointment in one's life project leads to a feeling of craziness. This feeling, that one is crazy, can be mastered by accusing others as willfully interfering with one's good-willed project. But accusing others for one's pain is the description of paranoia (Hegel 1977). Thus, already Hegel demonstrates that one serious mental illness, paranoia, could be connected with a defective mental attitude. I discuss this idea in chapter 8.

4. *DSM-V* continues as follows: "Differences are evident in multiple brain regions between groups of healthy individuals and persons with schizophrenia, including evidence from neuroimagining, neuropathological, and neurophysiological studies" (American Psychological Association 2013, 101–2); however, I like to mention that these differences might be attributed to the different lifestyles of people afflicted with schizophrenia.

5. For an article, long on criticism of the *DSM* approach, that also includes criticism of previous editions of the *DSM*, see Jacobs and Cohen 2003.

6. The case of John F. Nash is reported in the film *A Beautiful Mind.*

7. The claim that schizophrenia is incurable is also contradicted by the Finnish experience using the "Open Dialogue" method, where the following results are reported after five years of therapy: "Eighty-two percent did not have any residual psychotic symptoms, 86% had returned to their studies or a full-time job, and 14% were on disability allowance. Seventeen percent had relapsed during the first two years and 19% during the next three years" (abstract in article by Seikkula et al. 2006). Later in this conclusion, I also refer to this statistic as proof of the efficiency of talk therapy.

8. The Vermont experience confirms Hegel's theory that to be human is to be recognized (Hegel 1977, 111: "Self-consciousness exists in and for itself when, and by the fact that, it so exists for another; that is, it exists only in being acknowledged").

9. In their 2004 article, the authors argue against intermittent antipsychotic medication maintenance strategies (Lehman et al. 2004, Recommendation 7, 198).

10. I hereby repeat what I state in the introduction.

11. For full statement, see footnote 7 in this conclusion.

12. Irwin 2004 provides broader statistical proof for our conclusion, writing, "Randomized studies comparing psychosocial treatment programs without neuroleptics to drug-based programs were sought out for review, and six were found. Long-term outcomes were statistically equivalent or superior in the nondrug group in all six studies" (Irwin 2004, 99).

13. This feeling that the mother is perfect remains part of the structure of the unconscious. Thus, teenagers do personally criticize their mothers, but if another person criticizes their mother for the exact same characteristic, teenagers will not agree. Instead, the teenagers will angrily defend their mother. Hence, the will and need to keep the image of the ideal mother alive is still present in the teenage years.

14. The girl has to make an additional move. She must identify with the mother. This identification with the mother is normally not a regression to a position in which the mother is seen as omnipotent and able to do everything for the child, who is allowed to remain passive. At this point in the development of the girl, the identification with the mother is with a post-

Oedipal mother who is experienced as not being omnipotent, thereby giving the girl a task like, "I will be able to cook as well as my mother and even better." Here, too, the future is the important dimension in time.

15. I make use of the ideas of Corveleyn and Vergote, who both stress that aside from an improved relationship to language, people afflicted with schizophrenia also need an improved relationship to their body (see chapter 6).

16. For statistical evidence of the efficacy of ego-structuring, see Annika Stencrantz 1998 and Stencrantz and Malmgren 1997.

Bibliography

Alcorn, Marshall. 2002. *Changing the Subject in English Class: Discourse and the Constructions of Desire*. Carbondale: Southern Illinois University Press.

Allen, N. C., S. Bagade, M. B. McQueen, J. P. Ioannidis, F. K. Kavvoura, M. J. Khoury, R. E. Tanzi, and L. Bertram. 2008. "Systematic Metanalyses and Field Synopsis of Genetic Association Studies in Schizophrenia: The SzGene Database," in *Nature Genetics*, 40, no. 7, 827–34.

Allison, David B., Prado de Oliveira, Mark S. Roberts, and Allen S. Weiss. 1988. *Psychosis and Sexual Identity*. Albany: State University of New York Press.

Allison, P. J., C. Guichard, K. Fung, and L. Gilain. 2003. "Dispositional Optimism Predicts Survival Status One Year after Diagnosis," in *Head and Neck Cancer Patients*, 21, 543–48.

American Psychiatric Association (APA). 2000. *Diagnostic and Statistical Manual of Mental Disorders*, 4th ed (*DSM-IV-TR*). Text Revision. Arlington, VA: American Psychiatric Association.

———. 2013. *Diagnostic and Statistical Manual of Mental Disorders*, 5th ed. (*DSM-V*). Washington, DC: American Psychiatric Association.

Andreasen, N. 1999. "Understanding the Causes of Schizophrenia," in *New England Journal of Medicine*, 340, no. 8, 645–47.

Apollon, W. 1990. "Psychanalyse et Traitement des Psychotiques," in W. Apollon, D. Bergeron and L. Cantin (eds.), *Traiter la Psychose* (pp. 77–110). Québec: Gifric.

Apollon, W., D. Bergeron, and L. Cantin. 1990. *Traiter la Psychose*. Québec: Gifric.

———. 2008. *La Cure Psychanalytique du Psychotique*. Québec: Gifric.

Aronsson, B. G. 1994. *Norrgårdens behandlingenshem-6 år, en utvädering*. TIPS Report October 1994. Umeå University: Department of Applied Psychology.

———. 1999. *Behandling av schizofrena patienter—en utvärering av Norrgårdens behandlingshem*. TIPS Report nr 51. Umeå University: Department of Applied Psychology.

Arras, John D., and Nancy K. Rhoden (eds). 1989. *Ethical Issues in Modern Medicine*, 3rd ed. Mountain View, CA: Mayfield.

Artaud, A. 1976. *Selected Writings*, ed. S. Sontag, trans. W. Helen. New York: Farrar, Straus and Giroux.

Aulagnier, P. 1964. "Remarques sur la structure psychotique. I. Ego spéculaire, corps phantasmé et objet partiel," in *La Psychoanalyse*, 8, 47–67.

"Back from the Edge: A Dramatic Decline in Suicides." *Economist*, June 28, 2014, http://www.economist.com/news/china/21605942-first-two-articles-chinas-suicide-rate-looks-effect-urbanisation-back (downloaded August 27, 2018).

Bär, Eugen. 1975. *Semiotic Approaches to Psychotherapy*. Bloomington: Indiana University Press.

Baumeyer, F. 1956. "New Insights into the Life and Psychosis of Schreber," in *International Journal of Psychoanalysis*, 33, 140–56.
Benveniste, E. 1971. *Problems in General Linguistics*, trans. M. E. Meek. Coral Gables, FL: University of Miami Press.
Benvenuto, B., and R. Kennedy. 1986. *The Works of Jacques Lacan*. New York: St. Martin's.
Bergeron, D. 1990. "L'Enjeu de la cure du Psychotique," in W. Apollon, D. Bergeron, and L. Cantin (eds.), *Traiter la Psychose* (pp. 139–59). Québec: Gifric.
———. 2002. "The Work of the Dream and Jouissance in the Treatment of the Psychotic," in Willy Apollon et al. (eds.), *After Lacan: Clinical Practice and the Subject of the Unconscious* (pp. 71–88). Albany: State University of New York Press.
Bernet, R. 1996. "Over de Premissen van Lacan: Manifestatie en Terugtrekking van het Onbewuste in de Drift, de Voorstelling en het Affect," in N. Kok and K. Nuijten (eds.), *In Dialoog met Lacan* (65–85). Amsterdam: Boom.
Berthold-Bond, D. 1995. *Hegel's Theory of Madness*. Albany: State University of New York Press.
Bertilsson, G., and E. Berggren. 2000. *Utvärdering av de Första 46 Jagstrukturerande Psykoterpiera vid Psykiatriska Kliniken I Skellefteå*. Skellefteå: Psykoterpienheten.
Bettelheim, B. 1962. *Symbolic Wounds*. New York: Collier.
Blatt, S. J. 1995. "The Destructiveness of Perfectionism: Implications for the Treatment of Depression," in *American Psychologist*, 50, no. 12, 1003–20.
Blatt, S. J., Z. D. C. Sanislow, and Paul A. Pilkonis. 1996. "Characteristics of Effective Therapists: Further Analyses of Data from the National Institute of Mental Health Treatment of Depression Collaborative Research Program," in *Journal of Consulting and Clinical Psychology*, 64, no. 6, 1276–84.
Bleuler, F. 1950. *Dementia Praecox*, trans. Joseph Zinkin. New York: International Universities Press.
Boothby, R. 1991. *Death and Desire: Psychoanalytic Theory in Lacan's Return to Freud*. New York: Routledge.
———. 2001. *Freud as Philosopher: Metapsychology after Lacan*. New York: Routledge.
Borch-Jacobson, Mikkel. 1991. *Lacan: The Absolute Master*, trans. D. Brick. Stanford, CA: Stanford University Press.
Bowie, Malcolm. 1991. *Lacan*. Cambridge, MA: Harvard University Press.
Calligaris, C. 1991. *Pour une Clinique Différentielle des Psychoses*. Paris: Point hors Ligne.
Carver, C. S., R. G. Smith, M. H. Antoni, V. M. Petronis, S. Weiss, and R. P. Derhagopian. 2005. "Optimistic Personality and Psychosocial Well-Being during Treatment Predict Psychosocial Well-Being among Long-Term Survivors of Breast Cancer," in *Health Psychology*, 24, no. 5, 508–16.
Casey, Edward S., and J. Melvin Woody. 1983. "Hegel, Heidegger, Lacan: The Dialectic of Desir," in Joseph H. Smith and William Kerrigan (eds.), *Interpreting Lacan (Psychiatry and Humanities)* (pp. 75–112). New Haven, CT: Yale University Press.
Caskie, Susan. "The Rise of Youth Suicide in China." *Week*, November 1, 2013, https://theweek.com/articles/457373/rise-youth-suicide-china (downloaded August 27, 2018).
Chakos, M. H., J. M. J. Alvir, M. G. Woerner, A. Koreen, S. Geisler, D. Mayerhoff, and J. A. Lieberman. 1996. "Incidence and Correlates of Tardive Dyskinesia in First Episode of Schizophrenia," in *Archives of General Psychiatry*, 53, no. 4, 313–19.
Chauvin, R. 1941. "Contribution à l'étude physiologique de criquet pélerin et du déterminism des phénomènes grégaires," in *Annales de la Société entomologique de France*, 110, 113–272.
Clark, Michael. 1988. *Jacques Lacan: An Annotated Bibliography*. 2 vols. New York: Garland.
Corveleyn, J. 1998. "Délire à thème religieux: La psychose et l'hystérie," in D. Devreese, Z. Lothane, and J. Schotte (eds.), *Schreber Revisité* (pp. 185–209). Louvain: Presses Universitaires de Louvain.
Corveleyn, J., and P. Moyaert. 2003. *Psychosis: Phenomenological and Psychoanalytical Approaches*. Leuven: Leuven University Press.

Crump, C., M. A. Winkleby, K. Sundquist, and J. Sundquist. 2013. "Comorbidities and Mortality in Persons with Schizophrenia: A Swedish National Cohort Study," in *American Journal of Psychiatry*, 170, no. 3, 324–33.
Davoine, F. 1992. *La Folie Wittgenstein*. Paris: E.P.E.L.
Dean, Kimberlie, and Robin M. Murray. 2005. "Environmental Risk Factors for Psychosis," in *Dialogues Clin. Neurosci.*, 7, no. 1, 69–80.
Demoulin, C. 2009. *Se Passer du Père*. Toulouse: Editions Erès.
Deutscher, I. 1954. *I. The Prophet Armed: 1879–1921*. London: Oxford University Press.
———. 1959. *II. The Prophet Unarmed: 1921–1929*. London: Oxford University Press.
———. 1963. *III. The Prophet Outcast: 1929–1940*. London: Oxford University Press.
De Waelhens, A. 1972. *La Psychose*. Louvain/Paris: Nauwelaerts.
———. 1978. *Schizophrenia: A Philosophical Reflection on the Structuralist Interpretation of J. Lacan*. Pittsburgh, PA: Duquesne University Press. Introduction, explanatory footnotes, and a bibliography by W. Ver Eecke.
De Waelhens, A., and W. Ver Eecke. 2001. *Phenomenology and Lacan on Schizophrenia, after the Decade of the Brain*. Leuven: Leuven University Press.
Dixon, L. B., et al. 2009. "The 2009 Schizophrenia PORT Psychosocial Treatment Recommendations and Summary Statements," in *Schizophrenia Bulletin*, 24, no. 1, 1–23.
Dorman, D. 2003. *Dante's Cure*. New York: Other Press.
Douglass, Frederick. 1999. *Narrative of the Life of Frederick Douglass, an American Slave*. Electronic edition, *Documenting the American South*, http://docsouth.unc.edu/neh/douglass/douglass.html (downloaded January 6, 2017).
Ducrot, Oswald, and François Wahl. 1968. *Qu'est-ce que le structuralism?* Paris: Editions du Seuil.
Edenius, B. 1999. *Om en Teori för psykos utveckling av en behandlingsmetod*. Medical Dissertations, New Series, no. 597. Umeå: Umeå University.
Eigen, M. 1986. *The Psychotic Core*. London: Jason Aronson.
Erikson, E. 1959. "Growth and Crisis of the Healthy Personality," in *Psychological Issues*, 1, 50–100.
Evans, D. 1996. *An Introductory Dictionary of Lacanian Psychoanalysis*. London and New York: Routledge.
Fink, B. 1996. "The Subject and the Other's Desire," in R. Feldstein, B. Fink, and M. Jaanus (eds.), *Reading Seminars I and II: Lacan's Return to Freud* (pp. 76–97). New York: State University of New York Press.
———. 1997. *A Clinical Introduction to Lacanian Psychoanalysis: Theory and Technique*. Cambridge, MA: Harvard University Press.
Finkelde, D. 2017. *Excessive Subjectivity: Kant, Hegel, Lacan, and the Foundations of Ethics*. New York: Columbia University Press.
Flay, J. 1984. *Hegel's Quest for Certainty*. Albany: State University of New York Press.
Fort, D. C. 1990. "Parent–Child Effects on Performance, Thinking, and Communication in Families of Normal and Schizophrenic Sons," in A. S. Silver and Morton B. Cantor (eds.), *Psychoanalysis and Severe Emotional Illness* (pp. 73–98). New York: Guilford Press.
Freedman, A. M., H. I. Kaplan, and B. L. Sadock. 1975a. *Comprehensive Textbook of Psychiatry*, Vol. I, 2nd ed. Baltimore, MD: Williams and Wilkins Company.
———. 1975b. *Comprehensive Textbook of Psychiatry*, Vol. II, 2nd ed. Baltimore, MD: Williams and Wilkins Company.
Freud, Sigmund. 1901. *The Psychopathology of Everyday Life* (S.E. vol. 6). London: Hogarth.
———. 1905. *Three Essays on the Theory of Sexuality* (S.E. vol. 7). London: Hogarth.
———. 1911. *Psycho-Analytic Notes on an Autobiographical Account of a Case of Paranoia (Dementia Paranoides)* (S.E. vol. 12). London: Hogarth.
———. 1911–1913. *The Case of Schreber: Papers on Technique and Other Works.(S.E. vol. 12)* London: Hogarth Press.
———. 1920. "Beyond the Pleasure Principle," in *Standard Edition of the Complete Psychological Works of Sigmund Freud*, Vol. 18 (pp. 1–64). London: Hogarth.
———. 1930. "Civilization and Its Discontents," in *Standard Edition of the Complete Psychological Works of Sigmund Freud*, Vol. 21 (pp. 57–145). London: Hogarth.

———. 1953–1974. *Standard Edition of the Complete Psychological Works of Sigmund Freud*, vols. 1–24, ed. and trans. James Strachey. London: Hogarth.

———. 1958. "On Beginning the Treatment," in *Standard Edition of the Complete Psychological Works of Sigmund Freud*, Vol. 12 (pp. 121–44). London: Hogarth.

———. 1961. "Negation," in *Standard Edition of the Complete Psychological Works of Sigmund Freud*, Vol. 19 (pp. 233–39). London: Hogarth.

———. 1963. *Therapy and Technique*. New York: Collier.

Gadamer, H-G. 1975. *Truth and Method*. New York: Seabury Press.

Gaudelière, J. 1998. "Communication at the Lacan Clinical Forum," October 31, 1998–November 1, 1998. Stockbridge, MA: Austen Riggs Center.

Graham, G. 2013. *The Disordered Mind: An Introduction to Philosophy of Mind and Mental Illness*. New York: Routledge.

Green, A. 1986. *On Private Madness*. London: Hogarth Press/Institute of Psycho-Analysis.

Hackenesch, C. 2002. "Der subjective Geist: Hegels Begriff des Menschen," in *Hegel Jahrbuch*, 2, 280–305.

Harari, R. 2002. *How James Joyce Made His Name: A Reading of the Final Lacan*, trans. L. Thurston. New York: Other Press.

Harding, C. M. "Beautiful Minds Can Be Recovered." *New York Times*, March 10, 2002, http://www.nytimes.com/2002/03/10/opinion/beautiful-minds-can-be-reclaimed.html (downloaded December 18, 2017).

Harris, H. 1995. *Hegel: Phenomenology and System*. Indianapolis, IN: Hackett Publishing.

Heaton, J. 2000. *Wittgenstein and Psychoanalysis*. Cambridge, UK: Icon Books.

Hegel, G. W. F. 1967a. *The Phenomenology of Mind*, trans. J. B. Baillie. New York: Harper and Row.

———. 1967b. *Philosophy of Right*, trans. T. M. Knox. London: Oxford University Press.

———. 1977. *The Phenomenology of Spirit*, trans. A. V. Miller. New York: Oxford University Press.

Herold, R., T. Tényi, K. Lénard, and M. Trixler. 2002. "The Theory of Mind Deficit in People with Schizophrenia during Remission," in *Psychological Medicine*, 32, no. 6, 1125–29.

Hertenstein, Matthew J. "Social Referencing." DePauw University, https://www.depauw.edu/learn/lab/publications/documents/infant%20development/2010_Infant_development_Social_referencing.pdf (downloaded January 13, 2018).

Husserl, E. 1935. *The Child*. Ms K III 11 (pp. 4–7), in 1970, *Logical Investigations*, trans. J. N. Findlay. London: Routledge and Kegan Paul.

Hyppolite, J. 1946. *Genèse et Structure de la Phénoménologie de l'Esprit, I and II*. Paris: Aubier-Montaigne.

"Indexicals." *Stanford Encyclopedia of Philosophy*, September 14, 2001, https://plato.stanford.edu/entries/indexicals/ (downloaded January 11, 2018).

Insel, T. 2015. "Mortality and Mental Disorders." *National Institute of Mental Health*, https://www.nimh.nih.gov/about/directors/thomas-insel/blog/2015/mortality-and-mental-disorders.shtml (downloaded January 6, 2018).

Irwin, Matt. 2004. "Treatment of Schizophrenia without Neuroleptics: Psychosocial Interventions versus Neuroleptic Treatment," in *Ethical Human Psychology and Psychiatry*, 6, no. 2, 99–110.

Israël, H. 1989. *Schreber: Father and Son*. Madison, CT: International Universities Press.

Izcovich, Luis. 2017. *The Marks of a Psychoanalysis*, trans. E. Faye and S. Schwartz. London: Karnac.

Jacobs, David H., and David Cohen. 2003. "Hidden in Plain Sight: *DSM-IV's* Rejection of the Categorial Approach to Diagnosis," in *Review of Existential Psychology and Psychiatry*, 26, nos. 2 and 3, 81–95.

Jakobson, R., and M. Halle. 1956. *Fundamentals of Language*. The Hague: Mouton and Co.

Janik, A., and S. Toulmin. 1973. *Wittgenstein's Vienna*. Chicago: Ivan R. Dee.

Kain, P. 2005. *Hegel and the Other: A Study in the Phenomenology of Spirit*. Albany: State University of New York Press.

Kainz, H. P. 1976. *Hegel's "Phenomenology," Part I: Analysis and Commentary*. Tuscaloosa: University of Alabama Press.

———. 2008. *Hegel's Phenomenology of Spirit: Not Missing the Trees for the Forest.* Lanham, MD: Lexington.
Kant, I. 1929. *Critique of Pure Reason*, trans. Norman Kemp. New York: St. Martin's.
———. 1987. *Critique of Judgment*, trans. Werner S. Pluhar. Indianapolis, IN: Hackett.
Karon, B. P. 2003. "The Tragedy of Schizophrenia without Psychotherapy," in *Journal of the American Academy of Psychoanalysis and Psychodynamic Psychiatry*, 31, no. 1, 89–118.
———. 2018. *The Widening Scope of Psychoanalysis. Collected Essays of Bertram Karon.* M. Codgro & A. Widener (eds.). New York: IP Books.
Karon, B. P., and G. R. VandenBos. 1981. *Psychotherapy of Schizophrenia: The Treatment of Choice*. New York: Jason Aronson.
Kelly, G. A. 1972. "Notes on Hegel's 'Lordship and Bondage,'" in A. MacIntyre (ed.), *Hegel* (pp. 11–17). New York: Doubleday.
Kemp, S., and K. Williams. 1987. "Demonic Possession and Mental Disorder in Medieval and Early Modern Europe," in *Psychological Medicine*, 17, no. 1, 21–29.
Kirsch, I. 2010. *The Emperor's New Drugs: Exploding the Antidepressant Myth.* New York: Basic Books.
Kojève, A. 1969. *Introduction to the Reading of Hegel* (1947). Lectures on *The Phenomenology of Spirit*, assembled by R. Queneau. Edited by A. Bloom. Translated by J. H. Nichols Jr. New York: Basic Books.
Komisar, E. 2017. *Why Prioritizing Motherhood in the First Three Years Matters.* New York: Penguin.
Kreitmeyer, B., and G. Prouty. 2003. "The Art of Psychological Contact: The Psychotherapy of a Retarded/Psychotic Client," in *Person-Centered and Experiential Psychotherapies*, 2, no. 3, 151–61.
Kristeva, Julia. 1987. *In the Beginning Was Love: Psychoanalysis and Faith.* New York: Columbia University Press.
———. 1989. *Black Sun: Depression and Melancholia*, trans. L. S. Roudiez. New York: Columbia University Press.
Kroenke, C. H., L. D. Kubzansky, E. S. Schernhammer, M. D. Holmes, and I. Kawachi. 2006. "Social Networks, Social Support, and Survival after Breast Cancer Diagnosis," in *Journal of Clinical Oncology*, 24, no. 7, 1, 105–11.
Kroenke, C. H., C. Quesenberry, M. Kwan, C. Sweeney, A. Castillo, and B. J. Caan. 2013. "Social Networks, Social Support, and Burden in Relationships and Mortality after Breast Cancer Diagnosis in the Life after Breast Cancer Epidemiology (LACE) Study," in *Breast Cancer Res Treat*, 137, no. 1, 261–71.
Kuo, Lily. "China's Suicide Rate Has Plummeted Because of Urbanization, but It May Be Climbing Again." *Quartz*, June 27, 2014, http://qz.com/227136/chinas-suicide-rate-has-plummeted-because-of-urbanization-but-it-may-be-climbing-again/ (downloaded August 27, 2018).
Labarrière, P.-J. 1968. *Structures et Mouvement Dialectique dans la Phénoménologie de l'Esprit de Hegel*. Paris: Aubier.
Lacan, Jacques. 1932. *De la Psychose Paranoïaque dans ses Rapports avec la Personalité, suivi de permiers ècrits sur la Paranoïa*. Paris: Editions du Seuil.
———. 1966. *Écrits*. Paris: Seuil.
———. 1975. *De la Psychose Paranoïaque, suivi de Premiers Écrits sur la Paranoia.* Paris. Editions du Seuil.
———. 1975–1976. *The Seminar of Jacques Lacan, Book XXIII: Joyce and the Sinthome*, trans. C. Gallagher. Private.
———. 1981. *The Four Fundamental Concepts of Psycho-Analysis*. New York and London: W. W. Norton and Company.
———. 1988a. *The Seminar of Jacques Lacan, Book I: Freud's Papers on Technique, 1953–1954*, ed. J. A. Miller, trans. J. Forrester. New York: W. W. Norton and Company.
———. 1988b. *The Seminar of Jacques Lacan, Book II: The Ego in Freud's Theory and in the Technique of Psychoanalysis, 1954–1955*, ed. J. A. Miller, trans. S. Tomaselli. New York: W. W. Norton and Company.

———. 1993. *The Seminar of Jacques Lacan, Book III: The Psychoses, 1955–1956*, ed. J. A. Miller, trans. R. Grigg. New York: W. W. Norton and Company.

———. 2001. Autres écrits. Paris: Editions du Seuil.

———. 2004. *Anxiety: The Seminar of Jacques Lacan Book X*, ed. Jacques-Alain Miller, trans. A. J. Price. Cambridge, UK: Polity.

———. 2005. *Seminaire XXIII. Le Sinthome*, ed. J. A. Miller. Paris: Editions du Seuil.

———. 2006. *Écrits*, trans. B. Fink. New York: W. W. Norton and Company.

———. 2016. *The Sinthome: Seminar of J. Lacan, Book XXIII*, ed. J. A. Miller, trans. A. R. Price. Cambridge, UK: Polity.

Langdon, R., and M. Coltheart. 2004. "Recognition of Metaphor and Irony in Young Adults: The Impact of Schizotypal Personality Traits," in *Psychiatry Research*, 125, no. 1, 9–20.

Laplanche, J., and J. B. Pontalis. 1969. *Hölderlin et la Question du Père*. Paris: Presses Universitaires de France.

———. 1988. *The Language of Psychoanalysis*, trans. D. Nicholson-Smith. London: Karnac Books.

Lauer, Q., SJ. 1976. *A Reading of Hegel's Phenomenology of Spirit*. New York: Fordham University Press.

Laurin, C. 1964. "Phallus et sexualité feminine," in *La Psychanalyse*, 7, 14–54.

Leader, D. 2011. *What Is Madness?* London: Hamish Hamilton/Penguin Group.

Lear, J. 2017. *Wisdom Won from Illness: Essays on Philosophy and Psychoanalysis*. Cambridge, MA: Harvard University Press.

Lee, Jonathan Scott. 1990. *Jacques Lacan*. Amherst: University of Massachusetts Press.

Lehman, A. F., J. Kreyenbuhl, R. W. Buchanan, and L. B. Dixon. 2004. "The Schizophrenia Patient Outcomes Research Team (PORT): Updated Treatment Recommendations 2003," in *Schizophrenia Bulletin*, 30, no. 2, 193–217.

Lehman, A. F., and D. M. Steinwachs. 1998. "Translating Research into Practice: The Schizophrenia Patient Outcomes Research Teams (PORT) Treatment Recommendations," in *Schizophrenia Bulletin*, 24, no. 1, 1–10.

Lidz, Theodore. 1973. *The Origin and Treatment of Schizophrenic Disorders*. New York: Basic Books.

Loewenberg, J. 1965. *Hegel's "Phenomenology": Dialogues on the Life of the Mind*. La Salle, IL: Open Court.

Lopez, Donna. 1987. "The Oedipus Complex. A Lacanian Re-Reading." Unpublished manuscript.

Lothane, Z. 1989. "Schreber, Freud, Flechsig, and Weber Revisited: An Inquiry into Methods of Interpretation," in *Psychoanalytic Review*, 76, no. 2, 203–62.

———. 1992. *In Defense of Schreber: Soul Murder and Psychiatry*. Hillsdale, NJ: Analytic Press.

———. 1998. "Pour la défense de Schreber: meurtre d'âme et psychiatrie," in D. Devreese, Z. Lothane, and J. Schotte (eds.), *Schreber Revisité* (pp. 1–29). Louvain: Presses Universitaires de Louvain.

Mahler, M. S., F. Pine, and A. Bergman. 1975. *The Psychological Birth of the Human Infant: Symbiosis and Individuation*. New York: Basic Books.

Maine, M. 2000. "The Organized Categories of Infant, Child, and Adult Attachment: Flexible vs. Inflexible Attention under Attachment-Related Stress," in *Journal of the American Psychoanalytic Association*, 48, no. 4, 1,055–96.

"Major Depression." *National Institute of Mental Health*, https://www.nimh.nih.gov/health/statistics/prevalence/major-depression-with-severe-impairment-among-adolescents.shtml 2015 (downloaded January 6, 2018) .

Mannoni, M. 1964. *L'Enfant Arriéré et Sa Mère*. Paris: Éditions du Seuil.

———. 1972. *The Backward Child and His Mother*, trans. A. M. Sheridan Smith. New York: Random House.

Marini, Marcelle. 1986. *Lacan*. Paris: Pierre Belfond.

Marquet, J.-F. 2004. *Leçons sur la Phénoménologie de l'Esprit*. Paris-Bruges: Editions Ellipes.

Matthews, L. H. 1938–1939. "Visual Stimulation and Ovulation in Pigeons," in *Proceedings of the Royal Society of London, Series B*, 126, 557–60.

Meissner, W. W. 2003. *The Ethical Dimension of Psychoanalysis*. Albany: State University of New York Press.
"Mental Illness." *National Institute of Mental Health*, http://www.nimh.nih.gov/health/statistics/prevalence/any-mental-illness-ami-among-adults.shtml (downloaded January 6, 2018).
Michaud, G. 2004. *Essais sur la Schizophrénie et le Traitement des Psychoses. 1. L'Impossible Réalité*. Ramonville Saint-Agne: Érès.
Miller, J.-A. 1994. "Extimite," in Mark Bracher et al. (eds.), *Lacanian Theory of Discourse: Subject, Structure, and Society* (pp. 74–87). New York: New York University Press.
———. 1999. *La Psychose Ordinaire: La Convention d'Antibes*. Le Paon: Seuil.
———. 2009. "Ordinary Psychosis Revisited," in *Psychoanalytic Notebooks*, 19, 139–67.
———. 2013. "Ordinary Psychosis Revisited," in *Psychoanalytic Notebooks*, 26, 33–48.
Mills, J. 2002. *The Unconscious Abyss: Hegel's Anticipation of Psychoanalysis*. Albany: State University of New York Press.
———. 2010. *Origins: On the Genesis of Psychic Reality*. Montreal and Kingston: McGill-Queen's University Press.
———. 2012. *Conundrums: A Critique of Contemporary Psychoanalysis*. New York: Routledge.
Mishler, E. J., and N. E. Waxler. 1966. "Family Interaction Processes and Schizophrenia: A Review of Current Theories," in *International Journal of Psychiatry* 2, no. 4, 375–413.
Mitchell, S. A., and M. J. Black. 1995. *Freud and Beyond*. New York: Basic Books.
Mitchley, Nicola J., Joan Barber, John M. Gray, D. Neil Brooks, and Martin G. Livingston. 1998. "Comprehension of Irony in Schizophrenia," in *Cognitive Neuropsychiatry*, 3, 127–38.
Mo, S., Y. Su, R. C. Chan, and J. Liu. 2008. "Comprehension of Metaphor and Irony in Schizophrenia during Remission: The Role of Theory of Mind and IQ," in *Psychiatry Research*, 157, no. 1, 21–29.
Montejo, A. L., L. Montejo, and D. S. Baldwin. 2018. "The Impact of Severe Mental Disorders and Three Psychotropic Medications on Sexual Health and Its Implications for Clinical Management," in *World Psychiatry*, 17, 1.
Moskowitz, A., I. Schäfer, and M. Dorahy (eds). 2008. *Psychosis, Trauma, and Dissociation: Emerging Perspectives on Severe Psychopathology*. Hoboken, NJ: Wiley-Blackwell.
Moyaert, P. 1993. "Schizophrénie et Paranoia," in Antoine Vergote et al. (eds.), *Psychanalyse. L'homme et ses destins* (pp. 255–81). Louvain/Paris: Peeters.
———. 1994. *Ethiek en Sublimatie*. Nijmegen: Sun.
———. 1998. "Schizofrenie vanuit Psychoanalytisch Perspectief," in *Tijdschrift voor Psychoanalyse*, 4, no. 3, 132–49.
———. 2002. *Begeren en vereren. Idealisering en sublimatie*. Amsterdam: Sun.
Muller, John P., and William J. Richardson. 1982. *Lacan and Language: A Reader's Guide to Écrits*. New York: International Universities Press.
Murray, J. 2001. *Weathering the Storms: Psychotherapy for Psychosis*. New York: Karnac.
Nagel, T. 1997. *The Last Word*. Oxford, UK: Oxford University Press.
Niederland, W. 1974. *The Schreber Case: A Psychoanalytic Profile of a Paranoid Personality*. New York: Quadrangle.
Nobus, Dany. 2000. *Jacques Lacan and the Freudian Practice of Psychoanalysis*. London: Routledge.
Nuland, S. B. 2003. *Lost in America: A Journey with My Father*. New York: Alfred A. Knopf.
Panksepp, J. 1985. "Mood Changes," in P. Vinken, G. Bruyn, and H. Klawans (eds.), *Handbook of Clinical Neurology* (pp. 271–85). Amsterdam: Elsevier.
Peraldi, F. 1984. "L'attente du Père," in *Etudes freudiennes*, 23, 25–41.
———. 1987. "Krake/Krakra: A Case Study," in *PsychCritique*, 2, no. 1, 55–63.
Pinkard, T. 1996. *Hegel's Phenomenology: The Sociality of Reason*. Cambridge, MA: Cambridge University Press.
———. 2009. "Shapes of Active Reason: The Law of the Heart, Retrieved Virtue, and What Really Matters," in K. Westphal (ed.), *Blackwell Guide to Hegel's Phenomenology of Spirit* (pp. 136–52). Malden, MA: Wiley-Blackwell.

Plant, R. 1973. *Hegel*. Bloomington: Indiana University Press.

Prouty, G. 1994. *Theoretical Evolutions in Person-Centered, Experiential Therapy: Applications to Schizophrenic and Retarded Psychoses*. Westport, CT: Praeger/Greenwood Press.

———. 2003. "Pre-Therapy: A Newer Development of Schizophrenia," in *Journal of the American Academy of Psychoanalysis and Dynamic Psychiatry*, 31, no. 1, 59–73.

Prouty, G., D. Van Werde, and M. Pörtner. 2002. *Pre-Therapy: Reaching Contact-Impaired Clients*. Monmouth, UK: PCCS Books.

Read, J. 2007. "Why Promoting Biological Ideology Increases Prejudice against People Labelled 'Schizophrenic,'" in *Australian Psychologist*, 42, no. 2, 118–28.

Redmond, J. 2014. *Ordinary Psychosis and the Body: A Contemporary Lacanian Approach*. New York: Palgrave Macmillan.

Richardson, W. J. 1983a. "Lacan and the Subject of Psychoanalysis in Interpreting Lacan," in J. H. Smith and W. Kerrigan (eds.), *Psychiatry and the Humanities*, Vol. 6 (pp. 51–74). New Haven: Yale University Press.

———. 1983b. "Psychoanalysis and the Being-Question," in Joseph H. Smith and William Kerrigan (eds.), *Interpreting Lacan, Psychiatry, and Humanities* (pp. 139–60). New Haven, CT: Yale University Press.

Ricoeur, Paul. 1970. *Freud and Philosophy: An Essay on Interpretation*, trans. Denis Savage. New Haven, CT: Yale University Press.

Ritter, Alfons. 1936. *Schreber, das Bildungssystem eines Arztes* [PhD dissertation]. Erfurt: Ohlenroth.

Robbins, M. 1998. "Review of the Paradoxes of Delusion by Louis Sass," in *Journal of the American Psychoanalytic Association*, 46, 959–62.

———. 2002. "The Language of Schizophrenia and the World of Delusion," in *International Journal of Psycho-Analysis*, 83, 383–405.

———. 2011. *The Primordial Mind in Health and Illness: A Cross-Cultural Perspective*. New York: Routledge.

Roothaan, P. 1953. *Thesaurus Spiritualis Societatis Iesu*. Roma: Curia Praepositi Generalis.

Rosenbaum, Bent, Brian Martindale, and Allison Summers. 2013. "Supportive Psychodynamic Psychotherapy for Psychosis," in *Advances in Psychiatric Treatment*, 19, no. 4, 310–18.

Rosenbaum, Bent, and Harly Sonne. 1986. *The Language of Psychosis*. New York: New York University Press.

Rothgeb, Carrie Lee. 1973. *Abstracts of the Standard Edition of the Complete Works of Sigmund Freud*. New York: International Universities Press.

Russon, J. E. 2004. *Reading Hegel's Phenomenology*. Bloomington: Indiana University Press.

Saks, E. R. 1971. *The Center Cannot Hold*. New York: Hyperion.

Samuels, R. 1993. *Between Philosophy and Psychoanalysis: Lacan's Reconstruction of Freud*. New York: Routledge.

Sancipriano, M. 1965. "L' 'Urkind' di Husserl," in *Aut Aut*, 86, 7–26.

Sartre, Jean-Paul. 1966. *Being and Nothingness: An Essay in Phenomenological Ontology*, trans. Hazel E. Barnes. New York: Washington Square Press.

Sass, L. 1992. *Madness and Modernism: Insanity in the Light of Modern Art, Literature, and Thought*. New York: Basic Books.

———. 1995. *The Paradoxes of Delusion: Wittgenstein, Schreber, and the Schizophrenic Mind*. Ithaca, NY, and London: Cornell University Press.

———. 2003. "'Negative Symptoms,' Schizophrenia, and the Self," in *International Journal of Psychology and Psychological Therapy*, 3, no. 2, 153–80.

———. 2004. "'Negative Symptoms,' Common Sense, and Cultural Disembedding in the Modern Age," in Janis Hunter Jenkins and Robert John Barrett (eds.), *Schizophrenia, Culture, and Subjectivity: The Edge of Experience* (pp. 303–28). Cambridge, UK: Cambridge University Press.

Saussure, Ferdinand de. 1959. *Course in General Linguistics*, trans. Wade Baskin. New York: Philosophical Library.

Schatzman, M. 1973. *Soul Murder: Persecution in the Family*. New York: New American Library.

"Schizophrenia as a Health Disparity." *National Institute of Mental Health*, March 29, 2013, http://www.youngminds.org.uk/training_services/policy/mental_health_statistics (downloaded January 6, 2018).
Schreber, D. 1988. *Memoirs of My Nervous Illness* [with a new introduction by Samuel M. Weber], trans. I. Macalpine and R. A. Hunter. Cambridge, MA: Harvard University Press.
Scott, C. E. 1989. "The Pathology of the Father's Rule: Lacan and the Symbolic Order," in E. Wyschogrod, D. Crownfield, and C. A. Raschke (eds.), *Lacan and Theological Discourse* (pp. 76–91). Albany: State University of New York Press.
Searles, H. F. 1986. *My Work with Borderline Patients*. Northvale, NJ: Jason Aronson.
Seikkula, Jaakko, Jukka Aaltonen, Birgitta Alakare, Kauko Haarakangas, Jyrki Keränen, and Klaus Lehtinen. 2006. "Five-Year Experience of First-Episode Nonaffective Psychosis in Open-Dialogue Approach: Treatment Principles, Follow-Up Outcomes, and Two Case Studies," in *Psychotherapy Research*, 16, no. 2, 214–28, https://www.researchgate.net/publication/25265_five-year_experience_of_first-episode_nonaffective_psychosis_in_open-dialogue_approach_treatment_principles_follow-up_outcomes_and_two_case_studies (accessed October 9, 2017).
Seikkula, Jaakko, Birgitta Alakare, Jukka Aaltonen, Juha Holma, Anu Rasinkangas, and Ville Lehtinen. 2003. "Open Dialogue Approach: Treatment Principles and Preliminary Results of a Two-Year Follow-Up on First Episode Schizophrenia," in *Ethical Human Sciences and Services*, 5, no. 3, 163–82.
Shanshan, Wang. 2007 "Suicide the Major Cause of Death among Young People." *China Daily*, March 27, 2007, http://www.chinadaily.com.cn/china/2007-03/27/content_836869.htm (downloaded August 27, 2018).
Shedler, J. 2010. "The Efficacy of Psychodynamic Psychotherapy," in *American Psychologist*, 65, no. 2, 98–109.
Silver, A.-L., and M. B. Cantor. 1990. *Psychoanalysis and Severe Emotional Illness*. New York: Guilford Press.
Silverman lectures, Duquesne University. 1988 "Commentaries and Discussions, VI Annual Symposium, 1988." Transcript.
Simiu, D. 1986. *Disorder and Early Alienation: Lacan's Original Theory of the Mirror Stage* [doctoral dissertation]. Washington, DC: Georgetown University.
Sini, C., C. L. Cazzullo, and G. Invernizzi. 1985. "Sign, Symbol, Language," in *Schizophrenia: An Integrative View* (pp. 49–55). *Biological Psychiatry, New Prospects*, no. 6. London: John Ubbey.
Smith, Joseph H., and William Kerrigan. 1983. *Interpreting Lacan. Psychiatry and the Humanities*, no. 6. New Haven, CT: Yale University Press.
Soenen, S., and J. Corveleyn. 2003. "The Vicissitudes of Corporeality in Schizophrenia: A Psychoanalytic Approach," in Jozef Corveleyn and Paul Moyaert (eds.), *Psychosis: Phenomenological and Psychoanalytical Approaches* (pp. 27–42). Leuven: Leuven University Press.
Sokolowski, R. 2000. *Introduction to Phenomenology*. Cambridge, UK: Cambridge University Press.
———. 2002. "Language, the Human Person, and Christian Faith," in *Proceedings of the American Catholic Philosophical Association*, Vol. 76, 27–38.
Soler, Colette. 2014. *Lacan: The Unconscious Reinvented*. London: Karnac.
———. 2015. *Lacan, Lecteur de Joyce*. Paris: Presses Universitaires de France.
Solms, Mark, and Oliver Turnbull. 2004. *The Brain and the Inner World: An Introduction to the Neuroscience of Subjective Experience*. New York: Other Press.
Solomon, R. 1983. *In the Spirit of Hegel: A Study of G. W. F. Hegel's "Phenomenology of Spirit."* Oxford, UK: Oxford University Press.
Spitz, R. 1945. "Hospitalism: An Inquiry into the Genesis of Psychiatric Conditions in Early Childhood," in *The Psychoanalytic Study of the Child*, 1, 53–74.
———. 1957. *No and Yes: On the Genesis of Human Communication*. New York: International Universities Press.
———. 1965. *The First Year of Life*. New York: International University Press.

Stencrantz, A. 1998. *Jagstrukturerande psykoterapi—förändringar hos fyra unga psyykotiska patienter, del 2*. TIPS Report nr 50. Umeå University: Department of Applied Psychology.

Stencrantz, A., and B. Malmgren. 1997. *Jagstrukturerande psykoterapi med fyra schizofrena patienter, del 1—en processbeskrivning*. TIPS Report nr 49. Umeå University: Department of Applied Psychology.

Stern, R. 2002. *Hegel and the Phenomenology of Spirit*. London and New York: Routledge.

Stewart, J. 2000. *The Unity of Hegel's "Phenomenology of Spirit."* Evanston, IL: Northwestern University Press.

Strauss, M. 1987. "La vraie fonction du père, c'est d'unir un désir á la loi," in G. Miller (ed.), *Lacan* (pp. 59–76). Paris: Bordas.

"Suicide Rates Per 100,000 Population." *World Health Organization*, http://www.who.int/gho/mental_health/suicide_rates_crude/en/ (downloaded August 27, 2018).

"Suicides Increasing amongst Swedish Youth." *The Local*, November 26, 2018, https://www.thelocal.se/20181126/suicides-increasing-amongst-swedish-youth (downloaded August 27, 2018).

Sullivan, Harry Stack. 1974. *Schizophrenia as a Human Process*. New York: W. W. Norton and Company.

"Swedes and Suicide: A Fresh Perspective." *Inequality.org*, April 26, 2011, https://inequality.org/research/fresh-perspective-inequalitys-suicide-defense/ (downloaded January 6, 2018).

Thompson, M. G. 1985. *The Death of Desire: A Study in Psychopathology*. New York: New York University Press.

———. 1994. *The Truth about Freud's Technique*. New York: New York University Press.

Tienari, P. J. 1992. "Biological and Psychosocial Factors: Interaction between Genetic Vulnerability and Rearing Environment," in A. Werbart and J. Cullberg (eds.), *Psychotherapy of Schizophrenia: Facilitating and Obstructive Factors* (pp. 154–78). Oslo: Scandinavian University Press.

Tienari, P. J., J. Moring, A. Sorri, M. Naarala, and I. Lahti. 1992. "Adopted-Away Offspring of Schizophrenics: The Finnish Adoptive Family Study of Schizophrenia," in *Clinical Neuropharmacology*, 15 (Part B), 43B.

Tubridy, D. "'In His Second Mouth Language': Joyce and Irish Poetry." *Credo*, http://search.credoreference.com/content/entry/wileycjaj/in_his_secondmouth_language_joyce_and_irish_poetry/0 (downloaded August 28, 2018).

Vanderveken, Y. 2009. "Retour sur la Psychose Ordinaire," in *Quarto*, 94–95, 41–49.

Van Hautte, Ph. 2002. *Against Adaptation: Lacan's "Subversion" of the Subject: A Close Reading*. New York: Other Press.

Vanheule, Stijn. 2014. *The Subject of Psychosis: A Lacanian Perspective*. New York: Palgrave Macmillan.

———. 2017. "Conceptualizing and Treating Psychosis: A Lacanian Perspective," in *British Journal of Psychotherapy*, 33, 388–98.

Ver Eecke, W. 1983. "Hegel as Lacan's Source for Necessity in Psychoanalytic Theory," in Joseph H. Smith and William Kerrigan (eds.), *Interpreting Lacan* (pp. 75–112). New Haven, CT: Yale University Press.

———. 1984. *Saying "No": Its Meaning in Child Development, Psychoanalysis, Linguistics, and Hegel*. Pittsburgh, PA: Duquesne University Press.

———. 1988. "Phenomenology and 'Paternal Metaphor' in Lacan," in *Phenomenology and Psychoanalysis: The Sixth Annual Symposium of the Simon Silverman Phenomenology Center*. Pittsburgh, PA: Simon Silverman Phenomenology Center Duquesne University.

———. 1993. "Lacan and Schatzman: Reflections on the Concept of 'Paternal Metaphor,'" in David J. Boileau and John A. Dick (eds.), *Tradition and Renewal: Philosophical Essays Commemorating the Centennial of Louvain's Institute of Philosophy*, Vol. 2 (pp. 75–92). Leuven: Leuven University Press.

———. 1995. "Schreber and Hölderlin: The Concept of 'A-Father,' in B. Babich (ed.), *From Phenomenology to Thought, Errancy, and Desire: Essays in Honor of William J. Richardson, S.J.* (pp. 479–82). Dordrecht: Kluwer Academic.

———. 2001. "Lacan's Theory, Karon's Psychoanalytic Treatment of Schizophrenics," in *Psychoanalysis and Contemporary Thought*, 24, no. 1, 79–105.

———. 2002a. "A Lacanian Explanation of Karon's and Villemoes's Successful Psychodynamic Approaches to Schizophrenia," in *Journal of the American Academy of Psychoanalysis and Dynamic Psychiatry*, 30, no. 4, 633–43.

———. 2002b. "On Villemoes's Lacanian-Inspired Treatment Method of Schizophrenics," in *Collection of International Symposium of Psychoanalysis 2002 Chengdu* (pp. 287–99). Chengdu: University of Sichuan.

———. 2009 "Lacan'in Kompleks Psikoz Kuramina Dair Kuramsal ve Terapötik Çikarimlar," in *MonoKL*, 3, no. 6–7, 416–30.

Vergote, Antoine. 1973. "Raisons de la Déraison," in *Revue Philosophique de Louvain*, 71, 772–85.

———. 1976. "Névrose Dépressive," in *Topique*, 17, 97–126.

———. 1980. "Overview and Theoretical Perspective," in Antoine Vergote and Alvaro Tamayo (eds.), *The Parental Figures and the Representation of God* (pp. 185–225). Leuven: Leuven University Press.

———. 1983. "From Freud's 'Other Scene' to Lacan's 'Other,'" in Joseph H. Smith and William Kerrigan (eds.), *Interpreting Lacan in Psychiatry and Humanities* (193–222). New Haven, CT: Yale University Press.

———. 1984. "La Psychose," in G. Florival (ed.), *Études d'Anthropologie Philosophique* (pp. 311–28). Louvain-La-Neuve: Éditions de l'Institut Supérieur de Philosophie.

———. 1994. "La Constitution de l'Ego dans le Corps Pulsionnel," in G. Florival (ed.), *Dimensions de l'Exister* (pp. 178–94). Louvain: Editions Peeters.

———. 1998. "Le plaisir destructeur transfiguré en hiérogamie," in D. Devreese, Z. Lothane, and J. Schotte (eds.), *Schreber Revisité* (pp. 223–43). Louvain: Presses Universitaires de Louvain.

———. 2003. "Depression as Neurosis," trans. W. Ver Eecke, S. Sadowski, and L. Chwastiac, in *Psychoanalysis and Contemporary Thought*, 26, no. 2, 223–75.

Vergote, Antoine, and Alvaro Tamayo. 1980. *The Parental Figures and the Representation of God*. Leuven: Leuven University Press.

Villemoes, P. 1989. *Hur jaget strukturera*. Härnösand: Internet.

———. 1994. *Jagstrukturerande psykoterapi. Senare rön, 1989–94*. Härnösand: Internet.

———. 2000. E-mail, June 24.

———. 2002. "Ego-Structuring Psychotherapy," in *Journal of the American Academy of Psychoanalysis*, 30, no. 4, 645–56, www.jagstrukurerande.se (accessed October 9, 2018).

Wallerstein, J. S., J. M. Lewis, and S. Blakeslee. 2000. *The Unexpected Legacy of Divorce*. New York: Hyperion.

Waugaman, Richard M., and Harold F. Searles. 1990. "Infinite Reflections: The Opening Phase of Intensive Psychotherapy with a Chronically Schizophrenic Patient," in Ann-Louis S. Silver and Morton B. Cantor (eds.), *Psychoanalysis and Severe Emotional Illness* (pp. 99–114). New York: Guilford Publications.

Weber, S. M. 1988. "Introduction," in D. Schreber, *Memoirs of My Nervous Illness* (pp. vii–liv). Cambridge, MA: Harvard University Press.

Winnicott, W. 1965. *The Maturational Processes and the Facilitating Environment*. London: Hogarth.

———. 1990. *Home Is Where We Start From*. London: Penguin.

———. 1991. *Playing and Reality*. London: Routledge.

Wittgenstein, L. 1978. *Remarks on the Foundations of Mathematics*, ed. G. von Wright, R. Rhees, and G. Anscombe, trans. G. Anscombe. Cambridge, MA.: MIT Press.

———. 1981. *Zettel*, ed. G. von Wright, R. Rhees, and G. Anscombe, trans. G. Anscombe. Oxford, UK: Blackwell.

Zahavi, D. 1999. *Self-Awareness and Alterity: A Phenomenological Investigation*. Evanston, IL: Northwestern University Press.

Index

About the Author

Wilfried Ver Eecke, PhD, is professor at Georgetown University in the department of philosophy and adjunct professor in the department of psychology. He has been teaching there since 1967, the year after he had a postdoctoral year at Harvard University, where he studied with Erik Erikson.

Ver Eecke has edited, translated, and published seven books and almost one hundred articles. His publications have appeared in ten languages. Two of his books are translated into Chinese and a third is in the process of being translated.

He obtained his PhD at the University of Leuven, Belgium, with a doctoral thesis on Freud's ideas on negation as they relate to Hegel's ideas on negativity. As part of his preparation for his doctoral thesis, Ver Eecke studied in Paris with Hegelian philosopher Jean Hyppolite, psychiatrist Jacques Lacan, and linguist Emile Benveniste. In Freiberg, Germany, he studied with linguist Johannes Lohmann. Ver Eecke also became a Lacanian psychoanalyst, is associated with the Washington School of Psychiatry, and has a private practice.

www.ingramcontent.com/pod-product-compliance
Ingram Content Group UK Ltd.
Pitfield, Milton Keynes, MK11 3LW, UK
UKHW012036150926
475560UK00001B/38

9 781538 11800